DEVIL'S GATE

BRIGHAM YOUNG AND THE GREAT MORMON HANDCART TRAGEDY

DAVID ROBERTS

Simon & Schuster
NEW YORK · LONDON · TORONTO · SYDNEY

Simon & Schuster
1230 Avenue of the Americas
New York, NY 10020

Copyright © 2008 by David Roberts

First Simon & Schuster hardcover edition September 2008

SIMON & SCHUSTER and colophon are registered trademarks
of Simon & Schuster, Inc.

For information about special discounts for bulk purchases,
please contact Simon & Schuster Special Sales at
1-800-456-6798 or business@simonandschuster.com

Designed by Paul Dippolito

Manufactured in the United States of America

1   3   5   7   9   10   8   6   4   2

Library of Congress Cataloging-in-Publication Data
Roberts, David, date.
Devil's gate : Brigham Young and the great Mormon handcart tragedy /
David Roberts.
p.   cm.
Includes bibliographical references and index.
1. Mormon pioneers—West (U.S.)—History—19th century.   2. Mormon
handcart companies—History—19th century.   3. Mormons—Migrations—
History—19th century.   4. Disasters—West (U.S.)—History—
19th century.   5. Overland journeys to the Pacific.   6. Frontier and pioneer
life—West (U.S.)   7. Young, Brigham, 1801–1877.   8. Mormons—
West (U.S.)—Biography.   I. Title.
F593.R54   2008
978'.02—dc22   2008002286
ISBN-13: 978-1-4165-3988-9
ISBN-10:   1-4165-3988-3

For Sharon,
with love,
in this season of loss

CONTENTS

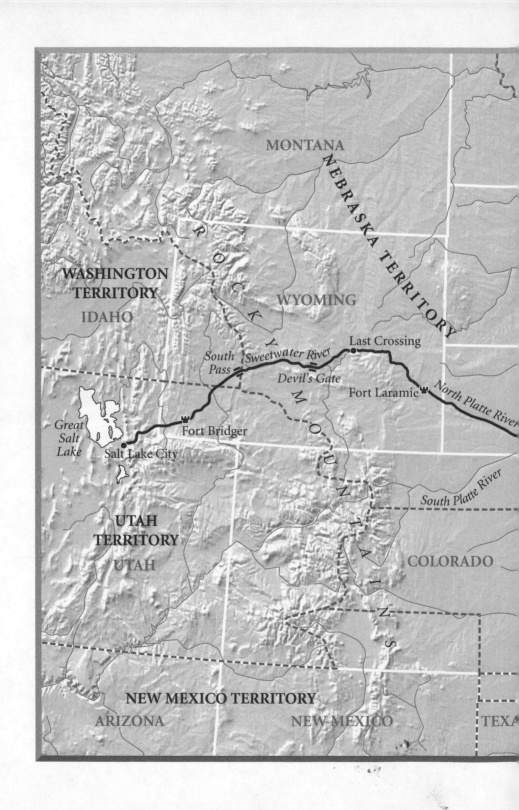

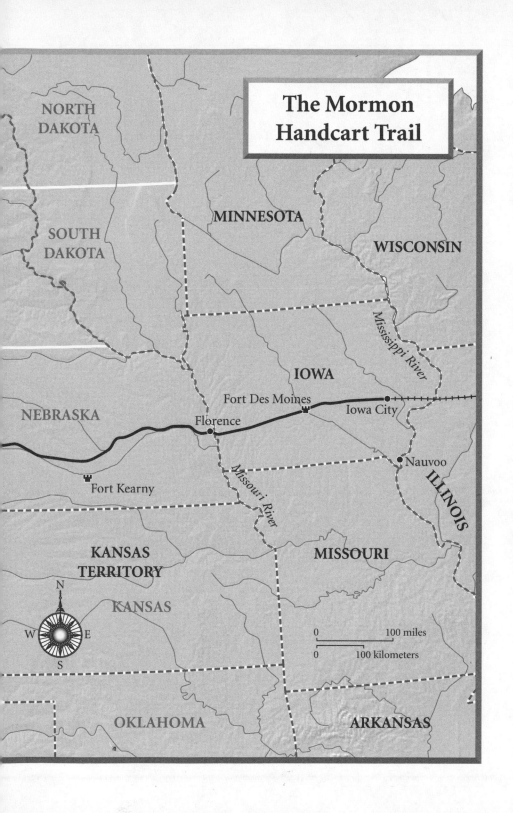

The Mormon Handcart Trail

NORTH DAKOTA

SOUTH DAKOTA

MINNESOTA

WISCONSIN

IOWA

NEBRASKA

Fort Des Moines

Florence

Iowa City

Mississippi River

Nauvoo

Fort Kearny

Missouri River

ILLINOIS

KANSAS TERRITORY

MISSOURI

KANSAS

N
W   E
S

0   100 miles

0   100 kilometers

OKLAHOMA

ARKANSAS

DEVIL'S GATE

PATIENCE

U p to that point, for Patience Loader, the journey had been chiefly exhausting. During the four weeks from July 25 to August 22, 1856, the company with which she traveled had covered 270 miles of trail from Iowa City to Florence, a fledgling community six miles north of Omaha, which itself had been founded just two years earlier. Averaging ten miles a day, the party of pioneers, some 575 strong, suffered the occasional delay due to thunderstorms or wayward cattle, but kept up their spirits with prayer services in camp each night and songs upon starting off each morning.

Yet even as the emigrants approached Florence, the trek, for twenty-eight-year-old Patience, took on an ominous new cast. Her fifty-seven-year-old father, James Loader, had been growing weaker by the day. Now his legs and feet swelled so badly that he had trouble walking. He was too feeble to help erect the big canvas tent under which twenty pilgrims slept wrapped in blankets on the ground. After mid-August, as he went to bed each night, James wondered whether he would be able to travel at all on the morrow.

Patience, her father, her mother, four of her younger sisters, and a younger brother were eight of some 1,865 Mormon emigrants engaged in what historians LeRoy and Ann Hafen call "the most remarkable travel experiment in the history of Western America." The Loaders and their fellow sojourners were traveling overland from eastern Iowa across the crest of the Continental Divide to Utah. The last four-fifths of that 1,300-mile trail, from Florence onward, had been traversed (though not

blazed, for thousands of settlers bound for Oregon and California—
including the ill-starred Donner party—had preceded them) by Brigham
Young's pioneer company of Mormons, who in 1847 had founded their
new Zion on the site that would become Salt Lake City.

In 1856, however, the emigrants were not traveling, as Brigham
Young's party had, in covered wagons pulled by oxen. Instead, they were
serving as their own beasts of burden. From Iowa City all the way to Salt
Lake City, they pulled and pushed wooden handcarts freighted with three
months' worth of clothing, gear, and sometimes food. A few ox-drawn
wagons accompanied the handcart train: in Patience Loader's company,
along with 145 handcarts, there were eight wagons to carry the heavy
tents, miscellaneous gear, and much of the food. The wagons could also
serve in extremis to carry a pioneer who was too weak or ill to walk.

The handcart "experiment" was Brigham Young's idea. Complicated
factors lay behind its genesis, but the bottom line was economic. By 1856,
Young's virtually autonomous empire on the edge of the Great Basin—
the self-proclaimed State of Deseret—was rife with fears of an impending invasion by the U.S. Army. Four years before, Young had gone public with a doctrine that had long been kept secret within the Mormon
hierarchy—what the Church of Jesus Christ of Latter-day Saints (as the
Mormons called themselves) referred to as "plural marriage." Polygamy,
in short, was not merely permissible in Utah: it was the sacred duty of
every God-fearing Saint. Young and his "Apostles" (the chief officers of
the Mormon theocracy) had lobbied in vain to have Utah admitted to
the union as a state. That very year of 1856, John C. Frémont, the first
Republican candidate for the presidency, had grounded his campaign
on the pledge to rid the country of "those twin relics of barbarism—
Polygamy and Slavery."

Deseret needed reinforcements. Meanwhile, thanks to nearly two decades of proselytizing so zealous there is no comparable achievement
in American annals, missionaries sent to Great Britain and Scandinavia
had converted thousands of the working-class poor to Mormonism. Not
only to strengthen the colony, but to ensure the converts' own spiritual
salvation, Young determined to get those Saints to Zion as quickly as
possible. And as cheaply as possible—for Deseret was in the midst of a
fiscal crisis. Handcart emigration, Brigham Young declared, could be ac-

complished even more easily than the usual trek by covered wagon, and at a fraction of the cost.

The handcart of 1856 was modeled on the kinds of luggage trolleys employed by railroad porters in the big cities of the Eastern United States. Its two wheels, about four and a half feet in diameter, were narrow hoops of wood, with thin wooden spokes radiating from the axle hub. The axle itself was made of hickory. The bed upon which the pioneers' goods were carried was a shallow, open, rectangular box, a little less than three feet wide by five feet long. From the front of the cart protruded a simple yoke made of thin, rounded sticks; two persons could stand inside this yoke, grasp the crosspiece with both hands at chest level, and push the cart along.

The Mormon handcart, designed to be as light as possible, weighed only about sixty-five pounds. In consequence, it was a fragile, rickety vehicle. The bane of the emigrants' existence was the constant breaking down of these handcarts, necessitating jury-rigged repairs along the trail.

On the average, four or five pilgrims pushed and pulled a single handcart. Each emigrant had been strictly limited to seventeen pounds of personal belongings, including clothes, bedding, and cooking utensils. The aggregate load, then, could be as little as eighty-five pounds, but it was usually much heavier, when logistical setbacks forced each handcart team to add a hundred-pound sack of flour to its load, or when a young child or failing grandparent for whom there was no room in the wagons had to be carried on the cart by his or her family.

From Iowa City to Florence, Patience and her father normally stood inside the yoke and pushed the cart by its crossbar. Sisters Maria (nineteen years old) and Jane (fourteen) pulled the cart by means of ropes tied to the shafts of the yoke. Sister Sarah, only twelve years old, pushed from behind the cart. Patience's mother, Amy, fifty-four years old; Patience's twenty-two-year-old sister, Tamar, who had fallen ill with the flulike malady the Saints called "mountain fever"; and her little brother Robert, who was nine, walked alongside. Before the family reached Florence, however, James Loader grew too weak to help with the pushing. Maria took his place inside the yoke, and the cart trundled on under the power of only four young women and girls.

The memoir of her life that Patience Loader wrote sometime after 1887, more than three decades after her handcart trek, is silent on the agonies of the initial 270-mile leg of the journey. They emerge, however, in the diary kept by another member of that party, forty-five-year-old Joseph Beecroft. Sample extracts:

August 1: About 9 aclock we started on our ardious journey. . . . We felt fateagued, got fires lighted water boiled, and our dry bred and tea. Between 3 and four we started for the next camp ground about 3 miles off which we reached very tired about 6 aclock. I thought I should have had to give it up, for I had a faint fit.

August 5: we were worse featuged than on any former perion [portion] of our jurney my wife was really finished. We had 2 carriages had their Axels broke in our company.

August 7: we rested near some water and being so near finished I could not fetch water. we started again and came to a place with which was secelected a camp. I[t] was nearly dark. . . . I could not help with tent.

August 10: I soon had breakfast and then went for an brought a large bundle of wood, which nearly murdered me. I came to tent and stayed in all day, and endured horrid pain in my limbs perticularly below my hips. My wife tryed to comfort me.

August 12: Soon after we started my goods had to be put in the waggon inorder that a young sister who could not endure the shaking of the waggon might be carried on in my cart. . . . Finding our queer position, and that I could bear to stand no longer, we moved on 100 yards came to a wood yard and in horrid pain we sat down leaving our selves in the hand of our father in heaven.

Unlike Beecroft, Patience Loader waited more than thirty years to record her story of the handcart trek. Yet among the scores of journals and memoirs written by the handcart pioneers that have come down to us, Patience's "Reccolections of past days" is the most vivid and eloquent. In an odd way, her account rings even truer thanks to her quirky spelling, erratic capitalization, and virtual absence of punctuation. Thus, describing James Loader's collapse on the approach to Florence, Patience writes:

> That afternoon we had not traveled far when My poor sick father fell down and we had to stop to get him up on his feet I said father You are not able to pull the cart You had better not try to pull we girls can do it this afternoon Oh he sais I can do it I will try it again I Must not give up the breathren said I shall be better and I want to go to the valley to shake hands with Brigham Young.

Even so, the Loader family came very close to terminating their journey in Florence. As the handcart train had crossed Iowa, it traversed a sparsely settled country, with many a roadside homestead and even a nascent village or two, such as Des Moines. Florence, however, stood on the edge of true frontier. On the thousand miles of trail stretching between that community and Salt Lake City, there were only three outposts of American civilization: the forts named Kearny, Laramie, and Bridger.

In that last week of August, not only was James Loader nearly unable to walk and Tamar racked with high fevers, but yet another Loader sister, twenty-five-year-old Zilpah—married to John Jaques, who had been a staff member in the Liverpool Mormon Mission—was within days of giving birth. The Jaqueses pushed their own handcart, but traveled in tandem with the Loader family.

It would not have been unreasonable for the Loader family to stay put in Florence and winter over, finishing their pilgrimage the next summer. In 1846, Brigham Young's vanguard party had originally hoped to go all the way to the Great Basin, but as the season grew too late to push on, the 148 pioneers who would found their Zion in the wilderness, along with many other Mormon emigrants, stopped just across the Missouri River from the border of the state of Iowa and threw together an instant village they called Winter Quarters (later renamed Florence). In doing so, they were in fact squatting on territory that had been ceded to the Omaha Indian tribe. Starting off again in early April 1847, the pioneer wagon train reached Utah in the height of summer.

In her memoir, Patience bitterly rues the decision not to stay in Florence. For in pushing on, the Loader family plunged into an utter catastrophe. By the time the last handcart pioneers straggled into Salt Lake on November 30, they had left some 220 of their brothers and sisters dead on the trail. Consequently the Mormon handcart tragedy of 1856 remains the greatest disaster in the whole pageant of westward migration across America.

The handcart catastrophe was, moreover, entirely preventable. What went wrong, and why?

BORN IN 1827, Patience Loader grew up in Aston Rowant, a small town in south-central England, "fifteen Miles from the City of Oxford," as she explained in the first paragraph of her memoir, "Which place is noted for its great educational coleges and old fashion buildings some which are black with age." As a member of the working class, she was typical of the legions of British converts with whom she would travel across the Great Plains. Yet compared to the coal miners and factory workers among that throng, Patience's father, James, occupied a relatively comfortable station in life, as private gardener to a baronet named Sir Henry John Lambert.

To follow Patience Loader's narrative of her journey to Utah is to retrace the steps of a representative handcart pioneer in the landmark year of 1856. And yet in other respects, Patience's experience was unique and poignant.

By the time she wrote "Reccolections of past days," Patience had been a steadfast Mormon for more than three decades. As far as we know, she never wavered in her faith or dreamed of returning to England. Yet one of the felicities of Patience's memoir lies in the fact that, despite her fidelity to the church, she seldom colors the past with retrospective pieties. She has a genius for remembering exactly how she felt.

Thus the gardener's cottage in which she grew up lingered long in her heart, an image of a lost Eden:

> the dear old house with a thatched roof and old fashion casements wendows with dimant cut glass and the verada in front with woodbrnes roses and honey suckles twing up to the upstairs

windows a beautifull flower garden on each side of the Walk from
the Street to the house a walk of red brick laid in on each side
with flints all kept so clean and free from weeds and gravle walks
all around the house to the back Whare we had a play ground a
beautifull green grass plate whare father had swings and jumps
batts and balls skiping ropes and everything to please his children
at home as he did not alow us to go out in the Street.

James Loader was what we would call today an overprotective father.
By the age of seventeen, Patience had apparently never spent a night
away from home. On October 10, 1844, under the mischievous sway
of her sister Ann (two years her elder), Patience indulged in what must
have been the most rebellious and hedonistic act of her young life, which
was to attend a county fair in the village of Thame, six miles from Aston
Rowant. "I never had been to a fare in My life," she later wrote, "as my
Parents would never alow me or My sisters to visit those places allthough
fares was verey comon in England in those days once a year an the young
Men and women go there to enjoy themselves together there thay dance
all day and sometimes up to a late hour at Night."

With their father's permission out of the question, Ann and Patience
sneaked away from the cottage. Patience tried to have fun at the fair,
but guilt laid its heavy hand on her spirit: "We had a verey good day
alltogether but to tell the truth I did not have any real enjoyment the
thoughts that we had run away from home unknown to our parents
spoiled all my pleasure."

James Loader, furious and worried, set out on foot to track down the
wayward girls, to no avail. At a late hour, the sisters stopped for the night
at their cousins' house in Kingston, closer to Thame than Aston Rowant.
In the morning, the girls faced the music, which was as discordant as
they had feared.

On October 11, the day the sisters returned home, Patience began
seven consecutive years as a domestic servant in various households. By
1845, invited by her older brother Jonas, she was installed in sprawling
London, then the most populous city in the world (and one of the most
sophisticated), but she remained a country girl through and through.
The constant theme running through her narrative of those years is

lonesomeness and homesickness. Jonas got her a job helping a young married couple run a dairy. But when Jonas left to get married and start his own business, Patience felt abandoned—and trapped in the dairy.

By 1848, as a skilled seamstress, Patience had seen her salary rise to £12 a year. No photograph of Patience Loader from her English years seems to have survived, but a picture taken in Utah in 1858, when at the age of thirty-one she married her first husband, reveals a pleasant, almost pixieish face, with a prim mouth but gaily curling hair.

The Loaders were staunch Anglicans. James and his wife, Amy, were so devout that as a child Patience found the churchgoing onerous: "Sometimes I use to get quite tiard and as I grew older I use to think it was alittle to much to have to go to church and Sunday school all day on Sundays when some of My companions could go and take a nice walk with there friends." In London, Patience had the misfortune to serve three years as a servant for an elderly "Maden Lady" and her equally superannuated housekeeper, who were fervent devotees of a splinter church calling itself the Independents.

> Between the two the Lady and her housekeeper I heard noth-
> ing but religion talked over and ever talking to get Me to join
> there church which in time I done. I must say More to pleas them
> than Myself for I realy fealt religion a burthen. . . . Thay allmost
> thought it a sin to laugh and thay considered it awfull to think of
> going to a theater.

From the employ of this odd couple, Patience passed, around 1848, into the service of the Maden Lady's sister, one Mrs. Henderson, and her husband. The Hendersons, who had served for years as missionaries in Russia, were also fiercely devout, imposing on their hired help as many as three church meetings each Sunday, Bible classes at home on Monday evenings, and prayer meetings on Thursday evenings. Mr. Henderson, a tutor at some sort of school or college, was often heard to swear that "he could not die happey if he did not visit Jerusalem."

For Patience, then, at age twenty-three, religion was apparently at best a pro forma exercise, at worst a tiresome obligation. One day in 1851, however, Mrs. Henderson, returning from a church meeting, took her servant aside. She "called me into her room and said do you know anything about the Mormons I answered no. Well she sais I have heard that your father and Mother have joined them and she said she was sorrey for them I told her I did not think it was so."

A measure of the integrity of "Reccolections" as a memoir is that Patience resists any temptation to gild this stunning revelation with complacent hindsight. Instead, she captures the full shock—indeed, the indignation—of that moment in Mrs. Henderson's room.

I wrote home to enquire of father and Mother and I found it was true that thay had been baptised and said thay was Latterday Saints Of course I did not know what it ment I wrote back and told them that thay must think themselves better than anyone else to be so conceited as to call themselves saints and I did not feel verey good over it either and I ask Mother if she thought that to be baptised by a Man was going to wash her sins away and told her I did not believe any such Nonsense as that and said I believed there was other churches just as good as theres and I said that I had found out by My Brother that there was none but poor folks that joined there church.

Patience does not reveal by whom or precisely when her parents were converted. Despite her ignorance of the Mormon creed, however, England at the time was abuzz with gossip about the upstart American religion, in large part because LDS missionaries had been so wildly successful at winning recruits among the poor of Great Britain.

Accepting what she could not change, Patience took a job as a dressmaker in Ramsgate, a seacoast resort town in Kent, not far north of Dover. More than a year passed before she paid her next visit to Aston Rowant. By that time, several of her sisters had also converted to Mormonism. Patience arrived at the gardener's cottage to find two Mormon missionaries from Utah, a Mr. Archer and a Mr. Dalling, visiting her father. They "came to My fathers house to preach," she recorded; but "I did not pay any great attention to their preaching."

The missionaries evidently saw a soul ripe for the plucking, for they went out of their way to invite Patience on walks in the garden and cooked her (and her family) a dinner of "roast Mutten and nice fresh vegetables." Mr. Archer was accompanied by wife and children; Mr. Dalling was alone. As the week wore on, Patience remembered,

> I had quite a pleasant visit with Mrs Archer . . . but not so pleasant with Mr Dalling for he set about to try to convert me to the Mormon faith of course this was his Mission he was sent out to do. but he was to tiresome he done Nothing but preach to me all the time and at that time I did Not want to be troubled so much about religion. and Mrs Archer seeing I did not like it came to my rescue. and she said to Mr Dalling I think you had better stop your preaching to Miss Loader she don't like so much of it You are enough to tire her out.

At this rebuff, Mr. Dalling shifted gears. "From this he did not talk so much of religion to me but commenced upon the subject of marriage. and let me know that he was without a wife in the world and that he would like to get accompanion before he returned to Utah." Patience declined the proposal.

Yet something "took" during this extended visit home. Whether it was Mr. Dalling's badgering or, more likely, the serene example of her parents and sisters, by the time she returned to a new job—this time in a posh London hotel—Patience, too, had become a Latter-day Saint. Perhaps at first hers was a conversion of complaisance, to please her family, as she had agreed to embrace the Independent church to ingratiate herself with her former employer. But probably not—for in her memoir Patience now insists that God's "watchfull care was over Me and he knew what was best for me and opened my eyes." This may well be the voice of retrospect speaking from sometime after 1887; but for the rest of her life, until her death in Utah in 1922 at the age of ninety-four, Patience would remain a steadfast Mormon.

Two days before she went off to the London hotel, she was baptized into the church. The chronology of the memoir is hazy here, but it seems that the conversion occurred sometime during 1853. More than two years would pass before the Loaders set sail for America. Meanwhile, in London, Patience kept her new faith a secret, for good reason.

At some point, a new housekeeper, who proved to be a thoroughgoing busybody, came to work at the hotel. Every Sunday, Patience would slip out to attend an LDS meeting. One Monday, as she started work, Patience bid a cheery good morning to the housekeeper.

She did not care to speak after a time she sais I hear you are a Mormon I answered Yes well She Sais we don't want no Mormons in this house and said I would have to leave I said I could do that I can get a nother place She said she did not think I could if she told people I was a Mormon. . . . She said She had heard that the Mormons was abad Set of folks.

The housekeeper's fear was that Patience might try to proselytize among her fellow maids at the hotel. Indeed, she had been doing just that, covertly inviting them to attend her LDS meeting and giving them "tracks" that laid out the principles of the church. She had already succeeded in winning over two of the maids to the Mormon faith.

Defiant to the end, Patience accepted her firing by the busybody housekeeper. As she walked down the long hall of the hotel for the last time, some of the manservants "sneared at me and said good bye old gal are you going to see old Joe Smith I said good bye don't you know Joseph Smith was killed by wicked men." (The founder in 1830 and first Prophet of the Mormon church, Joseph Smith, had been murdered by a mob in Illinois in 1844.)

Patience was even castigated by her own sister Eliza, who was staying with her during a visit to the hotel. Two years younger, Eliza had held out against the family drift toward the LDS church: she would never become a Mormon, and would spend all her life in England. Now Eliza "fealt as bitter towards me about My religion as the housekeeper did she would scarcely speak to Me and never came to bid me good bye."

Patience promptly found another job with a kindly old military veteran who, according to her, had "fought in the Battle of Watersoo." Her duties were to care for the ex-officer's invalid wife.

Meanwhile, Patience's parents were also bearing the brunt of the widespread English prejudice against the Mormons. At some point, Sir Henry John Lambert, the baronet whom James Loader had faithfully served as gardener for more than two decades, discovered their new religion. He gave them an ultimatum—to abjure their faith within a year or be evicted. The family refused to renounce the church.

It was not the prospect of losing his job, however, that set James Loader's eyes on the New World. Within a year after founding his church, Joseph Smith had proclaimed the solemn duty of every Saint to "gather to Zion." At the time, the Prophet had fixed Missouri as the land in which the elect must assemble. He had determined, in fact, that Jackson County, on the western edge of that state, was the original site of the Garden of Eden. Adam and Eve had been placed on Earth by God not in the Holy Land of the Near East, but in the middle of North America.

The apocalypse, or the second coming of Christ, was imminent, though Smith declined to specify a date. At the time of the apocalypse, only those gathered to Zion would be spared. All the rest of the world was Babylon, and on that ultimate day, in Smith's words, "tribulation and desolation [would] fall upon the wicked" who dwelled there.

By 1855, Zion had been relocated to Salt Lake City, or, more generally, the State of Deseret, in what the U.S. government called Utah Territory. The *Millennial Star,* the Mormon newspaper established by Brigham Young and his colleagues in 1840, published in Liverpool and read by every British Saint who could read English (the Welsh had their own language, and many of the converts were illiterate), was full of constant exhortations to gather to Zion. As early as 1848, in the pages of the *Star,* the faithful had absorbed Young's injunction, "To the Saints of England, Scotland, Ireland, Wales, and adjacent islands and countries, we say, emigrate as speedily as possible. . . . Come immediately and prepare to go West." And in September 1855, even as the Loaders prepared for their journey, they no doubt heeded the words of Franklin D. Richards, president of the European Mission: "Every impulse of the heart of the Saint, every hope of the future, says, 'Gather up to the land of America.'"

For most of the British Saints, the only obstacle to emigration was financial. The converts were expected to pay their own way to Zion, and for many of the working-class poor, the cost of passage amounted to a staggering sum. More than one family scrimped and saved for years to afford the long journey to Utah.

By December 9, 1855, James and Amy Loader, their daughters Patience, Maria, Jane, and Sarah, and their son Robert, had arrived at the harbor in Liverpool, ready to board the *John J. Boyd*, a sailing vessel bound for New York. Also booking passage were Patience's thirty-four-year-old brother, John, his wife, Harriet, and their two small children. None of those pilgrims would ever see England again.

PATIENCE ALMOST MISSED the trip. Having carried their baggage on board, the Loaders learned that the *Boyd* would not sail until the next day. Patience decided to use the free time to visit her twenty-four-year-old sister, Zilpah, the wife of John Jaques, who worked in the offices of the *Millennial Star*. Zilpah and John were planning to wait till the following June or July to sail to America, along with their twenty-two-year-old sister, Tamar.

There must have been some confusion, for when Patience returned to the harbor the next day, the ship was minutes from pulling out of the dock. Her family was screaming at the crew "to the top of there voice for the Lord sake bring My girl on the ship and dont leave her behind," but with hundreds of passengers on board, the *Boyd* was not about to delay its departure for a single tardy emigrant. A bare wooden plank was all that connected ship to shore: now, with a pair of sailors each holding one of her hands, one man walking ahead, one behind, Patience negotiated the gauntlet. Once on board,

> My dear good father sais God bless you My dear girl we was all afraid you would be left behind we watched for your coming so anxiously. and when the men began to take away the planks Your Mother began to frett and said oh what will we do Patience has not come and the vesel is ready to start out to sea and we will have to leave her behind. . . . There was great rejoicing when I was safe on the vesel with them all.

The journey from Liverpool to New York would take sixty-six days, unconscionably long even for a sailing ship in an age when steamships were already routinely making the passage in two weeks. But like nearly

all the European Saints bound for Zion, the Loaders could afford only
steerage on a sailing vessel.

A semiofficial report of the *John J. Boyd*'s passage that winter, written
by one of the emigration officers on board, was published in *The Mormon*
on March 1, 1856. That newspaper, launched only the previous year, New
York's answer to Liverpool's *Millennial Star*, was edited by John Taylor,
one of the Twelve Apostles, who were subordinate in rank in the church
only to Brigham Young himself. As president of the New York Mission,
receiving the Saints who came from abroad and sending them on to Iowa
City, Taylor would play a crucial role in the handcart campaign.

The résumé of the journey that appeared in *The Mormon* insisted
that "Notwithstanding that our company consisted of Danes, Norwe-
gians, Swedes, Icelanders, Italians, English, Irish, and Scotch, the rules
adopted proved efficacious in maintaining a strict *entente cordial[e]*
among us all." While acknowledging a fair amount of hardship and an
unspecified number of deaths (particularly among the Danes, due to
an outbreak of measles) during the journey, the correspondent struck a
jaunty tone. In a season plagued by storms that wrecked other ships on
the Atlantic, he bragged, "We had made the passage without the loss of
a single spar. Truly we can say that we have been blest, and that our long
voyage has been an advantage to us in many ways."

In her memoir, Patience left an account of the voyage on the *John J.
Boyd* that paints a far more ominous and vivid picture of the trip. "Never
will forget the first night on the ship," she vows.

> Not much sleep for any one that first night and we was orderd to
> go below we could not get a berth the first night So we had to lie
> down on the floor as best we could: I began to think we would
> smother to death before Morning for there was not abreath of air
> I made my bed on a large box I had abig loaf of bread in asack this
> I used for my pillow to make sure of having bread for breakfast
> this was not avery nice thing to do to sleep on my bread.

Such belowdecks chaos and squalor were far from uncommon on the
emigrant ships of the day. After the first night, a guard promised better
accommodations for the Loaders, and indeed, they were soon moved

to a higher deck with berths "just beneath the skylights and that was opened to give fresh air."

Patience claims that each emigrant was allotted only one pint of drinking water per day (which of course would have been inadequate for health in even the most sedentary passenger); "we had to wash in Salt water and cook our potatoes in salt water I said well one good thing we will not have to use any salt to our potatoes."

On board the ship, pitching with the waves through one storm after another, Patience, her mother, and all her siblings were seasick for six weeks running. The captain, whom Patience sized up as "avery rough cross man" and a drunken tyrant, was driven to distraction by his cargo of Saints.

> At one time the captain Said if we did not stop our d— preachen and praying we would never land in New York I told the Mate that was the only thing that Saved his vesell for he [i.e., the captain] was such awicked drinking Man and neglected his duty it was awounder that he was sufferd to live.

According to Patience, one night the captain, in a drunken stupor, knocked over the lantern in his cabin, which caught fire. The conflagration might well have set the whole ship ablaze had the crew not rushed to extinguish it.

Halfway through the passage, the *John J. Boyd* came in sight of a dismasted clipper ship bound from Baltimore to Liverpool that was on the verge of sinking: several crew members had already been washed away. The captain lowered lifeboats and rescued the survivors. This "one kind act he did," in Patience's phrase, had an ulterior motive:

> The Mate fetched in his boat the first time four poor Sick Men poor things thay looked so poor and waurn out two Men had two ribs broaken. . . . The other two poor Men Said to the captain sir we feel to thank you God bless you for coming to help us. the brute of a captain sais to them god d— you go to work that is all I want of You get up that riging I don't want to here no more of your talk.

(Even the correspondent to *The Mormon* admitted that the rescue was providential for the *Boyd,* whose crew was shorthanded from overwork.)

The captain of the clipper ship, his jaw broken, was beside himself with grief, for his sixteen-year-old son had been lost at sea on his first ocean voyage. The man had opposed his son's participation, but, in Patience's direct quote, the boy "beged So hard of his Mother to let him come with me and now this has happened. I have lost my boy my only child how can I go home to my wife without our boy."

According to Patience, there were five hundred Danish Saints among the company. As she reports,

> Good and kind was the dainesh brothers and sisters and we enjoid ourselvs together allthough we could not talk there langwage Neither could thay talk the English langwage but we could make each other understand thay would make up a dance as Many of the danish breathren had instruments with them and could play Many good dance tunes and the Young Men would come and envite us English sisters to there dance.

Yet there was no ignoring the tragedy that stalked the company on board the *Boyd*. Patience is the only witness who recorded the toll: "We had aterrable severe voiage Much sickness and Many deaths Numbering Sixty two in all." Among the victims was her own niece, Zilpah, the ten-month-old daughter of John Loader and his wife, Harriet King: "It did indeed seem verey hard to role her in ablanket and lay her in the big waves and see the little dear go floting away out of sight."

At her lowest ebb, however, Patience (who up to this point in her memoir has showed no instinct for the metaphysical) was visited with what she took to be a divine vision. During a night so stormy that "we had to hold on to the berth to keep from beign thrown out," as her mother voiced fears that "we would all be lost and drounded in the sea," Patience lay sleepless behind curtains her father had hung for privacy around her bed.

> Just when the ship was tosing and rolling the worst I opened my eyes we was all in darkness: but in amoment the curtens opened

and abeautifull lovely figure stood there oh such alovely countenance I had never seen before in all my life and the light was So
bright around him that I could See the calour of his eyes and heir
he had brown eyes and lovely brown heir and he spake the words
to me as I looked at him he sais fear not You shall be taken there
all safe then he left and the curtens was again closed. . . . I believe
I had seen the savior.

On February 15, 1856, the *John J. Boyd* at last lay at anchor in New
York harbor. The correspondent for *The Mormon* acknowledged that the
ship had only one day's drinking water left among its provisions.

As HAD BECOME routine, all the Saints who arrived in New York
were transplanted at once to Castle Garden, a gigantic refurbished opera
house that served as a temporary dormitory and processing center for
the emigrants. It was at this point that a colossal misunderstanding began to inflict its insidious harm upon the Loaders—a misunderstanding
that would have profound consequences for the tight-knit family from
Aston Rowant.

In her memoir, Patience recalls that President John Taylor visited
Castle Garden the morning after the arrival of the *John J. Boyd*, "to make
enquirey to findout who had Money and who had not those that was
able to go out and rent rooms for themselves had to do so."

The Loaders still had money. At once the family rented rooms in
Williamsburg, a section of Brooklyn just across the East River from
Manhattan. Within a short time (Patience simply says "soon"), the various Loaders had found paying jobs. James's expertise as a gardener won
him employment planting flower beds at "good wages." John got work
as a shoemaker. Patience and her sister Maria were hired by a clothing
store to make mantillas—long silk or lace scarves that hung down over
the shoulders. Jane and Sarah became baby-sitters. Nine-year-old Robert started attending school in Williamsburg.

The fact is that the Loaders had no intention of setting out at once
for Iowa City and thence to Zion. Instead, in Patience's testimony, "We
was all working and expected to stay here until the next year then we

thought we would make enough Money to buy an outfit to go to Utah."
That outfit would be a wagon and a team of oxen.

Such a plan was far from unusual among the European Saints arriving in the New World. Many would set down roots in New York (or
Boston or Philadelphia) that proved so tenacious they would never finish their pilgrimages to Salt Lake City. Others grew disillusioned with
the Mormon faith and eventually (in the opprobrious formula of the
church) "apostatized." And many worked for a year or longer, until they
could indeed afford an outfit, then made their way to Zion in covered
wagons, just as Brigham Young's pioneer party had done in 1847.

Not only had the Loaders no intention of gathering to Zion by handcart: it seems, astonishingly, that they had never heard of the handcart
plan. The grand scheme had been announced in a long article in the *Millennial Star*, but that manifesto had not been published until December
22, 1855—ten days after the *Boyd* had left Liverpool. It had likewise been
published in *The Mormon* on December 1, 1855, two and a half months
before the Loaders arrived in New York. Yet surely the Saints on board
the ship had gossiped and speculated about the prospect of their novel
"experiment" in crossing the plains. Even more surely, Patience's brother-in-law, John Jaques, as the associate of European Mission president
Franklin D. Richards, must have been intensely caught up in the details
of the handcart plan. How could he not have explained it to Patience, on
the very eve of her departure from England, when she spent the night
visiting Jaques and his wife, her sister Zilpah?

It is possible that Patience's memoir is disingenuous at this point—
or that the hindsight of three decades in Utah before she began to write
had retouched her memory. But "Reccolections of past days" is so art-
less a narrative that deliberate falsehood seems unlikely. Perhaps after
all the truth is that the Loaders had somehow remained ignorant of the
handcart scheme.

There is no getting around the family's shock and surprise at what
transpired in the spring of 1856. On March 29, John Jaques wrote James
Loader a letter, which he received on April 18. In no uncertain terms, the
epistle ordered the Loaders to leave New York at once and go by train to
Iowa, then by handcart to Zion. The orders, according to Patience, were
straight from President Richards.

Patience went to President John Taylor's office in New York to plead her case. "He knew that My father had only we fourgirls to help him as Mother was avery delicate Woman unable to take a journey by handcart across the plains." Taylor seemed sympathetic. "I ask Br Taylor if he would like to have his girls pull ahand cart across the plains he Said no."

Quite apart from the physical ordeal the emigration promised for her frail parents, Patience was disturbed by the indignity of such a means of travel. "I could not see it right at all," she wrote later, "to want us to do such a humeliating thing to be I said harnest up like cattle and pull a handcart loded up with our beding cooking utencels . . . and have to go through different towns to be looked at and Made fun of."

So deep was the family's alarm at this turn of events that Patience wrote her brother-in-law a letter of protest. Not only did John Jaques answer it in paragraphs that thundered with anger and contempt—he published the exchange in the *Millennial Star*, disguising Patience's identity only with the signature "P_____."

In English regularized with respect to spelling and punctuation, Patience appeared in the *Star* insisting that the family had been "somewhat surprised to find that we have to go by the hand-carts."

> Father and mother think this cannot be done, and I am sure I think the same, for mother cannot walk day after day. . . . If we girls were strong boys then I think it might be done, but father is the only man in our family. . . . Mother, I am sure, can never go that way. She says herself that she cannot do it. . . . Mother says that she must have a revelation before she can see this right. Why, we shall have to sell nearly all our clothes! And what shall we do for things to wear when we get to the Valley? Seventeen pounds weight each is very little.

(The last line reveals that the seventeen-pound personal baggage limit was announced in advance to the Loaders—as it would not be to many of the handcart Saints.)

John Jaques's rejoinder, addressed not to Patience but to her father, is a fanatical tirade. He insists he has read the letter from "P_____" half a dozen times, barely managing to suppress his incredulity.

There is not one atom of the spirit of Zion in it, but the very spirit of apostasy. I felt to exclaim in my heart, "Who has bewitched you . . . that you should so soon forget the goodness of the Lord in delivering you from this part of Babylon, and opening up your way to Zion?" . . .

Joseph Smith prophesied that those who would not gather to Zion when their way was open, should be afflicted by the devil. . . .

It astonishes me that you wish to stay in New York. After you have left one part of Babylon, I wonder how you can think of sitting down in another, when you have the privilege of bidding it farewell altogether. . . . I have heard you talk of saving all your family, and I know you desire to do so, but is this the way to do it? No, it is not, but is the way to make shipwreck of your own salvation, and your children's too.

(And so on, to the length of some 2,500 very public words.) Jaques softened the blow of his withering diatribe only by promising to emigrate with Zilpah and set out by handcarts with the Loader family in the summer of 1856.

The impact on James Loader of his son-in-law's savage dressing-down would have been devastating enough had it remained private. But one day in April or May a high official in the New York Mission office came to the Loaders' lodgings in Williamsburg. "He said did you know that your name is in the Mellinal star Br Loader," Patience later wrote. "You are thought to be apostizing from the Church & it sais father Loader has brought his family out of one part of Bablon and Now he wants to settle down in another part of Bablon."

The shaming was too much for James Loader. In Patience's words,

This hurt My poor dear fathers feelings very Much he said to Mother I cannot stand that to be accused of apostasy I will show them better; Mother I am going to Utah I will pull the hand cart if I die on the road. . . . So when father gave the word we all agreed to go with him and we commenced to make ready for the Journey.

It was a decision that would seal James Loader's fate, and change the lives of his family members forever.

THE LOADERS LEFT New York on July 3, 1856. They took a train across New York state to the town of Dunkirk, on the shores of Lake Erie, then a boat westward across that body of water to Cleveland. From Cleveland, they traveled once more by railroad, with stops in Chicago and Rock Island, before arriving in Iowa City.

Just as in England, in the United States Mormon converts were regarded as a curiosity, and sometimes taunted about their pilgrimage to Zion. In Davenport, Iowa, Patience reported, "agreat croud—gatherd around us casting slurs at us and asking father if he was going to take his fine girls to Utah and give them to Brigham Young for wives." The jeerers urged James Loader to stay in Davenport, "for girls was scarce in that neighbourhood and there was lots of Men that wanted wives."

Later, on the train between Davenport and Iowa City, "two big Men" forced their way into a car that the family had been told was reserved for them. (They may have been hobos, or simply local ruffians looking for amusement.) The men's intrusion was threatening enough that James Loader and his son John ordered them to leave, but only when John, "beign astaut Young Man, pushed them boath out of the car and closed the doors" was the family liberated from the menace.

Besides the stress of the journey itself, there was another reason it was wrenching for Patience to leave New York. In her brief résumé of the trip to Iowa City, she momentarily lifts the veil over her private life. In Williamsburg, she had been courted by a man named Alexander Ott. Thirty-three years old that July, Ott had first come to Utah by wagon in 1854; now he was serving as a missionary proselytizing in the East. Patience was now twenty-eight years old, but Ott is the first suitor mentioned in her memoir. She was in fact engaged to be married to the missionary. In Dunkirk, Patience took the time to write her beau a love letter.

Yet the romance came to a sour ending. In one brisk run-on sentence, Patience sketches its denouement: "I promised to become his wife when he came home [to Utah] that I would wait for him to return home as soon as he was releaced from his Mission but he prooved falce to me and Married a widow woman."

The Loaders arrived in Iowa City in mid-July. Here, along with all the other members of their handcart company, they camped on the ground under a big canvas tent. "The weather was dreadfully hott No shade whatever," Patience complains, "here we staid for three weeks before the company was ready to start."

In that laconic sentence, Patience records a delay that would prove to be the fatal flaw in the 1856 emigration. At the Iowa City camp, there were not nearly enough handcarts available to supply the hundreds of Saints bound for Zion. On the spot, using green wood culled from nearby forests, the best carpenters among the company had to build makeshift handcarts that would break down with infernal regularity on the trail.

During that extended wait, Patience's brother John and his wife, Harriet, decided not to continue to Utah. Having lost their infant daughter on the voyage of the *John J. Boyd*, the couple was expecting yet another newborn. As Harriet was "nearing her confindment," she and her husband deemed the handcart journey too arduous. John soon found a job in Iowa City. The couple and their children would gather to Zion only a decade later, after he had served as a volunteer in the Civil War and been seriously wounded in the Battle of Cedar Creek in Virginia.

To make up for that loss, the Loaders were reunited in Iowa City with John Jaques and his wife, Zilpah, Patience's twenty-five-year-old sister, as well as sister Tamar, two and a half years younger. Jaques had made good on his promise to emigrate to Salt Lake City with the Loaders by handcart. Zilpah herself was eight months pregnant, but, unlike her sister-in-law, was prepared to face the rigors of the trail in that condition. If at this reunion there was any lingering bad blood between Jaques and his father-in-law, on account of the humiliating broadside published in the *Millennial Star*, Patience does not record it. Instead, she remarks simply, "this was ahappy Meeting."

The handcart train of which the Loaders were members is known today as the Martin Company, after the man in charge of it, Edward Martin. Thirty-seven years old, born in Lancashire, he had emigrated to the United States in the 1840s and served in the so-called Mormon Battalion in the Mexican War. Having traveled with those troops to California and back, Martin was one of the most experienced voyagers among all the 1,800-plus handcart pioneers of 1856.

On July 25, the Martin Company at last moved out of its Iowa City camp. Decades later, Patience would look back on that departure as a grievous mistake: "At that time we did not know what hardships we would have to pass through before we came to the end of our Journey if we had known we may have backed out and Staid in Iowa which I think would have been better for us and would have been the means of Saving my dear fathers life."

In her memoir, Patience devotes only a few lines to the 270-mile month-long trek from Iowa City to Florence. In retrospect, no doubt the routine ordeals of that first leg of the journey paled in comparison with the horrors to come. It is only as the Martin Company neared Florence, and her father's legs swelled so much he had trouble walking, that her prose begins to prickle with alarm.

In a reminiscence published in the *Salt Lake Daily Herald* more than two decades later, with his former fanaticism mellowed out of him, John Jaques vividly conjured up the chaos of the Iowa City camp and the tortures of the first weeks on the handcart trail. That most of the pioneers had been told nothing about the seventeen-pound personal baggage limit is abundantly clear in the camp scene Jaques evokes:

> As only a very limited amount of baggage could be taken with the handcarts, during the stay in the Iowa camping grounds there was a general lightening of such things as could best be done without. Many things were sold cheaply to the residents of that vicinity, and many more things were left on the camping ground for anybody to take or leave at pleasure. It was grievous to see the heaps of books and other articles thus left in the sun and rain and dust, representing a respectable amount of money spent therefore in England, but thenceforth a waste and a dead loss to the owners.

As for the party's makeshift handcarts:

> Some of the axles broke in a few days, and mechanics were busy in camp at nights repairing the accidents of the day. . . .

Many were prostrated in the Iowa camp because unclimated and unaccustomed to the great heat. In starting from Iowa with the handcarts and dragging them over the sandy roads, it seemed like pulling the very pluck out of one, the pluck physical and corporeal. The pluck mental remained with the company much the same to the last. The carts were poor ones, with wooden axles, leather boxes, and light iron tires, and the squeaking of the wheels through lack of sufficient grease could often be "heard a mile."

John Jaques also kept a diary of the trek. Its entries are telegraphic, factual, and determinedly upbeat: "Good camping place, good feed, water a half mile off at a spring"; "wood, water and feed excellent." Yet here and there tribulation breaks through: "Two wagon loads of rough men came to our camp from Marengo with the intention of creating a disturbance, but they were unable to and went away in a short time shouting and yelling"; "The axle of two carts brokle down. Temporary axles were lashed on"; "Saw a wolf at the carcus of a calf, close to the road. I arrived after dark. Lame with fester."

Contemplating the character of the hundreds of handcart emigrants, one cannot help but be impressed by how tough these men, women, and children were. To be sure, lives of hard manual labor back in Britain or Scandinavia had inured many of them to weakness or fatigue. And their Mormon faith gave them a strength that cannot be measured in ergs.

But for the kind of effort an overland migration would require, these converts were woefully inexperienced. As Wallace Stegner writes in his pithy history *The Gathering of Zion*, "Most of them . . . had never pitched a tent, slept on the ground, cooked outdoors, built a campfire. They had not even the rudimentary skills that make frontiersmen. But as it turned out, they had some of the stuff that makes heroes."

By August 22, the last of the handcart emigrants had straggled into Florence, just across the Missouri River on the west. Built in 1846 as Winter Quarters by Brigham's pioneer party, the place had been abandoned in 1848. Then in 1854, when the former Omaha Indian territory was opened for settlement by U.S. citizens, Mormon entrepreneurs reestablished the outpost as Florence. By 1856, it was a thriving little tent city, with stores, warehouses, corrals, and a bowery or town hall for

meetings, all laid out in the orderly rectangular grid that would charac-
terize all Mormon settlements, including Salt Like City.

Here in Florence lay another opportunity to terminate the trek,
winter over, and head on for Zion the next spring. A general discussion
among the Martin Company emigrants was held on just this theme. But
a combination of fatalism and the by now ingrained exhortations of the
church officials turned nearly all the pioneers back to the trail stretching westward, where it plunged into real wilderness, traversed by at least
half a dozen different Indian tribes, none of which could be counted on
to be friendly.

On August 25, the company started off—dangerously late in the season, as more than one emigrant suspected. Within only three days, the
Loader family found itself in dire straits. By now, Zilpah was about to
give birth, and Tamar was incapacitated with "mountain fever." On the
morning of August 27, Captain Martin came to the Loaders' tent to tell
them to get ready to move on as soon as possible. But, in Patience's recollection, "There lay my Sister Zilpha on the ground just gave birth to
achild she was liing on some Quilts in one corner of the tent and My
sister Tamar liing on quilts in the other corner of the tent neither of the
poor things able to moove."

Martin assigned the two invalids and the newborn baby boy to one
of the team's eight wagons, but when Patience pleaded for a healthy sister to be allowed to ride with them to take care of Zilpah and Tamar, the
captain brusquely refused. Stubbornly, Patience then declined the offer
of wagon transport for her ailing sisters.

> I said thay will not go we will stay here for a day or two and take
> care of our two sick Sisters so we was left there all alone as the
> company started about seven oclock that morning we was there all
> day alone with our sick and when night came My poor father and
> brotherinlaw John Jaques had to be up all night to make big fires
> to keep the wolves away from us I never heard such terrable hawl-
> ing of wolfs in my life as we experenced that loansome night.

Only three days out of Florence, the Loaders had been left behind
by the Martin Company. The next day, a rider on horseback—Joseph

A. Young, one of Brigham's own sons—came galloping into the Loader camp. The main body of the party had seen the huge bonfire a few miles behind them and had worried that some accident had befallen the family.

> When he came into the tent and saw My sister with her new born babe liing on the ground on some quilts he was overcome with seympathy the tears ran down his cheeks then he bless my sister and tried to comfort and cheer her by saying well Sister Jaques I supose you will name Your boy handcart having begn born under such circumstances No she said I will want a prettyer name than that for him.

The boy, named Alpha Loader Jaques, would live to the ripe old age of eighty-nine. Before he died in December 1945, he had become the last surviving member of the Martin Company.

The handcart party, 575 strong, could not grind to a halt to wait for a single family to catch up. Accepting the inevitable, on August 28 the Loaders pushed on. On one handcart, along with the heavy tent, Tamar rode; on the other, Zilpah and her two children. The rest of the family pushed and pulled. In an incredible feat of perseverance and stamina, they traveled twenty-two miles that day, rejoining the main party only at 2:00 A.M., having navigated by moonlight. Patience saw the hand of God in the effort of August 28: "My poor father seemed better that day than he had been for aweek past surely God gave him new strength."

Before they could catch up with the company, however, the Loaders had their first Indian scare. As Patience tells it,

> Five great Indians came out of acave in the Mountains got on there horses and came to Meet us thay was all painted bare naked except there brich cloth had there tomahawks and hatchet bows an arrows thay stopt us in the road talked but we could not understand them when they saw our Sick and My sister with her New born babe thay mooved out of the road and motioned for us to go on I think this was as near to beign killed by Indians as I wished to be.

Those natives, probably Omaha Indians, seem to have been more perplexed by the sight of the struggling family than bent on bloodshed. Adds Patience,

> Thay was quite impodent in there Maners to us and Made fun of us pulling the handcart we was some what afraid of them and I daresay thay could see we was afraid of them. . . . I know it was nothing but the power of God that saved us from those Indians.

Eventually, both Zilpah and Tamar recovered sufficiently so that they could walk alongside the handcarts. (In his 1878 reminiscence, John Jaques insists that each sister was carried 150 miles, but this may be a retrospective exaggeration.) James Loader's strength held up for another two weeks or so. Patience remembered the agony of those days trudging across the plains and sand hills of Nebraska, and the faith that saw her through it: "Sometimes in the Morning I would feel so tiard and feel that I could not pull the cart the day through. then the still small voice would wisper in my ear as thy day thy strength shall be. this would give me new strength and energy."

Already the party's daily rations were proving inadequate. John Jaques's otherwise mundane diary records a consequence of the emigrants' ceaseless hunger that Patience's memoir omits. On September 22: "Cold, wet, rainy morning. Someone stole a cow's foot from my cart, also treacle, spice, meat, etc. from Brother John Oldham's cart and a meat dumpling from another brother's cart."

The 1878 reminiscence amplifies: "In some of the pinching times there would be a little petty pilfering going on in camp occasionally. The pilferings were usually of bread."

On the trail west, the Martin Company followed the Platte River along its northern bank. By mid-September, they had traveled some 275 miles from Florence, and were camped in what is now south-central Nebraska. On the 12th or 13th, they had passed Fort Kearny—a landmark that, curiously, neither Jaques's diary nor Patience's memoir mentions. The fort, established in 1848 to protect emigrants on the Oregon Trail, was one of only three places west of Florence where the Martin Company might have hoped to purchase supplies and food.

A pair of other diary-keepers in the party give clues to that omission. Wrote Jesse Haven, "Sept 12th . . . remained in Camp to-day did not travel. opposite to Fort Kerney I went over to the Fort and traded som Indians doing some depredations in this vicinity." And Samuel Openshaw recorded,

> Sept. 13—Started about half past 8 o'clock this morning, traveled until one o'clock when we stopped for dinner nearly opposite Fort Kearney where the soldiers are stationed, started again and traveled until five o'clock when we camped at the Platte River. A man fell down dead. The Indians are very hostile about here. They have attacted some of the immigrants who have passed through this season and rumor says that some have been murdered, but they have kept out of our way.

The chief reason that the Martin Company did not tarry at Kearny was not fear of Indians but the fact that the fort lay on the south—the wrong—side of the river. Crossings of waterways as broad and deep as the Platte were major undertakings. The detour to Kearny, even with its potential for trade, must have loomed as an unnecessary hiatus for the Saints as they hurried into autumn.

It was now that James Loader began to fail. A long, poignant passage in Patience's memoir chronicles his collapse:

> Some days he was not able to pull the cart but had to walk one evening when we goto camp he had walked seventeen miles with Mother helping him he sais My dear girls I was not able to get any wood to Make you afire and he fealt so bad about it I said never Mind father we have got some wood on the cart and we will soon have afire and make you a little warm grewel.

The Loaders and John Jaques got their tent pitched and carried James into it, swaddled in quilts.

> The next Morning I got very early to make afire and make him alittle more flour grewel that was all we had to give him but be-

fore I could get it ready for him My Sister Zilpha called to Saying patience come quick our father is dieing and when I got into the tent my poor Mother and all our family four Sisters My youngst brother Robert ten years old and my brother in law John Jaques was all kneeling on the ground around him poor dear father realizing he had to leave us he was to weak to talk to us he looked on us all with tears in his eyes then he said to Mother with great diffulcuty he said you know I love My children then he closed his eyes thees was the last words he ever said.

One of the sub-captains of the company, taking pity on the nearly comatose old man, offered to put him in a wagon as the party moved onward, but when Patience was rebuffed once more in her plea for one of the Loader sisters to ride with him, she again declined the offer. Instead, all day on September 23, the family pushed their two handcarts, atop one of which lay James Loader. "He did not seem to suffer pain he never opened his eyes," recalled Patience. "Many times dureing the day I spoke to him quite loud and ask him if he knew me or could he hear me but he never noticed me." The day's journey was a particularly arduous one, as the emigrants climbed and crested sand hills into which the handcart wheels sank as they gouged deep ruts.

That evening several Saints came to the Loader tent to give a last blessing to James. They moistened his mouth with anointing oil. To the family's amazement, James licked the oil from his parched lips. One of the watchers said, "We the servants of God seal him up unto God our Father," to which "my dear father amen said so plain that we could understand him and there lay with such asweet smile on his face that was the last word he said Amen to the blessing." He died at 11:00 P.M.

Another sub-captain, Daniel Tyler, who had also been made bishop of the Martin Company, tried to console the Loaders, calling James "afaithfull true servant of God" who "had laid down his life for the gosple sake he had died amarter to the truth," promising the family that "we will Meet our dear father again and be reunited with him to dwell in unity and love allthrough eternity. . . . Of course this was all very comforting to us but it did not bring our dear father back."

The burial, carried out at six the next morning, was agonizing for the family. "Two kind brothers" dug a grave deep enough so that the wolves would not dig up the corpse. Coffinless, wrapped in a quilt, James Loader was lowered into the hole "and the earth thown in upon his poor body oh that sounded so hard I will never forget the sound of that dirt beign shoveld anto my poor fathers boday it seemed to me that it would break every bone in his body."

John Jaques tersely recorded the gravesite as "west side of sandhill, 13 miles east of Ash Hollow." Jaques assigned "diarrhoea" as the cause of death.

After that, for the Loaders, there was nothing to do but to push on along the Platte with the rest of the company. During the first weeks of October, the days grew shorter and colder. James Loader was far from the only victim of this procession into an early winter. One day an emigrant named Jonathan Stone, about fifty-three years old, lay down beside the trail and fell asleep. It was some time before he was missed. According to Patience, "Some of the breathren had to go back in seach of him and when thay found him he was dead and nearly all eaten by the wolves."

The first snow fell on October 19. The timing was disastrous, for on that day the Martin Company had reached the point, not far from today's Casper, Wyoming, where the Mormon Trail left the Platte to follow the Sweetwater River toward South Pass and the Continental Divide. To pursue that route, all of the Martin Company had to ford the Platte, snowstorm be damned.

The team's few oxen were forced to swim, as the wagons were floated across, but the handcarts had to be pushed through the current by the terrified pilgrims. The mass ford quickly grew chaotic. Amy Loader was able to ride on the back of a mule making the crossing, but from the far bank she watched her children wading almost up to their necks. As Patience remembered,

> The water was deep and very cold and we was drifted out of the regular crossing and we came near to beign drounded the water came up to our arm pits poor Mother was standing on the bank screaming as we got near the bank I heard Mother say for Gods Sake some of you men help My poor girls.

One vignette glimpsed by Patience that day would haunt her for decades:

> When we was in the middle of the river I saw a poor brother car-
> reying his child on his back he fell down in the water I never Knew
> if he was drowned or not I fealt sorrey that we could not help him
> but we had all we could do to save ourselves from drownding.

Once on the far bank, with all their clothing soaked, the snow falling, and a bitter wind raking the plain, the emigrants were at immediate risk of fatal hypothermia. The company moved on for several miles before finding a campsite. The Loader children's clothing froze stiff. "Mother took of one of her under skirts and put on one of us and her apron for another," Patience later wrote. In camp that afternoon,

> It was to late to go for wood and water the wood was to far away.
> that night the ground was frozen to hard we was unable to drive
> any tent pins in as the tent was wett when we took it down in the
> morning it was somewhat frozen So we stretched it open the best
> we could and got in under it untill morning.

For the Loaders, and for the hundreds of other members of the Martin Company stranded in the middle of this increasingly desperate journey, the worst was yet to come.

CHAPTER TWO

FINDING ZION

The handcart trail to Zion was paved with two and a half decades of messianic visions on the part of Mormon leaders and relentless persecution at the hands of the church's enemies. What is today by far the most successful homegrown American religion, with nearly six million adherents in the United States and twelve million worldwide, might well have fizzled out early on, like such contemporary American faiths as the Millerites, the Campbellites, or the celibate Jemimaites. In his 1930 essay "The Centennial of Mormonism," Bernard DeVoto—born in Ogden, Utah, to a mother who had been raised in the LDS church—alluded sardonically to an "anonymous Frenchman" who had "remarked that America, which could contrive only one soup, had invented a hundred religions." (One wonders what soup the Frenchman had in mind.)

The very survival of the Church of Jesus Christ of Latter-day Saints in the nineteenth century, not to mention its burgeoning appeal at the beginning of the twenty-first, owes everything to the extraordinary characters of its first two Prophets, Joseph Smith and Brigham Young. (For its December 2006 issue, *The Atlantic Monthly* polled ten "prominent historians" to rank the one hundred most influential Americans in history. The list, headed by Lincoln, Washington, and Jefferson, included Joseph Smith [at number 52] and Brigham Young [at 74]. Only two other religious leaders made the list—Martin Luther King Jr. [8] and Mary Baker Eddy [86].) Indeed, during the 1860s and 1870s, many sagacious observers of the Mormon colony in Utah were quite certain that the religion would collapse shortly after the death of Brigham Young.

It is something of a coincidence—but something not—that while Joseph Smith and Brigham Young were both born in Vermont (in Sharon, in the eastern Green Mountains, and Whitingham, just north of the Massachusetts border, respectively), both moved while still in childhood to western New York state. Driven by poverty and illness, Smith's farming family resettled in 1816 in Palmyra, a town of about four thousand situated some twenty-five miles southeast of Rochester. Smith was ten years old at the time.

Born on June 1, 1801, Young was actually four and a half years older than the Prophet who would lead him into the church he would found in 1830. Like Smith's, Young's father was a down-on-his-luck farmer, a man who supplemented his earnings as a part-time carpenter. By 1804 the Youngs had moved to Sherburne, in central New York state; eight years later, when Young was eleven, they fetched up in the rural burg that is known today as Tyrone—fifty miles due south of the Palmyra to which the Smiths would emigrate in 1816, during the famous "year without a summer."

There was no more propitious time or place in American history for the concoction of new religions. During the first decades of the nineteenth century, Americans were hungry for millennial proofs that God was among us, watchful, punitive of sinners, but promising abundant and imminent rewards to the righteous. The whole country was lurching in violent counterreaction against the irreligion and moral looseness of Tom Paine's Age of Reason—itself a violent reaction against the Puritan thunderings of Jonathan Edwards and Cotton Mather a generation before.

Nowhere was that zeal for new faith more rabid than on the semi-frontier of western New York state. The region centering on Palmyra acquired among circuit-riders a sobriquet as "the burnt-over district." In biographer Fawn Brodie's gloss: "One revival after another was sweeping through the area, leaving behind a people scattered and peeled, for religious enthusiasm was literally being burnt out of them."

Latter-day Mormon hagiographers have tended to portray the young Joseph Smith as an upstanding teenage citizen of Palmyra with an insatiable curiosity about the metaphysical, but there is plenty of evidence that he had much of the scamp and scallywag about him, and even a bit of the con man. Brigham Young's iconoclastic 1925 biographer, Morris Werner, finds the flawed image of Smith more appealing than the gilded icon:

> The Mormons would do better to accept this picture of him, which wins our sympathy by virtue of his roguery. However, it outrages the moral sensibilities of stern religious enthusiasts to admit that Huckleberry Finn could have grown up into a Prophet of God.

Fawn Brodie, whose 1945 biography of Joseph Smith, *No Man Knows My History* (revised in 1970), remains the definitive life, concurs. She sees her subject in adolescence as "a likeable ne'er-do-well who was notorious for tall tales and necromantic arts." Later, after Smith became famous, a number of his erstwhile Palmyra neighbors published unflattering vignettes of the rogue who had grown up in their midst. One former friend wrote, "He was known among the young men I associated with as a romancer of the first water. I never knew so ignorant a man as Joe was to have such a fertile imagination."

Some of these retrospective slurs were solicited by anti-Mormon polemicists, and are thus perhaps no more to be credited than the hagiographers' rosy portraits. Among them is an affidavit signed by fifty-one Palmyrans asserting that Smith was "destitute of *moral character and addicted to vicious habits.*" It is a matter of record that at age twenty-one he was arrested for being "a disorderly person and an impostor." But the affidavit seems too harsh. Smith himself, in a church publication, admitted at the age of twenty-eight that in his teenage years "I fell into many vices and follies," but he insisted that "I have not . . . been guilty of wronging or injuring any man or society of men."

In any event, while still a teenager, he took up the hobby (a common one in the "burnt-over district") of digging for buried treasure, and soon he was selling his talents as a diviner of riches hidden in the earth to credulous neighbors. Brodie sees this avocation as initially the innocent outlet of a restless spirit: "Nimble-witted, ambitious, and gifted with a boundless imagination, he dreamed of escape. . . . He detested the plow as only a farmer's son can."

By his early twenties, Smith was over six feet tall, good-looking, and vigorously athletic (wrestling being one of his favorite pastimes, even after he had become the Mormon Prophet). In Brodie's sketch,

> He was big, powerful, and by ordinary standards very handsome, except for his nose, which was aquiline and prominent. His large blue eyes were fringed by fantastically long lashes which made his gaze seem veiled and slightly mysterious.

In the best-known portrait of the man, he is dressed to the nines in a collarless black frock coat worn over a white silk shirt and white tie. His wavy, combed-back brown hair has tints of auburn in it. The eyes stare unblinking and hypnotic at the viewer, but the mouth, pursed in a tight half-smile, exudes smugness. The overall effect of the likeness hovers on that ambiguous border between the strikingly handsome and the foppishly vain.

At the age of nineteen, on a wild-goose chase in search of a lost Spanish silver mine in the Allegheny foothills of western Pennsylvania, Joseph met and fell in love with Emma Hale, two years his elder. Brodie describes her as "a dark, serious-faced girl with great luminous hazel eyes." Against the unbending opposition of Emma's father, Joseph wooed her, ran away with her, and secretly married her in January 1827. In important ways, Emma would prove to be the bane of Smith's existence.

At some point, while still a teenager, as he dug a well for a neighbor, Smith discovered what he called a "seer stone" twenty-four feet underground. With this magical aid, he launched a serious if intermittent career as diviner of subterranean riches.

At this remove, it is perhaps impossible to judge whether Smith's treasure-hunting was a deliberate con game or sprang from sincere belief. The fact that he did little digging himself but charged others for his secret knowledge, and that he always had a ready excuse why days of shoveling turned up only rocks and dirt, suggests the former explanation. Yet legions of frontier settlers in places like western New York were utterly convinced that buried treasure abounded in their neighborhoods, a conviction reinforced by the prehistoric Indian mounds scattered across the landscape, in which diggers regularly hit paydirt of an artifactual sort.

Joseph Smith, however, would be forgotten by history, but for a pair of miraculous visitations that seized him, the first at age fourteen, the second at seventeen. In 1820, a latent religious instinct in Smith's soul was sparked by several recent revival meetings near Palmyra. One day the youth went into the woods alone to pray to God for guidance. Almost at once, as he later wrote, he was struck dumb by some "astonishing influence," and he found himself surrounded by "thick darkness." As he prayed now for deliverance from this "evil" miasma, suddenly all was light, and two "personages" stood before him. One pointed to the other, saying, *"This is my beloved Son, hear him."*

Smith's initial purpose in beseeching God in the forest was to get an answer to a question that was plaguing him: which of the many sects and denominations whose doctrines had been blazoned forth at the revival meetings was the true church? Now one of the personages told him that all those sects were wrong, that "all their creeds were an abomination in His sight," and that he must join none of them. "Many other things he did say unto me," Smith recorded years later, "which I cannot write at this time. When I came to myself again, I found myself lying on my back, looking up into heaven."

The second vision, which came to Smith on September 21, 1823, was even more vivid and revelatory. In his room at home, that night he knelt by his bed to pray to God "for forgiveness of all my sins and follies." Again, a light "brighter than noonday" suffused the room and a "personage" appeared, floating in midair. As Smith later recounted,

> He had on a loose robe of most exquisite whiteness. It was a whiteness beyond anything earthly I had ever seen; nor do I believe that any earthly thing could be made to appear so exceedingly white and brilliant. His hands were naked and his arms also. . . . His head and neck were also bare. I could discover that he had no other clothing on but this robe, as it was open, so that I could see into his bosom. Not only was his robe exceedingly white, but his whole person was glorious beyond description, and his countenance truly like lightning. . . .
>
> When first I looked upon him, I was afraid; but the fear soon left me. He called me by name, and said unto me that he was

a messenger sent from the presence of God to me and that his name was Moroni; that God had a work for me to do. . . . He said there was a book deposited, written upon gold plates, giving an account of the former inhabitants of this continent, and the sources from whence they sprang. He also said that the fullness of the everlasting Gospel was contained in it, as delivered by the Savior to the ancient inhabitants; also that there were two stones in silver bows and these stones, fastened to a breastplate, constituted what is called the Urim and Thummim deposited with the plates; and the possession and use of these stones were what constituted "Seers" in ancient or former times; and that God had prepared them for the purpose of translating the book.

Moroni (pronounced "Mo-ROAN-eye"; Mormon proper names ending in "i" almost always take the long form of the vowel) was not only an angel, but a prophet who had lived in America many centuries before the first Europeans arrived. It was Moroni, in fact, who had buried the golden plates around A.D. 421.

The very next day, Smith went out to work in the fields, but he was so weak, his father sent him home. On the way, he fell into a swoon, only to be visited again by Moroni, who now told him exactly where the plates were buried. "Convenient to the village of Manchester, Ontario county, New York," Smith later wrote, "stands a hill of considerable size, and the most elevated of any in the neighborhood. On the west side of this hill, not far from the top, under a stone of considerable size, lay the plates, deposited in a stone box." Smith dug up the box and, with the aid of a lever, pried it open. "I looked in, and there indeed did I behold the plates, the Urim and Thummim, and the breastplate." But just as he started to seize the plates, Moroni again appeared, warning Smith that he was not spiritually prepared to receive this testament of the true church.

As directed by Moroni, Smith returned to the hill once a year for four years on the anniversary of his discovery. Finally, on September 21, 1827, the angelic messenger allowed the youth (now twenty-one years old) to carry the plates away with him.

The hill, named Cumorah, stands a mere several hundred feet above the surrounding fields, just off State Highway 21, which connects Palmyra and Manchester. However unprepossessing it may be as a geologic eminence, Cumorah is today a prominent stop for Mormon history tours. Every July since 1937, a Hill Cumorah Pageant, lasting seven days, has attracted as many as ten thousand visitors (both Saints and non-Mormons) from all over the country and the world.

The golden plates were densely inscribed with a hieroglyphic script, a sample of which Smith later transcribed. But a condition of his custodianship of the sacred objects, Smith insisted, was that no one else be allowed to look at them. Somehow the young treasure-hunter recognized the language of the glyphs as what he called "reformed Egyptian." With the aid of his seer stones, the Urim and Thummim, he set out to translate the plates. His wife, Emma, was his first scribe, as he dictated out loud. Though the plates often lay on the table, wrapped in a linen tablecloth, she never saw them; she did, however, dare to handle them when she dusted the table, and later reported that the plates "seemed to be pliable like thick paper, and would rustle with a metallic sound when the edges were moved by the thumb."

Eventually Smith collaborated with a more credulous scribe, a farmer friend named Martin Harris, who in turn was succeeded by a schoolmaster named Oliver Cowdery. The procedure must have seemed a bit bizarre, even to true believers. With Harris, Smith sat in a room partitioned by a blanket thrown across a rope. Smith sat on one side, staring painfully at the plates with his Urim and Thummim, while Harris sat on the other side, writing down the sentences as Smith translated them. Smith repeatedly warned his scribe that "God's wrath would strike him down" should he even sneak a look at the plates.

By 1829, working with Cowdery, Smith had replaced the Urim and Thummim with the seer stone that he had found in the well, which he placed in an upturned hat. He then plunged his face into the hat, cutting off all surrounding light, as with the stone he deciphered the plates one character at a time. Starting on April 7, Smith dictated all 275,000 words of what would become the *Book of Mormon* in seventy-five days, at an extraordinary pace, averaging around 3,700 words a day.

Five thousand copies of the *Book of Mormon* were published by a local printer in 1830. On April 6 of that year, Smith formally founded his new church.

By then, in accordance with his promise to the angelic messenger, Smith had returned the golden plates to Moroni. No one would ever see them again.

To THE AGNOSTIC or the skeptic, virtually all religions may seem to be founded on events and concepts that are absurd and implausible. (The Trinity? The Virgin Birth? The Second Coming?) Yet from its inception, the Church of Jesus Christ of Latter-day Saints has been singled out for ridicule on account of the wildly far-fetched story of Joseph Smith and the golden plates. To Bernard DeVoto, for example, the *Book of Mormon* seemed "a yeasty fermentation, formless, aimless, and inconceivably absurd."

At first blush, there seem to be three separate and mutually exclusive explanations for what was going on in and around Palmyra, New York, in the 1820s. One is what twelve million Mormons steadfastly believe: that the angel and prophet Moroni really did appear to Joseph Smith; that the golden plates were not only real, but had inscribed on them the authentic gospel; that Smith translated them with the aid of various seer stones; and thus that the *Book of Mormon* corrected more than a millennium and a half of Christian error and gave the world the only true message of God's dispensation. All other religions are wrong.

For nonbelievers, however, two other explanations immediately present themselves. The first is that a teenage treasure-hunter and con artist set out to perpetrate a deliberate fraud, one that would become the most successful in American history. Fawn Brodie would seem to be of this camp. "Perhaps in the beginning," she writes in *No Man Knows My History*, "Joseph never intended his stories of the golden plates to be taken so seriously, but once the masquerade had begun, there was no point at which he could call a halt. Since his own family believed him (with the possible exception of his cynical younger brother William), why not the world?"

Brodie had grown up Mormon in Utah, but became more and more skeptical as she went through high school and college. At the University of Chicago, where she did graduate work, she lost her faith entirely. "It was like taking a hot coat off in the summertime," she told an interviewer in 1975. In 1946, the year after she published her biography of Joseph Smith, the church excommunicated her.

The alternative agnostic explanation is that, while the whole business about the golden plates was nonsense, Smith sincerely believed it—that he was in the grips of the sort of profound self-delusion that afflicts many religious visionaries.

At second blush, however, the three explanations turn out not to be mutually exclusive. Writes Morris Werner in his biography of Brigham Young:

> It is impossible to determine exactly whether the golden plates of the Book of Mormon were an imaginative delusion of Joseph Smith's, or whether they were a piece of conscious fakery instituted at first for fun and later developed for their financial possibilities. His later acts seem to favor the opinion that he had succeeded in deluding himself, however much he may have been interested at first in deceiving other people.

Some extraordinarily intelligent men and women have devoted the best parts of their lives to defending the authenticity of the *Book of Mormon* and the truth of the LDS church. One of them was Brigham Henry Roberts (1857–1933), whose six-volume *A Comprehensive History of the Church of Jesus Christ of Latter-day Saints* remains unparalleled. One scholar calls Roberts "intellectually the most eminent and influential of all the official leaders of the Church." Another hails him as "the greatest Mormon thinker of his generation, or perhaps any generation."

Around the turn of the twentieth century, Roberts vigorously and eloquently defended the *Book of Mormon* against its learned critics. The terms upon which the debates hinged seem quaint and hyper-scholastic today: whether, for instance, 553 years intervened between Zedekiah's reign as the last king of Judah and Christ's birth (the biblical version) or six hundred years, as the *Book of Mormon* specified. Yet in one controversy after another, Roberts reportedly put the doubters to rout.

Then, late in his own life, the great Mormon thinker was apparently assailed by his own doubts. He had always striven to reconcile science and religion; he believed passionately that one could be a devout Mormon and a rational pragmatist at the same time. In the 1920s, perplexed by how Darwin's theory of evolution and the discoveries of New World archaeologists seemed to contradict Mormon doctrine, he drafted a pair of manuscripts that he titled "A Book of Mormon Study" and "Book of Mormon Difficulties." Joseph Smith's gospel claimed that long before the first Europeans arrived, the natives of North America had possessed such domestic animals as horses, cows, sheep, and pigs, as well as weapons and tools of iron and steel, crops including wheat and barley, and wheeled vehicles. The archaeologists insisted that none of the above was true.

Roberts's superiors in the church deemed these late works too heretical to bring to light without major revisions. Roberts declined. The problematic manuscripts were not published until 1985—fifty-two years after Roberts's death.

There is a school of Mormon thought that in these late treatises, Roberts was not truly plagued by doubt, but was rather playing the devil's advocate, positing all possible rational objections to the *Book of Mormon* in hopes of finding the loopholes that would leave the LDS doctrine unscathed. Yet the problems Roberts raised remain unanswered: as far as we know, before Columbus, no Native American had ever seen a horse, a steel weapon, or a vehicle with wheels. The integrity of the greatest Mormon theorist's willingness, late in life, to open his mind to the fundamental historical problems raised by the *Book of Mormon* should win him admiration, not excuses.

Whether or not Joseph Smith concocted his 531-page gospel out of his own runaway imagination, or was simply the amanuensis for a divine revelation, the *Book of Mormon* is an astonishing performance. To be sure, it is not an easy book to read, and many a good Mormon has nodded off long before reaching the closing "Book of Moroni." Mark Twain famously called Smith's book "chloroform in print," and, singling out the work's recurrent verbal tic, added, " 'And it came to pass' was his pet. If he had left that out, his Bible would have been only a pamphlet."

The *Book of Mormon* is riddled with grammatical errors and apparent anachronisms of diction and style. Whole chapters of Isaiah are lifted verbatim from the Old Testament. One of the antagonists Roberts debated claimed that Joseph had quoted not only from the King James

version of the Bible (not published until 1611, or almost twelve centuries after Moroni supposedly buried the golden plates), but from Hamlet's famous soliloquy.

From almost the time it was first published until the present day,
the *Book of Mormon* has been accused of being a wholesale plagiarism,
either from the manuscript of a romance novel by one Solomon Spaul-
ding, or from a popular 1823 treatise written by a Vermont pastor named
Ethan Smith called *View of the Hebrews*, which advanced the then vogu-
ish theory that American Indians were the remnants of the lost tribes of
Israel. Neither plagiarism claim has been proved or disproved (Spaul-
ding's manuscript is apparently irretrievably lost), but B. H. Roberts
himself was sufficiently troubled by the similarities with *View of the
Hebrews* that he compiled a twin-columned document that he called "A
Parallel," laying without comment the overly close passages of the two
Smiths side by side. This study, too, was not published until 1985, but it
gives serious pause to anyone who peruses it today.

Quite aside from allegations of plagiarism, Smith has been long accused of recklessly borrowing not only doctrine, but later, ecclesiasti-
cal rituals from the secret practices of the Freemasons. Yet astonishing
the *Book of Mormon* remains, especially in view of the fact that its "author," having kicked around with his vagabond farming family through
the backwaters of Vermont and New York, had absorbed precious little
schooling by the age of twenty-four, when the new gospel was first published.

In the face of such early criticism, Smith obtained the written affidavits of eleven of his friends and Palmyra neighbors (including Martin
Harris and Oliver Cowdery), who swore that they had not only seen the
golden plates (despite Smith's initial warning against such a violation),
but also that "we did handle [them] with our hands," that "we have seen
and hefted" them. For the skeptic, it is curious that although several of
these witnesses later left the church, none ever recanted his testimony.
This fact bothers Brodie enough to make her speculate, "Perhaps Joseph
built some kind of makeshift deception. If so, it disappeared with his
announcement that the same angel that had revealed to him the sacred
record had now carried it back into heaven." Brodie and others have
wondered whether Smith in effect hypnotized his witnesses.

All this controversy would amount to a mere footnote to the history of the nineteenth century in America had Mormonism caught flame briefly and then flickered out, like so many other religions of the day. Whatever Smith's shortcomings as a prose stylist, he possessed in spades those two essential qualities of the messianic leader—charisma and oratorical eloquence. The testimonies to his ability to hold an audience spellbound when he preached are legion. One of his first and most important converts, Parley P. Pratt, related, "I have ever known him to retain a congregation of willing and anxious listeners for many hours together, in the midst of cold or sunshine, rain or wind, while they were laughing at one moment and weeping the next."

Traveling all over the region, Smith slowly but doggedly made converts. One of the first to fall under his spell was Brigham Young, who had moved in 1829 to Mendon, a village only fifteen miles southwest of Palmyra. Twenty-eight years old, married, with a three-year-old daughter, Young was eking out a living, like his father, making chairs and baskets that he sold door-to-door.

Young, however, was no instant convert. At age twenty-two, he had joined the Methodist Church, but he was far from satisfied with that faith, having also attended services in Mendon of half a dozen other Protestant denominations, ranging from Episcopalian to Quaker. One day in 1830, only two or three weeks after it had been published, a copy of the *Book of Mormon* was thrust into his hands by his brother Phineas. Brigham struggled with the dense tome for two years before he became convinced, as he later wrote, that "I knew it was true, as well as I knew that I could see with my eyes, or feel by the touch of my fingers, or be sensible of the demonstration of any sense."

An important and unresolved question about Brigham Young is how literate he was. By his own admission, he had received only eleven days of formal schooling in his life. The hundreds of letters that he "wrote" after he became Prophet of the church were all dictated to scribes. Some skeptical visitors to Salt Lake City during Young's heyday claimed that the official epistles he regularly issued were ghostwritten by his right-hand men, and that Young himself could scarcely write more than his own name. Such calumnies must be taken with a grain of salt, for the nineteenth-century authors of exposés of the Mormon empire had their own axes to grind. Many a close acquaintance observed him reading a book now and then, and even his ex-wife Ann Eliza Young, whose *Wife No. 19, or the Story of a Life in Bondage* is perhaps the angriest of all those exposés, wrote in 1875, "He loses his temper every morning over the *Salt Lake Tribune*—the leading Gentile [i.e., non-Mormon] paper of Utah."

On April 15, 1832, Young was baptized into the LDS church. A few months later, with his friend Heber C. Kimball, who would become one of the most important men in the Utah theocracy, he traveled to Kirtland, Ohio, to meet the Prophet. (Kirtland was the first of several places where Smith tried to establish an autonomous colony for the Saints, free from Gentile distractions and attacks.) Kimball and Young found Smith in the forest chopping wood. "He was happy to see us and bid us welcome," Young later testified. That evening, in Smith's house, the Prophet urged Young to get on his knees and pray. All at once, Young spontaneously began to speak in tongues.

This performance, which was to become a mainstay in the mystical apparatus of Mormon church services, is dryly explicated by Morris Werner, Brigham's skeptical biographer: "It consisted of a babble of incomprehensible sounds which were supposed to be the spirit of God resting upon the speaker, and these sounds were interpreted by another person in the congregation as soon as the speaker had uttered them."

THE DUTY OF every Saint to gather to Zion was announced by Joseph Smith within six months of the founding of his church. As befit a man who would set himself up with the formal title of Prophet, Seer, Revelator, and President (a title Brigham Young would inherit), Smith received frequent revelations from God. One of the first decreed: "And ye are called to bring to pass the gathering of mine elect . . . they shall be gathered in unto one place upon the face of this land." Moreover, "The glory of the Lord shall be there, and it shall be called Zion."

The only question was where Zion might prove to be. From the start, Smith looked westward, for the revelation also specified that the gathering place "shall be on the borders of the Lamanites."

According to the *Book of Mormon*, the Lamanites (pronounced "LAY-man-ites") were the American Indians. All the different tribes found in

North America were the descendants of Laman, one of the sons of Lehi, the patriarch who had built a ship and sailed with his people from the Holy Land to the New World around 600 B.C. Another son of Lehi was named Nephi.

By about A.D. 231, the followers and descendants of Laman and Nephi started a war with each other that lasted more than 150 years. Finally, the Lamanites—unbelievers in Christ (who himself had appeared in the New World between his resurrection and his ascent into heaven), reduced to the state of savages—wiped out the righteous Nephites. (Moroni, the last Nephite alive, buried the golden plates shortly before his death.) For their wrongdoings, God cursed the Lamanites with dark skin. The Lamanites of today, however, are not beyond redemption. If they accept the Christian God and convert to the LDS church, they can become in the next life "a white and delightsome people." (Later editions of the *Book of Mormon* changed the phrase to "a pure and delightsome people.")

The new faith got off to a slow but steady start. Founded with a congregation of only six adherents, the church plucked converts here and there from the towns around western New York and Pennsylvania, until by the autumn of 1830 Smith could count sixty followers. Having divined the prophecy that Zion would be located "on the borders of the Lamanites," Smith sent Oliver Cowdery, Parley Pratt, and two other disciples on a mission to the west, with instructions not only to preach to the Indians but to scout for a place to establish Zion.

On their mission, the scouts met thirty-seven-year-old Sidney Rigdon, a prominent preacher who had founded a utopian colony in Kirtland, only a few miles east of Cleveland. Reading the *Book of Mormon*, Rigdon was impressed, and started to doubt the validity of his own sect. Mormon history is full of narratives and parables that sound almost too good to be true. According to one of these, not only was Rigdon at once converted to the LDS faith, but so was every member of his colony.

Once Rigdon met Smith, the idea of Kirtland as the gathering place began to seem inevitable. Yet the Prophet had a hard time convincing his New York flock to pick up and move, for they would have to sell the homes and farms they had worked so hard to build and cultivate. To persuade the recalcitrant, Smith received another revelation, which proclaimed in part that Kirtland lay on the eastern edge of the promised land, which stretched all the way from Ohio to the Pacific Ocean.

Kirtland lasted as the Mormon stronghold for seven years, but almost from the start, serious problems arose there. Rigdon and Smith had minor fallings-out; a number of Rigdon's former congregation did not take easily to the younger man's assuming supremacy in the church; and curious nonbelievers flocked to the town to gawk at the Saints as they might animals in a zoo. Smith made the mistake of curing, in front of his congregation, a woman with a paralyzed arm. When the doubters later challenged him to perform other cures, he failed to make a lame man walk or to revive a dead child.

Antagonisms with non-Mormon Ohio neighbors sometimes erupted into violence. The nadir of Smith's Kirtland years came in March 1832, when a mob in the nearby town of Hiram broke into the house where he and Rigdon were sleeping and tarred and feathered them. In Fawn Brodie's vivid evocation,

> They stripped him, scratched and beat him with savage pleasure, and smeared his bleeding body with tar from head to foot. Ripping a pillow into shreds, they plastered him with feathers. It is said that Eli Johnson demanded that the prophet be castrated, for he suspected Joseph of being too intimate with his sister, Nancy Marinda. But the doctor who had been persuaded to join the mob declined the responsibility at the last moment, and Johnson had to be content with seeing the prophet beaten senseless.

Kirtland set the pattern for the first fourteen difficult years of the LDS church's existence in the United States. Loyalists tend to paint this period as a continuous ordeal of persecution of the Saints by intolerant neighbors, but there is abundant evidence that the Saints themselves often provoked those neighbors with aggressive actions of their own. For one thing, the Mormon colony sometimes behaved as though it were exempt from the laws of the state in which it resided. Thus in 1837, Smith organized the Kirtland Safety Society Bank Company and began to issue the church's own paper money. The Ohio legislature refused to incorporate the bank, and warrants for the arrest of both Smith and Sidney

Rigdon as counterfeiters were issued. (Rigdon was brought to court, and as a result, the Bank Company stopped making its own money. In January 1838, Smith fled Ohio rather than submit to arrest.)

Smith's solution to the Kirtland crisis was to announce a new locus for Zion. As early as 1831, Oliver Cowdery and Parley Pratt had pushed their mission to the Lamanites much farther west. They came back from Missouri raving about the felicities of Jackson County, on the western edge of the state, bordering the Missouri River, beyond which the Indian Territory stretched. Cowdery himself urged the fledgling town of Independence (founded only four years earlier) as the new seat of Zion.

Smith sent a small body of settlers west to establish a colony near Independence. Meanwhile, he was visited by further divine revelations. One of them delivered the surprising information that the Garden of Eden lay not in the Holy Land of the Near East, but in Jackson County, Missouri.

Yet Independence would never become the Mormon Zion. Frictions with neighbors there grew even more heated than they had in Ohio. In 1833, the colonists were driven out of their homes by a mob, and in November an armed battle that cost the lives of two Gentiles and one Mormon ended with the withdrawal of the Mormons from Jackson County. Most of the refugees moved to neighboring precincts to the north.

In August 1836, two of those refugees founded the town of Far West, about thirty-five miles north of Independence. Caldwell County was created from scratch to accommodate the Saints. Arriving there two years later, Smith declared that Far West lay in the exact place where Cain had slain Abel.

Smith was nothing if not ambitious. Even as the Kirtland colony was disintegrating before his eyes, in June 1837 the Prophet sent three of the church's leading missionaries to England to preach to the poor. Thus began the wildly successful campaign of conversion in Great Britain, which would send so many of the hundreds of pioneers to Utah in the 1850s, including the vast majority of the handcart emigrants of 1856.

The year 1838, by far the most troubled yet in Mormonism's brief existence, could well have seen the extinction of the church. In January, Smith abandoned Kirtland and moved to Far West. Brigham Young, by now one of Smith's most trusted aides, went with him. In July, the remaining Kirtland colonists, about five hundred to six hundred strong, traveled by wagon train to the new Zion in northwest Missouri.

During these tumultuous years, Mormonism's darkest secret was polygamy. There is good evidence that Smith practiced "plural marriage" as early as 1831, and that not long after that he gave orders to his closest lieutenants to do likewise. Rumors of the practice inevitably leaked out. In 1835, the church promulgated the first of its numerous official denials, in a resolution at its annual conference: "Inasmuch as this Church has been reproached with the crime of fornication and polygamy, we declare that we believe that one man should have one wife, and one woman but one husband, except in case of death, when either is at liberty to marry again."

For the next seventeen years, LDS authorities continued to deny that the church authorized polygamy, until Brigham Young came publicly clean in 1852. Brodie characterizes those denials as "a remarkable series of evasions and circumlocutions involving all sorts of verbal gymnastics."

Meanwhile, through the late 1830s and into the 1840s, Smith secretly married one wife after another, with a crescendo of such liaisons sanctified in 1843 and 1844. Brodie offers a list of forty-nine plural wives during Smith's lifetime; there may have been more. The man, of course, could hardly keep his polygamy secret from his first wife, Emma. From the start, she was intensely distraught over her husband's intimacies with other women, and could never be reconciled to his arguments in favor of the practice. Her obstinacy grew so truculent that in 1843, Smith put an extraordinary revelation in writing. In it, God spoke directly to Emma Smith, commanding her to "receive all those that have been given unto my servant Joseph." The punishment for her refusal was extreme: "But if she will not abide this commandment she shall be destroyed, saith the Lord; for I am the Lord thy God, and will destroy her if she abide not in my law."

Yet Smith and his high-level confederates managed to keep any confirmation of the rumors of polygamy away from the ears of the rank and file. One may credit the remarkable keeping of this secret for more than two decades to a sheeplike credulity on the part of ordinary Saints, or to a masterly job of spin control among its hierarchy. As late as the early

1850s, Fanny Stenhouse, an English Saint living in France, met with a group of fellow female believers in Boulogne-sur-mer to discuss the gossip. Their gathering was sternly admonished by Apostle John Taylor (later to play a critical role in the handcart emigration): "We are accused here of actions the most indelicate and disgusting, such as none but a corrupt and depraved heart could have contrived." Taylor went on to cite early proclamations from the Prophet himself about the sanctity of monogamous marriage, scolding the women for their lack of faith.

Skeptical observers of the church point to this twenty-one-year denial of polygamy as proof of the most arrogant hypocrisy on the part of Smith and his chief confederates. Defenders argue that "plural marriage" was so radical a doctrine in mid-nineteenth-century America that disclosure could have meant the dissolution of a faith that had already been hounded by its persecutors out of Ohio and Missouri.

Those camps divide along similar lines when it comes to the question of why Smith came up with the doctrine of polygamy in the first place. The skeptics see it as a simple rationalization of his own propensity for womanizing (evidence of which preceded the founding of the church). Brodie imagines "a man of Joseph's physical charm" growing tired of his older wife, worn out from childbearing; and "Kirtland was overflowing with women who idolized him." Smith is also reported to have confessed to a close friend, "Whenever I see a pretty woman I have to pray for grace."

Yet when Smith came to argue for the logic of plural marriage, he did so by citing the example of Old Testament patriarchs such as Abraham and Jacob, who took more than one wife. In a twist of Mormon doctrine, a woman's eternal salvation can be gained only through marriage. Polygamy could actually save the old crones and maiden ladies who might otherwise get passed over from exclusion from heaven. There are numerous later nineteenth-century testimonies by Mormon women defending polygamy, and of course there are breakaway Mormon groups today that practice polygamy.

AS THE NEW Zion, Far West, Missouri, would last less than a year. The Saints must have thought that by removing themselves to a sparsely settled region, they might flourish free from outside interference. Yet they could hardly have chosen a worse place. In the words of Brigham Young biographer Stanley Hirshson, "Within the state raged every imaginable conflict: slaveholder fought abolitionist; Indian battled white man; and Democrat clashed with Whig. To this was added another struggle: Saint versus Gentile."

By 1838 the numbers of Mormons in northwest Missouri had swelled to between eight thousand and ten thousand, 1,500 of them in Far West alone. It was too large a throng to be ignored. And the Saints did their part to stir up trouble. The paranoia engendered by very real persecution and vilification around Palmyra and Kirtland transmuted in Far West into grandiose assertions of superiority.

One of Smith's closest associates, Sampson Avard—Brodie calls him "cunning, resourceful, and extremely ambitious"—proposed forming a secret Mormon army. Rigdon was enthusiastic, and Smith listened.

Thus was born the most nefarious organization ever to coalesce within the Mormon church. Referred to at various early stages as the Brothers of Gideon, the Daughters of Zion, or the Sons of Dan, the band—less an army than a kind of secret police—soon became known as the Danites. They took their name from a verse in Genesis: "Dan shall be a serpent by the way, an adder in the path, that biteth the horse heels, so that his rider shall fall backward."

Men handpicked for their skill with guns and their courage, the Danites were sworn to secrecy and invested with cabalistic handshakes and signals. They would prove, across nearly half a century, well into Brigham Young's reign in Utah, a devastatingly effective cadre of assassins, targeting apostates, enemies, rich Gentiles, and even Indians—in effect, the KGB of the Mormon church. Both Smith and Young would aver that the Danites never existed. In 1859, the famous journalist Horace Greeley arrived in Salt Lake City and won from Young one of the first interviews he ever gave to a professional newspaperman. Greeley pressed the Prophet hard, asking, among other questions, "What do you say of the so-called Danites, or Destroying Angels, belonging to your church?" Brigham smoothly countered, "What do *you* say? I know of no such band, no such persons or organization. I hear of them only in the slanders of our enemies."

Leonard J. Arrington, whose *Brigham Young: American Moses*, published in 1985, is considered by orthodox Mormons to be the definitive life of the second Prophet, turns somersaults to deny the existence of the Danites in Utah. He insists that Young had instead "created a small force of Minute Men" charged with recapturing stolen livestock and establishing emigrant way stations, not with perpetrating murders and assassinations. As for the Danites, Arrington insists, "They played and continue to play a major role in western fiction, and many readers have imagined Brigham as a military dictator with a personal army of avengers who carried out his orders to capture, torture, and kill people who crossed him." (Many non-Mormons regard Arrington's voluminous biography as a partisan whitewash, and insist that the definitive life has yet to be written.)

There is simply far too much evidence not only of the existence of the Danites, but of the specific murders and assassinations carried out by thugs whose names and characters we can identify. One of the most notorious, Bill Hickman, who eventually fell out with Young, collaborated in 1872 with an anti-Mormon journalist to publish his confessions of many a murder and robbery ordered by the Prophet, under the lurid title *Brigham's Destroying Angel*. And from 1838, within weeks of the founding of the secret society, a text survives in which Smith himself sums up Avard's clandestine orders to his Danite captains. Among other duties, they were instructed "to go out on a scout of the borders of the settlements, and take to yourselves spoils of the goods of the ungodly Gentiles" and "you will waste away the Gentiles by robbing and plundering them of their property; and in this way we will build up the kingdom of God."

In the middle of 1838, Missouri settlers indeed began to complain of goods and livestock stolen, of barns and houses burned. On July 4, in front of a large congregation, the impetuous Sidney Rigdon gave a speech that would come to be known as the "Salt Sermon," as the orator elaborated on a passage from Matthew: "If the salt have lost its savor, wherewith shall it be salted? It is thenceforth good for nothing, but to be cast out, and to be trodden under the foot of men."

With fiery rhetoric, Rigdon made the threat to Missouri Gentiles explicit. He summed up the provocations the Saints had so far received at the hands of unbelievers, then vowed,

Our rights shall no more be trampled on with impunity. The man, or set of men, who attempt it, does it at the expense of their lives. And that mob that comes on us to disturb us, it shall be between us and them a war of extermination, for we will follow them till the last drop of their blood is spilled.

It was almost inevitable that fighting words such as Rigdon's would lead to real fights. The first outbreak of violence occurred on August 6, election day in Missouri. John D. Lee, who was Brigham Young's stepson and who later became famous for his part in the Mountain Meadows Massacre, left an eyewitness account of what would come to be known as the "election-day riot." In the town of Gallatin, in Daviess County, only a few miles northeast of Far West, as he lay in the grass awaiting his turn to vote, Lee heard one of the candidates for office stir up the crowd with derogations of the Saints: "They are a set of horse thieves, liars, and counterfeiters. . . . If you suffer the Mormons to vote in this election, it will mean the end of your suffrage."

Moments later, the first Mormon approached the polling booth. According to Lee, a man blocked his path and sneered, "Daviess County don't allow Mormons to vote no more than niggers." As the Mormon protested, the settler knocked him off his feet.

Lee swore that a Danite captain in the crowd gave the secret signal to his confederates. By the captain's own testimony, a supernatural power came to his aid, as the brawlers singled him out for attack. With a club, he leveled one Missourian after another. "I never struck a man the second time," the captain later wrote, "and while knocking them down, I really felt that they would soon embrace the gospel." No one was killed, but as the unbelievers fled, they left some nine men sprawled on the ground, seriously injured.

During the next two months, several pitched battles broke out between Mormons and Missourians, and the first fatalities occurred. The conflict culminated in the Haun's Mill Massacre. Founded in 1835, Haun's Mill was a small Mormon farming community well to the south of Independence. On October 30, a renegade militia from a neighboring county, two hundred strong, rode toward the defenseless settlement with mayhem on their minds. As the attackers came into sight, one Mormon ran out, waving his hat to sue for peace. It was to no avail. The militia-men started firing.

The women and children fled into the woods, while men and boys made a futile stand inside the blacksmith's shop. It was a poor refuge, for the logs of which it was built were so widely spaced, the attackers could fire through the gaps. Within hours, at least eighteen Mormon men and boys were dead, and thirteen more lay wounded. According to one Mormon witness, a nine-year-old boy named Sardius Smith tried to hide under the bellows. A militiaman found him and hauled him out. Another attacker pleaded, "Don't shoot, it's just a boy."

"It's best to hive them when we can," the first man answered. "Nits will make lice." Then he blew Sardius's brains out with his rifle at point-blank range.

Alarmed by the escalating bloodshed, Missouri governor Lilburn Boggs ordered his regular militia to drive all the Mormons out of the state or, if they would not leave, to exterminate them. As the troops approached Far West—ten thousand strong, according to the Prophet—Smith realized that his people had no choice but to flee.

What followed remains uncertain. One version is that Major General Samuel Lucas tricked Smith, Sidney Rigdon, Parley Pratt, and two other leading Saints into surrendering, under the pretense of a meeting to negotiate a truce. But John D. Lee insisted that, in an emotional speech to his followers, Smith announced that he would surrender himself to Lucas "as a sacrifice to save your lives and to save the Church."

With his five hostages under guard, Lucas was unbending. He issued a formal order to Brigadier General Alexander Doniphan: "Sir:—You will take Joseph Smith and the other prisoners into the public square of Far West, and shoot them at 9 o'clock tomorrow morning."

The history of the LDS church in America would be far different had Doniphan carried out his orders. Instead, risking a charge of treason, he answered in writing, "It is cold-blooded murder. I will not obey your order. My brigade shall march for Liberty to-morrow morning at 8 o'clock; and if you execute these men, I will hold you responsible before an earthly tribunal, so help me God."

Surprisingly, Lucas relented. The upshot was that Smith and his four fellow prisoners would languish for more than four months in the jail at Liberty, a small town about six miles north of Independence, as they awaited a trial that might yet levy upon them the death penalty.

Meanwhile, under a new de facto leader, Brigham Young, the Saints began their exodus from Missouri. The only direction that seemed possible for them to pursue was eastward into Illinois. Mobs of gleeful settlers descended upon Far West and ransacked it of everything of the slightest value. In Brodie's words, "Hogs and cattle they shot for sport."

Finally, in April 1839, Smith and the other incarcerated Mormon leaders were taken on horseback to Daviess County, the scene of their alleged crimes, to be tried by a jury of their supposed peers.

The trial never took place. With a bribe of $800 and a jug of whiskey fortified with honey that his brother Hyrum had smuggled into the midst of the caravan, Smith bought his freedom from a weak-willed sheriff. Once the man guarding him got drunk and fell asleep, Joseph and the other prisoners mounted horses and galloped north. They managed to catch up with the last stragglers from Far West and joined them as they crossed the border into Illinois.

The Garden of Eden lay behind them to the west. The new Zion of the Saints would never rise in Missouri.

STILL A MERE thirty-three years old as he entered Illinois, Joseph Smith would have only half a decade longer to live. Despite his people's ignominious flight from the Missouri mobs, in late April 1839 the Prophet remained as forward-looking as ever. Without hesitation, he chose an uninhabited neck of land protruding into a bend of the Mississippi River as the site for his next (and last) attempt to build Zion. That neck of land, ten miles north of Keokuk, Iowa (itself a fledgling village at the time), was dominated by a high hill, but surrounded by woods and swamps, the latter the breeding ground of hordes of malarial mosquitoes. Smith declared that the new town would be named Nauvoo—Hebrew, he told his followers, for "beautiful place" or "beautiful plantation."

Despite the topographic irregularities of the site, Smith laid out Nauvoo's streets and building lots in a rigid rectangular grid, oriented to the cardinal directions—just as Salt Lake City would be laid out in 1847, as well as virtually every other Mormon town in the West thereafter.

Within months, however, malaria started to take its toll. Smith himself lost his father, his youngest brother, and his youngest son.

Such setbacks in no way diminished Smith's ambitions. In November, "armed" (as Brodie writes) "with hundreds of affidavits and petitions," he traveled to Washington, D.C., to lay his grievances before President Martin Van Buren. Smith sought $2 million in damages from the state of Missouri. According to a reporter who was present, the president answered him with an exasperated refusal: "Help you!" he almost shouted. "How can I help you? All Missouri would turn against me." The two men argued bitterly before Van Buren stood up and left the room. Noting the president's corpulence, Smith told the reporter that he "hoped [Van Buren] would continue to grow fat, and swell, and before the next election burst!"

By now, Smith had organized his leading lieutenants under the lofty title the Twelve Apostles—the hierarchical designation that still obtains today. And only months after choosing the site for Nauvoo, in September 1839, he did an extraordinary thing. He ordered all twelve to go to England to make converts as fast as they could.

Brigham Young, one of the Twelve, was shocked and dismayed by the assignment. Neither he nor his second wife—the former Mary Ann Angell, whom he had married in 1834, two years after his first wife had died—had fully recovered from their malarial fevers, and only ten days before, Mary Ann had given birth to a baby. Yet, like every good Saint, Young obeyed the Prophet's order, and set out on the English mission without a murmur of complaint.

On September 18, with his longtime friend and fellow Apostle, Heber C. Kimball, Brigham left Nauvoo. When he arrived in Liverpool, he had only 75 cents in his pocket. In their penury, Young and Kimball followed what would become a sanctified tradition of missionaries hitting the road, in the Mormon phrase, "without purse or scrip" ("scrip" meaning money, "purse" something to carry it in), the better to put themselves at the mercy of the hospitality of potential converts.

Young had left Illinois full of doubts and insecurities. When he sought advice from Smith, the Prophet blithely instructed him, "When you reach England the Lord will teach you what to do, just as He teaches me how to act here."

The Apostles were stunned when they saw the conditions of the working-class poor in England. George A. Smith, Joseph's cousin, wrote in a letter home, "I have seen more beggars here in one day than I saw in all my life in America."

The Lord, however, must have worked just as Joseph had promised he would. During the single year they spent in England, the Twelve converted and baptized between eight thousand and nine thousand new Saints, published tens of thousands of tracts and copies of the *Book of Mormon*, and started the Liverpool-based *Millennial Star*: at first a monthly publication, it came out weekly starting in 1852. (The *Star* would cease publication only in 1970.)

The newspaper made honeyed promises about life in Illinois. The cost of a home there was only about one-eighth as much as it was in Britain. "Millions on millions of acres of land lie . . . unoccupied, with a soil as rich as Eden, and a surface as smooth, clear and ready for the plough as the park scenery of England." In and around Nauvoo, the *Star* boasted, there was room for "more than a hundred millions of inhabitants."

The first British converts, two hundred strong, arrived in Nauvoo in 1840. Two years later, the influx numbered 1,600. Nauvoo started to burst at the seams. In 1842, its population was counted at around seven thousand. In a mere three years of existence, the town had become the largest in Illinois. By 1844, Nauvoo's population would swell to twelve thousand.

Rebuffed by President Van Buren, Smith continued to nurse his grudge against Missouri. On May 6, 1842, something occurred that would have deep repercussions, setting in motion a chain of events that would end with the abandonment of Nauvoo. On a windy, rainy night, Lilburn Boggs, now ex-governor of Missouri, sat reading a newspaper in the study of his home in Independence. Nearby, his six-year-old daughter rocked the cradle bearing his newborn infant.

It was Boggs, of course, who had issued the infamous "extermination order," instructing his militia to drive the Saints out of Missouri or wipe them out. Suddenly, the windowpane shattered as pistol shots rang out. The governor was struck four times by buckshot, twice in the head and twice in the neck. Unconscious and bleeding profusely, he was not expected to live.

A crowd that quickly gathered discovered the pistol lying in the mud near the window, but the shooter had fled. Eight days later, Smith told his Nauvoo congregation that Governor Boggs had been killed. A collective gasp—perhaps a cheer—erupted. On May 28, the *Wasp*, the Nauvoo newspaper, editorialized, "Boggs is undoubtedly killed according to report; but who did the noble deed remains to be found out."

Amazingly, Boggs survived, even though two of the buckshot balls remained lodged in his brain. The case has never been conclusively proven, but the assassination attempt was almost surely carried out by one Orrin Porter Rockwell, a man who would go on to become the most notorious of all the Danites. In 1870, a journalist would accuse Rockwell of having carried out more than forty murders. Brigham Young biographer Stanley Hirshson describes this formidable gunslinger:

> Rockwell's appearance was enough to frighten to death most men. Of medium height, exceptionally strong and broad-shouldered, he possessed steely, searching blue eyes, a chest as broad as a barrel, hands as hairy and powerful as bear paws, and a heavy mane of braided hair he refused to cut after Smith told him it would render him, like Samson, unconquerable.

In an excellent surviving photograph, Rockwell's hair hangs loose, not braided, while his eyes have the blank, unyielding stare of a B-movie fanatic.

The dates of Rockwell's temporary absence from Nauvoo coincided neatly with a possible trip to Independence. Dr. John Bennett was an 1840 convert to Mormonism who quickly rose to prominence in Nauvoo, only to fall out with Smith, who excommunicated him in June 1842. In retaliation, Bennett wrote a series of letters that were later published in book form, with the subtitle *An Exposé of Joe Smith and Mormonism*. Bennett is thus perhaps an unreliable witness, but in one letter he swore that he had overheard Smith offer a $500 reward to anyone who would kill Boggs. The rumors about Rockwell having accomplished the deed were sufficiently rampant that Smith made a cryptic announcement (according to Bennett): "The Destroying Angel has done the work as I predicted, but Rockwell was not the man who shot. The Angel did it!"

Meanwile, in the *Wasp*, Smith denied any Mormon involvement, speculating that the assassination attempt must have been carried out by one of Boggs's political opponents.

That denial failed to satisfy the Missouri authorities, who in early August sent sheriffs to Nauvoo, where they arrested both Joseph Smith and Porter Rockwell. (Smith was arrested as "an accessory before the fact.") The Nauvoo municipal court issued a writ of habeas corpus that freed the two men, then appointed itself to conduct an independent inquiry of the attempted murder.

Meanwhile, Rockwell fled. He wound up near Philadelphia, where he stayed in hiding through the winter. And Smith went into hiding, too, though he was never far from Nauvoo. In Brodie's judgment, "Joseph had a thousand witnesses to prove that he had been in Nauvoo on the day of the shooting, but he was certain that extradition to Missouri meant death."

Disheartened by exile, Rockwell decided to return to Nauvoo early in 1843. In St. Louis, as he got off the steamboat to take a walk, authorities recognized him (how could they not, with his wild hair and penetrating stare?). He was arrested and sent to Independence, where he languished in prison, shackled in leg irons, infested with lice, for nine months. In May, with a fellow prisoner, he pulled off a jail break, sawing through his leg irons, overpowering the guard, whom the two men locked in their cell, then dashing across the yard and over a twelve-foot fence. But when Rockwell lingered to help his less athletic partner, sheriff's deputies recaptured both men.

Finally, in August, Rockwell was brought to circuit court, where to his astonishment he was told that the grand jury had refused to bring an indictment. When he finally returned to Nauvoo in December 1843, according to Brodie, he "was a frightening apparition. His hair hung down to his shoulders, black and stringy like a witch's; his clothes were filthy and tattered, his shoes in shreds."

Experts, including Rockwell's sympathetic biographer, Harold Schindler, lean toward the conclusion that the man was most likely the assassin. For one thing, several anti-Mormon writers later related scenes in which Rockwell bragged about the deed. But whether Smith ordered the attack is a far less certain matter. In Brodie's analysis, "Certainly he had nothing to gain from it but trouble. Since Boggs was no longer in power, there could have been no serious motive but revenge, and Joseph was not a vengeful man."

For his part, Smith soon wearied of his fugitive life around Nauvoo. With the characteristic fatalism that always counterbalanced his messianic zeal, he came out of hiding, submitted to another arrest, and was brought to Springfield, the capital of Illinois, for a trial based on the Missouri writ demanding Smith's extradition. It is not far-fetched to discern in the Prophet a longing, however ambivalent, for the martyrdom that would perfect his meteoric career. On January 5, 1843, in a packed courtroom, a judge who would later convert to the LDS faith declared the Missouri writ invalid. Smith was free once more.

During these tumultuous years in Nauvoo, a mass paranoia welded the community together. Yet any hope that the Mormons could live in peace, undisturbed by hostile neighbors, was dashed again and again— dashed as much as anything by Smith's grandiosity. In 1844, he had the audacity to run for the presidency of the United States.

He would not live to see the election.

THE FINAL UNRAVELING began with an internal schism. Though Illinois towns full of Gentiles that stood not far from Nauvoo, including Warsaw and Carthage, were growing increasingly hostile to the Saints, the trouble came from a man named William Law, whom in happier times Smith had appointed to the august post of Second Counselor, one of his highest-placed advisors. A rich Canadian, Law soon grew dismayed by the Prophet's demand that his followers pour their savings into a pair of ambitious construction projects—including a temple in which the sacred ordinances every Saint must undertake ought to be performed.

The final breach came, however, when Smith decided to take Law's wife, Jane, as one of his own plural wives. Jane was not interested, even after Smith allegedly spent two months trying to woo her. Fed up, Law threatened to expose the "debauchery" of the Mormon church to the whole world. In return, on April 20, 1844, Smith excommunicated both William and Jane.

Rather than leave Nauvoo, as most of the Saints whom Joseph expelled from the church did, the Laws lingered on, joining ranks with a number of other prominent but disaffected Mormons. It was not only polygamy that disturbed these Saints, but Smith's despotic absolutism, as if he had conjoined the role of Prophet to that of a king. Meeting in secret, these schismatics decided to buy a printing press to publish their own newspaper.

The first and only issue of the *Nauvoo Expositor* appeared on June 7, 1844. The most damning of the paper's assertions was contained in three affidavits signed by William and Jane Law and another man, each swearing that he or she had seen the written revelation about polygamy. (It will be remembered that Smith committed that revelation to print in 1843 only to silence Emma's objections to the practice. Despite the growing multitude of "plural" or "celestial" wives Smith had taken by early 1844, the revelation and the practice remained a secret shared only by the hierarchy.)

As Brodie dramatizes the events of June 7, "When the prophet read the *Expositor* through, he knew that he was facing the gravest crisis of his life. The paper had put him on trial before his whole people."

The retaliation Smith wreaked on the upstart newspaper, however, bespeaks a leader at once so grandiose and so paranoid that he seems to have been starting to lose control. He called a meeting of the city council, then steered it toward his preordained verdict: the *Expositor* was libelous and must be destroyed. Not simply the copies of the June 7 issue: the printing press itself.

On June 10, with Smith himself at the head, a legion of Nauvoo citizens marched to the offices of the offending newspaper. Its publishers refused to surrender the key. Harold Schindler, Porter Rockwell's biographer, describes what happened next:

> At a signal from the prophet, Rockwell kicked the door from its hinges and the posse entered. Seven men pulled the press into the street and smashed its bed beyond repair. The type was pied and battered, the chases were dumped on the remains of the press, and the entire pile of metal was soaked in coal oil and set aflame.

In addition, the "posse" seized and burned every copy of the June 7 edition it could find.

This violent episode did not take place in a vacuum. The citizens of nearby Warsaw and Carthage were well aware of the *Expositor*'s destruction. For them, it was the last straw. They held meetings, drafted resolutions calling for the citizens of Hancock County to "put an immediate stop to the career of the mad prophet," and sent a deputation to Springfield to petition Governor Thomas Ford to intercede. The *Warsaw Signal* editorialized for a more militant and immediate response: "War and extermination is inevitable! CITIZENS ARISE, ONE AND ALL!!! . . . We have no time for comments; every man will make his own. LET it be made with POWDER AND BALLS!!!"

Governor Ford, whose role in trying to defuse this explosive clash of frontier cultures seems to have been admirably fair-minded, rode at once to Carthage, only fifteen miles southeast of Nauvoo. Prepared to send the militia to the Mormon stronghold to demand the surrender of the press-smashers, he was alarmed to find that very militia on the verge of turning into a lynch mob. Instead, he wrote Smith a letter asking him to turn himself in. He did not mince words: if Smith refused, Ford warned, "I have great fears that your city will be destroyed, and your people many of them exterminated."

Smith made at least a token offer of surrender, under the condition that the Nauvoo legion ride with him to Carthage as an armed guard. Ford declined, apprehensive lest the confrontation of Mormons and Gentiles unleash all-out bloodshed. Instead, Smith prepared to flee once more.

The details of the Prophet's last two weeks alive are intimately documented by the friends and colleagues who were with him during that calamitous time. Their written accounts were later published in the compendious *History of the Church*, edited by B. H. Roberts. Vivid though these testimonies are, they give only the Mormon side of the story, and like so many other LDS narratives, they are encrusted with myth and legend.

In any event, we know that Porter Rockwell rowed Smith, his brother Hyrum, and one of the Twelve Apostles, Willard Richards, across the Mississippi River into Iowa Territory, starting at midnight on June 23.

Smith is supposed to have announced to Rockwell and other close confidants that his plan was to abandon Nauvoo and "strike out for the Rocky Mountains." (Was this the germ of the Saints' later exodus to Utah? Or had Smith long toyed with the idea of such a removal beyond the reach of the United States government?) The skiff in which the four men rode was so leaky, the river so swollen with rainwater, that it took all the rest of the night to reach the far shore.

Smith was in tears as he had parted from Emma, but they may have been tears of guilt as well as sorrow. He knew that he was turning his back on his people. And Iowa was no safe refuge: its territorial governor (Iowa would not be made a state until two years later) had in fact let it be known that he might well comply with the original Missouri extradition order. The Rocky Mountains were far away, and Smith had escaped with little more than the clothes on his back.

Conscience, the hard logistics of the Iowa wilderness, a letter of appeal from Emma delivered by a messenger, and his ever-latent fatalism conspired to change the Prophet's mind. Only a day and a half after he had fled, Smith recrossed the Mississippi and surrendered to Governor Ford's forces. It was not, however, an easy decision. The retrospective account recorded in the *History of the Church* has an ambivalent Prophet pleading, there in the woods on the west bank of the river, for advice from Rockwell and from Hyrum. Rockwell demurred, but Hyrum spoke out: "Let us go back and give ourselves up, and hear the thing out."

Smith was silent for a long time before answering, "If you go back I will go with you, but we shall be butchered."

"No, no," insisted Hyrum, "let us go back and put our trust in God, and we shall not be harmed. The Lord is in it."

On June 24, with the eleven other men charged with destroying the press, Smith started toward Carthage under the protection of a militia recruited not from Hancock County, but from the presumably less rabid McDonough County, adjoining Hancock on the east. To this escort (again, according to the Mormon record), Smith uttered a Christ-like premonitory lamentation:

> *I am going like a lamb to the slaughter, but I am calm as a summer's morning. I have a conscience void of offense toward God and toward*

all men. If they take my life I shall die an innocent man, and my
blood shall cry from the ground for vengeance, and it shall be said of
me, "He was murdered in cold blood!"

The journey was uneventful, but as the entourage entered Carthage shortly before midnight, rabble-rousers shouted out, "Goddamn you, old Joe, we've got you now"; and, "Clear the way and let us have a view of Joe Smith, the prophet of God! He has seen the last of Nauvoo. We'll use him up now, and kill all the damned Mormons!"

The story of Joseph's last three days on earth has been so mythologized that by now it is almost impossible to disentangle truth from Mormon fiction. The most careful recent study of what took place in Carthage from June 25 to June 27, 1844, appears in the pages of Jon Krakauer's *Under the Banner of Heaven*. According to Krakauer, ten of the arrested men posted bail and were set free, while Smith and Hyrum, charged with treason on top of the destruction of the press, were locked inside the Carthage jail.

This building, which still stands today (it was restored by the LDS church in 1938), was a two-story, six-room edifice built of locally quarried red limestone. The jailer, his wife, and seven children occupied four of the rooms; the other two were holding cells. Joseph and Hyrum were initially lodged in a downstairs room normally reserved for debtors. In Krakauer's assessment, "The jailer, George Stigall, was not Mormon, but he was a decent man, and he worried that his downstairs cell, with its large, ground-level windows, might provide insufficient protection from the enraged men outside who wished to harm his prisoners." So Stigall gave Joseph and Hyrum his own upstairs bedroom. He also allowed a stream of Mormon friends to visit the brothers, some of whom managed to smuggle a pair of lightweight pistols into the makeshift cell.

At this point, Governor Ford made a fatal miscalculation. He had ordered the hot-tempered Warsaw Dragoons (a volunteer militia) to leave Carthage. They had obeyed, but proceeded only a short way beyond the town limits. There, on the afternoon of June 27, 125 of these militiamen rubbed gunpowder on their faces in a token effort at disguise and marched back into Carthage. Guarding the jail was an inadequate force of only seven Carthage Greys.

According to Krakauer, even these guards were in cahoots with the attackers. They fired their muskets, loaded beforehand with blanks, at the attacking mob, in a charade of defending the prisoners.

At the moment, Apostles Willard Richards and John Taylor were visiting Hyrum and Joseph. The Dragoons stormed through the front door and up the stairs, their guns blazing. Taylor and Richards, armed only with walking sticks, stood on either side of the doorway, ready to lash out at the invaders, while Hyrum and Joseph lifted their puny pistols. The Dragoons shot straight through the door. One bullet struck Hyrum in the neck, killing him instantly.

In a matter of minutes, the mob forced the door open. Taylor—who would later play a crucial role in the handcart emigration of 1856—tried to jump out the window, but bullets struck him in the leg and chest and felled him. He started to crawl under a bed, but two more balls struck him in the pelvis and the forearm. Richards had the luck to be standing on the hinge side of the doorway, so that throughout the attack, he went unnoticed, hidden behind the flung-open door. He escaped the slaughter with only a grazed throat and earlobe.

Like Taylor, Joseph Smith attempted to jump out the window, but as he hovered above the sill, he was struck from behind by three bullets. As he fell out the window, he cried out his last words: "Oh Lord, my God!" He fell twenty feet to the yard, where he lay unmoving on his left side. At once he was shot several times by Dragoons outside the building.

Taylor's life had been spared by a freak happenstance: the bullet that struck him in the chest hit a watch he was carrying in his pocket. The watch stopped, he later noted, at precisely sixteen minutes and twenty-six seconds after five o'clock on June 27. Writes Krakauer, "Mormons the world over have committed this time and date to memory, marking the death of their great and beloved prophet. Joseph Smith was thirty-eight years old."

THE MEN WHO had murdered Joseph and Hyrum Smith were speedily tried and acquitted. John Hay, the future secretary of state, sardonically commented that it took three days to find twelve men ignorant enough to form a jury.

Brigham Young's biographer Stanley Hirshson makes the intriguing point that Joseph Smith was the first, and until Malcolm X's murder in 1965, the only American religious leader to be assassinated. From the distance of more than 160 years after the Carthage debacle, one might well wonder what it was about the Mormons that so inflamed the hatred of their neighbors—not only in Illinois, but in Missouri, Ohio, and New York state before that. Fawn Brodie ponders this question with her usual perspicacity. She concludes that it was not Mormon doctrine (not even polygamy) that aroused that hatred. It was instead, in her view, the "self-righteousness" of the Saints, their "unwillingness to mingle with the world," combined, in Nauvoo, with the wild expansion of their numbers, that actually frightened the settlers in towns such as Warsaw and Carthage. Further fueling the Gentile antagonism was the influx, starting in 1840, of thousands of British converts. Poor farmers and factory workers those emigrants may have been, but in American eyes, they were still monarchists. In 1844, only sixty-one years had passed since the Revolution that had won our freedom from the despot George III, only thirty-two years since the War of 1812. Of the Mormons' neighbors in western Illinois, Brodie writes, "To them the Nauvoo theocracy was a malignant tyranny that was spreading as swiftly and dangerously as a Mississippi flood and that might eventually engulf the very government of the United States."

At the time of the Prophet's martyrdom, most of the Apostles were scattered about the Eastern states. Brigham Young, who had risen to the rank of president of the Twelve, was in Massachusetts. Ironically, on July 1, four days after Smith's death, he and two other Mormon elders spoke at the Boston Melodeon, vigorously advancing the Prophet's candidacy for president of the United States. The speakers were drowned out by the jeers of their audience. Young did not learn of the murder in Carthage for another fifteen days. When he did, he immediately set out to return to Illinois, but it would not be until August 6 that he arrived in Nauvoo.

Sidney Rigdon was in Pittsburgh when he got the news. He, too, rushed at once to Nauvoo, arriving there three days before Young. Although Rigdon had had serious differences with Smith during the two years before the Prophet's death, he was still perhaps the logical candidate to succeed him. Rigdon had been with the church almost since the beginning; it was he who had inspired the move to Kirtland, Ohio, in 1831.

Meanwhile, Nauvoo was in chaos. Had the anti-Mormon forces around Warsaw and Carthage decided to attack, they might have wiped out the community, sending the faithful fleeing into the wilderness. But with the brutal murders of Smith and Hyrum, their vigilante zeal had been temporarily expended.

Pundits all over America predicted the collapse of the Mormon theocracy. On July 8, the *New York Herald* editorialized, "The death of the modern Mahomet will seal the fate of Mormonism. They cannot get another Joe Smith. The holy city must tumble into ruins, and the 'latter day saints' have indeed come to the latter day."

It was not until August 8 that the whole of Nauvoo assembled in a grove overlooking the Mississippi River to decide the future leadership of the beleaguered church. One of the most cherished of Mormon myths would attach itself to this gathering. According to this tradition, after other pretenders to the vacant throne of the Prophet had advanced their candidacies, Rigdon addressed the throng as the last speaker. By now he was fifty-one years old, decidedly portly, with an unimpressive bearing. But his smooth and tempered oration seemed to win the day, and the crowd was on the verge of conferring the leadership on Rigdon by unanimous acclamation.

But then, according to the myth, a cry rang out. A steamboat was approaching on the Mississippi River, with Brigham Young aboard. There would be one last speaker.

One historian calls Young's oration that August day the most famous speech in Mormon history. The mythologizing tradition has transformed it into a miracle. As Orson Hyde, a future Apostle, would recall it decades later:

> Well, he spoke, and his words went through me like electricity. "Am I mistaken," said I, "or is it really the voice of Joseph Smith?" This is my testimony; it was not only the voice of Joseph, but there were the features, the gestures and even the *stature* of Joseph before us in the person of Brigham. . . . Every one in the congregation . . . felt it. They knew it. They realized it. . . . When

President ᷍oung began to speak, one of them said, "It is the voice
of Joseph! It is Joseph Smith!"

(No mean feat, this transformation, for Young was not only four or five
inches shorter than the handsome patriarch with the piercing gaze, but
already, at forty-three, he had a jowly face, a double chin, and a thickset,
stocky build.)

We know that there was no last-minute arrival by steamboat: by the
time the open-air meeting was held, Young had been in Nauvoo for two
days. Whether or not the man was functionally illiterate, we have many
a later testimony to his eloquence as a preacher and orator. On August 8,
however, it may not have been eloquence so much as strategy that won
the day. (Indeed, a bishop who listened to the speech would later complain about Young's "long and loud harangue. . . . For the life of me I
could not see any point in the course of his remarks.")

Desperate to be anointed, Rigdon had shamelessly announced that
on the day of Smith's death, the Prophet had visited him in a vision and
entrusted him with governing the church in a proper manner. Young,
who did in fact speak last, took a clever tack. He began by scolding the
congregation for convening a meeting to decide Smith's successor, rather than mourning his death. He feigned disinterest: "I do not care who
leads this church. . . . You cannot fill the office of a Prophet, Seer, and
Revelator: God must do this. You are like children without a father."

Not once did Young advance himself as a candidate. Instead, he
subtly brought the congregation around to a black-and-white choice.
It was a question, as he framed it, of sustaining the Quorum of Twelve
Apostles, or of voting for Rigdon. Next he called for a show of hands:
how many would vote to sustain the Twelve? Nearly every hand shot up.
How many would not? Only a few dared raise their arms. Rigdon was
trounced before his candidacy could even come to a vote. As biographer
Morris Werner puts it, "The meeting then adjourned until the Church
conference of the following October, and the church was in the hands of
the Twelve, who were in the hands of Brigham Young."

Like Stalin deposing Trotsky, the supremely Machiavellian Brigham
Young at once set about discrediting his rival. On September 8, he managed to bring Rigdon to trial on charges ranging from illegally ordain-

ing priests to promulgating false revelations. Whether or not the gossip
was true, Young maintained that he had gotten wind of a plot in which
Rigdon was secretly organizing a schism, with plans to lead the Saints
to his own reformed LDS church near Pittsburgh. The upshot was that
Rigdon was not only excommunicated by the Twelve, but sent packing
as the congregation unanimously "delivered [him] over to the buffetings
of Satan."

Rigdon indeed decamped for Pittsburgh with a smattering of followers, and there established his "true" Mormon church. It flickered briefly,
then expired. The man himself lived on for decades, humiliated by his
failure. As late as 1871, from a farm in Pennsylvania, he sent a letter to
Young in Salt Lake City offering to help the church weather its latest
crisis. Young did not bother to answer.

THUS BRIGHAM YOUNG took control of the church he would head
for the next thirty-three years, until his death in 1877. He would become a Prophet, Seer, Revelator, and President even more autocratic
than Joseph Smith—the epithet "despotic" is not too strong. Yet during
the first two years of his leadership, it was all Young could do to hold the
battered, fragmenting community of Saints together. Besides the challenge briefly posed by Rigdon's breakaway church, a very strange vision-
ary Saint named James L. Strang apostatized and proceeded to set up
his own church in Wisconsin. By 1846, he reportedly had ten thousand
devotees in his flock—two-thirds as many as the faithful in and around
Nauvoo. The bizarre career of Strang and the Strangites deserves a book
in its own right.

The greatest threat to Brigham's supremacy, however, came in the
person of William Smith, one of Joseph's brothers. In the aftermath of
the Prophet's murder, their mother, Lucy Smith, claimed to have received
visions conferring the succession on William. In a gesture of apparent
modesty, William insisted that his tenure as Prophet would only be temporary, until Joseph's twelve-year-old son grew old enough to assume
the mantle. John D. Lee, in his late, embittered autobiography, claimed
that in Nauvoo Young himself had often sworn that the twelve-year-old
was destined to succeed his father. "He is too young to lead this people

now," Lee swore Young had averred to Lucy, "but when he arrives at mature age he shall have his place. No one shall rob him of it."

The feud between William Smith and Young intensified. In 1845, the former fled to St. Louis, where he began delivering public lectures attacking the "false" Prophet. Finally, in 1860, William established his own church, calling it the Reorganized Church of Jesus Christ of Latter-day Saints. Remarkably, the church still exists today as the Community of Christ, headquartered in Independence, Missouri. The chief doctrinal difference between the Reorganized branch and the mainstream LDS church was the denial, first voiced by William, that Joseph Smith had ever preached or practiced polygamy.

After a lull in the hostilities around Nauvoo, new frictions arose between the Mormon stronghold and the surrounding Gentile towns. They were brought to the flash point on September 16, 1845, when Porter Rockwell murdered Franklin Worrell, one of the leaders of the Carthage Greys, the militia that had collaborated with the Warsaw Dragoons in the killing of Joseph and Hyrum. Several prominent Mormons later admitted that this assassination was carried out by Young's leading Danite, though Harold Schindler, Rockwell's biographer, portrays the encounter as an act of self-defense on Rockwell's part.

In response, Gentiles attacked the Mormon town of Lima, burning down 175 houses. A handful of further killings on both sides ensued. A newspaper in Hancock County captured the mood of the day: "Every Saint, mongrel or whole-blood, and every thing that looked like a Saint, talked or acted like a Saint, should be compelled to leave."

In 1845, the Illinois legislature revoked the charter for Nauvoo. It was the crushing blow. Smith's "beautiful place" was doomed. Zion would have to be raised elsewhere.

Before fleeing Illinois, however, the Saints, under Young's energetic direction, did something that to outside observers must have seemed a very curious deed. Only months before abandoning Nauvoo, they erected its most spectacular building, a temple in which the sacred ordinances could be performed.

The temple, which Mormons claimed cost $600,000 (a wildly inflated figure), had been divinely ordained by God through Joseph Smith. The nature of the ordinances and "endowments," which persist today, and which still can be carried out only inside an LDS temple, have always been kept secret by the church, but many a nineteenth-century apostate gleefully detailed them. Morris Werner argues that a more pragmatic motive contributed to Young's zeal—the hope of selling the building for profit once it was built. The temple in fact was eventually put up for sale, but found no buyers.

Alas, the grandiose building was destined for a sorry end. A fire in 1848 and a tornado in 1850 destroyed much of it, and the citizens of what was left of Nauvoo pushed down its remaining walls. Between 2000 and 2002, under church auspices, the temple was completely rebuilt. Formally dedicated on June 27, 2002, by LDS president Gordon B. Hinckley, it serves today as a fully functioning temple.

During the last weeks in Nauvoo, more than a thousand Saints "received their ordinances" in the temple. Among them was Brigham Young, who was "sealed" to thirty-four of the thirty-five wives he had taken by early 1846. Young would always insist that when the doctrine of plural marriage was first revealed to him by Smith, he was revolted. "It was the first time in my life that I had desired the grave," he would later claim, "and I could hardly get over it for a long time."

No doubt there were dutiful aspects to Young's wife-taking, as in the fact that he was "sealed for time" to eight of Smith's widows (not all of whom were young or comely) so that they could be "sealed for eternity" to Smith in the afterlife. Yet if Young initially obeyed Smith's order to take many wives with reluctance, he would acquire a taste for the obligation. In Utah, quite a few of the brides he wooed, all but commanding them to marry him, were pretty, and some were as young as fourteen.

Early in February 1846, Young led some two thousand followers west across the Mississippi River, as they turned their backs on Nauvoo for good.

IF THERE IS a single narrative that validates the church today in the hearts and minds of Saints all over the world, it is the grand 1846–47 pageant of the pioneer trek from Nauvoo across the plains and through the Rocky Mountains to the Great Basin, where the faithful would finally build their Zion on the site of what is now Salt Lake City. The subtitle of

Leonard Arrington's comprehensive (if biased) biography of Brigham Young, *American Moses,* draws without irony a parallel between the second LDS Prophet and the Old Testament patriarch who led the chosen people out of bondage to the promised land. It was an analogy of which the Saints in that voyage were fully conscious, for they called themselves the Camp of Israel.

Yet fundamental ambiguities still linger about that landmark hegira. Chief among them is whether Young had his destination in mind from the beginning, or instead simply headed west along the Oregon Trail until he might stumble upon the proper place for Zion.

As he fled into Iowa to escape the militia in June 1844, one recalls, Smith had told his retainers that he would strike out for the Rocky Mountains. On the other hand, when Kentucky statesman Henry Clay had recommended Oregon as an ultimate destination for the Saints a few years earlier, Smith had replied with a sneering, indignant refusal.

We know that Young had read (or had had read to him) John C. Frémont's famous *Reports* detailing his 1842 and 1843 explorations along the Oregon Trail, during the second of which he had veered south through the Great Basin on his way to California. The reports were illustrated with Charles Preuss's exquisitely accurate maps. In fact, as it headed west, the Mormon caravan carried Frémont's books with them.

The most careful study of the question may appear in Will Bagley's introduction to *The Pioneer Camp of the Saints,* the edited journals of Thomas Bullock, a member of the pioneer party. Writes Bagley:

> Much speculation has gone into when LDS leaders picked the Salt Lake Valley as their ultimate destination. By January 1845, the Saints had stated their determination to go to California, but in 1845 "California" included everything west of New Mexico and the Rocky Mountains and south of Oregon. Until July 1847 when he actually looked at the Salt Lake Valley, Brigham Young's statements about his destination were ambiguous and wildly contradictory, perhaps intentionally so to deceive the government and Mormon political enemies about the precise location of the new Zion.

Before leaving Nauvoo, Young and some of the leading Apostles had sought out expert advice about a safe haven for the Saints from everyone from politicians to newspaper editors. The recommendations ranged from the mouth of the Colorado River to San Francisco Bay to Vancouver Island. Yet Bagley concludes,

> The Mormon leaders had determined to leave the United States and move into Mexican territory and had identified the Great Basin as their destination by the late summer of 1845, when they publicly announced their plans to abandon Nauvoo by the next spring. . . . On 9 September they resolved to send 1500 men to "Great Salt Lake Valley" to find a location for the saints.

If in fact Young hoped to lead such a multitude (let alone all two thousand who followed him out of Nauvoo) all the way to the Mormon promised land in one push in 1846, he soon grew discouraged at the prospect. In the feverish preparations for the exodus, the Saints bought and built their own wagons in a motley assortment of styles and makes. As early as October 1845, the Nauvoo newspaper had published a list of goods recommended to be carried in each of those wagons. It is a mind-boggling roster, including a thousand pounds of flour, twenty pounds of soap for each family, a gallon of alcohol, a pound each of cayenne pepper and cinnamon, "1 good seine and hook for each company," and "from 25 to 100 lbs. of farming and mechanical tools." (Such baggage was a far cry from the seventeen pounds per person to which the handcart pioneers of 1856 would be limited!)

It did not take long on the road for the wagons to groan under their excessive burdens. Write William Slaughter and Michael Landon in *Trail of Hope*, "As the long journey weakened and wearied the oxen, loads were lightened. Such heirlooms as prized furniture, book collections, china, and pianos were often abandoned along the trail. Sometimes precious items were left along the trail with the hope of picking them up at a later date."

Adding to the pilgrims' difficulties was the fact that they seriously underestimated Iowa. The iron cold of February gave way to drenching rains in March and April. The trail turned to impassable muck. Instead of proceeding in an orderly cavalcade, the hundreds of emigrants started to get spread out, according to their hardiness and the quality of their teams, across scores of miles. Young and other leaders were compelled to travel back all the way to Nauvoo to help the stragglers. The horde of two thousand that had crossed the Mississippi with Young starting on February 4 was but an advance guard: in their wake eventually followed the other ten thousand Saints exiled from Nauvoo. As it was, even an elite cadre of skilled travelers, pushing ahead of the disorderly caravan as a kind of advance scouting party, needed a full four months to cross Iowa and reach the banks of the Missouri River.

So halting and desultory was the Saints' progress across Iowa that they decided to build a pair of way stations for those too weak to go on. Garden Grove and Mount Pisgah, in central Iowa, quickly morphed from camps into bona fide villages. Between five hundred and six hundred settlers would spend the winter in Garden Grove. The population of Mount Pisgah eventually swelled to between two thousand and three thousand. Many of those homesteaders would push on to Zion only years later; others would never leave Iowa.

Despite the emigration's early start, by the beginning of summer Young was reconciled to the reality that he would never be able to transport as many as a thousand Saints to the Great Basin in one year. Besides the hardships of the trail itself, the pioneers suffered from alarming outbreaks of malaria and other diseases. A substantial wintering-over settlement would have to be built. Yet the Prophet still keenly hoped to push on with a small, handpicked advance party that summer and fall.

The decision to winter over was sealed by the arrival in Mount Pisgah, on June 26, of a four-man military delegation that had traveled east from Fort Leavenworth, in what is today Kansas. The Mexican War had broken out. Since taking office in 1845, President James K. Polk had agonized over the Mormon situation. Now he performed a brilliant stroke of co-option. The delegation brought the president's formal request for five hundred Mormon volunteers to join General Stephen Watts Kearny's Army of the West as it marched to Santa Fe and southern California. If Mormons could be coerced to serve the cause of the United States, that would seriously blunt the edge of their threat to flee the country's confines to establish their autonomous Zion in the wilderness.

In later years, Young would rail against Polk's interference. "There cannot be a more damnable, dastardly order issued than was issued by the Administration to this people while they were in Indian country, in 1846," he thundered in an 1857 speech. "That was President Polk; and he is now weltering in hell." Yet Young was every bit as Machiavellian as the president. The request for volunteers proved an unexpected windfall. The army pay for five hundred volunteers for a year's service amounted to $21,000, of which Parley Pratt, acting for Brigham, managed to secure as much as $6,000 in pledges to bolster the colony of over-wintering Saints. In addition, the army would effectively pay the way to Zion for five hundred Saints who would otherwise have had to finance their own pilgrimage.

The story of the so-called Mormon Battalion, many of whose members reached California, then made their way back to Utah to meet the pioneer trekkers in 1847, is a minor epic in its own right, about which numerous books and articles have been written. And attached to that story is the usual Mormon mythologizing. As Wallace Stegner sardonically sums up the response to the call for volunteers:

> Some orthodox histories say that Brigham at once found among his steadfast people the volunteers their ungrateful country called for—simply asked and saw the firm chins rise, the resolute figures step forward. The fact is that he asked from Miller's Hollow through Mt. Pisgah to Garden Grove, and in every place got mainly shuffling feet and mulish downcast looks.

In the fall of 1846, on either side of the Missouri River, the Mormons started building houses. On the east side, in Iowa Territory, they constructed Miller's Hollow, soon to be renamed Kanesville, then Council Bluffs. On the west side, in Indian Territory (and thus technically illegal), they started to build Winter Quarters, later renamed Florence.

At last Young had given up his dream of pushing on toward the Great Basin with an advance party in the fall of 1846. Instead, he settled in to run Winter Quarters. A year-end census of the fledgling village counted 3,483 people, of whom, thanks to the volunteers who had left with the Mormon Battalion, only 502 were men. The town was laid out in the by now standard Mormon grid. There were 538 wooden houses, most of them made of cottonwood, and eighty-three sod dugouts.

It was a hard winter, as cold and scurvy took their toll. No accurate death count can be retrieved today, but a commemorative LDS Web site sets the number of those who perished at 325.

The sufferings of one resident of Winter Quarters are brought vividly to life in her retrospective account:

> Winter found me bed-ridden, destitute, in a wretched hovel which was built upon a hillside; the season was one of constant rain; the situation of the hovel and its openness, gave free access to piercing winds and water flowed over the dirt floor, converting it into mud two or three inches deep; no wood but what my little ones picked up around the fences, so green it filled the room with smoke; the rain dropping and wetting the bed which I was powerless to leave.

ON APRIL 7, 1847—the day after the seventeenth anniversary of the founding of the church—Young set off westward with a handpicked party of 144 men. That number resonated throughout Winter Quarters: twelve men standing for each of the twelve tribes of Israel. In the end, however, one man backed out because of illness, while three women (including one of Young's wives, Clara Decker Young) and two children joined the entourage at the last minute.

It would take the pioneer party 108 days to travel the 1,031 miles from Winter Quarters to the site of their new Zion, an average of a little less than ten miles per day, though the procession actually moved faster, since every Sabbath was observed as a rest day. That 1847 journey has become the founding saga of the whole Mormon odyssey, endlessly retold and celebrated by the Saints. Stegner calls it "the most extensively reported event in western history." Burnished as myth, it seems to acquire the kind of heroic glow that Odysseus's voyage home from Troy to Ithaca forever radiates.

Yet in many ways the pioneer trek was a routine peregrination. South Pass in western Wyoming, the key to the easy crossing of the Continental

Divide, had been discovered (as far as Anglos are concerned) as early as 1812, by Robert Stuart, traveling east from Astoria, the famous outpost at the mouth of the Columbia River. After its rediscovery in 1824 by a party guided by Jedediah Smith, the pass became a regular itinerary for the mountain men. The first wagons crossed South Pass in 1832.

With the opening of the Oregon Trail in the early 1840s, the path along the North Platte, the Sweetwater River, and over South Pass became the standard route for emigrants flocking to homestead in what was still officially British territory (though Polk, running for president in 1844, would famously dispute the claim under the ringing campaign slogan "Fifty-four Forty or Fight"). In 1843 alone, some nine hundred emigrants traveled to Oregon along the trail. Though not published until 1849, Francis Parkman's enormously popular *The Oregon Trail* recounted the author's journey of 1846, a year before the Mormon exodus. The Donner Party also traveled along the trail that year, and in fact blazed the difficult route through the canyons of northeast Utah that Young's pioneers would follow in 1847.

Long before the tide of Oregon emigration in the 1840s, boosters of westward expansion had made a vogue of minimizing the difficulties of the trail. In 1813 the *Missouri Gazette*, published in St. Louis, announced that there was "no obstruction in the whole route that any person would dare to call a mountain." A Missouri senator in 1838 boasted of Oregon's "tropical" climate and claimed that the Rockies could be crossed even by "delicate females." The first Anglo women to cross South Pass, a pair of missionaries' wives, did so in 1836.

And indeed the pioneer party under Brigham Young proceeded westward with relative ease. The few encounters with Indians were peaceful. There were so many bison to shoot that Young eventually had to scold his followers for wasting so much meat, as they left carcasses to rot on the plains.

As mythologized by the Mormons, the pioneer hegira seems to take place in isolation, as if those 148 pilgrims were pushing along the Platte and Sweetwater like explorers penetrating an undiscovered country. In fact, that spring and summer there were no fewer than five thousand emigrants walking and riding westward toward their own promised lands. The trail was so crowded that on April 25, the Mormon company decided to cross the Platte and continue on its north bank, rather than follow the established and well-trodden route of the Gentiles on the south side of the river. That separation, so characteristic of the Saints, would persist through the following years, so that along the Platte the Mormon Trail came to be distinguished from the Oregon Trail proper.

Unlike the Donner Party, whose story will always remain fuzzy, thanks to a paucity of primary sources, the Mormon pioneer trek is well documented in some twenty-seven trail diaries kept by various members of the party. The best of them is William Clayton's voluminous journal, full of homely but welcome detail. A random sample, from April 21:

> One of the Indians presented several certificates from persons who had previously travelled through their village, all certifying that the Grand Chief of the Pawnees was friendly disposed, and they had made him presents of a little powder, lead, salt &c. Heber gave them a little tobacco & a little salt & President Young gave to the chief, some powder, lead, salt and a number of the brethren gave a little flour each. The old chief however did not seem to think the presents sufficient, and said he did not like us to go west through their cou[n]try, he was afraid we should kill their Buffalo and drive them off. Brother Shumway told him we did not like Buffalo.

It comes as no surprise that this obsessive recorder would set himself the task of measuring the distances the party traveled to the nearest foot. On May 8, Clayton gauged the circumference of one of Heber Kimball's wagon wheels, finding it to be precisely fourteen feet eight inches. A calculation revealed that exactly 360 revolutions of the wheel covered a mile of ground. So Clayton tied a red rag to one of the spokes, then counted every single revolution all day long. After a few days, the labor started to drive him crazy. With the help of a handy collaborator, he concocted an interlocking pair of wooden cogs attached to the wheel that did the counting just as efficiently as the red rag (a replica of this "roadometer" is on display in the Museum of Church History in Salt Lake City).

The upshot of this mania for measuring distances was not only that

Clayton could sum up the party's journey as exactly 1,031 miles long, but that he could rush into print in 1848 a slender book called *The Latter-day Saints' Emigrants' Guide*, a volume that every subsequent party of Mormon pioneers heading to Zion found invaluable. The entries are as quaint and useful as Clayton's diary. Tables taxonomize every conceivable landmark:

> Sandy Bluffs, west foot.
>> Two hundred yard further, is a creek five feet wide.
>>> From W. Qas. miles,   From C of GSL miles
>>> 370 ¼   660 ¾

The cavalcade on the Mormon Trail amounted to far more than men accompanied by three women and two children. The pilgrims traveled in seventy-two wagons pulled by sixty-six oxen and fifty-two mules, or rode on ninety-three horses, driving along nineteen cows, seventeen dogs, and some chickens. The three women, as Stegner notes, "might as well have been invisible," for they are mentioned only three or four times in all the journals. Of the whole menagerie, he adds, "It sounds like a dog's dream, that trip; but the journals don't mention the dogs much either."

To bring order to what might have been a ragtag parade, Young imposed a military discipline. The whole party was aroused at 5:00 A.M. by the peal of a bugle. The team started moving at seven after each wagon team had cooked a dinner to be consumed at noon. The wagons were parked at night in a precise configuration with the front wheel of one interlocked with the back wheel of another. Prayers were offered to God every evening at 8:30, and by nine everyone had to be in bed with the fires extinguished. Rules included a prohibition against wandering more than twenty rods (110 yards) from camp.

Even so, the men and boys seemed to be having too good a time on the trip. Buffalo-hunting had become an addiction, as well as cards and checkers in camp. On May 29, Young blew his stack. He assembled the whole expedition and harangued them about the "low, mean, dirty, trifling, covetous, wicked spirit dwelling in our bosoms." More than one diarist recorded Young's diatribe:

When I wake up in the morning, the first thing I hear is some of the brethren jawing each other and quarreling because a horse has got loose in the night. I have let the brethren dance and fiddle and act the nigger night after night to see what they will do. . . . Well, they will play cards, they will play checkers, they will play dominoes, and if they had the privilege and were where they could get whiskey, they would be drunk half their time.

By June 12, the trekkers had reached what would come to be known as the Last Crossing, near where the Sweetwater entered the North Platte. Later in the season, the Platte would be low and braided enough to ford, but now, swollen with spring snowmelt from its headwaters in the Medicine Bow Mountains, it was running a hundred feet wide and fifteen feet deep. It was here—ironically, in the center of today's Casper, Wyoming—where the Martin handcart company would start to come to grief nine years later.

In 1847, it took the pioneer party six days of perilous ferrying to get across the Platte. The Saints had had the foresight to carry with them a leather boat that they called the "Revenue Cutter," which could carry as much as 1,800 pounds. The "Cutter" was up to the job of getting all the baggage across the river, but the wagons themselves presented a major problem. The men experimented with log rafts lashed together out of native timbers, with rope systems to swing the wagons from shore to shore, and with attaching outrigger poles to the wagons in an attempt to float them across. Finally, their best-built raft proved barely adequate to carry a single wagon at a time; each ferry left the men holding their breath as they anticipated a capsize.

As he would throughout his tenure as Prophet, Young now turned adversity into a business opportunity. He ordered several of the men to stay behind at the Last Crossing, where they would charge $1.50 per wagon to ferry the scores of Gentile trains bound for Oregon across the flooding river.

Ascending the Sweetwater, which meandered in endless loops through a valley flanked on either side by granite outcrops and wooded hills, the Saints were forced to share the single trail with Gentile companies. The procession sometimes took on the character of a traffic jam, as parties often raced each other to snag the best campsites. Some of the trains were peopled with emigrants from Missouri. The Saints had fresh and bitter memories of being driven out of that state in 1838–39, so relations between them and these homesteaders now grew tense. The Mormon diarists reflect the contempt for the Missourians: in one train, the "men, women and children were all cursing, swearing, quarreling, scolding, and finding fault with each other and other companies."

The Mormon caravan trundled without serious incident up the Sweetwater valley. On June 27 the wagons crested South Pass, the 7,500-foot divide that is so gently inclined the men amused themselves by trying to determine the precise place where the Atlantic watershed gave way to the Pacific. The date was not lost on the Saints—it was the third anniversary of Smith's murder in Carthage.

A few miles beyond South Pass, the Oregon Trail parted from the far less traveled route that the Saints must follow to the Great Basin. Grateful to take their leave of the noisome Gentiles, the Saints nonetheless began to worry about getting lost. Fortunately, the very next day they encountered three strangers near the Little Sandy River. One of them was the most famous of all mountain men, Jim Bridger, nicknamed "Old Gabe." No one knew the country to which the Saints were headed better than he. Two decades before, leading a party of trappers, he had made what was probably the Anglo discovery of Great Salt Lake (which he mistook, because of its saline composition, for a bay of the Pacific Ocean). In 1841, as the beaver trade collapsed, he had built Fort Bridger, the only outpost of civilization in the huge wilderness that stretched away on all sides.

During subsequent years, relations between Old Gabe and the Mormons would so deteriorate that the mountain man would have to flee for his life from Saints (Danites among them) who took over the fort by force. But now, at first meeting, Bridger was happy to camp with Young's party and tell them all he knew about the Great Basin.

Another Mormon legend hovers about this important meeting. According to this tradition, Bridger was so pessimistic about the prospect of settling near the Great Salt Lake that he promised to give Young a thousand dollars for the first ear of corn he might raise there.

The diaries kept on the trail reveal a more nuanced appraisal on Old

FINDING ZION

Gabe's part. According to Wilford Woodruff, Bridger said of the Great Salt Lake Basin that "there was but one thing that Could operate against it becoming A great grain country & that wold be frost. He did not know but the frost would effect the corn."

Before parting, Bridger gave the Saints detailed directions as to how to penetrate the canyons guarding the Great Salt Lake on the northeast. He averred that "he was Ashamed of the Maps of Freemont for He knew nothing about the Country." Old Gabe's directions, however, proved so confusing that the Mormons would give up trying to follow them.

On June 30, as the Saints lingered on the east bank of the Green River to build more rafts for their last major stream crossing, they had an equally momentous rendezvous with three other men riding in from the west. One of them was a fellow Saint, Sam Brannan. This extraordinary traveler had sailed from New York in 1846 all the way around Cape Horn to California, where he arrived in time to greet the American squatters who had perpetrated the semi-comic Bear Flag Revolt, the first step in the seizure of California from its Mexican government. Having learned of the pioneer party's departure from Winter Quarters in April 1847, Brannan had come all the way east to the Green River to intercept Young's Saints and talk them into settling in golden California.

Brannan would grow indignant when Young ignored his propaganda in favor of the land of milk and honey. Yet as he had crossed the Sierra Nevada that spring, he had been one of the first travelers to come upon the wreckage and carnage of the Donner Party. Now he was the bearer of the shocking tidings of the disaster that had engulfed that emigrant train in the snows of the winter of 1846–47.

Another Mormon legend has it that the Donner Party was made up of the very men who had persecuted the Saints in Missouri and Illinois. Their terrible end was God's punishment for their sins. In reality, although the Donner Party had started west from Springfield, Illinois, its members had had nothing to do with the conflicts around Nauvoo that had led to Smith's martyrdom in Carthage.

It is beguiling to learn that this righteous Mormon myth had its origins not in a retrospective distorting of history, but on the very day Brannan met up with the Saints. One of the pioneers, Norton Jacob, so mangled what Brannan reported (unless Brannan himself mangled the truth) that that evening he wrote in his diary:

> Br Brannan fell in with a company of Emigrants who by quar-
> reling & fighting among themselves, delayed time until they got
> caught in the Snows on the Mountains last fall & could not entri-
> cal themselves.... Their sufferings were incredible manny of them
> perished with cold & hunger, all their cattle died & they compeled
> to eat the flesh of those that died among them! ... These are the
> men that have Mobed & killed the Saints!

Once across the Green River, the Saints had only 169 more trail miles to reach the site of their new Zion. Five-sixths of their long journey was over. But in that home stretch, they would encounter the hardest traveling of all—none of it more arduous than the last thirty-six miles as, finding faint traces of the Donner Party's passage the year before, they literally built a road down what would come to be called Emigration Canyon.

And now the pioneers' progress was slowed to a crawl by an out-break of what the Saints called "mountain fever." It was characterized by intense headache, severe pain in the joints, and fevers approaching the delirious. The Saints themselves blamed it on sudden alternations of heat and cold, or on alkali in their cooking water. Historians have puzzled as to the true nature of mountain fever. The best guess is that it was Rocky Mountain spotted fever, which is caused by ticks. According to Rock Springs, Wyoming, Bureau of Land Management archaeologist Terry Del Bene, "The sagebrush through which the pioneers moved in western Wyoming is a huge tick farm. The ticks have thermal sensors—they'll migrate straight toward you."

No one was stricken more seriously than Young himself. By July 19 he could no longer walk. Uncertain whether to halt the migration until its leader recovered, the Saints ultimately sent ahead an advance party of twenty-two wagons under Orson Pratt, while Young was carried slowly along on the bed of a wagon among the main party.

On July 21, Pratt's team broke through a last canyon barrier and sud-denly gained its first view of the Great Salt Lake basin spreading below. "We could not refrain from a shout of joy," Pratt wrote.

It is often overlooked or forgotten that in choosing to settle near the Great Salt Lake, the Saints were invading and occupying a foreign country. In July 1847, virtually all of the Great Basin was still Mexican soil, even while the United States' war against its southern neighbor waxed furious. It would not be until the signing of the Treaty of Guadalupe Hidalgo on February 2, 1848, that all of what are today Utah, Nevada, and California, as well as most of Arizona and parts of New Mexico, Colorado, and Wyoming, would be formally ceded to the United States.

This singular moment in LDS history furnishes the pedestal for the most potent and beloved of all the Mormon myths. According to that legend, on July 24, 1847, Brigham Young beheld the Great Salt Lake valley and at once announced, "This is the place." Today, July 24, known as Pioneer Day, is the occasion for gala celebrations not only in Salt Lake City, but in every Mormon community. It is the most important Mormon holiday, even more significant than Christmas.

On the outskirts of Salt Lake City today stands This Is the Place Heritage Park, a spacious memorial ground that includes an authentic full-size replica village of the new Zion as it looked during its earliest years. The park is dominated by a sixty-foot-tall pylon with statues of Heber Kimball, Wilford Woodruff, and Brigham Young on top, gazing out over the city below from the spot where the Prophet made his pronouncement.

Alas, Young never uttered his most famous utterance. Historian Dale Morgan, combing the records of the pioneer days, found that the "This is the place" formula does not crop up before 1880—thirty-three years after the pioneer party reached its Zion, and three years after Young's death.

The truth, always more mundane than the myth, is that when a prostrate Brigham Young was wheeled into sight of the promised land on July 24, the advance party had already plowed three acres of ground and planted the first seedlings, built a dam on what would be named City Creek, and diverted water to the fields by means of irrigation ditches. Wilford Woodruff's journal for that day notes only that the Prophet "expressed his full satisfaction in the appearance of the valley as a resting-place for the Saints, and was amply repaid for his journey."

CHAPTER THREE

THE DIVINE HANDCART PLAN

P atience Loader was still in Williamsburg, Brooklyn, making mantillas in a clothing store when the first Mormon handcarts set out from Iowa City. On June 9, 1856, a party of some 280 emigrants, nearly all of them from Great Britain, started pushing fifty-six two-wheeled wooden carriages westward. Under the command of thirty-seven-year-old Edmund Ellsworth, a son-in-law of Brigham Young who had been a member of the 1847 pioneer trek, the entourage was reinforced by a mere three wagons carrying the party's tents and other gear. Two days later, a slightly smaller team of similar composition—220 pilgrims pushing forty-four handcarts, supplemented by a pair of wagons—started west as well. They were led by Daniel McArthur, a thirty-six-year-old American of Scottish heritage who was also a veteran of the 1,300-mile-long trail, having traversed it in 1848 in the second season of Mormon emigration to Salt Lake City.

During the nine years since the founding of the new Zion in the wilderness, tumultuous events had buffeted the would-be autonomous colony. From the very start, Young's abiding goal had been to enlarge and expand what would soon become a mini-empire. Though still in poor health, he had rested only thirty-four days in Salt Lake City during July and August 1847 before setting out on the return trail to Winter Quarters, so that he might lead as many as 1,600 Saints to Zion in the wake of the vanguard of 148. Every convert in the eastern states or in Great

Britain and Europe must be gathered to Zion as soon as possible—for who could know how soon the apocalypse might arrive, subjecting every denizen of Babylon to the tribulations of the Last Days.

There were political as well as spiritual reasons for building up the frontier theocracy. In settling the Great Basin while it was still technically part of Mexico (though that country's hold on its northernmost provinces was feeble to the point of impotence), the Latter-day Saints had hoped, as they never could in New York, Ohio, Missouri, or Illinois, to flourish in splendid isolation, beyond the reach of their Gentile persecutors. But in the stroke of a pen, on February 2, 1848, the treaty of Guadalupe Hidalgo rendered Great Salt Lake City a breakaway colony planted on U.S. soil.

In March 1849, Brigham Young and his co-leaders declared the establishment of the State of Deseret (which Joseph Smith claimed meant "honey bee" and is pronounced DEZ-er-ette), with a "free and independent government." The grandiosity of Mormon ambitions spoke in the very size of the domain the Saints claimed for Deseret—a region a thousand miles long from north to south (from the Wind River Range in Wyoming to the Gila River in Arizona) and eight hundred miles from east to west (from central Colorado to the eastern slope of the Sierra Nevada of California). Deseret was twice as big as Texas.

In an uneasy 1850 compromise, the U.S. Congress whittled Deseret down to an official Utah Territory—still colossal, at 220,000 square miles two and a half times as large as the state of Utah today. The compromise appointed Brigham Young to a four-year term as the territory's first governor.

The dream of Mormon autonomy, however, would be dashed not by Congress so much as by a completely unforeseeable event—the California gold rush. For the hordes of fortune-seekers who streamed west in 1849, the most logical route to the gold fields was the Mormon Trail through Salt Lake City. Young tried at first to divert this throng of roughnecks toward an alternative route that passed through Fort Hall, the Hudson's Bay Company outpost in what is today Idaho. But it soon became clear that there were huge economic benefits to be gained from trade with miners who, desperate to get to California, found Salt Lake to be the only viable resupply point on the long and arduous trail. Charging these "golden pilgrims" what they regarded as exorbitant rates for flour and other basic foodstuffs, Utah settlers and merchants grew prosperous. In 1849 alone, more than ten thousand gold-seekers passed through Zion.

The official U.S. census for 1850 recorded the non-Indian population of the Utah Territory as 11,380. Only about half the inhabitants were living in Salt Lake City itself, for almost from the start Young had ordered the Saints to build new towns elsewhere in the territory. Within ten years of the pioneer party's alighting in the Great Basin in 1847, there were no fewer than ninety-six Mormon villages and settlements, stretching from Fort Bridger in Wyoming to San Bernardino in California, inland from Los Angeles.

Ultimately, Young would never be content simply to establish an independent city-state in the wilderness. From 1830 on, with Joseph Smith's founding of the religion after he had "translated" the *Book of Mormon* from the golden plates, the goal of the Saints was to convert the whole world. Young sincerely believed in such a destiny. In a typical 1855 pronouncement, he proclaimed, "We will roll on the Kingdom of our God, gather out the seed of Abraham, build the cities and temples of Zion, and establish the Kingdom of God to bear rule over all the earth."

As the gold-miners flooded through Salt Lake City in 1849, and paused there for as little as a day or as long as several weeks to recuperate, curiosity about the odd Mormon sect bred familiarity, and familiarity often gave birth to contempt and alarm. Accounts of life and manners in Salt Lake City began to appear in Eastern newspapers. The government surveyor and explorer Captain John W. Gunnison spent the winter of 1849–50 in Salt Lake City. Fascinated by the religion and the society it had spawned, Gunnison published in 1852 the first book-length account of the colony written by a Gentile outsider, *The Mormons, or, Latter-day Saints, in the Valley of the Great Salt Lake*. A remarkably balanced account, the book credits the Mormons with having established a "peaceful, industrious, and harmonious community." At the same time, Gunnison unambiguously testified to the practice of polygamy among the Saints, still officially denied by the church: "That many have a large number of wives in Deserét, is perfectly manifest to any one residing long among them."

In 1853, as he surveyed for a possible railroad route, Gunnison's party was ambushed in a desolate region of western Utah, near the present-day hamlet of Hinckley. The captain and seven of his men were killed, their bodies mutilated. The so-called Gunnison Massacre was almost certainly perpetrated by a band of Pahvant Utes, in retaliation for the murder of members of their own tribe by a California-bound emigrant train unrelated to Gunnison. Yet because of the revelations in Gunnison's book, and because the idea of a railroad running through Utah was anathema to Young (since it would jeopardize Zion's isolation from the rest of the United States), it was suspected at the time—and is still argued today—that the killings were either carried out by Mormons or by Indians acting under secret Mormon orders. Those dark suspicions were given further credence in 1855 when, after a trial conducted by Gentiles but convened in Utah found three Pahvants guilty of manslaughter, they were sentenced to three years in prison and promptly allowed to escape.

Testimonies such as Gunnison's about life in Utah, and particularly about polygamy, forced Young's hand. In 1852, after twenty-one years of strenuous official denials, the President finally acknowledged publicly that "plural marriage" was sanctioned by Mormon doctrine. Meanwhile, from 1849 through 1856, with a certain naïveté, Young continued to lobby the U.S. government for the admission of Deseret to the union. Polygamy was too much, however, for the average American to swallow. It will be recalled that John C. Frémont, running for president as the first Republican candidate in 1856—the same Frémont who had surveyed the route the Mormons followed to the Great Basin, and whose report Young carried with him on the pioneer trek—campaigned on the pledge to abolish "those twin relics of barbarism—Polygamy and Slavery."

As part of his statehood effort, Young conducted his own census of Deseret in 1856 and came up with a population of some 77,000. This number was wildly inflated: four years later, the U.S. census would count the true population of the Utah Territory at 40,273.

By 1855, a number of federal officials assigned to the territory had fled, their reasons ranging from sheer frustration to fear of being assassinated by Young's shadowy "avenging angels," the Danites. Tensions in the breakaway theocracy were stretched tighter than at any time since the pioneers had first arrived in the Great Basin. It was widely rumored that the U.S. government, instead of admitting Deseret to the union, would invade Utah with troops. This was no mere paranoid fantasy on the part of the Saints, for in 1857 just such an invasion would be launched by President James Buchanan.

In Young's mind, the best deterrent against such a conquest was sheer numbers. In Great Britain, and increasingly in Scandinavia (particularly Denmark), thousands of converts longed to gather to Zion. Only their own poverty stood in the way.

It was in this fraught climate of fear and defiance that Brigham Young came up with the "divine" handcart scheme.

BETWEEN THE PIONEER trek of 1847 and the last wagon train in 1855, no fewer than 150 separate companies of Mormon emigrants made the long voyage across the plains to Salt Lake City. Some of these parties carried mainly freight, but the majority of them brought the tens of thousands of faithful Saints to the only place on earth where they would be safe from the iniquities of Babylon. Every such journey was perilous, and it was the rare exception for a party to come through without suffering several or more deaths. Disease far outweighed accidents as a cause of mortality. John Unruh, whose *The Plains Across* (1979) is the seminal study of overland migration to the West between 1840 and 1860, concludes that in 1850 and again in 1852, more than two thousand emigrants (both Gentile and Mormon) died of cholera on the Oregon and California Trails, most of them before they reached Fort Laramie.

The dead were usually hastily buried by the wayside. One 1852 emigrant bound for Oregon recorded in her diary the location of 401 fresh graves along the trail, estimating that she had discovered only about one-fifth of these dolorous sites. Taking the twenty-year period from 1840 to 1860 as a whole, Unruh calculates that the average mortality rate for an emigrant party was about 4 percent.

For the ever pragmatic Young, however, the critical flaw in the mechanism of gathering to Zion was not the mortality rate, but an economic one. Saints arriving in the Midwest from the Eastern states or from Europe faced the necessity of buying wagons and oxen to continue their journeys beyond the reach of Mississippi and Missouri River steamboats or of the railroad to Iowa City. By the mid-1850s, a wagon typically cost $90, a yoke of oxen $70. Since it took three yokes to pull a fully loaded wagon, the cost of outfitting a family for the trail easily reached $300. This sum was beyond the means of most Saints, especially the working-class converts in Britain and Scandinavia, who had to pay for their journeys from Liverpool to New York or Boston and their transportation to Iowa or Missouri before even contemplating the purchase of a wagon train.

To solve this problem, in 1849 Young and his fellow leaders invented the Perpetual Emigration Fund. In effect, the PEF lent the necessary money for the journey to Zion as an advance to the indigent emigrant, who once in Salt Lake City would pay off his debt through labor. Church officials characterized the PEF as an altruistic outpouring of funds to enable emigration. Its backers promised the recipients, "This will make the honest in heart rejoice, for they love to labor."

What those backers failed to mention (and what PEF apologists today still minimize) were two mitigating circumstances. The first was that while church coffers supplied much of the money, a substantial part of it was raised by dunning all the less-than-impoverished Saints—especially in Britain and Scandinavia—to donate every shilling or krone they could spare to the PEF. Even more onerous was the fine-print stipulation that the loan would accrue an interest rate of 10 percent in Utah. Many a Saint would spend the rest of his life in the territory unable to pay back his PEF loan.

In sheer practical terms, the PEF worked: by the end of 1855, it had assisted 3,411 emigrants to get to Utah. But in that year Young reckoned the PEF debt as $100,000, owed to the church by 862 Saints who had not yet been able to pay back their advances. To the Prophet, this was an untenable situation.

As the Forty-niners had streamed through Salt Lake City on their way to the goldfields, the Saints had been astonished to see the odd but undeniably doughty fortune-seeker heading westward with nothing more than a shapeless pack on his back, or, even more bizarrely, pushing a wheelbarrow laden with his belongings. These tough eccentrics planted the germ of an idea. As early as 1852, Young had toyed with the handcart scheme, but it was not until 1855 that he announced it to his flock. As Apostle Franklin D. Richards, president of the European Mission, would rationalize the wheelbarrow-handcart comparison, "Many men have traveled the long and weary journey of 2000 miles from the Missouri river to California on foot, and destitute, in order to obtain a little of the shining dust—to worship at the shrine of Mammon. Who that appreciates the blessings of the Gospel would not be willing to endure as much and more, if necessary, in order to dwell with the righteous and reap the riches of eternal life?"

Adding urgency to Zion's looming economic crisis was a disastrous crop failure in 1855. Not only drought but a plague of "Mormon crickets" (wingless grasshoppers) ravaged the corn and wheat fields, reducing the harvest to as little as a third of the normal yield. By winter, many residents were near starvation, digging up thistle roots and pigweed to fill their bellies. In 1848, a similar infestation of grasshoppers had threatened to wipe out the crops, but as if out of nowhere, hordes of seagulls had descended upon the fields and gorged themselves on the noxious insects, saving the fledgling colony. The advent of the seagulls, considered a divine miracle at the time, did not recur in 1855. (The state bird of Utah today is the California gull, *Larus californicus*.)

On October 29, 1855, in the Thirteenth General Epistle (a kind of Mormon state-of-the-union address issued once a year), Young and his two chief counselors announced the handcart plan. A month before that, the Prophet had written Franklin D. Richards in Liverpool a letter outlining the scheme in detail. In the December 22 issue of the *Millennial Star*, Richards published the letter along with his own extended editorial on the matter. His audience—the British Saints who would make up the vast majority of the handcart companies—would be far more directly affected by the consequences of the plan than the Saints who had already made it to Utah. (It was that issue of the *Star* that Patience Loader's family had failed to read, as they sailed toward New York aboard the *John J. Boyd* in December.)

Whatever his faults, Brigham Young is widely credited with being a practical genius. Yet in retrospect, his September 30 letter to Richards reads as a triumph of starry-eyed wishful thinking over common sense. Retrospect may be an unfair lens through which to scrutinize what we now know as a catastrophe; but there is a strong and persistent belief in Mormon circles today that there was nothing intrinsically unsound about the handcart plan—that only the domino effect of a series of unlucky and unlikely events produced the disaster.

"I have been thinking how we should operate another year," Young mused in his letter to Richards.

> We cannot afford to purchase wagons and teams as in times past, I am consequently thrown back upon my old plan—to make hand-carts, and let the emigration foot it, and draw upon them the necessary supplies, having a cow or two for every ten. They can come just as quick, if not quicker, and much cheaper—can start earlier and escape the prevailing sickness which annually lays so many of our brethren in the dust.

From this guardedly optimistic prelude, Young soared into wild fancy:

> If it is once tried you will find it will become the favourite method of crossing the plains; they will have nothing to do but come along, and I should not be surprised if a company of this kind should make the trip in sixty or seventy days. I do know that they can beat any ox train crossing the plains.

The Prophet seems to have forgotten that in 1847 it had taken his handpicked pioneer party, nearly all of whom were men in the prime of life, 108 days to travel from Winter Quarters to the Great Salt Lake, over a trail three hundred miles shorter than the one the handcart pioneers would be required to traverse.

Onward into delusion:

> Fifteen miles a day will bring them through in 70 days, and after they get accustomed to it they will travel 20, 25, and even 30 with all ease, and no danger of giving out, but will continue to get stronger and stronger; the little ones and sick, if there are any, can be carried on the carts, but there will be none sick in a little time after they get started. There will have to be some few tents.

Young never claimed that the handcart plan was divinely inspired. Unlike Joseph Smith, who received direct revelations from God with startling frequency, Young would record only one in his lifetime—the original vision that the Saints would find their lasting Zion somewhere in the West.

Yet in the same issue of the *Star*, Richards leapt to the divine conclusion: "The plan is the device of inspiration," he told the British Saints, "and the Lord will own and bless it." Within months of its inception, the handcart scheme was widely believed by Mormons to have been passed down to Young in a revelation from God. Thus in the lyrics of a song written by Emily Hill Woodmansee (a twenty-year-old member of the fourth handcart company in 1856)—one of many songs the handcart pioneers would sing along the trail:

> *Oh, our faith goes with the hand-carts,*
>   *And they have our hearts' best love;*
> *'Tis a novel mode of traveling,*
>   *Devised by the Gods above.*

> Chorus:
> *Hurrah for the Camp of Israel!*
>   *Hurrah for the hand-cart scheme!*
> *Hurrah! Hurrah! 'tis better far*
>   *Than the wagon and ox-team.*

> *And Brigham's their executive,*
>   *He told us the design;*
> *And the Saints are proudly marching on,*
>   *Along the hand-cart line.*

In his December 22 editorial in the *Star*, President Richards eagerly expanded upon Young's enthusiasm for the "novel mode of traveling." His rhetorical device was to evoke the tribulations endured by the pioneers who had employed the old method of crossing the plains:

They alone can realize what it is to get up on a sultry morning— spend an hour or two in driving up and yoking unruly cattle, and while impatiently waiting to start on the dusty, wearisome road, in order to accomplish the labours of the day in due time, hear the word passed around that some brother has an ox missing, then another hour, or perhaps half a day, is wasted, and finally, when ready to start, the pleasantest time for travelling has passed, during which a company with hand-carts would have performed the greater part of an ordinary day's journey.

With only a few animals among their numbers, the handcart companies, Richards predicted, would present far less of a temptation to Indian raiders. The emigrants ought to be able to average fifteen miles a day, and so cover the trail in seventy days. (A curious calculation, this, for seventy times fifteen equals 1,050 miles—some 250 short, as Richards well knew, of the 1,300 miles that stretched between Iowa City and Salt Lake.) Like Young, Richards predicted that the handcart Saints would grow so fit they would actually speed up as they neared their goal, topping twenty miles per day. "We believe," the Apostle wrote, "that experience will prove sixty days to be about the medium time that it will require to cross the plains."

Above all, Richards emphasized, it was the sacred duty of the British Saints to travel by handcart. Invoking Muslim pilgrimages to Mecca and Hindu self-sacrifices in worship of their religion's "imaginary deity," he preached, "Then shall not the Saints, who have the revelations of heaven—the testimony of Jesus—the preludes of eternal joys . . . be ready to prove by their works that their faith is worth more than the life of the body—the riches of the world—the phantoms of paganism."

About one advantage of the handcart plan, Richards and Young were dead right: it was substantially cheaper than emigration by wagon and ox team. LDS scholar Andrew D. Olsen calculates that, compared to the $300 a family needed to spend to buy a team and wagon, a handcart for five cost only $10 to $20.

With the plan announced to the Saints in Utah, to the Saints in the Eastern states (via a bulletin published in the New York–based *The Mormon* on December 1, 1855), and to the British Saints in the *Millennial Star*, the great "experiment" (as it was alternatively called, even by Young) was launched. The Prophet put Franklin Richards in charge of organizing the emigration from Liverpool. Apostle John Taylor, the president of the Eastern Mission, based in New York City, was to be in charge of receiving the European Saints upon their arrival in the New World and sending them on their way to Iowa. Taylor, who had been severely wounded in the Carthage jail when the mob had burst in and killed Joseph and Hyrum Smith in 1844, took his duties seriously. At once he dispatched Elders William H. Kimball (Heber Kimball's son) and George D. Grant to Iowa City to superintend the building of the first hundred handcarts, then Elder Daniel Spencer, a missionary just returned from England, to take charge of the whole Iowa operation.

In the spring of 1856, however, at the very launching of the great handcart experiment, things started to go seriously wrong.

MORE MYTHOLOGIZING: according to a persistent legend, Edmund Ellsworth, who was finishing his two-year mission in England in 1855, had a dream in which he was called to lead a handcart party to Utah— this, before Young had announced his plan. Ellsworth's prescient vision would serve for the Saints to buttress the idea that the scheme was indeed of divine origin.

In this case, the source of the myth was Ellsworth himself, who spoke to a huge gathering in Salt Lake City only two days after his company arrived there. With Young in the audience, he quoted the Prophet's advice in the dream of more than a year before: "He further said, 'The powers of the wicked would be exerted against me, and the force of the elements would be combined to overthrow me, as was the case with the companies which first left Nauvoo'; and asked, 'Can you be faithful before God, and lead your brethren home to Zion by means of hand-carts?'"

Most of the British Saints in the Ellsworth and McArthur Companies sailed to America aboard the *Enoch Train*, arriving in Boston on April 30, 1856. By steamer they reached New York the following day, and the day after that set off by train for Iowa City, where they alighted, ready to begin their handcart trek, on May 12.

Except that there were no handcarts waiting for them—despite the efforts of Apostle John Taylor and other Mormon officials to contract for the building by local carpenters of that initial fleet of one hundred carriages. No scholar has yet explained this monumental oversight. Daniel Spencer had arrived in Iowa City on April 23, almost three weeks before the Ellsworth and McArthur emigrants. That very day, he wrote cryptically in his journal, "Examined the handcarts contracted by G. D. Grant which I did not much like." Did Spencer simply discard or refuse to pay for these inadequate vehicles?

In any event, after the five hundred Saints in the two companies reached Iowa City, they would be forced to linger there for four weeks as they built their own handcarts. Even the more sharp-eyed diarists among these pilgrims seem to have accepted this glitch with a glum fatalism. Thus Archer Walters, a skilled carpenter who would perform much of the building of the handcarts, to his diary:

Monday [May] 19th Went into the city of Iowa. Short of lumber. . . . [Tuesday] 20th Went to work to make hand carts. Was not very well. Worked 10 hours.

The most serious consequence of the handcart shortage was that the new, hastily constructed contraptions had to be built of green, not seasoned, timber. On the trail, the wood would warp, split, and shrink, necessitating frequent stops for jury-rigged repairs.

It is a testimony either to the converts' loyal obedience to their leaders, or to their utter ignorance of just what kind of ordeal lay ahead of them, that in all the diaries and reminiscences from the first two handcart companies later collected in the LDS Archives, there is scarcely a word of complaint (not to mention recrimination) about the failure of the officials to have handcarts ready in Iowa City, or about the obligation for the emigrants to build the carts themselves out of unseasoned wood. At last, on June 9, Ellsworth's party set off; McArthur's followed two days later.

Ellsworth would prove himself something of a tyrant on the trail, as well as a fanatic proponent of handcart travel once he reached Salt Lake City. McArthur seemed, in contrast, to lead by charismatic example. His team earned the nickname of the "Crack Company," in homage to its members' pluck, fitness, and high spirits. Ellsworth had demanded that his company be allowed to move out first, a preemption that McArthur bore with good grace. Even on the trail, Ellsworth had to be at the head of the caravan. On July 1, Archer Walters, the English craftsman whose diary rarely has a harsh word for anyone, complained about "Bro. Ellsworth always going first which causes many of the brothers to have hard feeling."

The Crack Company soon caught up with Ellsworth's slightly balkier entourage, and the two parties traveled together across Iowa. A friendly but heated rivalry between the two teams developed early on, accentuated by the makeup of their personnel—Ellsworth's mostly English Saints, McArthur's nearly all Scots. Indeed, the first and second companies would play a grueling game of tag and catch-up all the way to Salt Lake City.

The 270-mile passage across Iowa, known by now to be by far the easiest segment of the long trail, nonetheless unfolded in a grim procession, as with alarming regularity pilgrims (mostly children) died by the wayside. Archer Walters, whose duty it was to craft coffins for the victims, recorded their deaths (which began even before the party left Iowa City) in laconic diary entries:

Friday [June] 6th Made another child's coffin. . . .

Sunday 15th Got up about 4 o'clock to make a coffin for my brother, John Lee's son name William Lee, aged 12 years. Meetings as usual, and at the same time had to make another coffin for Sister Prator's child. . . . Went and buried them by moonlight at Bear Creek. . . .

Tuesday 17th Traveled about 17 miles; pitched tent. Made a little coffin for Bro. Job Welling's son and mended a hand cart wheel. . . .

Saturday 21st . . . Bro. (Jas.) Bower died about 6 o'clock; from Birmingham Conference. Went to buy the wood to make the coffin but the kind farmer gave me the wood and nails. . . .

Wednesday [July] 2nd Rose about 5 o'clock after sleeping in wet clothes, and made a coffin for Bro. Card . . . for his daughter named _____ Card, aged _____ . . . .

Thursday 3rd Ever to be remembered. Bro Card gave me ½ dollar for making his daughter's coffin.

With regularity, Walters records the nearly daily stops to repair broken handcarts. Ever the realist, McArthur was well aware of the inadequacy of his flimsy carriages. In a memoir written just a few months after he arrived in Salt Lake, the leader of the Crack Company vividly evoked this ordeal by repair:

> Our carts, when we started, were in an awful fix. They mowed [moaned] and growled, screeched and squealed, so that a person could hear them for miles. You may think this is stretching things a little too much, but it is a fact, and we had them to eternally patch, mornings, noons and nights.

Edmund Ellsworth, in contrast, was hard put to admit that anything was amiss. "June 9th 1856. At 5 P.M. the carts were in Motion proceeding zion wards," he crowed in the official journal, kept by scribe Andrew Galloway. "The Saints were in excellent spirits bound zion wards. the camp travelled about 4 Miles and pitched their tents. all well."

And when the Saints were not in excellent spirits, Ellsworth responded with a tongue-lashing. As John Oakley, a sub-captain of the company and Ellsworth's unwavering yes-man, recorded on June 11:

> Prest E spoke said he did not want to hear any more grumbling from this time on that the Em[igratio]n had cost more than expected consequently Prest Spencer was short of means so that we could not expect Sugar & Meat &c plentifully. said much depended on the success of this Co. if we failed it would throw a damper in the gathering of Israel we are responsible for it will be our own faults if we fail for the Prophet Brigham has Said it can be done. said he would rather the people of this camp would cut open his heart & drink his hearts blood than to hear any more grumbling for the judgements of the almighty would be upon us.

According to Oakley, who no doubt mirrored Ellsworth's views on the matter, when the handcarts broke down, it was due not to faulty design but to carelessness on the part of their handlers.

Along with deaths by the wayside, both parties suffered losses in the form of what Mormon leaders called "dropouts" or "backouts"—men, women, and children who, finding the toil unsupportable or their faith weakening, chose to return to Iowa City (or later, to stay in Florence) rather than complete the trek. That pressure from peers and leaders not to abandon the pilgrimage was intense emerges in the poignant early entries of one of the McArthur Company's most faithful diarists, Twiss Bermingham, an Irish Saint about twenty-six years old who was accompanied by his wife and three children aged eight and younger. On June 12, only the second day of his party's journey,

> We traveled 12 miles, starting at 9:30 o'clock and camped at 1 o'clock. The day was very hot and windy. The dust flew so thick that we could not see each other 1 yard distant. . . . This day was so very severe that Brother Larens and myself with our families thought we could not go on with safety to ourselves and families and drag hand carts with about 250 lbs. of luggage on them, and so determined to return to Iowa City to try and procure a [wagon] team to go through with.

Bermingham paid a teamster $5 to carry his family back to Iowa City. There, on the following day, a fellow Saint exhorted the man to get back on the trail. Without further comment in his diary, the Irishman harnessed his family back to their handcart. On June 14, the Berminghams caught up with the McArthur train, thirty-six miles out of Iowa City.

Since no comprehensive rosters of any of the handcart companies were ever compiled, it is very hard to calculate the number of dropouts. Combing genealogical records, historians LeRoy and Ann Hafen assert that the Ellsworth Company had thirty-three dropouts among its 280 emigrants. In a letter to the New York newspaper *The Mormon*, one J. H. Latey, a loyal Saint resident in Florence, estimated that the average backout toll was "from five to fifty in a company of 300." Latey was disgusted by these defections, editorializing,

> Those weak in the faith soon find those who will make them weaker; those who have backed out before them come up with

their long faces, smooth words, and melancholy tone, prating away their words of comfort (?), and if they will only go away with them there is no end of the money and comfort they are going to have, and a team, ONLY NEXT SPRING, to ride in and go to the Valley.

Since observers such as Latey and the Hafens were at pains to minimize dropping out, the actual number of backouts was probably higher than their estimates.

Among the leaders of the handcart companies, there was a prevalent conviction that the process of dropping out was the Lord's way of separating the chaff from the wheat. John Oakley, Ellsworth's sub-captain, captures this sanctimonious leitmotif as he records the sermons in which emigration officials harangued his company on June 6, three days before its departure from Iowa City:

> Eld: Spencer Tyler & Furgesen spoke of the high anticipation thought & solicitude for the hand cart co. & how thankfull those ought to be who were about to start out. Prest S said how softly we all ought to walk before the Lord & before angles who are watching us with most anxious solicitude especially for this company. Bro. Fergusen said shame on him or her who would propecy that the H Cart Co. would not go through when Bro. Brigham had said they shall—said it seem it may be now as it has been the Lord has killed off one half of the people to scare the other half to do right.

This vein of righteousness, which Brigham Young himself was wont to employ in his speeches in Salt Lake City, readily produced a kind of circular argument: whoever dropped out or even showed faintness of heart was judged to have been morally deficient from the start. Thus on June 20, in Oakley's diary, "One Bro Loyd and family (Welsh) Complained that the Hand Cart pulling was too hard & stoped after pulling to the top of a hill Bro. L likes a full belly & plenty of Whiskey." Five days later, Oakley joined another sub-captain and Ellsworth to deliver a homily on "lousiness" to that evening's camp meeting: "Cautioned against to freequent talking. & the purpose of the Lord in having us travel in this way it was not that He had not sufficient Cattle &c but He wished to decipline & prove us."

Heartless though it seems, Oakley's scorn for dropouts extended with a kind of Orwellian logic to those who were so faithless as to collapse and die along the trail. Thus:

Sun. [September] 7th . . . A Bro. Geo. Liddiard was taken verry ill & remained back some 5 mi. I took the horse & went after him found him dying. I hasted back to camp it was then dark—& came back in com. with Bro. Ira Hinkley & Thos Fowler with a waggon & fetched the body he died an hour after we put him in the waggon. . . . According to Bro. Liddiard's own testimony he has been a soldier in the British Army & lived a verry life of debauchery My opinion is that the remains of venereal disease & want of his accustomed stimulous drinks was the cause of his stopping here.

Sat. [September] 13th . . . A sis Mary Mayo died of disentery She had little faith & had grumbled much (age 65).

W. [September] 17th Bro Jas Birch died of disentery (age 28) burried him by the side of the road near the river on the bluff Came 11 mi. he had murmured considerable.

Adding to the emigrants' hardships were the chronically insufficient rations. The main daily staple for adults in the Ellsworth Company was between one-half and one pound of flour. In addition, the pilgrims were each given two ounces of rice, three ounces of sugar, and one-half pound of bacon per week. Children got even less food. Obviously, such a diet was far too little to maintain health even in sedentary humans, much less in those exerting themselves to the utmost every day.

Archer Walters's clipped diary entries capture the agonies of constant hunger. "Very faint for the (lack) of food," he reports himself on June 26, only a little more than two weeks along the trail. On July 1: "My children cry with hunger and it grieves me and makes me cross." At Fort Laramie on August 24, Walters traded a dagger he had carried all the way from England "for a piece of bacon an salt." He also spent a dollar and a quarter to buy bacon and cornmeal, "and Henry [Walters's sixteen-year-old son] and me began to eat it raw we was so hungry."

By August, hunger had driven some of the Ellsworth emigrants to stealing food from their supply wagons. When their leader discovered the thefts, he flew into a rage. John Oakley dutifully recorded Ellsworth's tirade on August 10: "Prest E told the camp he would lead them no further unless they would do better accused them of stealing one anothers provisions hipocritically pretending sick to ride & c & c told them to put the coat on if it fitted & he knew it did some. . . . The Camp voted to do better." Apparently the pilfering continued, however, for on August 24, Archer Walters quoted the company president as vowing that "those that had robbed the hand carts, or wagons, unless they repent their flesh would rot from their bones and go to Hell."

All five 1856 handcart companies suffered comparable shortages of food. What was the ultimate rationale for feeding the emigrants such inadequate provisions? In an iconoclastic study, historian Will Bagley declares that the bottom line was Brigham Young's "obsessive penny-pinching." But it may be that woefully short rations were built into the divine handcart scheme, since the carriages could carry only so much baggage and the few wagons that accompanied the trains were too full of tents and other crucial gear to take on the burden of additional tons of flour and sugar and bacon and rice. Archer Walters thought (or perhaps was told) as much, for on August 11 he sighed, "Very weak myself. I expect it is the short rations: ¾ of a lb. of flour per day. It is but little but it is as much as the oxen teams that we have could draw from St. Florence."

Similarly, all the handcart pioneers were strictly limited to seventeen pounds of personal baggage per man or woman, and as little as ten pounds per child. This draconian regulation would contribute even more fundamentally to the catastrophe that would soon unfold than would the shortage of food. One searches the voluminous documentary record of the handcart emigration in vain for a clear statement of how the seventeen-pound limit was arrived at, or who first imposed it. That it was rigorously enforced, however, emerges in many a diary entry. The punitive John Oakley, who performed some of the weighing, railed against "those whom we suspected of Keeping more than the 17 lbs & had Idols such as Boxes Books &c."

Nineteen-year-old Mary Ann Jones, however—one of two young Mary Anns who would marry Captain Ellsworth shortly after arriving in Salt Lake City—could see a certain humor in the Saints' struggle with the weight limit:

> We were allowed 17 lbs. of baggage each, that meant clothes beding cooking utensils etc, When the brethern came to weigh our things some wanted to take more than alowed so put on extra clothes so that some that wore real thin soon became stout and as soon as the weighing was over put the extra clothes in the hand cart again but that did not last long for in a few days we were called upon to have all weighed again & quite a few were found with more than alowed. One old Sister carried a teapot & calendar [collander] on her apron strings all the way to Salt Lake. Another Sister carried a hat box full of things but she died on the way.

ON JULY 8, the first two handcart companies finally reached Florence. They had been thirty (Ellsworth) and twenty-eight (McArthur) days on the trail across Iowa, averaging not the fifteen (or twenty or thirty) miles a day the Prophet had predicted, but only about nine. "On the arrival of the company in Florence," Twiss Bermingham of the McArthur Company dryly recorded, "the emigrants were, as a rule, very tired. We found some of Bro. Ellsworth's Company lying insensible on the road."

In Florence, the last bastion of Mormon settlement before Salt Lake, the Ellsworth Company laid over for nine days, as the Saints tried to fix their dilapidated carts. While in Florence, John Oakley engaged in an impromptu debate with several "apostates" and "half Mormons" who, appalled by the hardship of handcart travel, tried to "entice whom they could to stop in their glorious place showing especial regard for the sisters—one said to me God never required such hard things as drawing a hand cart." Oakley had a ready rejoinder: "I told him he had not read his Book right He required (what he the apostate would call hard) his Only Begotten to do a harder thing than draw a hand cart."

In Florence, the McArthur party tarried even longer than Ellsworth's—sixteen full days—as they repaired carts and nursed their bodies back to health. Once again, the company's leader gallantly acceded to Ellsworth's insistence on going first on the trail. When McArthur's party headed west on July 24, the Scots were a full week behind their English rivals.

Unlikely though it may seem, no author would publish a history of the handcart emigration before LeRoy and Ann Hafen's 1960 volume, *Handcarts to Zion*. The Hafens (brother and sister) performed a valuable service in gathering together original documents, although since 1960 many more primary sources have come to light. Their narrative, however, is cursory at best, and the whole book is vitiated by the Hafens' partisan point of view: they consistently minimize the horrors of the emigration, while striving to see it as a heroic rather than a tragic saga. (As a Swiss girl of six, the Hafens' mother had come to Zion in the last of all the handcart companies, in 1860.)

Sadly, we can be sure that nothing like a comprehensive history of the strangest "experiment" in all the annals of westward migration will ever be written. Too many details and episodes have fallen for good between the cracks. Yet in gathering together every scrap of firsthand testimony researchers can find, and in making those documents available to the general public (as they were not, for instance, in the 1960s, when Wallace Stegner wrote his mildly skeptical *The Gathering of Zion*), the LDS Archives in Salt Lake City have performed a noble service in the name of disinterested scholarship.

Thanks to those archives, and to the sharp eyes of weary pilgrims, poignant aspects of the handcart ordeal can be rescued from oblivion. In the McArthur Company, for instance, only a single diarist—Thordur Didriksson, from Iceland—bothered to record an aspect of the daily regimen that must have been heart-wrenching for every Saint in the party:

> There were 30 children in the company and early every morning
> they were sent on ahead of the grownups all in one bunch. Some
> of them had very little clothing but they all wore hats. They were
> driven along with willows and had to keep walking as long as they
> could. No use to cry or complain. But along during the day when

it was hot they were allowed to rest and were given food. They were often 2 or 3 miles ahead of us. It was hard for parents to see their little 5 and 6 year olds driven along like sheep.

Similarly, in Florence the Ellsworth Company took on some thirty new recruits. They are glancingly referred to as "Italian Saints," but the names of the few that have been preserved look French (e.g., an emigrant recorded as "Peter Stalle," whose real name was something like Jean-Pierre Staley). How the "Italians" got to Florence is lost to history: most likely they had come up the Mississippi and Missouri Rivers by steamboat. Their addition to the party is not even mentioned in the official Ellsworth Company journal, nor are their names on the partial roster in that journal.

The cold-eyed John Oakley, however, recorded on July 17, "Some 30 Italians were added to our Com. 14 cows added to our fit out also 9 beef cattle & team." Then, on August 17:

One Bro. Rosing an Italien much reduced for want of his accustomed beverage (Brandy) was left behind the teams having taken a different road I went back having taken the horse out of the team to do so intending to put him on the horse but found him to feeble after a thougher trial so I came to the waggons (1 mi.) took one the mule teams & came to get him had to lift him in he died an hour after I lifted him in the waggon.

It would remain for a single informant—a descendant of Jean-Pierre Staley named Margaret Barker, who was interviewed many decades later—to flesh out the picture of this shadowy cadre of "Italian" Saints:

The Mr. Ellsworth who had charge of the company, for some reason, badly mistreated the French saints, even depriving them of food. It is claimed, by the children of Pierre (Peter) Stalle that he died of starvation. It is claimed that Mr. Ellsworth sold part of the food that should have gone to the saints. When Pierre Stalle was dying, his wife climbed to the wagon to have a few last words with her husband. Ellsworth came with a rope and cruelly whipped her until she was forced to get down. This was verified by the

French families who came. "The captain was a very mean man. At one time a man died and they whipped and kicked him and threw him under the tent. His wife took his shoes to wear and some lady called her a dirty Italian."

In this reminiscence, Margaret Barker was no doubt calling upon tales handed down by family and friends among the French contingent, and so her own testimony about Ellsworth's brutal treatment of these foreigners may itself be unreliable. Yet even the loyal sub-captain John Oakley corroborates such a portrayal of Ellsworth, as in his September 12 diary entry: "I whiped a man for stubbornly refusing to walk this according to my presidents orders."

As July waned, both companies trudged on, following the Platte River, the Ellsworth party staying a few days ahead of McArthur's. The good trail the Saints had followed across Iowa gave out, as the emigrants battled with the notorious sand hills of Nebraska. In the worst of the going, the handcarts sank up to the wheel hubs in sand. The toil was terrible, as Twiss Bermingham's diary entry for August 3 makes clear:

We started at 5 o'clock without any breakfast, and had to pull the carts through 6 miles of heavy sand. Some places the wheels were up to the boxes, and I was so weak from thirst and hunger and being exhausted with the pain of the boils that I was obliged to lie down several times, and many others had to do the same. Some fell down.—I was obliged to take the children and put them on the handcart and urge them along the road in order to make them keep up.

On July 26, Henry Walker—a fifty-eight-year-old English laborer in the Ellsworth Company—was struck and killed by lightning. Wrote Archer Walters, "I put the body, with the help of others, on the hand cart and pulled him to camp and buried him without coffin for there was no boards to be had." Walker left his wife and children to push on toward Zion without him. Three other emigrants were injured by the lightning bolt, including a boy who was badly burned, but they survived and were able to continue.

On August 16, the McArthur party suffered what Twiss Bermingham called "the most severe day's journey we have had since we started"—twenty miles of arduous pulling across sand hills interspersed with frequent fords of streams tributary to the Platte. On that same day, a double calamity turned into what many of the Saints regarded as a double miracle.

First, an elderly Scotswoman named Mary Bathgate was bitten by a rattlesnake. "Before half an hour," Bermingham averred, "her leg had swelled to four times its thickness." In his account of the journey written a few months after arriving in Salt Lake, Daniel McArthur detailed the emergency treatment of the victim:

> Sister Bathgate sent a little girl back to me as quickly as possible to have me and Brothers Leonard and Crandall come with all haste, and bring the oil with us, for she was bitten badly. As soon as we heard the news, we left all things, and, with the oil, we went post haste. When we got to her she was quite sick, but said that there was power in the Priesthood, and she knew it. So we took a pocket knife and cut the wound larger, squeezed out all the bad blood we could, and there was considerable, for she had forethought enough to tie her garter around her leg above the wound to stop the circulation of the blood. We then took and anointed her leg and head, and laid our hands on her in the name of Jesus and felt to rebuke the influence of the poison, and she felt full of faith. We then told her that she must get into the wagon, so she called witnesses to prove that she did not get into the wagon until she was compelled to by the cursed snake. We started on and traveled about two miles, when we stopped to take some refreshments. Sister Bathgate continued to be quite sick, but was full of faith.

Another member of the party, one Mary B. Crandal, wrote a beguiling portrait of the Scotswoman in a memoir published almost forty years after the trek. "We all called her Mother Bathgate, for she must have been upwards of sixty," Crandal wrote. "She told me she had been in the coal-pits for forty years. She would travel on ahead and swing her cane and shout, 'Hurree for the handkerts.'" After she reached Salt Lake

City, Mary Bathgate lived on for many years. "She was a natural poet," Crandal recalled. "She composed some verses on her miraculous healing from the bite of the snake. I promised to write them for her but never did so. She could not write herself. How many things we neglect that we wish in after years we had not!"

Compounding the near-tragedy was the reckless act of Bathgate's best friend. In McArthur's telling,

> As the word was given for the teams to start, old Sister Isabella Park ran in before the wagon to see how her companion was. The driver, not seeing her, hallooed at his team and they being quick to mind, Sister Park could not get out of the way, and the fore wheel struck her and threw her down and passed over both her hips. Brother Leonard grabbed hold of her to pull her out of the way, before the hind wheel could catch her. He only got her out part way and the hind wheels passed over her ankles. We all thought that she would be all mashed to pieces, but to the joy of us all, there was not a bone broken, although the wagon had something like two tons burden on it, a load for 4 yoke of oxen. We went right to work and applied the same medicine to her that we did to the sister who was bitten by the rattlesnake, and although quite sore for a few days, Sister Park got better, so that she was on the tramp before we got into this Valley, and Sister Bathgate was right by her side, to cheer her up.

Among the emigrants in both the Ellsworth and McArthur Companies, there were quite a few such spunky, cheerful, and doggedly determined souls. Many of them were women. Twenty-one-year-old Mary B. Crandal (Mary Brannagan at the time), from Ireland, was one. Retrospect may have added a rosy glow, but in 1895 Crandal would look back on the trek and vow, "We all felt well and I enjoyed myself as well as I ever did in my life, only sometimes I would have liked something more to eat."

DESPITE THE JAUNTY memoirs of such pioneers as Crandal, it is clear that somewhere near the boundary between today's states of Nebraska and Wyoming, toward the end of August, both the Ellsworth and McArthur Companies were in serious trouble. What saved the parties was the single most vital (and most foresighted) component of the divine handcart plan.

In Salt Lake City, Brigham Young and his chief counselors had anticipated that the rations issued to the first two handcart companies would be inadequate to sustain them on the 1,300-mile journey to Zion. To relieve the shortage, the authorities had sent out wagon teams laden with supplies (mostly flour), traveling east along the Mormon Trail in expectation of intercepting the handcart companies.

On August 31, near Deer Creek, a small southern tributary of the North Platte, the resupply train met the Ellsworth party. The surviving diaries of the handcart pioneers are surprisingly matter-of-fact about this potentially life-saving rendezvous. Perhaps the morale of the company was so low at that point that not even the gift of a thousand pounds of flour could stir the emigrants to exultation. Deaths, in fact, had begun to seem almost routine occurrences. One poor Englishman, fifty-one-year-old Robert Stoddart, had the bad luck to die only an hour before the Ellsworth Company met the resupply train. He was buried at Deer Creek, leaving his wife, his fourteen-year-old son, and his ten- and six-year-old daughters to travel on to Zion without him. Two days later another Englishman, sixty-five-year-old Walter Sanders, died and was promptly buried beside the trail.

Today, on the site of the Deer Creek resupply, stands the sleepy town of Glenrock, Wyoming. Sylvan the place remains, a woody hollow of an oasis in the bleak prairie stretching north and south of the meandering Platte. The only historical monument in Glenrock, however, says nothing about the handcart companies, choosing instead to celebrate the trading post–cum–saloon of former mountain man Joseph Bissonette (built in 1857) and a short-lived Pony Express station from 1860 to 1861.

The resupply expedition was so well organized that another thousand pounds of flour was waiting for the McArthur Company when it reached Deer Creek on September 2. A few months later, McArthur would remember how this sudden (and apparently unexpected) boon had "caused the hearts of the saints to be cheered up greatly." Not content with a single mission of mercy, the authorities in Salt Lake had sent out a second wagon train a couple of weeks after the first. Thus, farther west along the trail, the Ellsworth and the McArthur Companies each received another thousand pounds of precious flour, the latter only twelve days after their first resupply, as they camped on Pacific Creek, now a mere 228 miles short of Salt Lake City.

Twiss Bermingham, however, recorded in his diary a detail about the resupply mission that neither the authorities in Salt Lake nor the two company captains bothered to mention. Once they arrived in Zion, the Saints would be expected to pay for the flour that had kept them alive, at the rate of 18 cents per pound.

The dates of the Deer Creek resupplies indicate that, having set out from Florence a full week after the Ellsworth Company, McArthur's Crack Company had been steadily gaining on its rivals, until now it was only two days behind. Exhausted though the emigrants were, stopping regularly to rest and bury their dead, the race between the English and Scottish Saints was on.

In early September, both parties at last left the North Platte to follow the Sweetwater River to its headwaters near South Pass. On September 11, having pushed hard into the night, the hares finally caught the tortoises, on Alkali Creek, about twenty miles west of today's nearly derelict one-horse town of Jeffrey City, Wyoming. With laconic resignation, Ellsworth dictated this turn of events to his company's official journal: "About 11 P.M. Brother McArthur's company came up. They had traveled nearly night and day to overtake us."

Perhaps magnanimously, McArthur declined to mention his catch-up feat in the reminiscence he wrote a few months later. But that it was a dramatically orchestrated coup emerges in the gloating memory of it that Phyllis Hardie Ferguson, a member of the McArthur Company, reported many years later. Ferguson claimed that her party traveled thirty-two miles that day and night to overtake the Ellsworth team.

> When it became quite dark, we reached the top of a high hill, where by Captain McArthur's instructions we left the handcarts, and quietly walked down towards the blazing camp fires. Just before we reached the Ellsworth company, we all began to shout, "Hurrah for the handcarts!"

Captain Ellsworth, thinking it was the overland mail coach, in which was Franklin D. Richards, the returning president of the European mission, and others who were expected, hurriedly called out the band to give them glad welcome. Imagine his chagrin when he discovered that his welcome was given to the Scotch handcart company, who had overtaken him! But he was a good man, and has long years ago ended his life's journey. Peace to his ashes! The English people, though just as good and zealous, had not the endurance that we had, and it was difficult for them to be first.

Ferguson goes on to claim that the McArthur party now camped for two weeks at Alkali Creek, once more granting Ellsworth the priority on the trail that he so fiercely craved. This cannot be true, however: McArthur's own report has his company reaching Pacific Creek, some forty miles west of Alkali, only three days after the surprise rendezvous.

For all the hijinks and spirited competition this race along the trail seems to imply, and despite the invigoration provided by the blessed gift of flour, both parties trudged on as many of their members grew weaker and sicker. Twiss Bermingham, who had so faithfully jotted his party's doings into his diary from the Iowa City start onward, found himself unable to make a single entry between September 5 and 21, and none after the 21st. Archer Walters, the Ellsworth Company coffin-maker, recorded the Wyoming toll:

Tuesday 2nd Platt River. Travelled 19 miles. Walter Sanderson, aged 56, died. . . .

Sunday 7th Travelled 26 miles. Bro. Nipras died. Left on the road. . . .

Sunday 14th Travelled 3 miles. Camped to mend hand carts and women to wash. Sister Mayer died.

After that September 14 entry, Walters's own diary breaks off, not to be resumed.

Galvanized by the humiliation of McArthur's catching him up, Ellsworth drove his company onward with furious resolve. On September

18, a party of missionaries from Salt Lake who were returning to England crossed paths with the Ellsworth entourage. Writing later for the *Millennial Star*, Thomas Bullock sketched a rousing vignette of this meeting on the trail:

> September 18th, we were very agreeably surprised by suddenly coming upon the advance train of hand-carts, composed of about 300 persons, traveling gently up the hill west of Green river, led by Elder Edmund Ellsworth. As the two companies approached each other, the camp of missionaries formed in line, and gave three loud Hosannahs, with the waving of hats, which was heartily led by Elder P. Pratt, responded to by loud greetings from the Saints of the hand-cart train, who unitedly made the hills and valleys resound with shouts of gladness; the memory of this scene will never be forgotten by any person present.

Ellsworth's pace, however, was taking its toll. On September 17, another English Saint, twenty-eight-year-old James Birch, died of diarrhea; on the 22nd, yet another, identified only as "one man of the Italian brethren." John Oakley, who had pitilessly attributed the weaknesses and even the deaths of others to moral failings, came close to death himself. On September 24, "I had to go back 3 mi. in the dark to look for one of the teams & waggon & felt all the time that some one might have to come to look after me for I was much exhausted through the severe toil of the day—my head was dizzy." Oakley attributed his survival to "much assistance from an unseen source." He did not speculate what sorts of character flaws might have contributed to his own debilitation.

With the scent of Zion in his nostrils, sometimes traveling miles ahead of the main body of his company, on September 25 Ellsworth drove his party twenty miles through Echo Canyon, crossing the stream eleven times, and then over a high pass. "Crossed the bigg Mountain in 2 hours & 55 minutes," he bragged in the official journal. Just how dangerous a passage this was emerges in a vivid account by William Butler, a thirty-year-old sub-captain:

> When we got to Echo Kanyon, there came another heavy thunderstorm. litghtening and heavy rains knight coming on and the

people very weary travelling. our Captain persisted in continuing our journey over a divide, which made it very hard to ascend and descend a distance of six miles, and all in the dark—and no light only as the lightening flashed the rain pouring down in torrents all the time.—I had been taken sick the day before which made me very weak and unable to follow the train and drive the stock. my wife Emma had to take and drive the stock for me.—I was left behind to travel or die.—after a while I rose on my feet and lifted my voice with uplifted hands in token of the priesthood, and said these words.—having been commissioned by the King of Kings.—I command this spirit to let loose his grasp. . . . from this very moment the pain left me and I was able to resume my journey, it being very dark, insomuch that I could not see the road. I fell down a great many times over all manner of rocks, steep places and holes, after awhile I came to an Italian with his little girl. I tried to get him to come along with his hand cart, but not understanding his language, nor he mine, so he did not follow me.—he died during the night, and they fetched him into camp in the morning.—soon after leaving the Italian I came across a young english girl by the name of Clark. who was alone and had lost her way—she was crying and in great trouble.—I went to her, and fetched her into Camp,—the gratitude of the girl and her parents and relatives was unbounded towards one for what I had done.—she considered that I had saved her life and next day we gathered up the dead and buried them.

By September 25, word was abroad in Salt Lake that the first handcart party was camped at the foot of Little Mountain, just a few miles northeast of the city. Resident Saints rode out to greet the Ellsworth Company and escort it the rest of the way. Brigham Young had organized a gala welcome. Charles Treseder, a young man living in Salt Lake, wrote his parents in New Jersey a letter detailing the arrival and reception:

Presidents Brigham Young, and H. C. Kimball escorted by the minute men and a company of Lancers, followed by as many of the citizens as could turn out—some in vehicles and some on foot, with the two bands, to welcome the hand-carts and they did not forget to take them something to eat.

President Brigham Young, and Kimball went part way up the little mountain in a buggy and met them coming down. Bro. Brigham was introduced to them as they formed in line, and he was so much affected with the spectacle, he could only say: My good people I am glad to see you, God bless you all. He hurried away, he could say no more. The Salt Lake Brethren then gave the emigrants plenty to eat and they once more went to their hand-carts and made the last start. As they came down the bench you could scarcely see them for the dust. When they entered the city, the folks came running from every quarter to get a glimpse of the long-looked-for hand-carts.

Like many another resident, Treseder was overcome by the joyous spectacle.

I shall never forget the feeling that ran through my whole system as I caught the first sight of them. The first hand-cart was drawn by a man and his wife, they had a little flag on it, on which were the words: "Our President—may the unity of the Saints ever show the wisdom of his counsels."

The next hand-cart was drawn by three young women. . . . The tears rolled down the cheek of many a man who you would have thought would not, could not, shed a tear; but the scene was exciting in the extreme and most everybody felt sympathetic and joyous. I could scare refrain from tears. Richard [Charles's brother] cried like a child, and amongst the women the crying was pretty near universal.

Mary Powell Sabin, a twelve-year-old Welsh girl in the Ellsworth party, later recalled that Brigham Young himself and several Apostles gave the emigrants their first food—watermelons: "Pres. Young told us to eat moderately of the mellon, to eat the pink, not to eat into the green." The Prophet then spoke to the whole company. "He told us that we had fulfilled a prophecy. He also said that although we had endured privations and hunger on the plains we should never again feel the pangs of starvation if we would do right and live right."

Only hours behind the Ellsworth train, the McArthur Company entered Salt Lake City in time to share in the celebration. Yet not every handcart pioneer's heart was filled with joy as he reached Zion. William Aitken, a thirty-six-year-old dentist in the McArthur Company, who had traveled with his eleven-year-old son and fourteen-year-old daughter, would apostatize within the year and flee Salt Lake City the next April. In a letter published in the *Edinburgh News* in 1857, Aitken described the emigrants as they entered Salt Lake as "wearied and worn down, the bones almost through the skin, not only of myself but of all that were in the company." He added that the party "were half starved to the bargain, our whole allowance being 12 ounces of flour per day, and we did not even get so much."

Aitken's most serious criticism is nowhere corroborated in the surviving records of the Ellsworth and McArthur Companies. It may be merely the bitter exaggeration of a disillusioned apostate. Yet if it is true, it indicates that the kind of sanctimonious judgments reflected in John Oakley's callous diary entries—if a Saint faltered or died on the trail, it was proof of moral failure—were built into the very handcart plan. "It is the policy of the Church," wrote Aitken, "to leave the weak, the infirm, and the old by the way, that they may have no paupers to support."

AN ACCURATE COUNT of the number of deaths within the Ellsworth and McArthur Companies will probably never be made. The official Ellsworth journal lists 272 Saints by name, of whom thirty-three are identified as "backed out," twelve as "dead." But as this list omits any mention of the thirty "Italian" Saints—at least four of whom are recorded in various diaries as dying along the way—that roster cannot be complete. McArthur acknowledged "only the loss of 8 souls. 7 died, and one, a young man, age 20 years, we never could tell what did become of him."

Hafen and Hafen fix the number of deaths as thirteen and seven, respectively. (The admitted disappearance of the twenty-year-old in the

McArthur Company is not counted by the Hafens as a death.) Without citing sources, the company narratives in the LDS Archives elevate the numbers slightly, to sixteen deaths in the Ellsworth Company, ten among the McArthur emigrants. In all likelihood, even these counts are too low. None of the diaries, for instance, mentions perhaps the cruelest death of all, that of John McCleve, an Irishman from Belfast traveling with his wife and seven children in the McArthur Company, who gave up the ghost on September 24, only two days short of Salt Lake City.

The original counts of 280 Saints in the Ellsworth Company, 220 in the McArthur, seem reliable. If we take fifty as a minimum estimate of dropouts between the two parties, and accept the LDS Archives' count of twenty-six dead, then the mortality rate in the first two handcart companies was about 6 percent. If we guess a hundred dropouts, that figure rises to almost 7 percent. Either rate is slightly above John Unruh's average of 4 percent among all emigrating parties between 1840 and 1860, but it remains a remarkably low toll, given the conditions under which the handcart pioneers traveled. Without the critical resupplies at Deer Creek and farther west, the mortality rate would have been much higher. But the ultimate credit for the Saints' survival must go to their genuinely heroic perseverance and fortitude.

In the days and weeks after the first two handcart companies reached Salt Lake, the colony engaged in an orgy of joy and self-congratulation. The *Deseret News* baldly asserted, "This journey has been performed with less than the average amount of mortality usually attending ox trains." In an emotional speech in the bowery meeting hall only two days after the companies' arrival, Heber C. Kimball, the church's First Counselor and Brigham Young's closest confederate, gave vent to a characteristically apocalyptic vision of future emigration:

> I am very thankful that so many of the brethren have come in with hand-carts; my soul rejoiced, my heart was filled and grew as big as a two-bushel basket. Two companies have come through safe and sound. Is this the end of it? No; there will be millions on millions that will come much in the same way, only they will not have hand-carts, for they will take their bundles under their

arms, and their children on their backs and under their arms, and flee; and Zion's people will have to send out relief to them, for they will come when the judgments come on the nations.

At the same meeting in the bowery, Young basked in the success of his "experiment":

I think it is now proven to a certainty that men, women and children can cross the plains, from the settlements on the Missouri river to this place, on foot and draw hand-carts, loaded with a good portion of the articles needed to sustain them on the way.

To me this is no more a matter of fact this morning, after seeing the companies that have crossed the plains, than it was years ago.

The Prophet elaborated in this I-told-you-so vein by spinning out an odd homily:

My reasoning has been like this: Take small children, those that are over five years of age, and if their steps were counted and measured, those that they take in the course of one day, you would find that they had taken enough to have traveled from 12 to 20 miles.

Count the steps that a woman takes when she is doing her work, let them be measured, and it will be found that in many instances she had taken steps enough to have traveled from 15 to 20 miles a day; I will warrant this to be the case. The steps of women who spin would, in all probability, make from 20 to 30 miles a day.

So with men, they do not consider the steps they make when they are at their labor; they are all the time walking. Even our masons upon the walls are all the time stepping; they take a step almost at every breath.

"I am not a good walker," the Prophet asserted, "though I have walked a great deal in the course of my life." He went on to recount the longest pedestrian journey of his life, an 1834 missionary tour, during which he claimed to have walked two thousand miles, averaging forty miles a day for weeks on end with little trouble. Young did acknowledge that "the hand-carts look rather broken up, but if they had been made of good seasoned timber, they would have come in as nice as when they started with them." And, "True, the brethren and sisters that came in with hand-carts have eaten up their provisions, and some have hired their clothing brought, and they had but little on their carts when they came in."

Yet the moral was plain. In the euphoria of the moment, Young was happy to voice it:

> As for health, it is far healthier to walk than to ride, and better every way for the people. . . .
> To have to walk a thousand miles?— Those who get into the Celestial Kingdom will count this a very light task in the end, and if they have to walk thousands of miles they will feel themselves happy for the privilege, that they may know how to enjoy celestial glory.

If anything, at that bowery meeting Young was upstaged by Edmund Ellsworth, who delivered a truly fanatical analysis of his company's success. Ellsworth sincerely believed that the devil was in his party's midst, causing all the troubles the pioneers faced, "using his influence and doing his best, with sickness, weakness, and fatigue, breaking down the carts, etc., to discourage the faithful and sink their spirits."

Given his druthers, Ellsworth would have accomplished the journey in even purer style. He told the bowery congregation:

> I regret that there was a wagon in our company, for I realized that wagons had a tendency to destroy the faith of our brethren and sisters; for if they were sick a little they felt that they could get into the wagons.
> I am persuaded that if there had been no wagons for such people, there would have been none sick, or weak, but that their faith would have been strong in the name of the Lord.
> A few deaths happened in our company, but this was doubtless due mainly to the fact . . . that it was in a great degree composed

of infirm people, and many of them had been accustomed to different kinds of labor to what they have experienced this year.

Some had been raised at work under ground all their lives, and been subject only to that kind of exercise, and through this they had accumulated diseases and their lungs had been affected; and some were nearly dead when they left the old country.

In a speech given two weeks after the monumental bowery meeting, Young boasted that "Br. Ellsworth performed the journey in 63 days and br. McArthur in 61½." This is so far from the truth that it can only be characterized as a deliberate lie. In reality, the Ellsworth Company, leaving Iowa City on June 9 and arriving in Salt Lake City on September 26, had been 110 days on the trail. The McArthur Company was a mere two days faster. But the average Saint in Salt Lake had little idea when the handcarts had departed from Iowa, and the congregation dearly wanted to hear what their leader was telling them.

Evidently, Young also wanted to pretend that his prediction of a sixty-odd-day passage by handcart had come to pass. In truth, the Ellsworth and McArthur Companies had averaged a little less than twelve miles a day—quite a creditable pace, but far short of the fifteen to twenty to thirty the Prophet had envisioned.

Among the new arrivals in Zion that September, there were some curious and poignant sequelae. Mary McCleve, a sixteen-year-old Irish girl who lost her father, John, only two days before reaching Salt Lake City, was married only six weeks after the end of her journey to a sixty-one-year-old man. "It was love at first sight," she would report seventy-six years later, "even though he had three grown girls older than myself. . . . Ten children blessed our union."

But William Butler, who had staggered through Echo Canyon in the dark, resigned himself to death, and had to turn over his stock to his wife, Emma, suffered a diametrically opposite denouement. As the couple neared Salt Lake, Butler later ruefully disclosed, "We were meet on our way going into the city by a woman wife of John Pannel Wright. from south willow creek.—she used her influence to induce my wife to leave me and go home with her. her Man was three days waiting in the City to take my wife home with him."

Twiss Bermingham, the scrupulous diarist in the McArthur Company, saw his faith quickly dissolve in Salt Lake City. The following year, he apostatized and returned to Florence, where he became a schoolteacher. A version of his diary that was not published until 1937, in the *American Legion Magazine*, reveals that the church was not above expurgating original documents as they were transcribed into the official LDS Archives. In Bermingham's last diary entry, on September 21, the sentence "Conduct of the men from the Valley who came to meet us was disgraceful" was struck from every version except the one finally published by the non-Mormon *American Legion Magazine*.

William Aitken, that much angrier apostate, rode out of Salt Lake City with three hundred other apostates in April 1857, well armed and apparently in fear of ambush on the trail. The men, women, and children were "all determined to get off or die," Aitken later wrote. After a hard journey through heavy snows, the apostates reached the safety of the States. "Thousands in Utah would be glad to be with us, though in the same condition," Aitken averred.

As for Archer Walters, the loyal carpenter and burier of the dead—he succumbed to dysentery only two weeks after reaching Zion. His death, according to contemporary experts, was "caused by eating corn-meal and molasses, and aggravated by his weakened condition and lowered resistance resulting from exposure, under-nourishment, and physical exhaustion during the thirteen hundred mile journey." Walters's five children remained loyal to the church, and by 1937 he had five hundred descendants in Utah.

Meanwhile, even as the Saints in Zion rejoiced in the arrival of the first two handcart companies, the portent that would ultimately develop into catastrophe was already coalescing hundreds of miles to the east. In New York City, President John Taylor had received more than 1,600 Saints who had sailed from Liverpool in May: 764 aboard the *Thornton*, 856 aboard the *Horizon*. He had sent them on to Iowa, not without worrying about the lateness of the season. The *Thornton* emigrants reached Iowa City on June 26, the *Horizon* Saints not until July 8. These pioneers would make up the fourth and fifth handcart companies of 1856.

Brigham Young would later claim to know nothing about these late-arriving pilgrims, not even of their existence, but this, too, is a demonstrable falsehood. On June 11, from Iowa City, William Woodward, one of the officials in charge of the eastern end of the handcart migration, wrote to Heber Kimball in Salt Lake City. His newsy epistle contained this pregnant paragraph:

> We have heard that another ship load of emigrants have arrived at New York by the ship "Thornton" numbering when they left Liverpool 764 souls. James G. Willie, Millen Atwood, & Moses Clough preside over the Thornton's company. We expect them at this point by the 16th or 17th of June.

When did this letter reach Salt Lake? Normally the arrival dates of such documents are by now impossible to determine, but in this case, a clerk in Young's office marked a filing notation on the back of the original letter: "Recd July 30/56, Eastern Mail."

The conclusion is inescapable: nearly two months before the arrival of the long-awaited Ellsworth and McArthur Companies, Heber Kimball and Brigham Young were fully aware that more than seven hundred more handcart Saints were preparing their journeys westward, dangerously late in the season. What those two men, as well as the rest of the Mormon authorities in charge of the emigration, did—or more precisely, did not do—in the face of this alarming development remains all but inexplicable today.

CHAPTER FOUR

SAVAGE ADVICE

Among the five Mormon handcart expeditions of 1856, by far the least well known and most poorly documented is the third, the Bunker Company. There is a logical reason for this: the vast majority of the 290-odd emigrants in that party (a larger number than traveled in either the Ellsworth or McArthur Companies) were from Wales. As they started out from Iowa City, almost none of them spoke English. Nor in later years did more than a handful of them choose to reflect in writing upon their experience crossing the plains.

The chaos in communication caused by that language barrier is hard to imagine, but it must have added a severe stress to the inevitable hardships of the trail. One member of the party, twenty-one-year-old Priscilla Evans, made the trek with her thirty-seven-year-old husband, Thomas. Though both Evanses were Welsh, only Thomas spoke the language. Almost sixty years after the marathon journey, Priscilla kept a fresh (and still indignant) recollection of that linguistic tribulation. "Dont you think I had a pleasant journey," she wrote in an autobiographical sketch penned around 1914, "traveling for months with about 300, people, of whose language I could not understand a word. My husband could speak Welch, so he could join in their festivities when he felt like it."

Edward Bunker, thirty-four years old that summer, was an American just returning from almost four years of missionary service in Great Britain. He had first emigrated to Zion by wagon train from Winter Quarters (Florence) in 1850, although in 1846, he had been a member of the staunch Mormon Battalion that had marched with General Stephen Watts Kearny's Army of the West to California. In mid-June of 1856, a church official helping oversee the launching of the handcart trains at Iowa City wrote to President John Taylor in New York, "Edward Bunker superintends the making of ox-yokes, ox-bows and the hauling of timber."

Bunker himself wrote almost nothing about the Welsh company's journey. His 1894 manuscript autobiography devotes a mere three short paragraphs to the trek. From that account, only two details of interest emerge. Very soon after the company left Iowa City, a torrential rainstorm leveled its camp. Thanks to the storm, writes Bunker, "I got a heavy drenching, which brought on a spell of rheumatism that confined me to my bed a portion of the Journey."

Bunker found the language barrier between himself and most of the Welsh Saints a trial: "The Welsh had no experience at all and very few of them could speak English. This made the burden upon me very heavy."

From the first-person accounts of pilgrims on the Bunker Company's trek, only the haziest portrait of its leader emerges. He seems to have been a stern disciplinarian along the lines of Edmund Ellsworth, without perhaps the latter's fanatical bent. Priscilla Evans claimed many years later that Bunker would allow none of the sick or lame to ride in the three wagons that accompanied the train; instead, they had to be carried on handcarts. Yet David Grant, a sub-captain whose fawning loyalty to his leader may render his testimony unreliable, wrote in a letter to England from mid-trek, "There are in the company those still more advanced in years, who ride in the wagons."

In the same letter, Grant also insisted, "This is so healthy a country, that our appetites are very good." And, "I am happy to say that we have been united in all things since we left Iowa City, and am glad in having such a man to lead us as our Captain."

Like the two parties before them, the Bunker Company arrived in Iowa City to find no handcarts ready for them. A delay of three weeks ensued while the carriages were once again slapped together out of unseasoned wood. At last the third company started rolling westward on June 23, two weeks after the Ellsworth procession had departed. In the end, it would take the Bunker Company 104 days to reach Salt Lake City; it thus completed the passage about a week faster than the Ellsworth and

McArthur parties, but still far more slowly than the sixty to seventy days predicted by Brigham Young.

From details in the scanty record of the pioneers' own writings, one divines that the Bunker party suffered much the same privations and ordeals as did the two companies that preceded them. Among the few vivid vignettes of daily life within the entourage are those concerning a single handcart, the one pushed and pulled by the Evans couple and by Elizabeth Lane, a woman traveling alone who was assigned to the Evanses' cart. We know almost nothing about Lane—neither her age nor her place of origin, even though she wrote a memoir of the trek in 1896. It contains this cryptic avowal: "I had always been isolated from the Church, so that I had not one particular friend; I seemed to travel all alone."

Priscilla Evans paints a woeful picture of the motley crew of twenty-odd comrades with whom she shared a tent each night: "There were in our tent a man with one leg (my husband) Two blind Thomas Giles being one of them, one man with one arm, and a widow with five children. The widow and her children and myself, were the only ones who could not speak the Welch language." Thomas Evans had lost his leg in an accident at the age of nine. Hobbling along on his wooden leg, he somehow covered the 1,300 miles from Iowa City to Salt Lake. His wife hints at the torment he underwent: "While walking 20 to 25 miles per day where the knee rested on the pad it would gather and break and was most painful, but he had to endure it or remain behind." Elizabeth Lane elaborates: "He soon gave out in the deep sands of Nebraska, and his wife and myself took the cart all the way to Laramie."

A slightly different version of Priscilla Evans's memoir adds the significant admission that she was at least five months pregnant toward the end of the journey. And this version makes it clear just how desperate Thomas's plight was:

When his knee, which rested on a pad, became very sore, my husband was not able to walk any farther and I could not pull him in the little cart, being so sick myself, so one late afternoon he felt he could not go on so he stopped to rest beside some tall sagebrush. I pleaded with him to try to walk farther, that if he stayed there he would die, and I could not go on without him. The company did not miss us until they rested for the night and when the names were checked we were not among the company and a rider on a horse came back looking for us. When they saw the pitiful condition of my husband's knee he was assigned to the commissary wagon.

If "assigned to" means "allowed to ride in," this version of Evans's memoir contradicts her other one. But if Bunker ever relented and let invalids mount the wagons, he apparently did so only rarely and grudgingly, for Elizabeth Lane wrote that after rheumatism in her ankles rendered her almost too lame to walk, a kindly fellow pilgrim named John Cousins "carried me on his back through many rivers, and when Captain Bunker put me out of the wagon at Laramie River, he picked me up and carried me through the water."

Several sources report that from the very start at Iowa City, the Bunker Company emigrants were issued only half a pound of flour per person per day "and a little Tea and shugar." This was only half the ration allotted to the Ellsworth and McArthur Companies on leaving Iowa City, a ration that those earlier emigrants themselves found pitifully inadequate. The rationale for this extreme economy of food is nowhere to be found in the record. Only after Florence was the daily issue raised to a pound of flour per man or woman per day. Even this, reported John Parry, was "not near enough," as he remembered an ordeal during which "little Children 6 years of age did use to walk 26 miles p[er] day."

The Bunker Company would most likely have faced mass starvation had another timely resupply wagon train out of Salt Lake City not intercepted its path. Only Parry's account even mentions this heaven-sent intervention, as he places it at "the uper crossing of the Platt River," possibly at or near present-day Casper, Wyoming.

The record of the Bunker Company offers posterity only a glimpse here and there of its three-month odyssey. A few moments verge on the comical. "Indians met us some times," John Parry noted, "and helped us to pull our Carts, which was a great fun for them." Despite his ceaseless suffering, Thomas Evans was not above a practical joke. Priscilla relates how it backfired:

Some Indians came to our camp, and my husband in a joking way told an Indian, who admired me, that he would trade me for a Pony. He thot no more about it. But the next day, here came the Indian with the Pony, and it was no Joke with him. I never was so frightened in all my life. There was no place to hide, and we did not know what to do. The Captain was called, and they had some dificulty in settling with the Indian with out trouble.

The Bunker Company was fortunate not to encounter freezing weather before completing its trek, though one diary mentions a six-inch snowfall thirty miles west of Fort Laramie. Despite the resupply at the Platte crossing, the company ran short on food long before reaching Salt Lake City. One emigrant, Samuel Orton, later claimed that while the party was still two or three hundred miles east of Salt Lake, the daily flour ration was cut to a quarter-pound per adult. Hunger once again reduced the emigrants to desperate straits. Twenty-three-year-old Eleanor Roberts had married a fellow emigrant while the company waited in Iowa City for the hand-carts to be built. According to a secondhand source, somewhere along the trail (perhaps at Fort Bridger) she traded her wedding ring for flour.

Eleanor also purportedly lost her shoes en route, when she took them off to cross the Missouri River but forgot and left them on the near bank. "She walked the rest of the journey bare-footed," claims the source. By his own account, Robert Roberts's boots gave out somewhere near Independence Rock in central Wyoming and he had to walk the last eight hundred miles barefoot. (The actual distance from Independence Rock to Salt Lake City is only 332 miles.)

As late as August 30, the loyal sub-captain David Grant could blandly write, "We travel together in peace and harmony. . . . Elder Bunker has proved himself a father to his people, and I know that the Holy Spirit has been with him and aided him in leading them all the time."

But other pilgrims in the Bunker Company were beginning to give out, and more than one prepared for death. The loner Elizabeth Lane later recalled,

We finally came to Green River, and I was behind the camp; there was no one in sight and it was near sundown. I sat down and thought this is the last. After a while I began to ask myself what brought you here? I called myself a coward. So I got up and asked the Lord to help me, and prepared to wade the river; and the Lord did help me, and I got safe to the camp just as they were preparing to come after me. But the next morning I could not stand; I had been chilled through.

Others also attributed their survival in extremis to divine intervention. Thomas Giles, one of the blind men in the party, was traveling with his wife, two young sons, and a baby girl. The infant died early on during the trek and was buried beside the trail. Near Fort Bridger, only 113 miles short of Salt Lake, Giles collapsed with illness. Bunker delayed the company for two days, hoping the blind man would recover, but when he did not, the captain ordered the party to continue. He allegedly left two men behind to bury Giles after he died.

During this wait, leading Apostle Parley Pratt passed by on an eastward journey to the States. Pratt had known Giles in Wales. According to a secondhand account, Pratt administered a blessing to the blind man, making the following promises: "that he should instantly be healed and made well, that he should rejoin his company and arrive safely in the Salt Lake Valley; that he should there rear a family; and that because of his faithfulness he would be permitted to live as long as he wanted."

All the promises came true. Giles recovered, caught up with the company, and made it to Salt Lake City. He would live another forty years, gaining a genial reputation as the Blind Harpist for his talents as an itinerant musician.

After the daily ration had been reduced to a quarter-pound of flour, Samuel Orton also lingered on the edge of death, only to undergo an even more mystical salvation than Giles's. In his own words:

I soon became very weak and sick so that I had to leave my handcart and travel behind the company. I was so sick I thought I should die, and I asked the Lord that I might die. All at once a voice spoke to me as plain as I ever heard a voice in my life and said, "Sam are you here?["] I turned around and answered "yes" but could see no one. which surprised me very much. I went on and caught up with the company took hold of my handcart and my sickness left me.

That voice out of nowhere plunged Orton into a deep meditation: "I made up my mind if the Father and the Son did appear to the Prophet Joseph Smith and reveal the gospel unto him, and that Brigham Young was his Lawful successor I wanted to see the Halo of light around his head like there was around the head of the Saviour on nearly all of the pictures we see."

A few days after Orton reached Salt Lake, he attended a meeting in the bowery. Sure enough,

Looking toward the stand there I saw President Young with the rays of light around his head as I had asked for on the plaines, and the same voice as spoke to me on the plaines said, "Now Sam if ever you apostatize here is your condemnation." I looked around me to see if the people heard it, but, I thought they did not.

So fragmentary is the record of the Bunker Company's journey that no accurate death toll has ever been compiled. Without citing their sources, Hafen and Hafen reckon a total mortality of "less than 7."

One of the emigrants, Robert Roberts, flatly contradicts this sanguine conclusion. "This hand cart journey," he later wrote, "was a very severe and trying experience in which many lost their lives." All the way to Salt Lake, the nineteen-year-old Welshman had guided his nearly blind uncle, who in exchange had paid his nephew's passage across the Atlantic and to Iowa City. But only a few days after reaching Salt Lake, the uncle died "on account of the hardships of the hand cart journey."

On October 2, the Bunker Company staggered into Salt Lake City, to a celebration only slightly less frenzied than the one the first two handcart companies had touched off a week earlier. The jubilation ringing throughout Zion, however, would come to an abrupt end two days later.

NOT ONLY THE genesis of the handcart plan in Young's imagination, but the very spirit in which it was carried out, has everything to do with what was going on in the Utah Territory at the time.

By early 1856, the Mormon authorities knew that Deseret's hopes of winning statehood were doomed on the floor of an unsympathetic Congress. Polygamy, out in the open since 1852, was simply too repulsive a practice for mainstream America to countenance. Meanwhile, the apprehension that federal troops might invade the territory and wrest control from Young and his lieutenants was growing weekly. The need to bring thousands of converted Saints quickly and cheaply across the Atlantic from Europe and Great Britain had everything to do with the dream of building up a Zion that could repel such an invasion.

Out of this climate of fear and righteous indignation was born what remains by all odds the strangest cultural convulsion in LDS history. The Mormons themselves called it the Reformation. Its author was Young's Second Counselor, a forty-year-old man named Jedediah Grant. He was known to the faithful as "the sledgehammer of Brigham," while he liked to style himself "Mormon Thunder." More familiarly, the Saints called him "Jeddy."

Historian David L. Bigler describes Grant's appearance as "not unlike a young Abraham Lincoln."

> He stood over six feet tall, his build was lanky, his eyes deep-set, complexion swarthy, jaw square, and face long. Perhaps to a combative nature may be attributed his crooked nose which bent somewhat to his left from an old break near the bridge. But his smile was natural and his face not at all unpleasant. Behind the smile was an enigmatic figure, one untroubled by doubt, driven to enforce righteousness.

A *New York Times* reporter visiting the territory painted a less flattering portrait of Grant, as "a tall, thin, repulsive-looking man, of acute, vigorous intellect, a thorough-paced scoundrel, and the most essential blackguard in the pulpit."

According to several sources—Saints who later turned apostates, but whose testimony on this matter seems reliable—the Reformation germinated out of a trivial event. Grant was attending a church meeting in Kaysville, a small town about twenty-five miles north of Salt Lake City. Having invited several elders to come to the meeting, he had lent one of them a mule. That man (his name has not come down to us) prided himself on his riding skills, so he set out for Kaysville at a full gallop, compelling his colleagues to follow at an equally frantic pace.

By the time the horses and mules arrived in Kaysville, they were "heated and tired." Grant opened the meeting "pleasantly enough," as the various elders took turns offering testimonies of their faith. But when the "sledgehammer" rose to speak, he allegedly "became quite excited and then proceeded to accuse every one present of all sorts of wrong-doing. . . . He denounced them for their inconsistency and hypocrisy, and bitterly upbraided them for running his own mule and their own beasts in such a manner."

Such a tantrum ought to have spent itself in a few minutes at the Kaysville meeting. But Grant went on in his vituperative vein, "call[ing] upon everybody to repent, and 'do their first works over again,' or the judgment of God would speedily overtake them."

The zeitgeist of Zion was primed for this outburst. Grant's "spirit of fiery denunciation" sparked the wildfire that would quickly sweep across Deseret. Meetings followed weekly, during which "the mutual accusations of those who were present became, if possible, more bitter than before; the 'Saints' were denounced as the vilest of sinners and they were all commanded to be re-baptized." (Rebaptism, in Mormon doctrine, accomplished "remission for one's sins.") According to Fanny Stenhouse, the first baptisms occurred on a cold night, during which Jeddy not only immersed others with vigorous enthusiasm, but "remained in the water so long that he got a thorough chill and contracted the disease of which he died." Indeed, Grant would suddenly die on December 1, 1856, of typhoid and pneumonia, the latter in all probability brought on by the nocturnal baptisms.

Almost at once, Young followed his "sledgehammer's" lead and took up the cudgel of denunciation. In a speech on September 14, just twelve days before the Ellsworth and McArthur Companies would roll into Salt Lake, he "worked up the people with his tongue" (in the words of the Apostle who summarized the harangue for the *Deseret News*). Young "justly, Strictly & strongly chastized & rebuked" the Saints who formed his audience, "for lying, stealing, swareing, commiting Adultery, quarelling with Husbands wives & children & many other evils."

Of course no such large-scale reform movement can truly be born solely from an overheated mule. Gustive Larson, an LDS scholar who sees the Reformation in a mostly positive light, points out that a full year earlier, on July 13, 1855, Grant had warned a Provo congregation that "The Church needs trimming up, and if you will search, you will find your wards contain branches which had better be cut off." In that speech, Grant first used the word by which the movement would come to be called: "I would like to see the works of reformation commence, and continue until every man had to walk the line."

Larson and others see the Reformation as ultimately having its roots in the disastrous crop failures of 1855 and 1856. To devout Mormons, such punishments betokened not simply the ravages of grasshoppers, but divine retribution for unacknowledged sins.

For weeks after the mass rebaptism, Grant addressed the congregation in the Tabernacle every Sunday. According to one witness,

> The bishops were "whipped" for dereliction of duty, for being "old fogies," and not being strict in making the Saints pay their tithing to "the Lord." All were called upon to confess their sins, and to make known to God's servant the crimes of which they were guilty. . . . Individuals were hinted at and sins imputed to them which they dared not deny, nor even attempt to defend themselves, however innocent they might be.

The tithing, an obligation that persists today in the LDS church, was a mandatory contribution (usually 10 percent) of one's earnings and property.

On November 3, in dramatic fashion, Young added what would come to be known as the catechism to the rhetorical thunder of the Reformation. Inside the Social Hall in Salt Lake City, he had the doors locked, then pulled from the breast pocket of his coat a long piece of paper. Reading from it out loud, he dunned the audience with the following list of questions:

1. Have you shed innocent blood or assented thereto?
2. Have you committed adultery?

3. Have you betrayed your brother?
4. Have you borne false witness against your neighbor?
5. Do you get drunk?
6. Have you stolen?
7. Have you lied?
8. Have you contracted debts without prospect of paying?
9. Have you labored faithfully for your wages?
10. Have you coveted that which belongs to another?
11. Have you taken the name of the Lord in vain?
12. Do you preside in your family as a servant of God?
13. Have you paid your tithing in all things?

Later the catechism would be expanded with such questions as, "Do you pray in Secret?" and "Do you wash your bodies once a week?" (The Prophet himself was obliged to confess that he sometimes failed to observe this last commandment. He did not bathe once a week, Young admitted, although "he had tried it.")

The catechism was no mere laundry list of admonitions for the Saints to dwell upon in the privacy of their consciences. It was the text for an inquisition. With the Reformation underway, a pair of church officials visited every household in the territory and grilled its inhabitants under oath. If too many wrong answers escaped the trembling lips of a Saint being examined, he or she might be summarily cut off from the church.

The Mormon Reformation is often compared to the Salem witch trials of 1692. As at Salem, in Utah brainwashed citizens confessed to sins they were not in fact guilty of. At one all-male meeting in the Social Hall, according to an eyewitness, Young suddenly announced, "All you who have been guilty of committing adultery, stand up." To his astonishment and chagrin, more than three-fourths of the congregation promptly got to their feet.

The preoccupation with adultery may seem to modern readers a curious one. Yet in the orthodox Mormon thinking of the 1850s, sleeping with another man's wife, or with an unmarried woman, was the polar opposite of polygamy. Adultery, in fact, was so serious a sin that it could be punishable by death.

The bizarre but logical consequence of the Reformation's focus on adultery was to touch off an epidemic of plural marriages. One scholar demonstrated that "there were sixty-five percent more [plural] marriages during 1856 and 1857 than in any other two years of this experiment." By 1859, after the Reformation had sputtered out, the number of polygamous marriages dropped to one-fifth of the 1857 total.

Young himself was fully aware that many wives in Utah felt only misery in having to share their husbands with other women, but he had little sympathy for their unhappiness. On September 21, he announced that he would give all Mormon plural wives two weeks to decide whether or not to accept their fate with good cheer. "If they decided to stay with their husbands," he decreed, "they should keep the law of God & not murmur or Complain." If not, "I will set all at liberty"—i.e., grant the recalcitrant wives divorces and probably excommunicate them.

On November 5, 1856, the *Deseret News* published a "psalm" in praise of the Reformation, written by one W. G. Mills. It began, "The reformation has commenced,/ All hail! the glorious day," and contained two stanzas that celebrated plural marriage in much the same vein as Young's lecture:

> *Now, sisters, list to what I say,*
> *With trials this world is rife*
> *You can't expect to miss them all,*
> *Help husband get a wife!*
> *Now, this advice I freely give,*
> *If exalted you would be*
> *Remember that your husband must*
> *Be blessed with more than thee.*
>
> *Then, O, let us say,*
> *God bless the wife that strives*
> *And aids her husband all she can*
> *T'obtain a dozen wives.*

The Reformation's emphasis on cleanliness seems to have been Jedediah Grant's peculiar crotchet. In one tirade, he lashed his congregation thus:

Do you keep your dwellings, outhouses, and door yards clean? The first work of the reformation with some should be to clean away the filth about their premises. How would some like to have President Young visit them and go through their buildings, examine their rooms, bedding, &c.? Many houses stink so bad that a clean man could not live in them, nor hardly breathe in them. Some men were raised in stink, and so were their fathers before them.

If the Reformation took on the character of a general inquisition, its most frightening aspect was the doctrine of blood atonement, the joint brainchild of Grant and Young. This principle was first announced by the Prophet and his Second Counselor in a meeting in the bowery on September 21, 1856. According to historian David Bigler, this neo-biblical doctrine "was founded on the belief some sins were so serious they could not be cleansed by the blood of animals or even Christ's sacrifice."

At the bowery meeting, Young urged the Saints not only to report on one another, but to participate in the "shedding of blood" of the male-factors—which the audience clearly understood to mean execution. Asked the President,

Will you love your brothers or sisters likewise, when they have committed a sin that cannot be atoned for without the sheding of their blood? Will you love that man or woman well enough to shed their blood? That is what Jesus Christ meant.

Grant then elaborated on this doctrine in more lurid language, urging sinners to seek their own punishment. He advised the guilty to present themselves to the Prophet "and ask him to appoint a committee to attend to their case; and then let a place be selected, and let that committee shed their blood." The "sledgehammer" continued, "And you who have committed sins that cannot be forgiven through baptism, let your blood be shed and let the smoke ascend, that the incense thereof may come up before God as an atonement for your sins, and that the sinners in Zion may be afraid."

This was the doctrine of blood atonement. That it intimidated the Saints in Zion, there is no denying. Yet ever since the 1850s, scholars have argued over how much blood was actually shed during the brief spasm of the Reformation. The literature of future apostates is rich in sensational accounts of the carrying out of sentences of blood atonement. Thus Fanny Stenhouse:

> The wife of one Elder, when he was absent on a mission, acted unfaithfully to him. Her husband took counsel of the authorities, and was reminded that the shedding of her blood alone could save her. He returned and told her, but she asked for time, which was readily granted. One day, in a moment of affection, when she was seated on his knee, he reminded her of her doom, and suggested that now when their hearts were full of love was a suitable time for carrying it into execution. She acquiesced, and *out of love* he cut her throat from ear to ear.

Yet one LDS theologian, Bruce R. McConkie, writing of blood atonement, denies that "there has been one event or occurrence whatever, of any nature, from which the slightest inference arises that any such practice existed or was taught."

Was the doctrine, then, merely an empty threat, a rhetorical tactic aimed at terrorizing potential sinners into toeing the line? From the vantage point of a century and a half of history, we cannot solve this question. It seems likely, however, that the mid-1850s witnessed a proliferation of real acts of terror on the part of the notorious Danites, Young's secret police. The President himself (as noted above) denied that any such band existed. But there are too many accounts of beatings, robberies, and assassinations carried out in the territory during these years to ignore the phenomenon. A few of those accounts were written by Danites themselves.

Among the most notorious was Bill Hickman, who late in life published a startlingly candid memoir, under the title *Brigham's Destroying Angel*. In matter-of-fact prose, Hickman describes the first assassination he carried out under Young's orders, that of an Indian in 1848. This unnamed victim had converted to the church, but after an unhappy meeting with the President at Winter Quarters, had left in a rage, threatening publicly to enlist Indian allies to the west who would help him scalp Young. According to Hickman,

> Brigham sent me word to look out for him. I found him, used him up, scalped him, and took his scalp to Brigham Young, saying: "Here is the scalp of the man who was going to have a war-dance over your scalp; you may now have one over his, if you wish." He took it and thanked me very much. He said in all probability I had saved his life, and that some day he would make me a great man in the kingdom.

(By 1848, the phrase "use him up" already had long standing as Mormon shorthand for murder.)

In Salt Lake City, Hickman continued his useful services to the Prophet, using up a horse thief in 1852, another shortly thereafter. The destroying angel's unquestioning loyalty to Young sprang, by his own testimony, from a conviction that had become general in the Utah Territory by 1854: "The satisfied point and undoubted fact that God had established His kingdom in the mountains, and Brigham was conversant with the Almighty, was a settled question."

Sometimes the victim was a Gentile, such as a young, good-looking lawyer named Hartley, who had come to Utah from the Oregon Territory and married "a respectable lady of a good family" from Provo. For some reason, Hartley aroused Young's wrath: at the April General Conference, the Prophet thundered denunciations against the lawyer, declaring "that he ought to have his throat cut." Fearing for his life, Hartley fled toward Fort Bridger, but he was followed by Hickman.

Hickman's orders came from Apostle Orson Hyde, who was also stalking Hartley, and who said he in turn was acting under the Prophet's command. In East Canyon, not far from Salt Lake, as Hartley, on horseback, forded the stream, Hickman and another Danite ambushed the lawyer and shot him dead. "When I returned to camp," Hickman later wrote, "Orson Hyde told me that was well done; that he and some others had gone on the side of the mountain, and seen the whole performance."

Hickman continued his assassinations into the 1860s, well after the Reformation had run its course. But then he and Young had a serious falling-out, which led to the gunslinger's being disfellowshiped from the church (disfellowship being a less severe punishment than excommunication, because it could be reversed). Orthodox Mormon historians have tended to dismiss *Brigham's Destroying Angel* as pure fiction, concocted by an embittered ex-lieutenant as revenge against the Prophet. The memoir, which was published in 1872, was in fact dictated from prison to a rabidly anti-Mormon editor, J. H. Beadle.

That very imprisonment throws a monkey wrench into the theory that Hickman's memoir was fiction. At the time, the Danite was awaiting trial for the murder of a trader named Richard Yates. In Hickman's telling, Young ordered the assassination because he suspected that Yates was a spy for the U.S. Army, which was nearing Utah. After the Danite fell out with the President, Young (according to Hickman) hung him out to dry by sanctioning the trial. There is no doubt that a sense of betrayal colors every page of *Brigham's Destroying Angel*. But it is hard to come up with an explanation as to why Hickman would have murdered Yates—a man with whom he had no apparent quarrel—on his own.

The killings most often associated with the doctrine of blood atonement—a complicated chain of events about which historians still argue today—are known as the Parrish-Potter murders. They were triggered by the tragic fate of one of the handcart pioneers.

On Christmas Eve 1856, in an eastern suburb of Salt Lake City, a woman who had come by handcart to Zion allegedly committed suicide by slitting her throat. Indian agent Garland Hurt—no friend of Brigham Young—testified that she had taken her life rather than be forced into a polygamous marriage with the head of the household in which she had been lodged upon her arrival in Salt Lake. According to Hurt, she was told she would be denounced as a prostitute and refused food and shelter if she did not submit to marriage. (Hurt gave the woman's last name as Williams, but she cannot be conclusively matched with any of the Williams women in the rosters of the five 1856 handcart companies in the LDS Archives.)

Even at the time, there were suspicions that the suicide was actually a murder. That was the interpretation of William Parrish, living in Springville, a town fifty miles south of Salt Lake. Though a practicing Mormon, Parrish had heard about (and been appalled by) the doctrine of "killing to save." With his two sons, aged eighteen and twenty-two, Parrish attempted to flee the territory under cover of darkness in March 1857. The guide he entrusted to lead him planned instead to march the three Parrishes into an ambush. In the ensuing gun battle and knife fight, William Parrish and his older son were killed, as was the treacherous guide, Gardner Potter, by mistake. No one was ever brought to trial for the killings.

Whatever the reality of blood atonement as a practice rather than merely a doctrine, there is no gainsaying the pall of fear and recrimination that the Reformation cast over Zion, beginning in September 1856. Yet in Young's view, that pall was a blessing. All through the autumn months of 1856, as he dictated letters to his far-flung aides while he tried to manage the handcart migration, he inserted in virtually every epistle a paragraph proclaiming the moral improvement the Reformation was working. An example:

> There is quite a reformation springing up in many of the Settlements. . . . A General desire to renew their covenants and live nearer to the Lord, to serve him more perfectly and to be more Circumspect and alive to the interests of Zion. . . . This awakening spirit is much needed, as it is too unusually the case that when the Elders come home they throw off their armour, and the people too frequently follow their example. . . . Now that much of the chaff of the winters threshing floor has been floated off by the summer breezes, we trust that the Saints who are really such will awake from their lethargy.

Viewed in retrospect, the Mormon Reformation can well be seen as an episode of mass hysteria. Morris Werner, Brigham Young's skeptical 1925 biographer, characterizes the movement as "the height of fanatical Puritanism." Werner adds:

> But the worst effect of the Reformation was its influence on the state of mind of the community. Murder became a righteous

duty at times, and against sinners and enemies it was no longer regarded as a sin. Obedience to the leaders of the Church was considered a supreme duty, and the entire Mormon population was keyed up to a pitch of fiery faith by the psychological effect of the terrifying doctrine of blood atonement.

Mormon apologists, on the other hand, downplay or deny the murders and emphasize the moral improvement. Thus Gustive Larson: "The call to repentance in the Reformation was generally heeded, and as a result, in the words of historian Andrew Neff, 'the spiritual tone of the entire Mormon commonwealth was markedly raised.'"

One strategy for dealing with the Reformation as a potential embarrassment to the church is to ignore it altogether. Leonard J. Arrington manages in his 522-page *Brigham Young: American Moses* to mention blood atonement not once, the Reformation itself in only a single sentence, as he waves it aside as a minor historical nuisance: "During the Reformation of 1856 the Saints got carried away by the hellfire and damnation sermons of Grant, George A. Smith, and others."

In his speeches and letters, Brigham Young again and again resorted to the metaphor of separating the wheat from the chaff. In the territory, the Reformation "floated off by the summer breezes" the chaff of apostates, unwilling plural wives, sinners of all stripes, and the merely fainthearted, lazy, or unclean. The thresher ranged from disfellowship to excommunication to banishment to murder.

Such a set of mind helps to explain Young's often coldhearted attitude toward the handcart pioneers. Like the Reformation, the ordeal by handcart (in Wallace Stegner's phrase) separated the wheat from the chaff. Those who "backed out" in Iowa City or Florence, those who despaired of finishing the trek, even those who collapsed and died along the trail, were perhaps not worthy of Zion after all.

ON MAY 4, 1856, the sailing ship *Thornton* pulled out of Liverpool harbor. On board were 608 English and Scottish Mormons intending to emigrate to Zion, as well as 162 Scandinavian Saints, the vast majority of them Danes. With them sailed Franklin D. Richards, president of the European Mission, who had done so much to recruit British converts and start them on their way to Utah. During the Atlantic crossing, Richards served as captain over the throng of European emigrants. From Iowa City, however, he planned to ride by light carriage with a small contingent of fellow returning missionaries, making a far more rapid journey to Salt Lake City than the handcarts could accomplish.

The Atlantic crossing was largely uneventful, except for the day on which, as twenty-five-year-old Susannah Stone would recall many decades later, "the people's galley or cock [cook] house took fire and burned down which caused a great excitement." Stone added, "But through the blessings of the Lord we were saved." According to a Danish passenger, John Ahmanson, during the month-long passage six Saints died, three infants were born, and two marriages were celebrated.

Yet another Danish passenger, Peter Madsen, summarized in his journal a stern lecture on morals delivered to the Saints by President Richards in mid-voyage:

> 5 o'clock the president held council and instructed the brothers who had watch at night to have close supervision over the young people that no unallowable association and coming together would take place. It was discovered that such had taken place among the English; and an unclean spirit was found which should be rectified. On the other hand such lewdness was not found at all among the Danish saints.

Despite the lapses of the English young people, so well behaved were the passengers that on June 11, with New York City almost in sight, the ship's captain declared that "no company which he had transported to America could compare with them."

The *Thornton* arrived in New York on June 14, where the 770 Saints were greeted by President John Taylor. With some misgivings about the lateness of the season, Taylor sent 450 of the emigrants on by railroad and steamboat to Iowa City, which they reached after another eleven days. Back in April, Taylor had already gone on record as saying, "I wish the passengers, on their arrival at the place of outfitting, to be prepared to start the next day, or, in a day or two, at furthest."

But it was the same old story: when the *Thornton* Saints arrived in Iowa City, no handcarts were waiting for them. According to forty-six-year-old emigrant William James, whose testimony was passed down to a descendant, "When the company saints from Liverpool on the ship Thornton arrived in Iowa Camp quite a stir was created of great concern for they were totally unexpected." Workers superintended by master carpenter Chauncey Webb hastily cobbled together about a hundred handcarts. These carriages were even more rickety than the ones the first three parties had pushed and pulled westward, for "There was a scarcety of seasoned wood and other materials. They frantically gathered together what was available and went to work."

By now, Webb was deeply disheartened by his weeks of handcart-building. According to his daughter, who would later become one of Brigham Young's wives, Webb was not only thwarted by the insufficient supply of good timber, but by the same ruthless parsimony on the part of the Iowa City officials as would stamp the whole pageant of the handcart emigration.

> The agents all talked economy. . . . They did not want to furnish iron for the tires, as it was too expensive; raw hide, they were sure, would do just as well. . . . A thorough workman himself, [my father] wanted good materials to work with; but the reply invariably was, "O, Brother Webb, the carts must be made cheap. We can't afford this expenditure; you are too extravagant in your outlay."

The new company of Saints had to wait three weeks before they could be outfitted with handcarts. That delay would prove hugely consequential. "When William first saw the carts he wanted to laugh and then he wanted to cry," reported William James's descendant. "How could such a contraption get his family to Zion?"

One of the men in the company saw these hardships as an opportunity for building character. "Here is the place to try a man what he is," he wrote to President John Taylor in New York. "If a brother comes in camp and don't catch hold of an axe and cut down a tree for to make hand carts, or break in a pair of oxen, or make himself useful in some way, he is but little respected. This is the place to make a man know himself."

According to Peter Madsen, it was only on June 30, after the Saints had lingered for almost a week in Iowa City, that the agents in charge informed the emigrants about the strict handcart weight limit. As Madsen wrote in his diary:

> It was announced to the handcart company that no person would be able to bring more than 17 pounds per person on the carts. The remaining goods could be transported to the valley for _____ dollars per 100 pounds by some of the inhabitants. Some people sold their clothes in Iowa. . . . Sold flour to Line Larsen for 35 cents. At 8 o'clock prayer meeting. Speeches by Ahmunsen, Christiansen, and Larsen were given against grumbling, dissatisfaction and complaining which had crept in among some of the company's members who had not yet learned their duties and obedience to God's law and his servants.

The hardship that this unforeseen restriction worked on Saints who had hauled their most precious belongings all the way from Britain or Denmark to Iowa is made clear in a rueful July 5 entry in Madsen's diary (which was not translated until the twentieth century):

> At 8 o'clock some of the brethren went to Iowa with transport handcarts loaded with bedding and other items to sell. Some went through the city and sold a few items for a low price. Brother Ahmunsen, who was present, had discovered an auction place and showed the brethren where it was and helped with the sale there. The bedding was sold for 27 to 55 cents per pound. Linen and clothing did not sell well. We have much to do to be able to dispose of our surplus items in order to recover what was paid for the extra weight to this place. I have to pay $8 for 105 pounds of weight. The freight from here to the valley is so high that it has to be materials of good quality in order to pay for itself.

No doubt this draconian edict contributed to a lowering of morale among the handcart Saints, for the leaders kept scolding them in camp meeting lectures. Madsen again, on July 7: "The health of the company is good. To the contrary, it is difficult to preserve a good spirit when many false teachings creep in. This causes the authorities to have much to combat and watch over."

Finally, on July 15, about five hundred Saints were ready to set out from Iowa City. This fourth handcart company was under the leadership of James G. Willie, a forty-one-year-old Englishman who had come to America and joined the church in New York in 1842. Four years later, he and his American fiancée set out for Nauvoo, but when they found the Mormon stronghold nearly abandoned, they pushed on to Winter Quarters, where, with the hundreds of Saints under Young's leadership, they spent the winter of 1846–47. The next summer they traveled on by wagon train to Salt Lake City, arriving only three months after Young's pioneer company.

In 1852, Young ordered Willie back to his native country to serve as a missionary. By now, Willie and his wife had three small children. He was forced to leave them behind during the four years he served his mission in England. A condition of his release in February 1856 was that he take a leadership role in the handcart emigration.

It is hard to glean just what sort of man Willie was. Apparently he never wrote a word about the fateful trek he led, even though he lived to the age of eighty, dying in Cache Valley, Utah, in 1895. The official journal of the company, written by William Woodward, may reflect Willie's views. Judging from the comments of emigrants in his company, Willie seems to have been a stern taskmaster in the mold of Edmund Ellsworth and Edward Bunker. In one of the few extant photographs of the man, taken late in life, he is nearly bald. His mouth is fixed in a crooked down-turning rictus, and his eyes have a haunted, far-away stare. It is easy to imagine that in this portrait Willie still bears the pain of the ordeal he survived in 1856.

Willie's second-in-command, Millen Atwood, was also a mission-ary returning from four years in England, though he had been born in Connecticut. Only a week after arriving in Salt Lake City, Atwood would rise in the Tabernacle to deliver an "account of his mission." This remarkable speech reveals a loyal champion of the divine hand-cart plan every bit as fanatical as Edmund Ellsworth. In Atwood's view, despite all the suffering and death they would undergo on the plains, the English Saints were lucky to have been called to Zion. Serving his mission, he recalled,

> I have seen some so tired in England, after traveling only 5 or 6 miles to a conference, that they would have to go to bed and be nursed for a week. We stimulated the hand-cart companies with the words of br. Brigham, which went through me like lightning. . . .
>
> But when br. Brigham offered his property so liberally, and the word came that they should gather from England, it ran like fire in dry stubble and the hearts of the poor Saints leapt with joy and gladness; they could hardly contain themselves.

Back home, Atwood insisted, the working-class Saints were so destitute that "we had to buy everything for them, even to their tin cups and spoons. And let me tell you, the fare they had on the plains was a feast to them." In general, Atwood's testimony is so zealously upbeat that modern psychology would declare the man to be in denial. "I never enjoyed myself better than in crossing the plains in a hand-cart company," Atwood proclaimed in the Tabernacle. "The Spirit of the Lord did accompany us and the brethren and sisters enlivened the journey by singing the songs of Zion. They would travel 16, 18, 20, 23, or 24 miles a day and come into camp rejoicing, build their fires, get their suppers, rest, and rise fresh and invigorated in the morning."

The other sub-captains in the Willie Company, each in charge of his "hundred," were the young William Woodward, official company clerk; Levi Savage; John Chislett; and John Ahmanson. The latter trio were among the most interesting and articulate of all the thousands of hand-cart pioneers in 1856. Chislett and Ahmanson would both later apostatize, leaving behind coolly neutral accounts of the company's ordeal that pointedly undercut the fanatical mythologizing of a Millen Atwood.

Ahmanson's lot was a particularly hard one. A relatively well-to-do Dane, he had planned to purchase a wagon and oxen in Iowa City and travel with his wife by traditional means to Salt Lake City. But on board the *Thornton*, President Richards had discovered that among the 162 Danes, Ahmanson was the only one who spoke competent English.

Richards then "requested" (the word is Ahmanson's) the man to forgo wagon transport and lead a company of ninety-three Scandinavians pulling handcarts. That request was tantamount to an order. With heavy heart, Ahmanson bade goodbye to his wife, who with other relatively affluent Scandinavians set off for Zion by wagon team, as he took charge as sub-captain of the fifth "hundred" in Willie's company.

After he left the church, Ahmanson would live in Omaha, where he worked variously as a hardware merchant, a grocer, and a doctor dispensing homeopathic medicine before his death in 1891. In 1876, he wrote in Danish a memoir of his Mormon years, under the title *Vor Tids Muhamed.* The book was not translated into English until 1984, as *Secret History,* by which time LDS scholars could find only three extant copies of the original volume. Ahmanson's memoir is an important contribution not only to the handcart story, but to an understanding of the Mormon kingdom during the mid-1850s, for it adumbrates one of the most trenchant critiques of the faith and its President in all the voluminous (and too often sensationalistic) apostate literature.

As with the Welsh Saints in the Bunker party, the Scandinavians in the Willie Company suffered not only the tribulations of the trail, but the confusion of an all but unbreachable language barrier. And the record of the Scandinavian Saints' experience in 1856 remains woefully thin. Within the Willie Company, it amounts to scraps of later reminiscence by Mettie Rasmussen and Jens Nielson (himself an extraordinary pioneer, of whom more below), Peter Madsen's invaluable diary, and Ahmanson's percipient *Secret History.*

With some five hundred emigrants, about a hundred handcarts, and five wagons, the Willie entourage was nearly twice as large as any of the three handcart companies that had headed west before it. It would take the company twenty-eight days to cross Iowa and reach Florence, on the west bank of the Missouri River, as it completed the passage in exactly the same time span as the McArthur Company had a month earlier. Along the way, passing through small towns and semi-settled countryside, the Saints were the constant object of curious gawkers. Diaries and memoirs recount the occasional kindness bestowed upon the pioneers by Iowa residents, such as the donation of fifteen pairs of children's boots on July 31 by a "respectable gentleman" from Fort Des Moines.

Yet the company was also cruelly taunted by onlookers. According to George Cunningham, fifteen years old at the time,

> While traveling along, people would mock, sneer, and deride us on every occasion for being such fools as they termed us, and would often throw out inducements to get us to stop. But we told them that we were going to Zion, and would not stop on any account. When we went through a town or settlement, pulling our handcarts as we always had to do, people would turn out in crowds to laugh at us, crying gee and haw as if we were oxen. But this did not discourage us in the least, for we knew that we were on the right track.

On July 25, near Muddy Creek, a bizarre episode occurred. It is documented in the official company journal:

> The weather being very warm just before we encamped we were overtaken by the Sheriff with a warrant to search the waggons, &c. under the idea that women were detained contrary to their wish with ropes. After showing their authority, they had permission to examine any part of the Company & were fully satisfied that the report was without foundation & left us.

At the height of summer, the traverse of Iowa was carried out in blazing heat. The official company journal did its best to emphasize high morale among the company, as on July 18: "All are well and in first rate spirits." But even in this record, William Woodward could not overlook the hardships of the voyage, as he reported five days later, "The sun was excessively hot. We then continued our journey as far as Brush Creek, 13 miles, where we arrived at 7 p.m. with a great many sick & tired out."

Within five days of starting from Iowa City, the first dropouts left the company ranks. No accurate count of their number is even suggested by the various diaries and reminiscences. There were also deaths along the way. The most curious of them occurred on July 23, the day of "excessively hot" sun, when "Sister Mary Williams from the Worcester Branch of the Worcestershire Conference died on the way, supposed from eating green plums."

Looking back many years later, a few of the Saints in the Willie Company could gloss over the tribulations of Iowa, claiming, in the words of one, that "the first 200 miles of our journey was filled with pleasant memories." Another, Sarah Moulton, could even brag in a letter written to a friend from mid-trek, "I never had my health so well in my life before I walked about three hundred miles and pulled the hand cart all the way and we walked sometimes 20 & 17 miles a day and I never had a blister on my foot."

More typical, though, was the indelible ordeal recorded decades later by Agnes Southworth, who was nine years old at the time: "I can yet close my eyes and see everything in panoramic precision before me—the ceaseless walking, walking, ever to remain in my memory. Many times I would become so tired and, childlike, would hang on the cart, only to be gently pushed away. Then I would throw myself by the side of the road and cry. Then realizing they were all passing me by, I would jump to my feet and make an extra run to catch up."

Even the blindly partisan Millen Atwood was moved to observe:

I have walked day by day by the side of the hand-carts as they were rolling, and when the people would get weary I have seen them by dozens on their knees by the road side crying to the Lord for strength. . . . So long as you kept the bundle on the hand cart and stimulated them to lay hold of it, they were filled with the Holy Spirit and it seemed as though angels nerved them with strength.

As in all three of the handcart parties that had preceded them, a primary cause of fatigue and illness among the Willie Company was the inadequate food supply. John Chislett later cogently appraised the impact of this deficit:

Our rations consisted of ten ounces of flour to each adult per day, and half that amount to children under eight years of age. Besides our flour we had occasionally a little rice, sugar, coffee, and bacon. But these items (especially the last) were so small and infrequent that they scarcely deserve mentioning. Any hearty man could eat his daily allowance for breakfast. In fact, some of our men did this, and then worked all day without dinner, and went to bed supperless or begged food at the farmhouses as we travelled along.

Exhausted and underfed or not, the bedraggled emigrants still managed to spark their leaders' wrath. According to the official journal, on August 5, "In the evening Elders Willie & Atwood reproved the Saints for being so dilatory & told them if they did not repent they would not have the blessings of the Lord & would not get through this season."

On August 11, the Willie party finally reached Florence. By that date, a general apprehension had seized the company as to whether it was too late in the year to try to push on across the plains and over the Continental Divide to Salt Lake City. If the snows of winter came early, the company might find itself stranded somewhere in the mountains of Wyoming.

In the end, about a hundred of the Saints dropped out in Florence, electing to stay there for the winter, or even to settle there more permanently. About these backouts, Millen Atwood later sneered, "Those who were good for nothing left us at Florence."

The apprehension lingered. On August 13, a conference of the fewer than four hundred Saints still in the company was assembled. During that meeting, the most prescient counsel offered by any Saint in any of the handcart parties was put forth, only to be ignored. As a result, the single most tragic decision in the whole 1856 handcart campaign set in motion the catastrophe that would ensue.

Many years later, the granddaughter of one of the Willie party Saints insisted that "almost the entire company felt they should winter [in Florence] and start early in the spring," but this is probably hindsight passed down as memory. At the August 13 meeting, one by one the company leaders rose to speak. Captain Willie himself and his lieutenant, Millen Atwood, argued forcefully in favor of continuing the journey. So did two high church officials who happened to be present, George Grant and William Kimball. Grant and Kimball would soon join Franklin Richards and other returning missionaries in their high-speed, light-carriage dash to Utah.

Among the Saints remaining in the Willie Company, however, only four had ever been to Salt Lake. Three of them were Willie, Atwood, and William Woodward, the company clerk and official journal-keeper. The fourth was Levi Savage.

Born in Ohio, Savage was thirty-six years old that summer. Ten years earlier, like Edward Bunker, he had served in the Mormon Battalion that had traveled all the way to California in General Kearny's army. From California he had made his way east to Salt Lake the following year. There he had married and sired a young son, but only eleven months after the birth, his wife had died. Less than a year thereafter, in 1852, Young called Savage to go on a mission—not to Great Britain, but to far-off Siam (as Thailand was then called). Without questioning the Prophet, Savage set off for the Far East, leaving his sister to take care of a son still not two years old.

Bureaucratic snafus kept the missionary from even getting to Siam. Instead he ended up serving a frustrating two years in Burma, where he never learned the language and made virtually no converts. As a weary Levi Savage returned to the United States in early 1856, he wanted only to get back to Salt Lake City and his son and sister. It was his bad luck to arrive in Iowa City just four days before the Willie party set out. Valuing Savage's vast experience, Willie conscripted him to be sub-captain of the second hundred. Savage accepted the onerous post without demurral.

Now, however, at the August 13 meeting, Savage arose and spoke. With tears streaming down his face, he pleaded against continuing the journey—the sole voice among the leaders to argue for wintering over in Florence. In his own journal, Savage recorded this courageous deed:

> Brother Willey Exorted the Saints to go forward regardless of Suffering even to death; after he had Spoken, he gave me the oppertunity of Speaking. I said to him, that if I Spoke, I must Speak my minde, let it cut where it would. He Said Sertainly do so. I then related to the Saints, the hard Ships that we Should have to endure. I Said that we were liable to have to wade in Snow up

to our knees, and Should at night rap ourselvs in a thin blanket. and lye on the frozen ground without abed; that was not like
having a wagon, that we could go into, and rap ourselves in as
much as we liked and ly down. No Said I.—we are with out waggons, destitute of clothing, and could not cary it if we had it. We
must go as we are &c. The hand cart Sistem. I do not condemn. I
think it prcfcrblc. to unbrokc oxcn, and uncxpriancced tcamstcrs.
The lateness of the Season was my only objection, of leaving this
point for the mountains at this time. I Spoke warmly upon the
Subject, but Spoke truth, and the people, judging from appearance and after expressions, felt the force of it.

For his pains, Savage was instantly rebuked by the other company
leaders and church officials. Captain Willie was particularly scathing. As
one emigrant later recalled, "At the conclusion of his discourse, James G.
Willie denounced him as a recreant to the cause of truth and a disturber
of the peace of the brethren and an opposer of those who were placed
over him and called upon him to repent."

Savage himself recorded the captain's rebuke thus: "Elder Willey
then . . . Said that the God that he Served was a God that was able to
save to the utmost. *that* was the *God* that *He Served;* and he wanted no
Jobes co[m]forters with him." Stung, Savage offered to give up his sub-
captainship, but Willie did not accept the resignation.

Heaping further scorn on Savage's misgivings, church official William
Kimball now promised the Saints that he would "stuff into his mouth all
the snow they would ever get to see on their journey to the valleys!"

In his journal, Savage did not bother to record the further heroism of
his acquiescence. It would be left to John Chislett to capture it. Accepting
defeat, Savage addressed the meeting:

"Brethren and sisters, what I have said I know to be true; but,
seeing you are to go forward, I will go with you, will help you all
I can, will work with you, will rest with you, will suffer with you,
and, if necessary, I will die with you. May God in his mercy bless
and preserve us. Amen."

The Willie Company lingered three more days in Florence, as the Saints made desperately needed repairs to their handcarts. The recurrent problem was that sand caught between the axles and hubs ground the wood away. Again and again the weakened axles broke at the shoulder.

On August 16, the company started west out of Florence, pulling and pushing their dilapidated carts toward the very fate that Levi Savage had foreseen.

CHAPTER FIVE

TROUBLES ON THE PLATTE

O n July 9, 1856, as the Willie Company Saints lingered in Iowa City waiting for their handcarts to be built, William Woodward recorded an alarming development in the official journal: "A company of Saints arrived that came in the *Horizon* from Liverpool numbering some 800 souls came up this evening in the midst of a terrible storm, and we as well as the other Companies accommodated them the best in our power."

The sudden advent of the additional throng of Saints who had come across the Atlantic on the *Horizon* would now tax to the utmost the talents and energy of Chauncey Webb and his carpenter assistants. Yet more unseasoned wood had to be found and crafted to make carriages for what would become the fifth, last, and largest of the 1856 handcart companies.

The *Horizon* had departed from Liverpool on May 25, three weeks after the Willie Company's *Thornton*. With 856 Saints on board, the *Horizon* sailed to Boston, rather than New York. Some two hundred emigrants stayed on in Boston or other cities along the route, as the Saints rode by train through Albany, Buffalo, Cleveland, Chicago, Rock Island, and at last to Iowa City.

Eventually a company of about 650 emigrants would shove off from Iowa City on July 25, ten days after the Willie Company's departure. Thanks to straying cattle, they covered only seven miles during their first seven days. Most of the Saints in this party had come across the Atlantic on the *Horizon*, but their numbers were swelled by other emigrants such as Patience Loader and her family, who had reached the Eastern Seaboard earlier and now belatedly joined the last handcart party on the plains.

At first that company was split into two contingents, but it ultimately coalesced as one, under the charge of thirty-seven-year-old Edward Martin. Of all five leaders of the handcart parties, he had the longest tenure in the church and the greatest experience as a traveler. Born in Preston, a factory town in Lancashire, one of the English counties in which the Mormon missionaries had their greatest rates of recruitment, Martin was in the first wave of British converts, joining the church in 1837 at the age of eighteen. With a new bride, the former Alice Clayton, he traveled to Nauvoo in 1841 and came to know Joseph Smith well.

After the Prophet's martyrdom, the Martins, with their two surviving children (the firstborn had died in 1845), joined the exodus to Winter Quarters led by Young in 1846. There their younger child died. Only six days later, Martin was conscripted to serve in the Mormon Battalion, leaving his grieving wife behind, who was already pregnant with the couple's fourth child. He served faithfully in General Kearny's Army of the West, even though it meant an absence from Alice of eighteen months. During that time, she gave birth to a son who lived only five months.

In 1848, Edward, Alice, and their sole surviving child set out for Utah by covered wagon. As if the couple had not already been afflicted by enough tragedy, a fifth child was born en route in Wyoming, only to die within two weeks of the family's arrival in Salt Lake City. Another daughter, born in Salt Lake, died after a single year.

None of this shook Martin's faith. In a letter to a friend in England, he vowed, "Our God is a merciful God, and he will hear the cries of his children."

In 1852, Martin was called by Brigham Young to return to his native Britain to serve as a missionary. During his absence, Alice's seventh child, a son, also died after only a year on earth. Of the couple's seven children, only one survived infancy.

Martin spent almost four years in his missionary service, mostly in Scotland. A poignant letter from his eleven-year-old daughter, written in

1855, after her father had been gone for three years, laments, "It would be pleasing to me to see you once more, but as the time has not come I must be contented. It seems as if I never had a father."

Recruited by President Franklin D. Richards in Liverpool to help oversee the massive emigration of 1855, Martin was finally allowed to come home, as he sailed with his fellow Saints aboard the *Horizon*, then made his way to Iowa City. In a photograph preserved in the LDS Archives, Martin gazes down at the camera with a look that could be taken for disdain, or, alternatively, for the weariness of a man who has endured untold hardships. His chin is supported by a starched, upturned collar. A receding hairline is counterbalanced by almost dandyish curls bedecking both temples. His cheeks and chin are badly scarred, perhaps by smallpox or acne.

Among the five leaders of the 1856 handcart parties, Martin was, with Daniel McArthur, arguably the most skilled and the most humane. He certainly had the hardest job of all, for the Martin Company not only contained an unwieldy multitude of emigrants, pushing the most dilapidated handcarts, but fully three-quarters of their number were women, children, and old people. President Richards, who would see them off from Florence, admitted that "They have a great proportion of crippled and old gray-headed men."

It is a testament both to Martin's leadership and to the pluck and will of the average Saint in the party that despite these circumstances, the fifth company covered the 270 miles between Iowa City and Florence in about four weeks, just as fast as the four healthier companies that preceded it. It will be recalled that in her "Reccolections of past days," Patience Loader devoted only a few lines to the Iowa passage, those dealing chiefly with her alarm as her father's legs started to give out with the company almost in sight of Florence.

A few of the Martin Company Saints could even gaze back, from the vantage point of decades of retrospect, and remember the party in Iowa as "as happy a lot of people as ever crossed the plains." The words are those of Margaret Clegg, sixteen at the time, writing in 1906, a full half-century after the ordeal. "It never occurred to my young mind," Clegg would add, "that we should experience ought but joy and happiness on our long pilgrimage to that promised land."

Yet the diary of Jesse Haven, second-in-command, who led an advance guard across Iowa a few days ahead of the main company under Edward Martin, is a litany of aggravations:

July 27th Sunday. Saints in rather bad perdicament being without tents all their things got wet. . . . The Saints last night and this morning found much fault grumble much about me blamed me becaused the tents were left behind In the evening had a meeting. . . . I told them if they did not scese their groumbling that sickness would get into their midst and they would die off like rotten sheep. but if they would be humble and keep united the blessings of the Lord should attend them. . . .

Aug. 2nd . . . Saints much fatiged—Some got into camp late. Some did not come in at all. . . .

Aug 9th . . . Saints traveled badly to-day—much scatered, after we got into camp—11 left us.

As the last entry so laconically records, there were many backouts along the Iowa trail. Other Saints were disfellowshiped for one offense or another and banished from the company.

The Iowa traverse was a gauntlet of searing heat punctuated by violent thunderstorms. On July 22, Jesse Haven's thermometer recorded 108 degrees in the shade. More than half a century later, John Southwell vividly recalled an August downpour:

On the following day, when half mile from camp, one of the most horrible electric storms I ever saw fell upon us accompanied with hail and rain. It proved a perfect deluge. In this flat clay soil in the space of ten minutes the roads became almost impassable and oh what a scene to behold. Four hundred men, women and children struggling to keep their feet. Here was no sign of a shelter. Our tents were rolled up in the wagons. After everyone was drenched and many were unable to move out of their tracks the captain gave orders to pitch camp and set up the tents the best they could in the mud and quick as possible this was done. It proved a temporary shelter for the old people and children. They were protected from the rain but they were still ankle keep [deep] in the mud.

On August 3, the Martin Company witnessed a much rarer atmospheric phenomenon than a thunderstorm, as in midday a meteor blazed through the sky. As Samuel Openshaw described it, "We beheld a ball of fire brighter than the sun before us in the air and came within about three yards of the ground and then drew out in the form of a spear and vanished out of our sight." Some of the Saints regarded the meteor as a divine portent.

Like all four handcart parties before them, the Martin Company emigrants were underfed. Fifteen-year-old Aaron Giles, who despite his name was a Polish Saint traveling without his family, blamed his hunger on "2 sisters Jemima Coock & Hannah Wardell [who] behaived themselves very unkind to me. . . . The 2 sisters never gave me victules enough. and never gave me my full Raitions of provision; so when I found out that they served me so I left them and drawed my Raitions with another man for they never gave me enough to keep my body up."

But even those assured of full rations found the food supply inadequate. Many Saints fell ill before reaching Florence. More than sixty years later, Langley Bailey, eighteen years old at the time, remembered that

> I was taken down with hemerage of the bowles. I was unable to walk, had to be hauled on Bro. Isaac J. Wardle and my brother's John's cart. After reaching Florence a Doctor was consulted said I must not go another step or I would die and be burried on the road side. A captain named Tune would not administer to me, said he did not have faith enough to rais the dead.

The last of the Martin handcarts crossed the Missouri River and straggled into Florence on August 22. The Willie Company had departed six days earlier. Concern about the lateness of the season was widespread, but in the Martin Company there would be no Levi Savage to plead tearfully against continuing the journey that year.

On August 24, a Sunday, a general meeting of the company was convened. One after another, the leaders rose and addressed the question of whether to go on or to winter over in Florence. Only one man counseled the latter choice: Chauncey Webb, the tireless builder of handcarts, who, after his summer's toil turning green wood into carriages, had joined the Martin Company, bound for Zion.

The diaries of the Martin pioneers, however, contain not even a paraphrase of Webb's argument. If, like Savage, Webb vividly evoked the scenario of emigrants trudging knee-deep through the Wyoming snows, succumbing to cold and hunger, that speech is lost to history. Even Webb's daughter, Ann Eliza Young, whose 1875 memoir is one of the angriest of all Mormon apostate works, says only, "My father strongly objected to any of them starting after the last of June; but he was overruled."

The last person to speak at the August 24 meeting was Franklin Richards, president of the European Mission, who was about to launch out with fellow returning missionaries on his light-wagon dash to Salt Lake City. As one of the Twelve Apostles, Richards was by far the highest ranking Mormon at the meeting. One member of the assembly later recalled the man's fervent exhortation:

"I hear that there are saints here who fear on account of the lateness of the season and may suffer in the crossing of the Rocky Mts. in snow storms. This I will say as the saints have braved it this far and has anything come to hurt or mar the peace and safety of anyone, therefore, I prophesy in the name of 'Isreals God' through the storms we may come from the east, the west, the north, or the south God will keep the way open to the faithful at heart and we'll arrive in the valleys in safety and hoped that the saints would be blessed with health & strength to pursue unto the journey's end and there to meet with the Lords anointed and be saved with the just in the Eternal world."

After Richards had finished, church officials put the question to the meeting in a show of hands. A fifteen-year-old boy in the crowd, Josiah Rogerson, would recall fifty-one years later, "The vote was called, and with uncovered heads and uplifted hands to heaven and an almost unanimous vote, it was decided to go on."

BY THE TIME the Martin party set out from Florence on August 25, the Willie Company had reached the Loup Fork, a northern tributary of the Platte, in what is today eastern Nebraska. The fourth handcart company was thus 133 miles ahead of the fifth. So the two parties would proceed during the following two months, with the Willie Company usually a little more than a hundred miles ahead of the Martin.

One reason President Richards and the Martin Company leaders may have felt sanguine about the late start across the plains was that, by design, two fully equipped wagon trains took up the rear. The William B. Hodgetts Company, comprising 150 emigrants with about thirty-three wagons, set out from Florence on August 28. Three days later, it was followed by the much larger John A. Hunt Company, with three hundred individuals and some fifty-six wagons. Yet as it turned out, these two caravans straggled along, making no better progress than the women, children, and aged in the Martin Company, as they were beset with problems of their own. The Hodgetts and Hunt Companies played almost no part in mitigating the catastrophe that was soon to unfold.

Having left Florence on August 16, a week before the Martin Company, Willie's party, now reduced to 404 individuals with eighty-five handcarts, traveled at first in high spirits. Many years later, Mary Ann James, who was eleven at the time of the journey, recalled, "When we started out on the trail each morning there was always something new to see. Maby it was a bird running along the road which was chased but never did catch. The[re] were always flowers and pretty rocks to pick. This land was so different from the one in England that it kept us interested."

Even John Chislett, who would later apostatize, remembered the departure from Florence as a happy time: "Everything seemed to be propitious, and we moved gaily forward full of hope and faith. At our camp each evening could be heard songs of joy, merry peals of laughter, and *bon mots* on our condition and prospects. Brother Savage's warning was forgotten in the mirthful ease of the hour."

The Saints invented many songs to chant as they trundled their rickety carts, the most popular of which became known simply as "The Hand-cart Song." The verses were written by J. D. T. McAllister, who had been appointed commissary of the McArthur Company. The first stanza goes:

> Ye Saints that dwell on Europe's shores,
> Prepare yourselves with many more
> To leave behind your native land
>   For sure God's Judgments are at hand.
> Prepare to cross the stormy main
> Before you do the valley gain
> And with the faithful make a start
>   To cross the plains with your hand cart.

The chorus to "The Handcart Song" became the most beloved and often recited of all the ditties along the trail—a kind of Mormon "Row, row, row your boat" (though not, apparently, a round):

> Some must push and some must pull
>   As we go marching up the hill,
> As merrily on the way we go
>   Until we reach the valley, oh.

From the start, the Saints were also indefatigable composers of hymns. Along with "The Handcart Song," the emigrants in the Willie and Martin Companies sang "Come, Come, Ye Saints," which after its composition in 1846 had quickly become the most popular of all Mormon hymns (earning the sobriquet, "the Mormon 'Marseillaise' "). It was composed along the trail in Iowa by William Clayton, the fanatically precise mileage-measurer on Brigham Young's pioneer trek to Zion. In today's hymnal it is given a metronome marking of 66 to 84 for a quarter note, which would make it a brisk marching tune. The epigraphic inscription urges the faithful to sing the hymn "With conviction."

The fourth and last stanza of "Come, Come, Ye Saints" gives an eerie insight into the fatalistically pious spirit that drove the whole Mormon emigration, and it has an especially grim resonance for the disaster that awaited the last two handcart companies in Wyoming:

And should we die before our journey's through,
  Happy day! All is well!
We then are free from toil and sorrow, too;
  With the just we shall dwell!

Cheerful and melodic those first days out of Florence may have been, but the toil was at once more severe than what the Saints had borne across Iowa. As John Chislett explained, "Our carts were more heavily laden, as our teams could not haul sufficient flour to last us to Utah; it was therefore decided to put one sack (ninety-eight pounds) on each cart in addition to the regular baggage. Some of the people grumbled at this, but the majority bore it without a murmur."

"Grumbling" and "murmuring" were of course significant Mormon sins, earning a leader's tongue-lashing, such as the one Captain Willie delivered on September 7, as he announced that he "would like to see all the grumblers, pilferers, liars and so forth if any were still so in their hearts immediately stand by themselves aside from the rest so that the Brethren might better know them."

During those first weeks, as the company followed the north bank of the Platte River across Nebraska Territory, there were the usual mishaps. The official journal records that on August 22, with the company only seventy-five miles out of Florence, "Sister Sophia Geary had her left foot run over by Bro. Wilford's waggon. She was administered to in the evening by Bros. Siler, Cantwell and Geary, Capt. Siler officiating. He sealed the blessing of health and strength upon her and promised that inasmuch as she would exercise faith she should walk tomorrow." Sure enough, the next day, "Sis. Geary walked a considerable distance pursuant to Bro. Siler's promise."

Retrospective accounts of the journey are full of similar exempla of faith triumphing over adversity. Seventeen-year-old Joseph Wall nearly drowned crossing one of the tributaries of the Platte. He became too ill to walk, and the company leaders urged leaving him behind for the Martin Company to pick up. But Joseph's sixteen-year-old sister, Emily, could not stand to be parted from her brother, so for several days, she and another girl carried Joseph along on their handcart.

The onerous sand hills of Nebraska gave the company some of its sternest challenges. The official journal tersely notes that on August 25, "Had to double teams up a steep sandhill between 2 bluffs." Normally a team of six oxen was yoked to each of the seven wagons; if the journal is accurate, doubling a team would mean that a full dozen oxen were required to haul each wagon up the dune.

Levi Savage's journal routinely recorded the arduous labor of traversing the sand hills: "After noon we commenced to ascend the Bluffs. The ascent was Sand; it caused very hard puling." On the following day, "Both people and teams are much fatigued by the hea[v]y Sandy roads." And the day after, "Just before the camp got under way, a colde, and Strong wind arose from the N.W. This togeather with the hea[v]y Sand, made our progress very Slow, and exstreanly laborious. Several were obliged to leave their carts and they with the infirm, could Scarcely Get into camp."

Adding to the misery was the wretched condition of the handcarts. John Chislett would later eloquently analyze their failings:

> The axles and boxes being of wood, and being ground out by the dust that found its way there in spite of our efforts to keep it out, together with the extra weight put on the carts, had the effect of breaking the axles at the shoulder. All kinds of expedients were resorted to as remedies for the growing evil, but with variable success. Some wrapped their axles with leather obtained from bootlegs; others with tin, obtained by sacrificing tin-plates, kettles, or buckets from their mess outfit. Besides these inconveniences, there was felt a great lack of a proper lubricator.... The poor folks had to use their bacon (already totally insufficient for their wants) to grease their axles, and some even used their soap, of which they had very little, to make their carts trundle somewhat easier.

Despite all their hardships, by September 3, the Willie Company had reached central Nebraska. By their own reckoning, they had covered 265 miles from Florence in eighteen days, averaging a creditable fifteen miles a day.

Then an unmitigated disaster struck. The company had reached buffalo country. Many years later, Emma James, seventeen years old during the emigration, would recall the sight of a mass of bison in full stampede:

> One evening as we prepared to stop for the night a large herd of buffalo came thundering toward us. It sounded like thunder at first then the big black animals came straight for our carts. We were so scared that we were rooted to the ground. One of the captains seeing what was going on, ran for the carts which were still coming in, jerked out some of the carts to make a path for the steady stream of animals and let them go through. They went passed us like a train roaring along. I'm sure that but for the quick thinking of these men that many of us would have been trampled to death. The animals acted as if they were craz[y] the way they ran. We hoped that we wouldnt meet such a large herd soon again.

In the morning, the emigrants discovered that thirty of their forty-some cattle had disappeared—most of them the vital oxen that were used to pull the supply wagons. Captain Willie called a halt. For three days, the best scouts in the party searched far and wide for the missing livestock, without discovering a single "milch" cow. The storm had washed away the tracks of the straying beasts—if the ground trampled by hundreds of buffalo hooves had not in fact obliterated them.

Chislett describes the woeful solution the company was forced to resort to:

> We had only about enough oxen left to put one yoke to each wagon; but, as they were each loaded with about three thousand pounds of flour, the teams could not of course move them. We then yoked up our beef cattle, milch cows, and, in fact, everything that could bear a yoke—even two-year-old heifers. The stock was wild and could pull but little, and we were unable, with all our stock, to move our loads. As a last resort we again loaded a sack of flour on each cart.

On September 7, a Sunday, Captain Willie and his second-in-command, Millen Atwood, called the whole company together for a

meeting intended to boost its sagging morale. In typical fashion for this
iron-willed taskmaster, Willie castigated the throng even as he exhorted
the men, women, and children to superhuman efforts. He insisted on
"the absolute necessity for doing away with the spirit of grumbling,
strife, pilfering and disregard of counsel which was now on the increase
in the Camp and substituting in its place the spirit of contentment,
peace, union and strict obedience." Determined to keep up a rate of ten
to fifteen miles a day, Willie "said he would not enter into full particulars
of the plan of operations which he contemplated further than by saying
that if the Brethren or Sisters drawing handcarts should be required by
their Captain to draw 4 or 5 hundred of flour they must do it cheerfully."
It is a tribute to the sheer pluck and fortitude of the Saints that during
the next four days, they did indeed average just under ten miles a day.

By September 12, the Willie Company had reached the North Bluff
Fork of the Platte, 320 miles west of Florence. That evening they were
surprised by the sudden appearance of Franklin Richards's team of elite
returning missionaries. Besides the president of the British Mission,
their number included William Kimball, who in Florence had jauntily
promised the company that he would "stuff into his mouth all the snow
they would ever get to see on their journey to the valleys"; Joseph Young,
Brigham's oldest son; George Grant, who would later play the leading
role in a desperate rescue mission; and several other dignitaries. With
their light wagons and sturdy mules and horses, Richards's team had
left Florence on September 4, almost three weeks after the Willie Company, but, averaging a remarkable forty miles a day, had caught up to the
handcart train in western Nebraska.

According to the official journal, Richards and his colleagues "were
loudly greeted by the hearty hurrahs of the Saints whom they met after
supper." Willie called a meeting so that Richards could deliver a stirring
pep talk.

> Prest. Richards then addressed the Saints expressing his sat-
> isfaction at their having journeyed thus far & more especially
> with handcarts. . . . God being their helper and that if a Red Sea
> whould interpose they should by their union of heart & hand
> walk through it like Israel of old dryshod. On the same condi-

tions he promised that though they might have some trials to endure as a proof to God and their Brethren that they had the true "grit" still the Lamanites heat nor cold nor any other thing should have power to seriously harm any in the Camp but that we should arrive in the Valleys of the Mountains with strong and healthy bodies and that this should be the case with the aged the sick and the inform [infirm].

Richards repeated the by now widely accepted assertion that the hand-cart plan was of divine origin. He "said although it was a scheme at which many had already scoffed and which they were yet deriding it was nevertheless the Lord's plan, a plan which would first puzzle and aston-ish the nations and then strike terror into their hearts."

Richards was not content, however, simply to praise and encour-age the Willie Company. The next morning, with the wagons hitched to their makeshift teams, the handcarts loaded, and the company ready to move out, Richards and Willie called another meeting. The purpose was to give Levi Savage a thorough dressing-down in front of his fellow Saints. Savage recorded this public humiliation in a defensive journal entry, under the surface of which he seethes with outrage:

> I supposesd [the meeting] was for prayers. After Singing and prayers Brother Richards commenced to Speak. And I Soon per-ceived that the meeting was called in consequence of the wrong impression made by my expressing myself So freely at Florance, concerning our crossing the plains so late in the Season. The im-pression left, was, that I condemned the hand cart Skeem, which is aradiculy [ridiculously] wrong. I neaver conveyed Such an ideah, nor felt to do so, but quite to the conturary. I am infavor of it.

The tirade continued, with Willie taking up the cudgel: "Brother Rich-ards reprimanded me Sharply. Bro Willey Said that the Spirit that I had manifested from Iowa City. This is something unknown to me and Something he nevour before expressed I had always the best of feelings toward him, and Supposed he had toward me until now."

Before riding onward in advance of the handcart company, Richards promised the Saints that they would be resupplied "with provisions, bedding, etc." at Fort Laramie, about two hundred miles farther west. And also before departing, the missionaries enacted a tableau of such arrogance that John Chislett would remember it bitterly for the rest of his life:

> These brethren told Captain Willie they wanted some fresh meat, and he had our fattest calf killed for them. I am ashamed for humanity's sake to say they took it. While we, four hundred in number, travelling so slowly and so far from home, with our mixed company of men, women, children, aged, sick, and infirm people, had no provisions to spare, had not enough for ourselves, in fact, these "elders in Israel," these "servants of God," took from us what we ourselves so greatly needed and went on in style with their splendid outfit, after preaching to us faith, patience, prayerfulness, and obedience to the priesthood.

AFTER VOTING ALMOST unanimously to push on from Florence, the Martin Company had set out on August 25. The tribulations and minor triumphs of this sprawling caravan of Saints closely mirrored those of the Willie party a week ahead of them, though the Martin Company suffered no mass stampede of cattle. Like the Willie emigrants, the Martin pioneers had to add a ninety-eight-pound sack of flour to each handcart after Florence. The team's progress was even slower than that of the Willie Company, thanks to the large numbers of elderly, infirm, and ill in their ranks.

Patience Loader, her family, and her brother-in-law, John Jaques, were members of the Martin Company. Their ordeal, culminating in the death of Patience's beloved father, was but one of countless personal dramas unfolding among the 575 Saints in the last handcart company of the year, as the weary pioneers trudged across the plains.

James Bleak (pronounced "Blake") was a twenty-six-year-old Englishman who had risen from impoverished orphanhood to become a branch president in the London LDS church. In 1856, he originally planned to come to Zion with his wife and four children, who ranged from infancy to six years old, by conventional wagon team. He was wealthy enough to afford such means of transport. But the zeal of President Richards and other high officials, urging men such as Bleak voluntarily to forgo wagon teams and travel by handcart, pricked the man's conscience. The money he saved was donated to allow much poorer Saints to gather to Zion with their own handcarts.

On the trail, Bleak kept a journal that was as laconic as it was dutifully regular. Sometimes he noted nothing more than the day's mileage, and those entries serve as a memorandum of the Martin Company's fitful progress. From September 4 through 8, for instance, the daily toll was fifteen, six, eight, sixteen, and eighteen miles. The six-mile day was shortened "in consequence of a violent thunderstorm."

On the last of those five days, September 8, Bleak recorded, "No watering place on the road. Considerable murmuring in Camp." The very next day: "At the meeting this morning President Martin and Elder Tyler gave the murmurers a good chastising."

Bleak was as stoic about his own suffering as he was about the party's discontent:

Sunday [September] 14th We travelled 13 miles. While I was on Guard last night I was attacked with Bloody Flux. Have been very ill all day.

Monday 15th We travelled 22 miles. I began to draw the Handcart this morning but was obliged to leave it. Br Francis Webster very Kindly persuaded me to get on his handcart and drew me 17 miles. . . .

Tuesday 16th We travelled 9 miles. I through the blessing of God was able to draw the Handcart to day, but am still very ill. The brethren were out Buffalo hunting to day but returned unsuccessful.

Wednesday 17th We travelled 15 miles. I feel better to day.

Like James Bleak, thirty-seven-year-old Elizabeth Sermon initially planned to gather to Zion by wagon. She was so determined that she overcame the objections of her fifty-four-year-old husband, who would have preferred to stay in their home just outside London. The couple, and four of their five children, ended up in the Martin Company.

Temperamentally, Elizabeth Sermon was the polar opposite of James Bleak. Though she apparently did not keep a journal during the trek, many years later she left a reminiscence of the journey. What Bleak telegraphically understates, she brings into vivid relief. Like many another pilgrim, Sermon was shocked upon arriving at Iowa City to learn that she would have to sell or abandon most of the belongings she had hauled all the way from England. Still, she put a brave face on the sacrifice:

My bed, sixty pounds, was sold for four dollars, my sheets, boots, shoes and my clothing, but a basque were sold. I remember my old dress split every time I stooped. I had no stockings or shoes. Well, I kept up pretty well; work was hard, bed was hard, but still my shoulders were to the wheel and I think I pulled first fate [rate] for a beginner in shafts. They said, "Sister Sermon will get to Zion; she draws well." I think it was my faith did it mostly, but it weakened some before my journey was completed, but not lost.

Crossing Nebraska, the Sermon family began to break down:

We were very hungry, but did not dare touch only our allowances, one pound for each adult and one fourth for each child. I would make a scone cake, but we could eat it all in one meal. My husband's health began to fail and his heart almost broken to see me pulling in shafts. Myself and children hungry, almost naked, footsore, and himself nearly done for. Many trials came after this. My oldest boy had the mountain fever, we had to haul him in the cart, there was no room in the wagon. One day we started him out before the carts in the morning to walk with the aged and sick, but we had not gone far on our journey before we found him lying by the roadside, unable to go farther. I picked him up and put him on my back and drew my cart as well, but could not manage far, so put him in the cart, which made three children and my luggage. My husband failing more each day, the captain

put a young man to help me for a short time. My other son Henry
walked at seven years old.

Even at the remove of decades, a lingering sense of indignation in-
fuses Sermon's reminiscence:

> I will here state there was no time crossing the rivers to stop and
> take off clothing, but had to wade through and draw our carts at
> the same time with our clothes dripping wet had to dry in the sun
> and dust as merrily on our way we go until we reach the valley,
> oh, like a herd of stock or something worse. I was thinking the
> handcart system was not very pleasant, yet I thought it was the
> fault of the captain.

(Even her paraphrase of "The Handcart Song" has a derisive ring.)

It was not long before the daily grind of hunger tempted some of the
Martin Company Saints to steal food from one another. In his diary for
September 21, John Jaques glumly recorded, "Cold, wet, rainy morning.
Someone stole a cow's foot from my cart, also treacle, spice, meat, etc.
from Brother John Oldham's cart. and a meat dumpling from another
brother's cart." In an 1879 reminiscence published in the *Salt Lake Daily
Herald,* Jaques recounted in much greater detail a petty theft that would
seem comical were the emigrants' hunger at that point not so dire:

> In one family there were two or three grown-up girls, and one of
> them attended much to the cooking. One evening she had made
> and baked a very nice cake before going to prayers, and she set
> it up on edge against the tent while she went to prayer meeting.
> When she got back to her tent she went for her cake. On picking it
> up it seemed diminished marvellously in weight. Presently she ex-
> claimed, with tears in her eyes, "Oh, mother, somebody has been
> and taken every bit of crumb out of my cake and left the crust!"
> Some sharper, who either had not been to prayers, or who had
> loiteringly delayed his going, or had got through them with singu-
> larly swift dispatch for his own ulterior purposes, had discovered
> the girl's cake, taken a fancy to it, pulled it in two, eaten the soft

and warm inside, put the two crusts together again, and reared them carefully against the tent as they were. The poor girl thought that was really too bad, yet no doubt she felt thankful to get even the crust of her cake back again from that hungry pilferer.

Once the company reached the buffalo country, it ought to have been able to supplement the meager daily ration of flour with bison meat. But the British and Danish Saints were novice hunters. What is more, at least two of the pioneers recorded that the party was not allowed to shoot buffalo, because to do so would antagonize the Indians who depended on the herds as a staple part of their diet. One of those two informants elaborated, "We saw a great many buffalo as we traveled up the Platte River. The people were forbidden to kill them, as it made the Indians angry. So they hired the Indians to kill what they needed to eat. An Indian sold a man a whole buffalo for five cents' worth of tobacco. Both parties were satisfied."

As the grassy plains of eastern Nebraska gave way to prairie farther west, stands of timber grew increasingly scarce. Material for campfires was often hard to come by, so the pioneers went to bed supperless, or cooked dinner on smoldering piles of buffalo chips. Despite the fact that the party was following the North Platte River, sand hills and other obstacles often forced them far from its banks, and water was frequently hard to find. On more than one occasion the company pushed on well into the night to reach water, and some of the sources were barely potable.

Many years later, Josiah Rogerson, fifteen at the time, reconstructed the morning routine that preceded the Martin Company's setting out on the trail:

John Watkins was our bugler, and his cornet was heard every morning to "wake up" between 5 and 6 o'clock. Then again we heard his cornet to "strike tents" and to meeting—not later than 6 or 7 a.m.

These meetings every morning lasted from fifteen minutes to half an hour, when prayer was offered, a verse or two sung from one of our hymns, then a few remarks from Captain Martin, Tyler and the captains of the hundreds as to the health and condition of their companies and suggestions as to facilitating our progress; then our breakfast cooked and partaken of with haste; the tent poles and (about this date) the tents were taken to the four-mule team, the bedding rolled up, the cart packed, and we were generally in line in single file and on our journey by 7:30 to 8 a.m. at the latest.

Also many years later, John Southwell could not banish the sound of that "cornet" from his memory: "But oh! That bugle, that awful bugle. How disgusting it was to the poor, weary souls who needed rest rather then to hear the tirade of abuse uttered by that man who liked to talk and call down the curses of Almighty God upon the disobedient after a hard days march." (It is not clear if this tyrant was Edward Martin or one of his sub-captains.) "Tired and weary as they were, some of the older people would lie down on their hard beds and almost instantly be in the land of dreams. Than that accursed bugle would blow the call for prayers."

Many of the pilgrims were already weak or ill as they left Florence, and their numbers swelled with the hardships of the voyage. The tales of invalids being carried by their relatives and friends on their hand-carts challenge our modern imagination. Forty-one-year-old Margaret McBride, traveling with her husband and five children, ages two to six-teen, became too ill to walk not far out of Florence. About a dozen years after the trek, her son Heber recalled,

I being the oldest boy just past 13 years and my sister 3 years older than me we had to pull the handcart all the way but Mother being sick and nothing for her comfort she failed very fast she would start out in the morning and walk as far as she could then she would give out and ly down and wait till we came along, and we would take her on our cart and haul her along till we came to camp.

On September 7, twenty-two-year-old Samuel Openshaw had to pull a cart on which lay his two sisters, aged fourteen and twenty: "Eleanor has the Ague and Diree and is so badly that we had to pull her in the

hand cart. Eliza also is yet so weak that we had to pull her also in the
hand cart which made it just as much as we could pull." Eleanor recovered, but a week later Eliza was still prostrate on the cart.

One of the bravest emigrants was a crippled boy, whose "lower limbs
were paralyzed and his body badly deformed but he was strong in the
faith. He was able to propel himself with surprising speed with the use
of crutches." Fifty-seven years after the journey, John Southwell would
recall his fate on the Nebraska trail:

> On the road the old father missed him. The road followed down
> an old dry bed of a creek but finally crossed on to the other side
> where we expected to get back of him. There were, on the road
> he was traveling, faint tracks that had been used by stock, per-
> haps buffalo, and the poor fellow followed those tracks instead
> of crossing on the other side. We camped for noon near the loup
> part of the Platt River. Myself and two other men, taking a hand
> cart, went back to where we left the buffalo tracks and followed
> down about a mile when to our horror we saw around an old tree
> two large gray wolves prowling around, and half a dozen eagles
> hovering over the tree waiting for him to quit his screams and
> gestulations with his crutches so they would pounce upon him
> and devour him in his cramped position under the roots of the
> tree, screaming out his death knell.
>
> We arrived in time to save him from his pending fate, took
> him out and placed him on the cart we had brought, placed him
> in position to ride back to camp. How the poor fellow begged us
> to let him walk, as he said he had promised brother Tyler when
> we started on our trip that he would walk every foot of the way
> to Salt Lake City.

The rescue, alas, went for naught. Southwell: "We only saved him to
travel a few days longer, which at the close of the sixth days march his
trouble in this world came to an end and he was buried on the banks of
the Elkhom River where one other passed beyond the veil of tears."

Through the month of September, the Martin Company suffered a
number of other deaths. The count is uncertain, but decades later, Josiah

Rogerson reckoned it at about a dozen. The terse, numbed phrases with which various emigrants recorded these deaths indicate just how fatalistically the company took the toll for granted. "A man fell down dead." "An old sister died this morning, which delayed us until 10 o'clock." "A change for worse occurred and at three o'clock the old man breathed his last. He was taken from the van and the old lady became so prostrated she became unconscious. She lived until seven o'clock, when she joined her husband in the land of spirits."

Perhaps the strangest of all the deaths in the Martin Company during this period was recalled in considerably fuller detail many years later by Josiah Rogerson:

> Two bachelors, named Luke Carter, from the Clitheroe branch, Yorkshire, England, and William Edward, from Manchester, England, each about 50 to 55 years of age, had pulled a covered cart together from Iowa City, Ia., to here: slept in the same tent, cooked and bunked together, but for several days previous unpleasant and cross words had passed between them.
>
> Edwards was a tall, loosely built and tender man physically, and Carter more stocky and sturdy: he had favored Edwards by letting the latter pull what he could in the shafts for some time past. This morning he grumbled and complained, still traveling, about being tired, give out, and that he couldn't go any farther. Carter retorted: "Come on. Come on. You'll be all right again when we get a bit of dinner at noon," but Edwards kept on begging for him to stop the cart and let him lie down and dee (die). Carter replying, "Well, get out and die then." The cart was instantly stopped. Carter raised the shafts of the cart. Edwards walked from under and to the south of the road a couple of rods, laid his body down on the level prairie, and in ten minutes he was a corpse.

Like the three handcart parties that had crossed the plains before them, the Willie and Martin Companies were constantly worried about running into hostile Indians. Not long after setting out from Florence, the emigrants were warned by the relatively docile Omaha tribe that

Cheyennes farther west were on the rampage. The report was probably accurate, for not long before, soldiers stationed at Fort Kearny in central Nebraska had skirmished with the Cheyennes, killing ten of their men.

From that conflict springs the vexed and convoluted saga of Almon W. Babbitt. The true story of what happened at the end of August 1856 in Cheyenne country will never be sorted out, but both the Willie and Martin Companies became intimately involved with Babbitt's death.

Babbitt had been a leading member of the LDS church as early as the Nauvoo days. When the Saints abandoned that Illinois stronghold to set out for Zion, Babbitt was one of three trustees left behind to try to sell off the land and buildings, including the grandiose new temple. In 1851, he himself emigrated to Salt Lake City as the captain of a 150-wagon-strong team. Even before that, in 1849, Brigham Young had appointed Babbitt as delegate to Congress, during the first of the church's several fruitless efforts to win statehood for Deseret. In Utah, Babbitt became one of the first mail carriers, in which service he got to know the Mormon Trail as well as or better than any other Saint.

Babbitt, however, was evidently as flamboyant and reckless as he was talented. In 1851, he was disfellowshiped from the church, under the official charge of "profanity and intemperance in the streets of Kanesville, and for corrupting the morals of the people." Despite that disgrace, Young later reinstated the man, finding him so useful that in 1852 Babbitt began to serve as secretary for the Utah Territory, making many trips to Washington, D.C., where, according to one historian, he further "incurred Young's displeasure by carousing around the nation's capital with the abandon of a French sailor."

In the summer of 1856, after one such visit to Washington, Babbitt outfitted a wagon in Florence with such luxuries as books, stationery, and a carpet for the Salt Lake statehouse, then sent it west with four men to drive the ox team, and a certain Mrs. Wilson and her child as passengers. Babbitt's plan was to set off in a lightweight wagon and catch up with the rest of his entourage somewhere along the trail. A rumor had it that the secretary carried with him $20,000 in cash.

The heavier wagon, loaded with goods, left Florence before the Willie party. On August 29, the Willie's Saints camped with Indians whom one pioneer, James Cantwell, identified as Pawnees (they may have been

Omahas). According to Cantwell, "They informed us that the Cheyennes had killed 4 men and a child and taken a woman prisoner. Her name was Wilson but she was never heard from afterwards."

The next day, the Willie Company came upon the graves of the four teamsters, whom (according to Cantwell) the Pawnees had buried "so shallow that the wolves were digging them up." (The child may have been kidnapped along with his mother, rather than killed.) Another diarist recorded, "Passed the graves of Babbitt's teamsters—our men covered up the graves with soil as considerable stench arose from the dead."

According to Cantwell, "On the 31st Almon Babbit overtook us. He was carrying the mail and had a man with him as guard by the name of Sutherland. when he was [saw] what the Cheyennes had done he was wild with rage, and swore he would kill the first Cheyenne he was [saw]." Despite warnings from the Willie Company, Babbitt set off ahead of the handcart train with only Thomas Sutherland as his companion.

Here the plot thickens. Arriving at Fort Kearny, Babbitt allegedly purchased additional supplies to replace the goods he had lost to the Cheyennes. At the fort, however, he met a party of Mormons also bound for Salt Lake, under the command of Abraham O. Smoot. Theirs was largely a freight mission, as they hauled tons of goods that Young had ordered to be delivered to the territory. One of the men in Smoot's party was Orrin Porter Rockwell.

Rockwell, of course, had already earned his reputation as perhaps the fiercest and most fearless of all the Danites, Brigham's secret police. Now a very strange transaction took place. According to an affidavit later sworn by Rockwell, Babbitt hired Rockwell to carry his goods to Salt Lake, since he was determined to push on as fast as he could in his light wagon. The affidavit claimed a staggering total of 5,643 pounds of supplies, including "thirty-three cases of books." For the hauling, Rockwell was to be paid 14 cents a pound. Indeed, Rockwell eventually collected exactly $790.02 from Babbitt's estate.

Where did all those goods come from? Had the Cheyennes killed the teamsters and kidnapped Mrs. Wilson and her child, only to leave all the booty on the plains? Granted, thirty-three cases of books would have been of little value to the Indians, but in the wagon there must have been other goods that they would have coveted. (When the Martin Company came upon the site of the Cheyenne attack on September 23, they found only the burnt remains of Babbitt's heavy lead wagon.)

Harold Schindler, Rockwell's sympathetic biographer, insists that both the Kearny soldiers and the Smoot party begged Babbitt not to push on virtually alone. Schindler admits that "no satisfactory explanation has ever come to light regarding Babbitt's seemingly unreasonable haste to reach Utah." Nonetheless, Babbitt set out on September 6 in his light wagon, with only Sutherland and another shotgun guard to accompany him.

When Babbitt's small party failed to show up at Fort Laramie, it was generally assumed that Cheyennes had murdered them as well. Enter, at this point, another emigrant with a keen eye for fishy details. Caleb Green had been hired by Smoot as clerk and assistant commissary for his freight-heavy wagon train. After five months in Salt Lake, Green would grow disenchanted, apostatize, and flee the territory. The diary he kept during the 1856 expedition, though never published, is a fascinating document. Soon after Babbitt's hasty departure from Fort Kearny, Green noted,

> Rockwell + Smoot left camp at night and returned in the morn. the next day. Smoot left the road with some other men and brought a waggon out of the thicket which skirts the Platte at this point we suspected that it was Babbetts as it was very similar.

The suspicions about Rockwell and Smoot were not confined to Green and the one or two other skeptics in the Smoot party. When Rockwell arrived in Fort Laramie hauling more than two tons of Babbitt's goods, several of the residents of the trading post wondered whether "the Mormon Destroying Angel had notched another victim, an accusation which eventually would reach Washington." Caleb Green's diary adds that the scouts at Fort Laramie insisted that the only Indians then at war with whites were two hundred miles away, on the Arkansas River.

It is possible that Cheyennes were guilty of the murders and kidnapping of Babbitt's advance party, as well as of the killing of Babbitt and his two guards. It may be that the first attack was perpetrated by Indians, while Rockwell orchestrated the assassination of Babbitt and his guards, then stole their goods. And it is conceivable that all the murders and depredations were carried out by Rockwell and a fellow Danite or two in the Smoot party. In the darkest scenario, Rockwell would have wiped out Babbitt's party, and then helped himself not only to the $790.02 in freight-hauling charges, but to whatever cash (whether the rumored $20,000 or far less) the secretary was carrying on his person.

In 1862, Brigham Young cast a possibly unintentional light on this murky episode when he spoke in anger to a federally appointed justice of the Utah Supreme Court. If government officers, the Prophet threatened, "undertake to interfere in affairs that do not concern them, I will not be far off. *There was Almon W. Babbitt. He undertook to quarrel with me, but soon afterwards was killed by Indians.* He lived like a fool, and died like a fool" (emphasis in original).

Until very recently, historians of the handcart emigration have ignored the Abraham Smoot expedition sharing the Mormon Trail in 1856. Only in 2006 did the iconoclastic historian Will Bagley ferret out details of the freight-hauling enterprise that have important and possibly sinister relevance for the catastrophe in Wyoming.

THE WILLIE COMPANY arrived at Fort Laramie on October 1. To the shock of the emigrants, the "provisions, bedding, etc." promised by Franklin Richards were nowhere to be seen. Levi Savage recorded his disappointment in a single bitter sentence: "B[r]other Richards has no cattle provided for us here, & no other provisions made."

The Fort Laramie of 1856 stood not on the site of present-day Laramie, Wyoming, but eighty miles to the northeast, on a bench a mile south of the North Platte River, just east of today's town of Guernsey. It was not a military establishment, but a trading post, whose hazy origins dated from fur trappers' cabins built in the 1830s. At the fort, there was a very limited amount of food available for sale, but at exorbitant prices: 20 cents a pound for flour, in contrast with the 3 to $3\frac{1}{2}$ cents per pound that the company had paid in Iowa City. In any event, nearly all the Saints were too poor to purchase much of anything. Levi Savage wrote in his diary that he sold his $20 watch for $11, with which in turn he bought a $6 pair of boots and unspecified other articles.

In the end, Captain Willie was able to buy four hundred pounds of "hard bread"—i.e., soda crackers. One pound of crackers per man, woman, and child in the company amounted to but a feeble boost in provisions. By now, Willie had calculated that the flour supply remaining in the wagons would last only another eighteen days. Salt Lake City was still 509 miles away.

For the first time, Willie realized that drastic measures were called for. He called a meeting of the whole company, at which he offered the estimate that at their present rate of travel, the party would run out of food 350 miles short of Salt Lake. As John Chislett remembered the meeting, "It was resolved to reduce our allowance from one pound [of flour] to three-quarters of a pound per day, and at the same time to make every effort in our power to travel faster."

The failure of the Fort Laramie resupply has never been adequately explained. Historians struggle to come up with an explanation less damning than sheer negligent indifference on the part of the team of high-ranking missionaries speeding toward Salt Lake City.

Meanwhile the Martin Company, still lagging about a hundred miles behind their brethren in the Willie party, also decided to reduce their rations. In a diary entry on October 3, the anxiety leaks from Samuel Openshaw's pen: "We continued our journey as quick as we possibly could. The cold increasing upon us. It is severe nights and mornings. Our provisions are running out very fast so that our rations are reduced to 12 ounces of flour per day."

On October 4, the Willie Company camped thirty-one miles west of Fort Laramie. The official journal laconically recorded: "Benjamin Culley, aged 61, from Sprowston, Norfolk, England, died; also George Ingra, aged 68, from Bassingbourne, Cambridgeshire, England died; also Daniel Gadd, aged 2, from Orwell, Cambridgeshire, England, died. A cow was killed in the afternoon."

That same night the Martin Company pitched its camp two miles west of the prominent landmark of Scottsbluff, some twenty miles east of what is today the Nebraska-Wyoming border. Jesse Haven's diary recorded the death of Thomas Tennant at 1:30 in the afternoon. Among the Martin Company Saints, he was one of the most beloved. Certainly no single emigrant did more to advance the cause of the handcart enterprise of 1856. Unlike the vast majority of the Saints, Tennant was a rich Englishman, but he was so stirred by the news of the "divine" handcart plan that he chose to pull his own carriage rather than gather to Zion in a lavishly appointed wagon. And before leaving England, he accepted Young's offer to buy a house in Salt Lake City for $25,000, the whole sum of which went to the Perpetual Emigration Fund, thereby enabling scores of paupers to join the exodus.

On that same day, October 4, Franklin Richards's speedy caravan of light wagons drawn by mules rolled into Salt Lake City. What Richards told Brigham Young would shock Zion to the core.

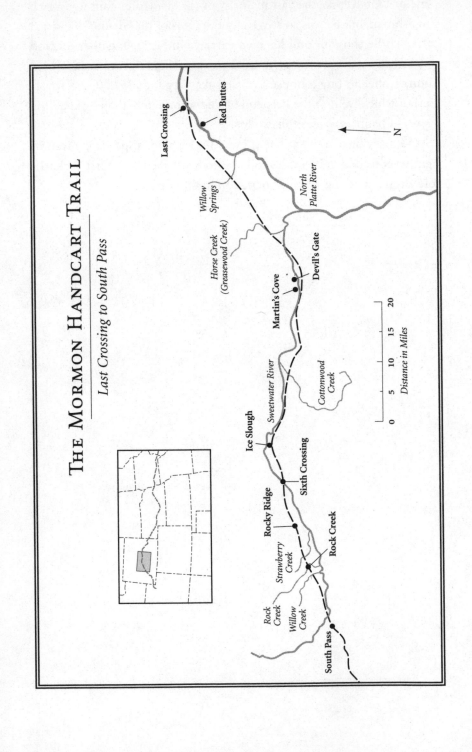

THE MORMON HANDCART TRAIL

Last Crossing to South Pass

Last Crossing

Red Buttes

Willow Springs

North Platte River

Horse Creek (Greasewood Creek)

Martin's Cove

Devil's Gate

Sweetwater River

Ice Slough

Cottonwood Creek

Sixth Crossing

Rocky Ridge

Strawberry Creek

Rock Creek

Rock Creek

Willow Creek

South Pass

N

0 5 10 15 20
Distance in Miles

CHAPTER SIX

ROCKY RIDGE

The message that Franklin Richards delivered to the Prophet that October day was that, among the Willie and Martin handcart companies and the Hunt and Hodgetts wagon trains, there were some 1,300 Saints still scattered along the Mormon Trail. At the time, and ever after, Young insisted that he had no knowledge even of the existence of the hundreds of emigrants who had crossed the Atlantic on the *Thornton* and *Horizon*, and who had proceeded to Iowa City to begin their long, arduous trek to Zion. We know that the Prophet's protestation is untrue, however, because of the existence of the June 11 letter from William Woodward to Heber Kimball announcing the imminent arrival in Iowa of the *Thornton* Saints, with the note on the back indicating its receipt in Young's office on July 30.

Nonetheless, historians have blithely accepted the Prophet's convenient fabrication. For example, as Andrew Olsen writes in *The Price We Paid*, on receiving the news from Richards on October 4, "Brigham Young was stunned."

The Prophet did react to the message forcefully and with alacrity. The very next day, he convened a meeting in the bowery attended by many of the Salt Lake Saints. Young himself spoke first. After a stern preamble warning mothers in the audience to shush their babies and the whole congregation to refrain from whispering and "shuffling of the feet" (in the day before microphones, orators at such large gatherings had virtually to shout to be heard in the back rows), the Prophet announced the "text" for the day. "On the 5th day of October, 1856," he proclaimed, "many of our brethren and sisters are on the plains with hand-carts, and probably many are now 700 miles from this place." (The Martin Company at that moment was actually 560 miles east of Salt Lake City.)

"That is my religion," Young continued; "that is the dictation of the Holy Ghost that I possess, it is to save the people. We must bring them in from the plains." Ever the pragmatist, he proceeded at once to specify the logistics of the rescue expedition he was prepared to launch. The Salt Lake Saints must furnish "60 good mule teams and 12 or 15 wagons"; also "12 tons of flour and 40 good teamsters." Young wanted "good horses and mules" to pull the wagons, not oxen. The former carpenter went on to itemize the gear each wagon team required: "harness, whipple-trees, neck-yokes, stretchers, lead chains, &c."

The Prophet thundered on: "Go and bring in those people now on the plains, and attend strictly to those things which we call temporal . . . otherwise your faith will be in vain; the preaching you have heard will be in vain to you, and you will sink to hell, unless you attend to the things we tell you."

After Young finished, Daniel Spencer, one of the returning missionaries in Richards's entourage, rose to speak. Despite the looming catastrophe, Spencer felt the need to voice his unswerving confidence in the handcart plan. "Many thought it impossible," he asserted, "but the faith that the people had in the works of President Young caused them to come forward, and we now feel convinced that it is the best way of emigrating the Saints to this city." Spencer's exhortations for rescue volunteers were expressed in a softer tone than Young's commands: "Well, now, we feel for those brethren and sisters that are still upon the plains, for we have been with them in the old countries and seen their faith and diligence, and now we feel to plead with you to assist them. . . . You must recollect this is a great work which they are performing, and they have done this to honor our Prophet and to carry out his designs."

Yet as to what had gone wrong, Spencer could only express bafflement—or perhaps he kept his finger-pointing in his pocket. "The emigration is late, quite late," he told the congregation, "but it is useless for me to undertake to explain why it is so."

And then, after Spencer, Franklin Richards addressed the meeting. Of the three speakers, he seemed the least capable of grasping the gravity of the situation. In words that would come to haunt him, he blandly averred, "The Saints that are now upon the plains, about one thousand with hand-carts, feel that it is late in the season, and they expect to get cold fingers and toes. But they have this faith and confidence towards God that he will overrule the storms that may come in the season thereof and turn them away, that their path may be free from suffering more than they can bear. They have confidence to believe that this will be an open fall."

The response to the rescue appeal on the part of the rank-and-file Saints was extraordinary. Despite the crop failures of the previous year, the faithful readily donated the tons of flour Young had specified. They also offered horses and mules, wagons, and all kinds of warm clothes and bedding. And there was no shortage of volunteers—in the Prophet's formula, "good young men who know how to drive teams"—to set out almost at once on the return trail. Six of the volunteers, in fact, came from Richards's party, who spent only a few days in Salt Lake before heading east again.

October 6, the day after the bowery meeting, happened to be the date of the semiannual General Conference of the church. Young seized the occasion to organize the rescue mission even more vigorously. The minutes of the conference reveal a charade of noblesse oblige that opened the proceedings, as the Prophet "called upon those who were willing to go, or send teams, to come to the stand and report; saying that if there were not enough teams, teamsters, &c., volunteered, he would close the conference, and, with br. Kimball, start back to help those companies.

"Pres. Kimball remarked, it is moved and seconded that Brigham Young, Heber C. Kimball, and Jedediah M. Grant go back to help the P. E. Fund Emigrants. Unanimously negatived." Thus the congregation enacted the charade, voting unanimously against sending the three highest-ranking officials in Zion to hit the rescue trail themselves. (After the pioneer trek to the Great Basin in 1847 and the Prophet's return journey the next year to gather more Saints from Winter Quarters, Young would go on only two extended trips during the rest of his life—a reconnaissance mission into Idaho in 1857 to ascertain whether the whole Mormon colony might take refuge there, should the U.S. Army invade Utah Territory, and an 1870 tour of Mormon colonies in Arizona and Southern Utah.)

Yet even as the colony awoke to the potential for a catastrophe on the plains, speakers at the General Conference, such as the leaders of the first and third handcart companies, felt the need to reassert their faith in the "divine" plan. According to the minutes,

> Elder Edward Bunker sketched the travels of his hand-cart company, and alluded to their having been led by the Lord all the way.
> Elder Ellsworth sung, "Hand-carts rolling."

On October 7, the first rescue wagons lumbered out of Salt Lake City, heading up Emigration Canyon toward Fort Bridger. They were led by George D. Grant, who, after several years of missionary work in England, his return to the United States, and his lightning-quick journey in the Richards party from Florence to Zion, got to spend only three days in Salt Lake City before setting out on what would prove to be a grim and grueling mission of mercy. Before the end of October, not twelve or fifteen wagons, but several score, would be rolling eastward to try to save the handcart Saints.

Some LDS historians and scholars see Young's prompt and ambitious launching of the rescue effort as the Prophet's finest hour. Even T. B. H. Stenhouse, that influential and articulate later apostate, gave Young the highest praise for his response to Richards's message:

> When the news reached Brigham Young, as already stated, he did all that man could do to save the remnant and relieve the sufferers. Never in his whole career did he shine so gloriously in the eyes of the people. There was nothing spared that he could contribute or command.

Leonard Arrington, author of *Brigham Young: American Moses*, manages to avoid altogether any mention of the handcart emigration and disaster, except in one paragraph in an epilogue aimed at fixing Young's legacy for the posterity of Utah and the church. There Arrington cites the rescue mission as a prime example of the Prophet's concern for "temporal salvation" as opposed to "spiritual"; i.e., saving people's lives as well as their souls.

Whether or not the launching of the rescue was Young's finest hour, to see it simply as a statesman's bold and prescient answer to a looming crisis is to obscure other vexing and as yet unsolved questions about the chain of events that led to that crisis. Only a few days after the Willie Company reached Fort Laramie to discover that Richards's party had failed to provide the expected resupply, the company was granted a second promise. According to John Chislett, "About this time Captain Willie received a letter from apostle Richards informing him that we might expect supplies to meet us from the valley by the time we reached South Pass." How this letter was conveyed to Willie remains unexplained, though sometimes messages were simply tacked to signboards erected along the trail. In any event, this second promise boded a desperately hungry onward march of another 275 miles.

Why did Franklin Richards make these promises, unless he thought he could fulfill them? Even for a man with his almost blind faith in the power of God to keep the storms away from the late-arriving pilgrims, it would seem heartless in the extreme to dangle imaginary carrots in front of the famished emigrants. Instead, Richards must have believed in the promises. Yet for the rest of his life, as far as we know, the Apostle never publicly explained why the resupplies failed to materialize.

The first three handcart parties, under Captains Ellsworth, McArthur, and Bunker, it will be recalled, had been successfully resupplied by substantial wagon trains heading east out of Salt Lake, carrying hefty loads of flour. Those rendezvous, which undoubtedly saved many lives, took place as far back along the trail as Deer Creek in eastern Wyoming.

Where were the resupply caravans for the Willie and Martin Companies? On the face of it, the apparent absence of such resupply trains might be construed to buttress Young's claim that he had no idea the Willie and Martin Companies were on the plains.

Here, however, the documentary record gets truly murky. In the *Deseret News* on October 22, 1856, Franklin Richards and Daniel Spencer published a very cursory account of their rapid jaunt from Florence, which gives a few salient details of the team's doings between September 13, when it parted from the Willie Company at the North Bluff Fork of the Platte, and October 4, when it arrived in Salt Lake City. In fact, during that ride, the returning missionaries encountered three separate resupply trains headed east along the trail. They seem to have been much smaller outfits than the teams that had so vitally resupplied the first three handcart companies earlier in the summer: one is described as consisting of only three men and "2 wagons of flour for the companies."

Richards's party met the first of these resupply teams at Independence Rock, the second fifteen miles east of Pacific Springs, and the third at the Big Sandy crossing west of South Pass. At the times of those encounters, the resupply teams had thus traveled 332, 243, and 196 miles, respectively, from Salt Lake. They were weeks ahead of the first rescue team, which would not be launched until October 7. On September 24, when Richards's party met the first resupply team at Independence Rock, the wagons with their precious flour stood only 244 miles west of the Willie party. Had the handcart company pushed on westward at a rate of only ten miles a day, while the resupply train continued eastward at fifteen miles a day, the two would have closed the gap and met only ten days later. Even a few wagonloads of flour would have meant a life-saving difference for the Willie Company.

The tragic fact, however, is that none of the three resupply teams ever met up with the Willie Saints, let alone with the Martin Company. The reasons for those failures are hard to divine. Richards and Spencer's account in the *Deseret News* indicates somewhat cryptically that "Br. Smith returned with us"—John Smith being the leader of the three-man team met at Independence Rock. Did the other two men push on eastward with the flour? As for the second resupply party, whom Richards met near Pacific Springs, the Apostle urged the team (likewise composed of only three men) to "cache their flour and go on to meet Br. Willie." This was truly puzzling advice: what good would the resuppliers do the Willie Saints without the essential flour? How much faster might they travel after caching it? As far as we know, the cached flour was never reclaimed. On meeting the third resupply party on September 28, Richards and Spencer gave the team leader "the same counsel, to go on with his teams to help br. Willie."

Tackling this thorny problem, LDS historian Andrew Olsen speculates that the resupply flour might have gone not to the handcart parties, but to the several wagon trains that were weeks or days ahead of the Willie Company—including Abraham Smoot's freight-hauling caravan. But Olsen also points to the diary of Robert T. Burton, one of the rescuers in the vanguard party under the charge of George Grant. On October 13, just east of Fort Bridger, Burton reported crossing paths with "some teams returning that had been back on the road and got tired of waiting." "Waiting"—the word itself is disturbing. Instead of pushing on to meet the starving handcart pioneers (for after meeting Richards, the resuppliers would have known that the Willie Company was woefully short on rations), did the feckless men with their wagons full of flour simply camp out and wait for the handcarts to come to them? And then, when the rendezvous did not take place as soon as they expected, did they simply turn around and head back to Salt Lake City?

AT FORT LARAMIE in the beginning of October, the Willie Company saw the last of its backouts leave the party, as several women chose to remain at the fort, and at least two men returned to it after proceeding only a few days farther west. These "deserters" simply vanish from the historical record. It is evident that some of the women were wooed by denizens of the fort in search of potential brides.

On October 4, the day the rations were reduced to twelve ounces of flour per adult, with the party camped thirty-one miles west of the fort, Levi Savage wrote in his journal, "Some Stealing is practiced by Some, consequently we put all the provisions into three wagons, and placed a gard over them." The calculus of starvation is as simple as it is cruel. Even with their full ration of a pound of flour per day, plus a little bacon, sugar, and tea, the handcart Saints were ingesting no more than 1,500 calories per day. The exertions of even a moderate day on the trail caused each adult emigrant to burn a minimum of four thousand calories. By October 4, the Willie Saints were fifty days out of Florence, eighty-two out of Iowa City.

During the numerous expeditions undertaken by covered wagon between 1847 and 1856, the Saints from Brigham Young down to the poorest emigrant learned from their own experiences on the trail just how much food it took to gather to Zion in good health. Although the concept of the calorie would not be defined until 1880, the Saints in Zion knew well the size and weight of the provisions needed to keep hunger at bay along the trail.

Once more, an obvious question has a tangled answer. Why did the church authorities, from the very start of the handcart "experiment," limit the daily ration to no more than a pound of flour per man and woman per day, plus a measly supply of other foodstuffs? There are several possible contributory factors. In estimating the rate of passage from Iowa City to Salt Lake by handcart at sixty days, Young radically underestimated the actual time those journeys would require. It was widely hoped that the companies could supplement their flour rations with game killed along the trail—particularly buffalo. But besides being for the most part inept hunters, the European-born Saints could ill afford to halt along the trail for whole days while their sharpshooters went off in pursuit of wild game. The odd berry patch or wild onion field raided along the way made only the paltriest boost to the pioneers' nutrition.

A more cynical calculation no doubt entered into the deliberate underfeeding of the emigrants. Young had concocted the handcart plan mainly to save money. The less spent on food, the cheaper the "experiment."

The overriding factor, however, was in all likelihood built in to the handcart expeditions by the very nature of the carriages the Saints pulled and pushed. Like the seventeen-pound baggage allowance, a one-pound flour ration stretched the carrying capacity of each company to the limit. One could counter by arguing that adding ten or twelve more wagons to each company would have allowed for the transport of far more food, but once again, economy dictated otherwise.

The very nature of zealous faith played its part, too, in the shortfall. Young, the Apostles, and the company leaders believed that hardship was a noble test. If an emigrant truly put his trust in God, hunger would be only a necessary privation, not a cause of death. A faithful Saint might arrive in Zion a bit leaner than when he left Iowa, but the trial would provide its own lasting spiritual reward.

Yet in sending out the massive resupply wagons that intersected with the Ellsworth, McArthur, and Bunker Companies, Young seemed to recognize that the handcart Saints were under-provisioned. All the more inexplicable, then, the tiny size and faint resolve of the three resupply missions Richards's party encountered between Independence Rock and the Big Sandy crossing.

Both the diaries kept during the journey by the Willie Saints and their reminiscences dictated as long as decades later abound in poignant tableaux of the ravages of hunger within the company after October 4. Many of them come from the voices of Saints who were only children at the time. John Oborn, then twelve, spoke for all of them when he later recalled, "Our scant rations had reached the point where the amount ordinarily consumed for one meal now had to suffice a full day. From here on it is beyond my power of description to write. God only can understand and realize the torture and privation, exposure and starvation that we went through."

Michael Jensen, an eleven-year-old Dane in the party, recollected eating roots, the bark from trees, and cactus. "Prickly pears were gathered, the stickers burned off in the fire, and then they were prepared, by being cut into pieces then boiled, then eaten. Sometimes they were baked, then eaten."

The livestock themselves were giving out, along with the emigrants. On several occasions, Captain Willie had a cow slaughtered for food, but to divide one scrawny animal's meat among more than 350 Saints made almost no dent in their hunger. On October 12, Levi Savage recorded the gruesomely comic demise of one heifer: "One of the cows, that was over run with work tho drove less could not be got within a mile of Camp. By Bro Willies order, Several of the Brothren went back to kill her, for the peop[le] to eat, (if they wanted it) They Struck her twice in the head, with an ax. She got up & run into camp, where She was Shot, dressed, and ishued out; The people have Sharp apatites." Five days later, a calf gave out, but was devoured by wolves before the Saints could claim it for food.

Fifteen-year-old George Cunningham remembered twenty years afterward how every scrap of a slain cow was rendered edible:

We used to boil the bones and drink the soup and eat what little meat there was. We greedily devoured the hides also. I myself have took a piece of hide when I could get it, scorched off the hair on the fire, roasted it a little on the coals, cut it in little pieces so that I could swallow it and bolted it down my throat for supper and thought it was most delicious.

Eighteen-year-old Sarah James later recalled,

How good the soup tasted made from the bones of those cows
although there wasn't any fat on them. The hides we used to roast
after taking all the hair off of them. I even decided to cook the
tatters of my shoes and make soup of them. It brought a smile
to my father's sad face when I made the suggestion but mother
was a bit impatient with me and told me that I'd have to eat the
muddy things my self.

Ann Rowley was a forty-eight-year-old English widow traveling with
her seven children, ages seven to nineteen, and an adult stepdaughter.
She later conjured up the truly extreme measures to which hunger drove
some of the children: "Rawhide strips was used to wrap the iron rims
to the wheels and the wood would shrink and the rawhide would come
loose. It hurt me to see my children go hungry. I watched as they cut loose
rawhide from the cart wheels, roast off the hair and chew the hide."

Sarah James's were not the only shoes reduced to tatters. According
to one emigrant, "Clothing was in rags, especially shoes. Any piece of
rags, burlap or canvas was tied around the feet. All too soon this was
chewed through by the tortorus terrain. It was not uncommon to take
the clothing from the dead to cover the living."

On October 15, Willie convened a council to take stock once more
of the provisions. The whole company expected to be resupplied near
South Pass, now less than a hundred miles away. Yet despite the Saints'
desperate hunger, the conclusion was almost foregone. In the official
journal, William Woodward wrote, "It was unanimously agreed to reduce the rations of flour one fourth—the men then would get 10½ ozs.
per day; women, & large children 9 ozs. per day; children 6 ozs. per day;
& infants 3 ozs. per day each." In the same entry, he noted, "Many of the
company are sick & have to ride in the wagons."

It was inevitable now that emigrants began to die. In the first week of
October, six Saints perished, equaling the toll of the whole six previous
weeks on the trail. Several families were hit particularly hard. Within
eight days, Robert Reeder witnessed the deaths of his father and his sister. Years later, he would poignantly reconstruct those losses.

My father, David Reeder, would start out in the morning and pull
his cart until he would drop on the road. He did this day after day
until he did not arise early on 7 October 1856. He was found dead
in his bed and his fellow bedmate had not heard a thing during the night. Sister Eliza wrapped a cherished sheet around him
and we placed him in a shallow grave hoping the wolves would
not disturb. We must go on our way in silent mourning and in a
weakened condition.

Then,

My younger sister, Caroline, 17 years old, after traveling all day
and seeing the camp being made for the night took off her apron
to tie some sage brush in to bring into the camp. She sat down
to rest, leaning on her bundle, exhausted. They found her chilled
and dying and carried her to camp. She died without gaining con-
sciousness. She, too, was placed in an unmarked grave near Three
Crossings—Sweetwater. She died the evening of 15 October 1856.

Also within days, the Gadd family lost three of its members—
two- and ten-year-old boys and their father. Ann Rowley, the matriarch
traveling with her seven children and her grown stepdaughter, saw the
latter steadily decline. "I watched with alarm, my stepdaughter Eliza,
grow weaker each day," Rowley later wrote. "She was never very strong. I
had always devoted a lot of love and care to her, but she passed away one
day and was buried off to the side of the trail. Her long journey was at
an end, but ours had a long way yet to go."

Many of the journals and reminiscences record the constant crying
of children from hunger and cold. Some pilgrims lay down and gave up,
but then found the courage to go on. Susannah Stone, twenty-five at the
time, later remembered:

Only once did my courage fail. One cold dreary afternoon, my feet
having been frosted, I felt I could go no further, and withdrew from
the little company and sat down to wait the end, being somewhat
in a stupor. After a time I was aroused by a voice, which seemed as

audible as anything could be, and which spoke to my very soul of the promises and blessings I had received, and which should surely be fulfilled and that I had a mission to perform in Zion. I received strength and was filled with the spirit of the Lord and arose and traveled on with a light heart. As I reached camp I found a searching party ready to go back to find me dead or alive.

Yet the legacy of her ordeal would be that "My frosted feet gave me considerable trouble for many years."

Sometimes only brutal treatment kept the weakest Saints from giving up. Ann Rowley witnessed an instance involving her ten-year-old son: "I watched John, so cold, drowsy and sick, want to lie down in his tracks, never to rise again. I had to stand helplessly while Captain Willie whipped him, to make him go on. Gladly would I have taken the whipping myself."

On October 14, the Willie Company finally left the banks of the North Platte to follow its western tributary, the Sweetwater River, to its headwaters at South Pass. For a day or two, crossing a neck of land between the rivers, the party found only alkaline water to drink, which further weakened their constitutions. The Sweetwater itself was (as the name may indicate) eminently potable, but the stream meandered so broadly between low mountain ranges that the company would be forced to ford it nine times. (An old legend had it that the river was named by French voyageurs who lost a pack mule loaded with sugar crossing the river.)

In the midst of all this suffering, there were acts of uncommon heroism. Robert Reeder swore that James Hurren carried four hundred pounds of cargo on his handcart, and to aid in one ford of the Sweetwater, crossed the stream some twenty times, carrying the ill and weak on his back.

There also occurred what the Saints could only regard as miracles. The pious Ann Rowley recalled one such event many years later:

Night was coming and there was no food for the evening meal. I asked God's help as I always did. I got on my knees, remembering two hard sea biscuits that were still in my trunk. They had been left over from the sea voyage, they were not large, and were so hard, they couldn't be broken. Surely, that was not enough to feed 8 people, but 5 loaves and 2 fishes were not enough to feed 5000 people either, but through a miracle, Jesus had done it. So, with God's help, nothing is impossible. I found the biscuits and put them in a dutch oven and covered them with water and asked for God's blessing, then I put the lid on the pan and set it on the coals. When I took off the lid a little later, I found the pan filled with food. I kneeled with my family and thanked God for his goodness. That night my family had sufficient food.

By contrast, William Woodward's official journal records the deaths in deadpan notations:

Thursday [October] 9th . . . Samuel Gadd, from Orwell, Cambridgeshire, England died in the afternoon, aged 42 years. . . .

Monday 13th . . . Paul Jacobsen, from Lolland, Denmark, aged 55 died this evening. . . .

Wednesday 15th. Early this morning, Caroline Reeder, from Linstead, Suffolk, England, aged 17 years, died. . . .

Thursday 16th . . . George Curtis, from Norton, Gloucestershire, England, aged 64 years died; Lars Julius Larsen, who was born July 5th, 1856 in camp at Iowa City died. John Roberts from Bristol, Somersetshire, England, aged 42 years died. The camp rolled on, roads hilly & sandy.

It would remain for John Chislett, writing years later, to summon up most eloquently the full horror of those October days in Wyoming:

We had not travelled far up the Sweetwater before the nights, which had gradually been getting colder since we left Laramie, became very severe. The mountains before us, as we approached nearer to them, revealed themselves to view mantled nearly to their base in snow, and tokens of a coming storm were discernible in the clouds which each day seemed to lower around us. . . .

Our *seventeen pounds of clothing and bedding* was now altogether insufficient for our comfort. Nearly all suffered more or less at night from cold. Instead of getting up in the morning strong, refreshed, vigorous, and prepared for the hardships of another day of toil, the poor "Saints" were to be seen crawling out from their tents looking haggard, benumbed, and showing an utter lack of that vitality so necessary to our success. . . .

Death was not long confined in its ravages to the old and infirm, but the young and naturally strong were among its victims. . . . Weakness and debility were accompanied by dysentery. This we could not stop or even alleviate, no proper medicines being in the camp. . . . Many a father pulled his cart, with his little children on it, until the day preceding his death. I have seen some pull their carts in the morning, give out during the day, and die before next morning. . . .

Each death weakened our forces. In my hundred I could not raise enough men to pitch a tent when we encamped, and now it was that I had to exert myself to the utmost. I wonder I did not die, as many did who were stronger than I was. When we pitched our camp in the evening of each day, I had to lift the sick from the wagon and carry them to the fire, and in the morning carry them again on my back to the wagon. When any in my hundred died I had to inter them; often helping to dig the grave myself. . . .

We travelled on in misery and sorrow day after day.

On October 19, the Willie Company set out from its camp at the fifth crossing of the Sweetwater. Only a single day's worth of flour remained in the wagons. Suddenly, around noon, a violent snowstorm engulfed the party. The storm had come unseasonably early, but it was far from unprecedented for that part of Wyoming, as previous parties could attest.

The company could not afford to stop and pitch camp, for the next site furnishing both wood and water lay sixteen miles ahead. So the Saints trudged on into the teeth of the blizzard.

By the next morning, snow lay more than a foot deep on the ground. The October 19 storm, and the bad weather that continued thereafter, would infinitely deepen the already desperate predicament in which the Willie Company found itself.

IF ANYTHING, THE tribulations of the Martin Company in early October were even more severe than those undergone by the Willie Company. Although they had suffered no major loss of livestock, as the Willie party had in the stampede, the Martin Saints composed an even larger entourage (well more than five hundred men, women, and children), of whom an inordinate number were ill, infirm, or elderly.

On October 4, the company camped two miles west of Scottsbluff, about a hundred miles behind their brethren in the Willie party. One of the keenest observers of the Martin Saints was not even a member of the company. John Bond was a twelve-year-old English youth traveling in the Hodgetts wagon company with his parents and five siblings. Many years later he wrote a graphic account of his journey, titled "Handcarts West in '56." The narrative circulated for years in manuscript form, until it was privately published in 1945. That edition, however, was heavily expurgated. Fortunately, the original was preserved, and the full, unexpurgated text is now available in the LDS Archives.

On October 4, the Hodgetts Company, which had lagged behind since leaving Florence, caught up and camped with the Martin Company near Scottsbluff. Bond remembered his shock at seeing the "sunken eyes and emaciated forms" of the handcart Saints after their six weeks on the trail out of Florence. But he marveled at the compassion and care that dictated a practice that by this point had apparently become commonplace within the Martin Company, although few members of the party recorded it. In Bond's words, "In an exausted condition on arriving in camp [the handcart emigrants] miss the loved ones, though fatigued themselves they return back on the plains to find them on the road powerless to go on farther, put them on their carts, pull and tug with them until they arrive in camp near midnight."

Bond further noticed that "their shoes were worn out, their toes protruding from the shoes in a bleeding condition. In the same way some were compelled to stay on the way and pull sand burrs from their feet shedding many tears." And Bond was moved by the courage of mothers traveling with infants: "Alas! it was painful and sorr[ow]ful to see the mothers carry their babes on the way giving them the bosom in languid and tired steps with sorrowful hearts."

The chief reason Bond's manuscript was expurgated in the 1945 edition was that, unlike Levi Savage, Bond—in retrospect, at least—was ready to condemn the handcart scheme itself. As he awkwardly expressed his censure many years later, "Whatever was on the agents minds were in regards the council to the saints to cause the trials and sufferings and heart burnings of an innocent and God fearing saints following should have been more careful in giving them advice as those anxieties with self confidence has rendered untold hardships, broken hearts and so many deaths of loved ones."

The constant hunger felt by the Martin Saints was comparable to that among the Willie party. As John Jaques remembered in 1878, "You feel as if you could almost eat a rusty nail or gnaw a file." Vignettes evocative of that hunger range from the poignant to the terrible. Peter McBride, only six years old during the journey, recalled that a passing party of Gentiles stopped to talk to his family. "They gave my baby sister some cookies. She carried them in her little pocket, and I was always with her and would tease for a bite. She would give me a taste once in a while, and it was so good. No cake I ever tasted since was ever so good."

Josephine Hartley remembered a small but significant deed on Edward Martin's part: "The captain was very kind to mother and gave her some of the flour sacks to scrape off with a knife for what little flour was left along with the lint. With this, she was able to make cakes and mush to help sustain life."

The most harrowing testimony to hunger among the Martin Company comes from Sarah Crossley. Twelve years old at the time, she watched as her nineteen-year-old brother steadily weakened and succumbed to the cold.

His suffering was over one morning as we found him frozen in his bed. We were so numbed with our suffering and the sight of death that I think we were almost glad he had gone. We felt that he had gone only a little ahead of us, that we would soon be with him. I did pray though that the commissioner of provisions would not know of it until I had received Joseph's portion of flour. I cannot tell you the pang that smote my heart as he counted out the spoons full and when he came to Joseph's he said, "Oh Joseph died last night didn't he"? I had lost my brother's portion and it hurt me worse than it did to first look upon his still white face.

Historians and even anthropologists have noted the fact that in all the handcart parties, more men than women died. A chief reason for this is that, on the whole, the men performed the most grueling labors on the trek. One of the most taxing came each night, when guards kept watch over the camp—vigilant not only against Indians (whose attacks never materialized), but against wolves. Several Saints recorded the toll of guard duty: "The hardship on the men having to stand guard six hours every other night was beyond human endurance."

Fifteen-year-old Albert Jones later recalled how one of the strongest men in the party was reduced to a walking cripple:

A Brother Blair, one of the Royal Life Guards Blue of her majesty, the British queen, was with us, whose grand physique and gigantic frame was the admiration of us boys of the London branch, whenever he attended meeting in his regimentals. With the lack of proper nourishment, he dwindled down to a wreck, both mind and body; his wife, to keep him from giving up, willow in hand, drove him about camp to fetch wood or water, as she required it for camp use.

Margaret Clegg remembered the comparable collapse of her father, who

took sick and he had to ride in one of the wagons, that had provisions. One day he felt a little better and thought that he would try and walk, but he could not keep up as he had rheumatism so bad he could not walk, and he took hold of the rod at the end gate of the wagon to help him along and when the teamster saw him, he slashed his long whip around and struck father on the legs and he fell to the ground. He could not get up again.

According to Margaret, her father was thus abandoned by the company, but, following the wagon tracks, he "crawled on his knees all the way to their camp. He was so badly frozen when he got there, they did all they could for him."

If his own testimony is to be believed, Aaron Giles, the solitary lad from Poland, was indeed abandoned by the company. In a letter to Brigham Young that he wrote just two months later, Giles recounted that, while the company was still about a hundred miles short of Fort Laramie,

> I was so sick that I was oblidged to lay down for I could not walk no farther and thay would not let me ride in the Waggon so I was oblidged to stop so I was so sick that I fell asleep by the Road side. they travelled on and left me. and when I awake I found that I was alone, so I tried to get up and try to overtake them, but I could not move so I sat up to think what I should do, out in the open plain. no house no where to go to, and among woolves and among the Indians to be killed—some time in the afternoon I got very thirsty so I tried to go towards the Platte River which was about 1 Mile from the road an in about an hour I got there. when I got there I drank as much as I wanted and I went to walk to go farther, but I could not, so I sat down to think what I should do. so while I was thinking I fell asleep, and before I slept long I heard some trampling of horses so I awake. and saw a man on horse back and he was a Waggon Master of a Compeny of soldiers going to Laramie with the pay Master—and he asked me how I came there I told him I was left behind by the mormons and I was sick and could not go no farther; so he put me on his horse and had me up to the waggons and put me in one of the waggons.

In the end, Giles left the Martin Company and stayed on with the soldiers at Fort Laramie. Yet despite the harsh treatment by his fellow Saints, Giles apparently did not apostatize, for his letter closes with a wish to come on to Salt Lake with a wagon company at some future date.

The Martin Company, as noted, reduced its daily rations even before reaching Fort Laramie. Samuel Openshaw's diary places the first reduction, from a pound of flour per adult per day to twelve ounces, as early as October 3, though it may have been later. According to John Jaques, before October 19, "The pound of flour fell to three fourths of a pound, then to half a pound, and subsequently yet lower."

Elizabeth Sermon would later claim, "The food rations were reduced to ¼ lb. per adult and 2 oz. for the children—per day. Starvation to us but not so to the Captains. By our going around camp at night where cooking pots of some of the Captains could be seen, they looked pretty full and smelled quite savory. In fact, the Captains fed well while we drank *ours* in porridge for I could not make bread with the small allowance of flour." No other diary or reminiscence, however, corroborates this aspersion.

On October 8, the Martin Company reached Fort Laramie. Like the Willie Company before them, the Martin Saints found none of Franklin Richards's promised resupply provisions waiting for them. The company spent two days at the fort, trying to trade valuables for food. As Josiah Rogerson remembered,

> During the afternoon, while resting here, numbers, if not all that had any money left, went to the fort and purchased from the sutler there, some tea, coffee, sugar, Babbitt's saleratus and soda, black and cayenne pepper, crackers, bacon, etc., of which our supply that we had brought from Florence, Neb., had been getting short for the past week or two. Hints were made to us while here as to the early fall of snow, which we might look for in the next 120 to 150 miles.

Although Fort Laramie was a nonmilitary trading post, that autumn there were quite a few soldiers billeted there. Their presence is explained by John Bond: "Here the government stationed the troops to guard the overland road to California and the northwest territory." Presumably, the need to guard the trail arose from rumors of hostile Indian tribes in the area.

Added Bond, "Here rest two days to wash the clothing, shoe the animals and make other repairs and receive council to go to the westward." At the fort, several backouts elected to leave the company and winter

over with the traders and soldiers, many of whom encouraged the Saints
to do so. Though only fifteen at the time, Josiah Rogerson vividly remembered the appeal of that proposition half a century later: "The comfortable adobe quarters, and the snug and warm log rooms were quite
tempting for a winter's rest, with plenty to eat."

But the vast majority of the company chose to push onward on
October 10. For the first time, the Saints saw real mountains looming
ahead. "Laramie's Peak, in the distance," noted John Jaques, "gave the
first adequate idea of the Rocky Mountains—grand, gloomy and mys-
terious." John Bond took in the same view with a sense of foreboding:
"The wind is blowing hard and the snow is seen on the Larimie Peak in
the distance which gave every indication that a snow storm was near at
hand." At the moment, Laramie Peak rose almost fifty miles away to the
west, but at 10,240 feet, it towered a full vertical mile above the banks of
the Platte. Bond further observed, "The wolves are following the trains
making their monotonous howlings in all directions a hideous sound
to the ears."

It was during these days that the daily rations were successively reduced. On October 17, the company reached Deer Creek. This was the
site where the McArthur Company had rendezvoused with the flour-
laden resupply wagons, which had covered no fewer than 410 miles from
Salt Lake. Here, five weeks later, Captain Martin and his co-leaders made
a momentous decision.

Even with reduced rations, Martin deemed that the handcarts were
moving too slowly. The solution was a radical one. As John Jaques remembered twenty-two years later, "Owing to the growing weakness of
emigrants and teams, the baggage, including bedding and cooking utensils, was reduced to ten pounds per head, children under 8 years five
pounds. Good blankets and other bedding and clothing were burned,
as they could not be carried further, though needed more than ever, for
there was yet 400 miles of winter to go through."

Half a century later, Josiah Rogerson could still see the casting off of
baggage as a reasonable stratagem: "The wisdom of this timely counsel was soon afterward realized. When many of the canvas bags were
opened it was readily seen that the heads of many families were hauling

and pulling luggage in the shape of books, trinkets and half worn-out clothing that could be dispensed with beneficially."

Yet others were appalled. In his journal, William Binder wrote, "This action of the Elders in charge seemed to us a terrible hardship, as we were only very scantily provided with clothes and bedding, and to stand by and see our bits of clothing and bedding burned on the spot caused anything but a good feeling to exist in our hearts towards our leaders."

The obvious question presents itself: why burn the baggage, rather than cache it, in case the Martin Saints changed their minds, perhaps in a return to Fort Laramie, so that as the season grew colder, they might retrieve the precious clothes and bedding? The reminiscence of one Saint seems to give the answer. "A council was called," wrote John Watkins, "at which they all decided, under the circumstances, to lighten the loads to a few pounds each, which was w[e]ighed out to them with a pair of scales, leaving out quilts and blankets, overcoats, cooking utensils and everything that could be dispensed with which were put in a heap and set fire to for fear some one would be tempted to pick out something that they needed so badly." On a much smaller scale, then, Captain Martin's order to burn the discarded baggage was like Cortés's burning his ships on the Mexican coast in 1519, so that his conquistadors could not succumb to the temptation to return to Cuba.

Two days later, on October 19, the bedraggled Martin Company came to its last crossing of the Platte, after which the Saints would cut the corner to the Sweetwater and try to follow it to South Pass. The timing could not have been worse, as the first snowstorm struck while the emigrants were fording the difficult river—the same snowstorm that engulfed the Willie Party between the fifth and sixth crossings of the Sweetwater, some hundred miles farther west.

A bitter irony is attached to that fording of the Platte. Five miles east of where the Saints waded into the water, a bridge built by a French voyageur spanned the river. As with all such bridges in the West, its owner charged a toll, which the Martin Saints were simply too poor to afford.

Given the conditions, the ford quickly turned desperate—as was so vividly recalled many years later by Patience Loader, in the passages from

her memoir quoted at the end of Chapter One. Other Saints who made
the crossing also left eloquent accounts of that misadventure. Wrote
John Jaques in 1878:

> The river was wide, the current strong, the water exceedingly cold
> and up to the wagon beds in the deepest parts, and the bed of
> the river was covered with cobble stones. Some of the men car-
> ried some of the women over on their backs or in their arms, but
> others of the women tied up their skirts and waded through, like
> heroines as they were, and as they had done through many other
> rivers and creeks. The company was barely over when snow, hail,
> and sleet began to fall, accompanied by a piercing north wind,
> and camp was made on this side of the river.

Thomas Durham wrote in his journal,

> We had a very heavy hail storm that day and the river was very
> high and the water very cold. It was all I could do to stand it.
> My woman and her sister Eliza crossed it sticking hands or they
> could not have stood up in it at all. All the sick that could walk at
> all had to get out of the wagons and walk through the river, some
> of them falling down in the river several times, not being able to
> stand up in it being so weak.

In this crisis, heroes emerged. Twelve-year-old John Bond, traveling
in the Hodgetts wagon company, which made the ford at the same time
as the Martin handcarts, remembered their names many years later:

> The captain repeated, "Have faith in God and you will not take
> cold," while he sat on his mule and saw those innocent ones, who
> had pleaded so, fall in the river as the current was carrying the
> weak ones off of their feet, but with the stronger and manly aid
> and courage of John Laty, T.J. Franklin, John Toon, Geo. Hains,
> Geo. Dove Sr, and others the helpless and weakened ones were
> taken to the opposite bank of the river and were given all the care
> they could when brought from the icy cold water. Those noble

heroes went backward and forward several times carrying them on their backs, the weaker ones, which is worthy of commendation for their kindheartedness and worthy to be handed down to future generations.

The snowstorm was no passing squall. With their clothes soaked and no way to get dry, with what we now call hypothermia menacing every Saint in the party, the Martin Company staggered on a single mile and camped near midnight. On October 20 it snowed continuously, as the Saints covered only five miles before camping again. By sunset, twelve inches of snow lay on the ground.

Inevitably, death now started to take a grim toll among the underfed, ill-clothed, and exhausted emigrants. Heber McBride, thirteen years old at the time, wrote more than a decade later about seeing his father die. The day after the last crossing of the Platte, "Father was very bad this morning could hardly sit up in the tent we had to travel that day through the snow I managed to get Father in to one of the wagons that morning and that was the last we ever saw of him alive." The next day,

> we went to try and find father but the wind was blowing the snow so bad that we could not see anything and the wagons had not got into camp and it was then after dark so we did not find him that night and the next morning the snow was about 18 inches deep and awful cold but while my sister was preparing our little bite of breakfast I went to look for Father and at last I found him under a wagon with snow all over him and he was stiff and dead. I felt as though my heart would burst I sat down beside him on the snow and took hold of one of his hands and cried oh Father Father.

Perhaps the most poignant, and certainly the most macabre, of the deaths that night befell thirty-one-year-old Aaron Jackson. Years later, his wife recounted Jackson's passing in wrenching detail:

> My husband had for several days previous been much worse. He was still sinking, and his condition became more serious. As soon as possible, after reaching camp, I prepared a little of such scant

articles of food as we then had. He tried to eat, but failed. He had not the strength to swallow. I put him to bed as quickly as I could. He seemed to rest easy and fell asleep. About 9 o'clock, I retired. Bedding had become very scarce, so I did not disrobe. I slept until, as it appeared to me, about midnight. It was extremely cold. The weather was bitter. I listened to hear if my husband breathed—he lay so still. I could not hear him. I became alarmed. I put my hand on his body, when to my horror I discovered that my worst fears were confirmed. My husband was dead. He was cold and stiff—rigid in the arms of death. It was a bitter freezing night and the elements had sealed up his mortal frame. I called for help to the other inmates of the tent. They could render me no aid; and there was no alternative but to remain alone by the side of the corpse till morning.

The night was enveloped in almost Egyptian darkness. There was nothing with which to produce a light or kindle a fire. Of course I could not sleep. I could only watch, wait and pray for the dawn. But oh, how those dreary hours drew their tedious length along. When daylight came, some of the male part of the company prepared the body for burial. And oh, such burial and funeral service. They did not remove his clothing—he had but little. They wrapped him in a blanket and placed him in a pile with thirteen others who had died, and then covered him up in the snow. The ground was frozen so hard that they could not dig a grave.

Other Saints confirmed that fourteen members of the Martin Company died during that single, terrible night.

At this point, the company ground to a halt. For days, they did not stir out of their wretched camp beneath the Red Buttes, a small outcropping of ruddy sandstone that loomed to the south. Effectively snowbound, the Martin Saints were too cold and hungry and worn out to travel onward. All they could do was hope for a spell of Indian summer to thaw the landscape and give them the motivation to strike the trail once more—or hope beyond hope that someone was coming from the west to rescue them.

But in the next week, no rescuers appeared, and the weather did not relent. As John Jaques pithily put it twenty-two years later, "Winter came on all at once."

MOST OF THE volunteers who joined the rescue mission out of Salt Lake City were young men serving in local Mormon militias: each town had such a corps of standing troops. Others, however, were ordinary citizens. Large though the force eventually became that set out eastward along the Mormon Trail to render aid to the handcart emigrants, the mission remains poorly documented in terms of primary sources. For the most part, the rescuers must have felt too pressed by the urgency of the moment to keep diaries.

Two of the men who would emerge as heroes of the rescue, however, later left colorful memoirs of that campaign. A comparison of the two reveals the very different ways in which rescuers were recruited. Ephraim Hanks was a footloose frontiersman who had sometimes served as a Mormon scout. In early October 1856, he was at Utah Lake, thirty miles south of Salt Lake, fulfilling a commercial fishing contract for the city's markets. According to his retrospective account, he had heard rumors about the handcarters on the plains, which troubled his sleep. One night, as he tossed and turned in his bed, he heard a disembodied voice call out his name three times. The third time, he answered, "Yes, yes. Is there something I can do for you?"

The voice intoned, "That handcart company is in trouble. Will you help them out?"

Hanks leapt from his bed. At dawn, as he entered Salt Lake City, he was intercepted by a messenger from Brigham Young requesting the very service he had divined in his dream. Shortly thereafter, the Prophet blessed Hanks by laying hands on his head, then sent him on his way.

The process by which Daniel W. Jones signed on was somewhat less inspired. A veteran mountain man and Indian fighter who had converted to the LDS church, Jones came to Salt Lake in early October to attend the General Conference. There, he heard Young announce the emergency and call for volunteers. Jones, however, did not immediately raise his hand. In his own telling, as he drifted out of the conference,

"Brother Wells spoke to me saying: 'You are a good hand for the trip; get ready.' Soon after Bishop Hunter said the same thing to me. Also Brother Grant met me and said: 'I want you on this trip.' I began to think it time to decide, so I answered, 'all right.'"

The first team to move out of Salt Lake City on October 7, under the command of George Grant, was composed of twenty-seven men and sixteen wagons. Among the six returning missionaries who were willing, after their high-speed journey to Zion, to turn around at once and head back into an early winter, Grant and William Kimball may have been motivated by something like guilt for their blithe assertions as they had passed the handcart pioneers on the plains that the latter would have no trouble completing their journey.

Yet those six missionaries also included Chauncey Webb, the master handcart craftsman. After joining the Martin Company, with whom he traveled from Iowa City to Florence, where he had been the sole voice pleading against continuing the journey, Webb had jumped into Franklin Richards's light-wagon caravan to complete the passage. It is curious, and perhaps telling, that Richards himself declined to set out back along the trail, for he more than any other church official had been responsible for urging both the Willie and Martin Saints to push on from Florence.

Even in Salt Lake City, Richards consistently underestimated the seriousness of the crisis. After uttering his soon-to-be infamous phrase in the bowery predicting that the handcart pioneers would suffer nothing worse than "cold fingers and toes," Richards advised Grant that his advance team of rescuers ought to run into the Willie Company somewhere near the Green River crossing, well to the southwest of South Pass.

Traveling fast, Grant's entourage reached Fort Bridger (two days' travel west of the Green River) on October 12. There they heard no news of the handcart companies, not even a rumor. Even more ominously, that same day the rescue party crossed paths with Abraham Smoot's freight train of wagons. Worn out themselves, Smoot's team had no news of either the Willie or the Martin Companies.

Alarmed, Grant immediately dispatched four men to speed ahead with fast horses and a single light wagon laden with a minimal cargo of flour, as a scouting party to determine the whereabouts of the missing handcart parties. Meanwhile the main caravan pushed on, averaging almost twenty miles a day. On October 15, the team reached the Green River. Still no sign or news of the Willie Company. Wrote Daniel Jones later:

> We began to feel great anxiety about the emigrants as the weather was now cold and stormy, and we, strong men with good outfits, found the nights severe. What must be the condition of those we were to meet? Many old men and women, little children, mothers with nursing babes, crossing the plains pulling hand-carts. Our hearts began to ache when we reached Green river and yet no word of them.

Although there was no way to know it, as the express team of four— Joseph Young (the Prophet's oldest son), Cyrus Wheelock, Stephen Taylor, and Abel Garr—moved out ahead of Grant's rescue team, the Willie Company was a full 160 miles to the east, struggling up the Sweetwater River in the vicinity of Independence Rock. Grant's team pushed on through intermittently stormy weather, reaching South Pass on October 17. Daniel Jones later remembered that a severe snowstorm hit the party head-on on the pass. But Robert Burton, one of the few men in Grant's party to keep a diary, noted:

> Friday, Oct. 17. Started late; camped on Little Sandy. Feed scarce; looked like a storm.

> Saturday, Oct. 18. Clear and fair, storm passed to the right and left us. Camped tonight on the head of Sweet Water. Good feed and wood. Looked like a storm.

Burton's is almost surely the more accurate record, indicating that Grant's team passed over South Pass without being struck by a storm. But in any event, by the 18th, Grant had adopted a curious strategy, which was to drop off splinter groups from his rescue team to set up stations along the trail and wait for the handcart emigrants to come to them. Subsequent wagon teams in the wake of Grant's advance guard were likewise counseled to stop and set up stationary resupply depots.

With all the advantages of hindsight, historians Rebecca Bartholomew and Leonard Arrington second-guess Grant's decision: "Had anyone in the relief party foreseen the condition of either of the handcart companies, they would have gathered all the stores and teams at Fort Bridger, Green River, and South Pass and traveled day and night until their animals broke. It was just as well they did not know, for the relief effort would already require more strength and supplies than they carried."

Yet how could they not know? Already, on finding no sign of the handcart parties at Green River, the rescuers' "hearts began to ache" as they contemplated the emigrants' plight. Was the dropping off of sub-parties to set up stationary depots a kind of laziness on the rescuers' part? Even worse, did it represent a certain failure of commitment, akin to that of the earlier resupply teams Franklin Richards's party had met along the trail? Grant's team crossed paths with these fainthearted returnees on October 13 as they headed back to Salt Lake because, in Robert Burton's dry diary entry, they "got tired of waiting."

Meanwhile, the condition of the Willie Company had begun to slide from the merely desperate to the almost hopeless. Deaths occurred daily. The details of many of them have escaped the historical record, but here and there, a vignette of piercing sorrow emerges, as in the recollection of Sarah James, eighteen at the time. On the morning of October 18, as the company broke camp, Sarah noted, "As usual there were dead to be buried before we could go on." Her father and her fourteen-year-old brother, Reuben, lingered to help with the interment detail.

> After a short services we with light cart went ahead to catch the rest of the company and mother and Rueben started to follow. Father collapsed and fell in the snow. He tried two or three times to get up with mother's help then finaly he asked her to go on and when he felt rested he would come on with Ruben. Mother knew in her heart that he had given out but perhaps she said in a few minutes with some rest he could come on she took the cart and hurried to follow us.

But by that evening, there was no sign of Sarah's father or brother.

> When we stopped for the night we made inquiries about our people but nothing had been heard of them. Since there were

some who had been a few hours behind us we felt that they would come with the next group. All night we waited for word. Toward morning some of the captains who had gone out to gather up the stragglers came into camp bearing the dead body of my father and the badly frozen body of my brother Rueben. His injuries were so bad that he would suffer from them for the rest of his life. When morning came Father's body along with others who had died during the night were buried in a deep hole. Brush was thrown in and then dirt. A fire was built over the grave to kill the scent to keep the wolves from digging up the remains.

On October 19, as the Willie Company forced its passage across the sixteen miles between the fifth and sixth crossings of the Sweetwater, the violent snowstorm struck almost without warning. The party had reached a marshy lowland known as the "Ice Slough" or "Ice Spring," an anomalous tundralike meander where thick grasses kept the winter's ice beneath frozen well into each following summer. Oregon Trail pioneers had come to count on the Ice Slough as a source of clear, cold water even in July or August.

In the midst of the storm, as Sarah James remembered, "Suddenly we heard a shout." Mormons have always been partial to premonitory dreams, but twenty years later, George Cunningham, fifteen years old during the trek, would swear that the previous night

I dreamed a dream. That morning had come, the storm had sub-sided some and that we had started out on the road. I thought that I saw two men coming toward us on horseback. They were riding very swiftly and soon came up to us. They said that they had volunteered to come to our rescue and that they would go on further east to meet a company which was still behind us and that on the morrow, we could meet a number of wagons loaded with provisions for us. They were dressed in blue soldier overcoats and had Spanish saddles on their horses. I examined them, particu-larly the saddles as they were new to me. I also could discern every expression of their countenance. They seemed to rejoice and be exceedingly glad that they had come to our relief and saved us.

Indeed, in the midst of the October 19 snowstorm, the express rescue train of Young, Wheelock, Taylor, and Garr rode into view. Various Saints recorded their reactions. The Dane Michael Jensen, only eleven at the time, recalled, "How we laughed and cried, sang and praised the Lord!" And John Chislett averred, "More welcome messengers never came from the courts of glory." According to some, the rescuers were equally moved. Euphemia Bain remembered that Cyrus Wheelock was the first rescuer to close ranks with the company: "He stood by and said how he never expected to see brethren and sisters in such a condition as we were. Tears ran down his cheeks as he spoke to us and encouraged us, saying help would reach us in two hours, and we should have plenty to eat."

In the official journal, William Woodward reported the rendezvous in less emotional terms:

> The company rolled on again, & were soon met by Cyrus H. Wheelock & Joseph A. Young & two other brethren from the Valley, bringing us the information that supplies were near at hand, the camp halted, a meeting was called. Bro. Wheelock informed us of the liberality of the Saints in the Valley, of Bro. Brigham Young's kindheartedness in speaking in behalf of the Handcart companies now on the Plains, & of himself fitting up ten teams & wagons & supplying them with flour, &c., & others in proportion.

For all the joy the meeting brought, however, it did not pose an immediate solution to the company's plight. Within hours, the express train moved on eastward in search of the Martin Company, which, the four scouts now realized, must be in an even more perilous predicament than the Willie party. According to Chislett, "As they went from our view, many a hearty 'God bless you' followed them." No Saint's diary or reminiscence records receiving even a scrap of food from the express train.

Euphemia Bain's memory of promised relief within two hours is undoubtedly wrong. Chislett recorded, "They informed us that a train of supplies was on the way, and that we might expect to meet it in a day or two."

That night, buoyed by wild hopes, the Willie Company camped on the banks of the Sweetwater at the sixth crossing. The last stragglers did not come in until 10:00 P.M. But hope was no antidote to utter debilitation: that day and night and following morning, five more Saints died. The official journal dutifully recorded, "During the day Eliza Smith, from Eldersfield, Worcestershire, England, aged 40 years died; also John Kockles, from Norwich, Norfolk, England, died; also, Daniel Osborn, from Norwich, Norfolk, England, died; also Rasmus Hansen, from Falster, Denmark, died. . . . Monday 20th This morning. . . . Anna F. Tait from Glasgow, Scotland, aged 31 years died." Chislett elaborated on that stormy bivouac:

> We finally, late at night, got all to camp—the wind howling frightfully and the snow eddying around us in fitful gusts. But we had found a good camp among the willows, and after warming and partially drying ourselves before good fires, we ate our scanty fare, paid our usual devotions to the Deity and retired to rest with hopes of coming aid.

In the morning, new snow lay heavy on the ground: Chislett says a foot deep, Woodward's journal only four inches. The last ration of flour had been issued the day before. Captain Willie now distributed what was left of the "hard bread" (soda crackers) he had bought at Fort Laramie, but that paltry breakfast did nothing to allay the emigrants' hunger.

On October 20, for the first time during the whole journey, the Willie Company found itself unable to move forward. Wrote Chislett, "Being surrounded by snow a foot deep, out of provisions, many of our people sick, and our cattle dying, it was decided that we should remain in our present camp until the supply train reached us." It was also decided, however, that Captain Willie and one of the strongest Saints, Joseph Elder, should set out westward on horseback to try to find the rescue wagons. It would turn out to be a providential mission.

What no one could know at the time was that George Grant's rescue team had stalled in the same storm. On October 19, the remaining men and wagons had turned into a brushy stand and set up their own camp on Willow Creek, twenty-five miles west of the sixth crossing where the

Willie Company was marooned. Robert Burton's noncommittal journal notes only:

> Sunday, Oct. 19. Killed one beef. Started in the afternoon in p.m.; camped below the mouth of Willow Creek. Tonight commenced storming; very cold; good feed.

> Monday, Oct. 20. Stayed in the same place today.

In their camp at the sixth crossing, instead of waiting two hours, or even a day or two, for the blessed rescue, the Willie Company spent three days without relief. The journals and reminiscences from this vigil spell out the erosion of hope. Ann Rowley, the widowed matriarch, swore that for forty-eight straight hours during those three days, the Saints ate nothing. Levi Savage's journal entry for October 20 is a quiet testament of despair:

> This morning when we arose we found Several inches of Snow on the ground; and is yet Snowing. The cattle, and people, are so much reduced with Short food and hard work. That except we get assistance, we Surely, can not move far in this Snow.
>
> Brothers Willey and Capt, and Elder, Started on horseback, about 10 oclock. To cerch for the wagons. Wagons that Whee-lock reported, a Short distance in our advance. This morning we isued the last bread, or breadstuffs in our possession. It continued Snowing Severely during the day. We expected Bro Willey would return this evening, but he has not come.

Twelve-year-old John Oborn later remembered October 20 simply as "the most terrible experience of my life."

SETTING OUT ON horseback on the morning of October 20 to try to intercept the rescuers, Captain Willie and Joseph Elder expected to find the flour-laden wagons within a few hours and a few miles. But after covering twelve miles and finding no sign of the party under the leadership of George Grant, the two scouts grew deeply alarmed. Ahead

Joseph Smith, founder and first Prophet of the Church of Jesus Christ of Latter-day Saints.
(COURTESY OF THE LDS CHURCH HISTORY LIBRARY)

Brigham Young, the second Prophet of the church and the man who led the Mormon emigration to what is now Utah. Young was also the architect of the handcart plan of 1856.
(COURTESY OF THE LDS CHURCH HISTORY LIBRARY)

Franklin D. Richards, president of the European mission in England, superintended the departure of thousands of handcart Saints from Liverpool in 1856. That summer, traveling in fast carriages with other returning missionaries, he passed the Willie and Martin Companies on the plains and urged them on. (COURTESY OF THE LDS CHURCH HISTORY LIBRARY)

James G. Willie, leader of the fourth handcart company. (COURTESY OF THE LDS CHURCH HISTORY LIBRARY)

Edward Martin, leader of the fifth and last handcart company of 1856, the one that suffered the greatest number of casualties. (COURTESY OF THE LDS CHURCH HISTORY LIBRARY)

As they traversed Iowa, the handcart Saints were sometimes cheered, sometimes taunted by the settlers of the villages they passed through. (COURTESY OF THE LDS CHURCH HISTORY LIBRARY)

Patience Loader, whose memoir of the trek is the most vivid account written by any of the handcart Saints, and her brother Robert, later in life. (SPECIAL COLLECTIONS, GERALD R. SHERRATT LIBRARY, SOUTHERN UTAH UNIVERSITY)

A William Henry Jackson painting, faithful to the last detail, of one of the handcart companies passing Devil's Gate. (SPECIAL COLLECTIONS, GERALD R. SHERRATT LIBRARY, SOUTHERN UTAH UNIVERSITY)

Captain George D. Grant, who led the rescue expedition that set out from Salt Lake City in October to try to find and save the Willie and Martin Companies. (COURTESY OF THE LDS CHURCH HISTORY LIBRARY)

Nellie Pucell Unthank, a nine-year-old Saint in the Martin Company, lost her lower legs to frostbite but lived to the age of sixty-nine. According to a friend, "She never knew a moment of freedom from pain." (SPECIAL COLLECTIONS, GERALD R. SHERRATT LIBRARY, SOUTHERN UTAH UNIVERSITY)

A replica of *The Handcart Pioneer,* the famous sculpture cast in 1926 by Torleif S. Knaphus. (COURTESY OF THE LDS CHURCH HISTORY LIBRARY)

One of the last surviving authentic handcarts, from a slightly later expedition, conserved in the Museum of Church History and Art in Salt Lake City.

A modern replica of an 1856 handcart.

Devil's Gate, the 300-foot-high notch carved through a granite ridge by the Sweetwater River in western Wyoming. Near here the Martin Company suffered its most desperate days.

Members of the West Valley, Utah, stake, in period garb, pulling a replica handcart at the Mormon Handcart Visitors' Center.

In Martin's Cove, where their ancestors came to grief, members of the West Valley stake pay homage to their memory.

A simple concrete marker indicates the Mormon Trail as it crosses Rocky Ridge, the hardest pull along the whole 1,300-mile gauntlet from Iowa City to Salt Lake City.

In many places in Wyoming, the old ruts of the
Mormon Trail are still visible.

The Sweetwater River in winter, looking much as it did when the Willie and
Martin Companies crossed it in October 1856.

of them loomed Rocky Ridge, a barren, five-mile-long series of hills that rises more than six hundred feet to an altitude of 7,300 feet, one of the highest eminences on the whole Mormon Trail. The climb of Rocky Ridge had become part of the standard itinerary, a northern detour to avoid a stretch where the Sweetwater carves a narrow and all but impassable gorge.

The scouts felt they had no choice but to tackle this daunting obstacle. Wrote Elder later, "The snow and an awful cold wind blew in our faces all day." On the far side of the summit, the two men on horseback descended to the banks of the Sweetwater, but still found no sign of their potential rescuers. Elder swore that he and Willie rode twenty-seven miles during that single day. But just as they were beginning to give up hope, a providential piece of luck—or, rather, a canny deed of logistical forethought—saved their mission. Willie and Elder stumbled upon a makeshift signboard on the trail.

On the evening of October 19, Grant's party had veered off the trail to camp in a clump of bushes on Willow Creek, a small northern tributary of the Sweetwater, where they found shelter. In that camp, Grant's team remained throughout the 20th, waiting out the storm. But it occurred to one rescuer, twenty-year-old Harvey Cluff, that the willow-shrouded camp could not be seen from the trail. Anticipating the return of the express team—Young, Wheelock, Taylor, and Garr—Cluff realized that they might ride past Willow Creek without knowing the main party was camped nearby, in which case the four men might continue westward, missing Grant's team altogether. Sometime during the 20th, then, Cluff erected his signboard, which directed passersby to the hidden camp.

Willie and Elder found the signboard and veered up Willow Creek to Grant's camp. The meeting was joyous. "When they saw us," wrote Elder, "they raised a shout and ran out to meet us. . . . They could scarcely give us time to tell our story, they were so anxious to hear all about us." Church historian Andrew Olsen takes the measure of Cluff's vital act:

His sign was the means of salvation not only for James Willie and Joseph Elder but perhaps also for the Willie company. Had James Willie and Joseph Elder bypassed the camp, the rescuers might have stayed there another two or three days while awaiting better weather.... [T]he Willie company would have been three or four days without a particle of food.

Meanwhile, back at the sixth crossing camp, the Willie Saints sank into despair, for they, too, had anticipated an early connection with the rescue team that the four scouts had told them was not far to the west. John Chislett, who had been put in charge of the company's virtually empty commissary, later conjured up the woeful scene:

> The scanty allowance of hard bread and poor beef . . . was mostly consumed the first day by the hungry, ravenous, famished souls. . . .
>
> During that time I visited the sick, the widows whose husbands died in serving them, and the aged who could not help themselves, to know for myself where to dispense the few articles that had been placed in my charge for distribution. Such craving hunger I never saw before, and may God in his mercy spare me the sight again.
>
> As I was seen giving these things to the most needy, crowds of famished men and women surrounded me and begged for bread! Men whom I had known all the way from Liverpool, who had been true as steel in every stage of our journey, who in their homes in England and Scotland had never known want; men who by honest labour had sustained themselves and their families, and saved enough to cross the Atlantic and traverse the United States, whose hearts were cast in too great a mould to descend to a mean act or brook dishonour; such men as these came to me and begged bread. I felt humbled to the dust for my race and nation.

Chislett records the momentous return of Willie and Elder with Grant's rescue train:

> On the evening of the third day after Captain Willie's departure, just as the sun was sinking beautifully behind the distant hills,

on an eminence immediately west of our camp several covered wagons, each drawn by four horses, were seen coming towards us. The news ran through the camp like wildfire, and all who were able to leave their beds turned out *en masse* to see them. ... Shouts of joy rent the air; strong men wept till tears ran freely down their furrowed and sun-burnt cheeks, and little children partook of the joy which some of them hardly understood, and fairly danced around with gladness.

The myth that has come down to present-day Mormons who are aware only of the general outlines of the handcart story is that the rescuers saved the Willie party. Even historians succumb to this simplifying temptation, as, for instance, do LeRoy and Ann Hafen in *Handcarts to Zion*, titling a section of the relevant chapter "Willie's Company Carried to Safety."

To be sure, the rescuers made a monumental difference. Without their help, it is possible that nearly all the members of the Willie Company might have died. Yet the inescapably tragic fact is that for many, the rescue came too late. More Saints in both the Willie and Martin Companies died after the rescuers reached them than during all the previous weeks of their trek from Iowa City to western Wyoming.

Daniel Jones, the former mountain man in the rescue party, recognized this fact the moment he rode into the Willie Company camp at the sixth crossing:

On arriving we found them in a condition that would stir the feelings of the hardest heart. They were in a poor place, the storm having caught them where fuel was scarce. They were out of provisions and really freezing and starving to death. The morning after our arrival nine were buried in one grave. We did all we could to relieve them. The boys struck out on horseback and dragged up a lot of wood; provisions were distributed and all went to work to cheer the sufferers. Soon there was an improvement in camp, but many poor, faithful people had gone too far—had passed beyond the power to recruit. Our help came too late for some and many died after our arrival.

Only now did Grant's rescue team learn that the Martin Company—larger in numbers than the Willie party, and no doubt in an even more desperate situation—lagged far behind the emigrants whom the team had found so wretchedly camped at the sixth crossing. Captain Willie could tell Grant nothing about the whereabouts or condition of the Martin Company, for Willie and Martin Saints had last overlapped during a single week in July, in Iowa City. All that Willie could say was that Martin's party must be straggling along somewhere to the east of the sixth crossing. And somewhere out there to the east must be the Hunt and Hodgetts wagon teams, as well. (In fact, at the moment, stranded in snow under Red Buttes, the Martin Saints were camped almost exactly a hundred miles to the east.)

Grant now performed a kind of triage: he left six wagons for the Willie Company, whom he put under the charge of William Kimball, to try to rally the ill and exhausted and carry them forward to Zion. With the bulk of his team, he forged on eastward along the trail to look for the Martin Company. Grant knew that in his wake, other teams out of Salt Lake must be coming, potential reinforcements to help pull the Willie Company to its ultimate destination.

Kimball, of course, was the official who had bragged in Florence about eating all the snow that should fall on the handcarters' path between there and Utah. He was despised by some within the Willie Company. In John Ahmanson's private memoir, not published in English until 1984, he sardonically referred to Kimball as "the snow prophet."

The first few days of that forced march under Kimball's leadership would prove to be the Willie Company's calvary. In his journal, Levi Savage glumly recorded,

We traveled about 10 miles and camped at the foot of what is called the Rocky Ridge. I had charge of the teams; because of their reduced Strength, and heavy loads,—a large number of Sick, and Children were in the Wagons—I did not arive in camp until late at night. The wind blew bleek and colde, and fire wood very scarse. The Saints were obliged to Spread their light beding on the Snow, and in this colde State, endeavored to obtain a litle rest. Sister Philpot died about 10 oclock P.M. leaving two Father-less girls, also Several others died during the night.

If the haul to the base of Rocky Ridge was bad enough, the ascent of that naked series of swales on October 23 would try the party to its very limits. Savage, again, in his longest journal entry in more than a month:

This was a Severe day. The wind blew awful hard, and colde. The ascent was some five miles long, and Some places, Steep and covered with deep Snow. We became we[a]ry, Set down to rest, and Some become chilled, and commenced to frieze, Brothers Atwood; Woodard; and myself; remained with the teams, they being porfer loaded down with the Sick, and children. So thickly Stoed, I was fearful, some would Smuther. About 10 or 11 oclock in the night, we came to a creek that, we did not like to attempt to cross without help, the [creek] being ful of ice and freezing colde. Leaving Bros Atwood; and Wooderd with the teams, I started to the camp for help; I met Bro Willey coming to look for us, he turned for the camp as he could do no good a loan. I passed Several on the road, and arived in camp after about four miles travel. I arived in Camp; but few tents were pitched, and men, women, and Children Sit shivering with colde around their Small fires. Some time alapsed when two teams Started to bring up the rear; Just before daylight they returned, bringing all with them, Some badly frozen; Some dying, and Some dead. It was certainly heartrending to hear Children crying for mothers, and mothers, crying for Childrin. By the time I got them, as Com-fortably Situated as circumstances could admit. (which was not very comfortable) day was dawning. I had not Shut my eyes for sleep, nor lain down. I was nearly exhosted with fatigue, and want of rest.

Two days later, Savage would find himself too worn out to continue keeping the diary he had written faithfully since the start of the trek. Its last entry, dated October 25 but written after the journey, sums up the final two weeks of the ordeal in the pithy formula, "Nothing of much note transpired excepte the people ded daily."

Other Saints vividly remembered Rocky Ridge for the rest of their lives. Michael Jensen, only eleven at the time, later recalled,

> My father was very weak from lack of food and so the men in charge of the wagons fastened our handcart to one of the wagons and told father to hang onto the wagon. He was walking between our handcart and the wagon when he slipped and fell, and before anyone could reach him, the handcart had passed over him as he lay on the ground. They picked him up and put him into the wagon and we went on until dark and then camped for the night. Sometime during that night my father died and next morning they buried him beside the road.

As usual, John Chislett had the most comprehensive view of that terrible traverse:

> The day we crossed Rocky Ridge it was snowing a little—the wind hard from the north-west—and blowing so keenly that it almost pierced us through. We had to wrap ourselves closely in blankets, quilts, or whatever else we could get, to keep from freezing. . . . The ascent of the ridge commenced soon after leaving camp, and I had not gone far up it before I overtook a cart that the folks could not pull through the snow, here about knee-deep. I helped them along, and we soon overtook another. By all hands getting to one cart we could travel, so we moved one of the carts a few rods, and then went back and brought up the other.

Through a superhuman effort, Chislett rallied perhaps a dozen Saints who would have otherwise given up and died, helping pull their carts and even supporting them bodily until they reached the summit. From there, he remembered, the carts "trotted on gaily down hill." Chislett's entourage caught up with the ox-drawn wagons, "all so laden with the sick and helpless that they moved very slowly."

On the far side of Rocky Ridge, however, the emigrants ran into a stream that was newly frozen over. The oxen could not be forced across it: "No amount of shouting and whipping could induce them to stir an inch." By now, despite Kimball and Willie's leadership, the company was stretched out across miles of terrain, and it was growing dark. Trying to rally the stragglers, Chislett finally went ahead to locate the camp. He reached it only at 11:00 P.M., where he roused other strong-bodied Saints to go back and gather up the weakest pioneers. "It was 5 A.M.," remembered Chislett, "before the last team reached camp."

Trail historians argue to this day about the location of this camp. Most place it on Rock Creek, but others believe the company reached Willow Creek, a little more than two miles farther west, and reoccupied the site where Grant's party had stalled on October 19. In any event, whatever its true location, that camp would witness the single most devastating episode in the Willie Company's long ordeal.

William Woodward, in the official journal entry for October 24, summed up the toll that crossing Rocky Ridge had taken in his usual laconic register-book fashion:

It was concluded to stay in camp today & bury the dead as there were 13 persons to inter. William James, from Pershore, Worcestershire, England, aged 46 died; Elizabeth Bailey, from Leigh, Worcestrshire, England, aged 52 died; James Kirkwood from Glasgow, Scotland, aged 11 died Samuel Gadd, from Orwell, Cambridgeshire, England, aged 10 died; Lars Wendin, from Copenhagen, Denmark, aged 60 died; Anne Olsen, from Seeland, Denmark, aged 46 died; Ella Nilson, from Jutland, Denmark, aged 22 years, died; Jens Nilson, from Lolland, Denmark, aged 6 years died; Bodil Mortinsen from Lolland, Denmark, aged 9 years, died; Nils Anderson from Seeland, Denmark, aged 41 years died; Ole Madsen from Seeland, Denmark, aged 41 years died; Many of the Saints have their feet & hands frozen from the severity of the weather.

Chislett described the mass grave and the ceremony of interment:

We had a large square hole dug in which we buried these thirteen people, three or four abreast and three deep. When they did not fit in, we put one or two crosswise at the head or feet of the others. We covered them with willows and then with earth. When we buried these thirteen people some of their relatives refused to attend the services. They manifested an utter indifference about it.

Only seven years old at the time, Mary Hurren remembered being hoisted to the shoulder of one of the men to observe the burial. Nineteen-year-old Robert Reeder explained the purpose of that deed: "My brother-in-law James Hurren held out his [seven]-year old girl Mary to see her playmate lying among the dead. They were laid in the clothes they wore, in a circle with feet to the center and heads out. We covered them with willows and then earth and slid rocks down the hill to keep the wolves from disturbing them." Reeder further remembered, "Two of the men who helped dig the grave died and were buried in another near by."

In addition to the fifteen dead, according to eleven-year-old Mettie Mortensen, "A big strong looking Sweedish woman who was in our tent, lost her mind." Yet Mettie's most indelible memory of that grim day was a testament to her insatiable hunger: "The thing I regret most in all that terrible time was, taking a piece of bread from a dead womans pocket. She was a woman I had walked with day after day and I knew she had this bread she had not eaten."

Despite the intercession of Grant's rescue team, with its bounteous supply of provisions, and despite the arrival on October 24 of a second rescue team—six wagons under the command of Reddick Allred—on Rock (or Willow) Creek, fifteen men, women, and children died in a single night and day. It is a powerful testimony to how memory reshapes events that several of the Willie Saints later wrote about the crossing of Rocky Ridge and the mass interment in camp the next day as if both had happened before the arrival of Grant's rescue team. Whatever aid and sustenance Kimball, Allred, and the other men with the rescue wagons were able to render, it was not enough to save those fifteen.

And according to Chislett, the burial failed to serve its lasting purpose. "I learned afterwards," he later wrote, "from men who passed that way the next summer, that the wolves had exhumed the bodies, and their bones were scattered thickly around the vicinity."

On October 25, the company started in motion once again. For the first time in weeks, the Saints now received a ration of a full pound of flour per adult. Yet from that date on, according to Chislett, "two or three died every day." Woodward's official journal records the seesaw swing of health and illness through the following week. On the 25th he recorded the deaths of four more men, ranging in age from twenty-two to sixty-five. Three days later, he wrote, "Weather fine. Saints improving in health." But two days after that, "Many persons were sick & it was late before they were in camp." On November 2, he observed that the captain himself had become crippled: "Bro. Willie's feet were in such a bad condition from frost that he was unable to walk to the Camp; a wagon was sent for him."

On top of all their other miseries, the Willie Company Saints had become infested with lice: "We were dirty & Lousy," Woodward remembered fifty-one years later, though he never mentioned the fact in the official journal. "Body lice by the hundreds were on our people."

During these days of dogged progress, despite the aid of increasing numbers of wagons sent out from Salt Lake, most of the Saints still pushed and pulled their handcarts. There were small moments of kindness and cruelty, the one sometimes masquerading as the other. Years later, the eleven-year-old Danish boy, Michael Jensen, would remember that after his father had died,

Mother sat on a large kettle turned upside down weeping bitterly, I and [nine-year-old brother] Anthony stood beside her not knowing what to do. One of the men who was helping to manage the company came along just then and he had a walking stick in his hand. He struck Mother across the back with his stick and said in a sharp voice, "Get up and go on, you cannot sit here crying. We have to go at once or we will all die." Oh, how I wished I were a man so I could fight for my mother! I never forgave this man. . . . Now in my late years as I look back, I see things more clearly and I see that sternness was our only salvation and the only thing we could stand as it roused us from our misery and had the leaders allowed us to grieve we could not have endured the hardships left to us when we had to go on alone.

Also years later, Agnes Caldwell, nine at the time, recounted the parable of her salvation:

> When the wagons started out, a number of us children decided to see how long we could keep up with the wagons, in hopes of being asked to ride. At least that is what my great hope was. One by one they all fell out, until I was the last one remaining, so determined was I that I should get a ride. After what seemed the longest run I ever made before or since, the driver, who was [William] Kimball, called to me, "Say, sissy, would you like a ride?" I answered in my very best manner, "Yes sir." At this he reached over, taking my hand, clucking to his horses to make me run, with legs that seemed to me could run no farther. On we went, to what to me seemed miles. What went through my head at that time was that he was the meanest man that ever lived or that I had ever heard of, and other things that would not be a credit nor would it look well coming from one so young. Just at what seemed the breaking point, he stopped. Taking a blanket, he wrapped me up and lay me in the bottom of the wagon, warm and comfortable. Here I had time to change my mind, as I surely did, knowing full well by doing this he saved me from freezing when taken into the wagon.

During these onerous days, John Ahmanson, the Danish sub-captain who would later apostatize, came to hate the handcarts, which he later referred to as "two-wheeled man-tormentors" and "two-wheeled infernal machines invented by Brigham Young." He also remembered the cold treatment of a fellow countryman meted out by, of all people, Levi Savage:

> There was a Dane named Niels Andersen, who had shown himself during almost the entire trip to be one of the strongest and bravest in the entire train. He had often loaded his fourteen-year old daughter on his cart when she was tired, and yet he still drove ahead just as happily with her. But more recently he had been attacked by dysentery, which had begun to spread to an alarming extent. By this day it had befallen Christiansen's group, and

his wife had to pull their cart by herself. Naturally she had fallen behind, and I therefore gave her a helping hand until we reached our camp location. It went pretty well that way, but we could not overtake the caravan. It was just about noon however, when we came up to her husband, who was tottering along the road and seemed as helpless as a child. He broke out with heartrending lamentation when he saw us. His wife comforted him as well as she could and gave him some food, which he ate ravenously. We stopped in order to wait for some wagons that were still farther behind, to have them pick him up as they drove by. Finally Savage came, the captain of the wagons, with a ox-drawn wagon; but he refused to take Niels Andersen up because the wagon, as he said, was already overloaded.

Eventually, however, Ahmanson persuaded Savage to give the played-out Dane a place in the wagon. It was too late: the next morning, Andersen was found frozen to death in camp.

As usual, John Chislett had the keenest eye for the sufferings of the Saints during the week beginning October 25. It was the custom, he remembered, to scavenge the clothes of the dead for the living to wear. Burying one man, however, Chislett could not bring himself to steal his "medium-heavy laced shoes."

> I wanted them badly, but could not bring my mind to the "sticking-point" to appropriate them. I called Captain Kimball up and showed him both, and asked his advice. He told me to take them by all means, and tersely remarked, "They will do you more good than they will do him." I took them, and but for that would have reached the city of Salt Lake barefoot.

On another day, Chislett had to bury two of the dead. "This I did before breakfast. The effluvia from these corpses were horrible, and it is small matter for wonder that after performing the last sad offices for them I was taken sick and vomited fearfully."

On November 2, the company reached Fort Bridger. At last there were enough rescue wagons so that all the Saints could ride. The two-wheeled man-tormentors were abandoned, after the Willie Saints had pushed and pulled them almost 1,200 miles from Iowa City. A cherished piece of Mormon folklore is dramatized by Wallace Stegner in *The Gathering of Zion*:

> Margaret Dalglish of the Martin company, a gaunt image of Scottish fortitude, dragged her handful of belongings to the very rim of the valley, but when she looked down and saw the end of it she did something extraordinary. She tugged the cart to the edge of the road and gave it a push and watched it roll and crash and burst apart, scattering into Emigration Canyon the last things she owned on earth. Then she went on into Salt Lake to start the new life with nothing but her gaunt bones, her empty hands, her stout heart.

Thirty-one-year-old Margaret Dalglish was actually Irish, not Scottish, and traveled in the Willie rather than the Martin Company. If, like the other Willie Saints, she abandoned her handcart on the grassy plain at Fort Bridger, there was no steep incline down which to push her cart and watch it smash to pieces. Church historian Andrew Olsen believes the tale is probably apocryphal, passed on to posterity by Dalglish's granddaughter.

Susannah Stone, twenty-five during the journey, later swore that "When we were within about a hundred miles from Salt Lake our captain had a dream that a company was coming from Salt Lake to meet us." The company came, according to Stone, the next day. This anecdote, too, must be apocryphal, or at least muddled in Stone's memory, for Fort Bridger lies 113 miles from Salt Lake City, and by the time the Saints reached it, they had been accompanied by rescuers for eleven days.

Despite finally having enough food to eat, and the luxury of riding in wagons, Saints continued to die during the week it took to cover those 113 miles. Dysentery seems to have been the main cause of mortality. Woodward's journal systematically records the passing of from one to three emigrants virtually every day. The last of those deaths, and therefore the most poignant, occurred on November 9, the very day the Saints finally reached Zion. Woodward's entry: "Rhoda R. Oakey from

Eldersfield, Worcestershire, England, aged 11 years died this morning." Chislett would later write that two or three Saints in the company died after arriving in Salt Lake City.

With Salt Lake City almost in sight, some of the women in the Willie party began to worry about the sorry appearance they might present. Euphemia Bain recalled that "When I left Scotland I had five pairs of shoes, but when I reached Salt Lake City I had to tie grass around them to hold them together." Susannah Stone later remembered, "When we got near the City, we tried to make ourselves as presentable as we could to meet our friends. I had sold my little looking glass to the indians for buffalo meat, so I borrowed one and I shall never forget how I looked. Some of my old friends did not know me. We were so weather beaten and tanned."

As the Saints entered the city, John Ahmanson later claimed, "the prophet did not honor us with a personal visit; presumably he was ashamed to look upon our miserable and wretched condition, the result of his own shortsighted and ill-conceived plan." But Susannah Stone remembered, "When we got near Salt Lake Valley, President Young with a company of our brethren and sisters came out to meet us, and bade us welcome."

In any event, the main greeting party was made up of Mormon bishops, who had been assigned the task of finding families to take in all the Saints who did not already have relatives living in Salt Lake. The reminiscences of the Willie Saints are uniform in expressing gratitude for the hospitality that was immediately lavished upon them. Of both bishops and families, Chislett wrote, "Their kindness . . . *cannot be too highly praised.*"

Along with joy at the Willie Company's arrival, the citizens of Salt Lake felt shock at seeing the condition to which the emigrants had been reduced. Captain Willie, the proud leader, still unable to walk, appeared with his legs wrapped in burlap. The horror of the toll that frostbite had taken among the party is captured in a vignette in the family history of the Reeder clan. George Reeder, living in Salt Lake, had come out to greet his relatives, including his brother-in-law, James Hurren. "Presently George inquired, 'What is this odor I can smell?' 'Little Mary's legs are frozen', replied James." A doctor was consulted, who recommended amputation of both legs to save the seven-year-old's life.

No definitive count of the number of dead in the Willie Company will ever be reckoned. Saints in the party put the toll generally in the range from sixty-six to seventy-seven, though Robert Reeder, nineteen during the journey, believed that one hundred had died. In *Handcarts to Zion*, LeRoy and Ann Hafen, who are inclined to underestimate, list the deaths as sixty-seven. After careful research, church historian B. H. Roberts fixed the number at seventy-seven. Andrew Olsen, in his recent *The Price We Paid*, totals up seventy-four, including deaths incurred between Liverpool and Iowa City.

The already embittered Danish sub-captain John Ahmanson resolved to file a formal complaint against the "snow prophet," William Kimball, with Brigham Young himself. He apparently did so, for in his *Secret History*, Ahmanson writes ruefully, "Oh, you trusting simpleton! The prophet laughed right in my face."

In the immediate aftermath of the Willie Company's arrival, church authorities went out of their way to minimize the tragedy. Millen Atwood, Willie's fanatical second-in-command, rose in the Tabernacle a week after the party came in and told a large congregation, "We did not suffer much; we had a little bit of snow, but that was nothing; and we had enough to eat as long as it lasted, and when that was gone you furnished us more; we fared first rate."

And on November 12, just three days after the frostbitten and emaciated Saints had arrived in Salt Lake, the *Deseret News* editorialized,

> After all the hardships of the journey, mainly consequent upon so late a start, the mortality has been far less in br. Willie's company, than in many wagon companies that have started seasonably and with the usual conveniences for the trip. The eminent feasibility of the hand-cart movement had been previously demonstrated; its healthfulness is now proven by the experience of this company.

CHAPTER SEVEN

MARTIN'S COVE

Acurious footnote to the rescue mission launched on October 7 is the fact that, six days later, Brigham Young indeed set out on the trail, hoping to reach Fort Bridger and greet the handcart Saints as they came in. That the Prophet himself, like Franklin Richards, seriously underestimated the gravity of the situation emerges in the makeup of the party: along with eight men, Heber Kimball and Young each took along a favorite wife, as if the trip were as much picnic lark as errand of mercy. In any event, the presidential train got no farther than East Canyon Creek, just a few miles outside Salt Lake City, when Young became violently ill.

A brief notice of this aborted expedition appeared in the *Deseret News* on October 22:

> RETURN. On the morning of the 15th inst., and while encamped on East Kanyon Creek, en route for Green river, Governor Young was suddenly seized with so severe an attack of illness that it was deemed unadvisable to prosecute the journey, and the party arrived in this city on the evening of the above date. Since then the Governor's health has improved rapidly, and is now in a good degree restored.

A much more elaborate and bizarre version of Young's short-circuited trip that October has been handed down by the family of Arza Erastus Hinckley, who may have also played a crucial role in the rescue of the Martin Company. As told by descendant Earl S. Paul, the party consisted only of the Prophet and Hinckley, who had often served as Young's carriage-driver. In this version, the two men travel along in silence, each preoccupied with fears about the fate of the handcart companies. Suddenly Young says, "Arza, I have been having some trouble lately with my stomach. The terrible worry is causing me to feel sick."

"We are just about to Canyon Creek," Arza answers. "When we get there we had better stop."

That bitterly cold evening, camped in a tent, Young begins to shake all over with fever. His solicitous attendant serves him herbal tea, piles quilts on the invalid, and builds up the fire. Finally Hinckley takes a bottle of consecrated oil out of his handbag.

Arza got the oil and anointed him then laid hands on his companion's head and blessed him asking his heavenly Father to relieve him of his suffering. After Arza had completed the administration, President Young seemed to be much better, a calmness came over him, he went to sleep and when he awakened in the morning his pain was gone.

Nonetheless, the two men decide to return to Salt Lake. On the way back, Young voices out loud the moral lesson of his sudden illness:

"After the time I have had I can realize more fully how the handcart people are suffering, even more than I have. . . . After my experience in this storm they would not be able to carry the needed protection in the small handcarts. Their small children, babies and elderly people must be freezing. They should not have left so late in the season, they should have waited until spring."

Probably this version, which has never been published, is apocryphal, or at least much embroidered with retrospective pieties as it was handed down from one generation to the next. Yet the dates jibe with the *Deseret News* account, the treatment with consecrated oil was standard Mormon practice, and just possibly Hinckley was the "doctor" dispatched from Salt Lake City mentioned in other accounts.

. . .

AFTER MAKING INITIAL contact with the Willie Company in the midst of the October 19 snowstorm, the express rescue train—Young, Wheelock, Taylor, and Garr—hurried on to search for the Martin Company and the Hodgetts and Hunt wagon companies, of whose whereabouts Captain Willie knew nothing. During three days of constant storm, pushing through deepening snow, the rescue team covered forty-five miles, reaching Devil's Gate. A striking landmark along the Mormon and Oregon Trails, the Gate is a three-hundred-foot-high sheer cleft in a granite ridge, carved by the Sweetwater as it turns briefly north in its generally eastward course.

George Grant had ordered the express train to stop near Devil's Gate. Precisely why is unclear: in a November 2 letter sent to Brigham Young from that camp, Grant vaguely remarks, "Not thinking it safe for them to go farther than Independence Rock, I advised them to wait there." (Independence Rock is a low granite dome covered with trail signatures; it lies five miles east of Devil's Gate. The latter, however, offered the express train a far better camping place, for the half-decrepit remains of Fort Seminoe, a trading post built by French voyageur brothers in 1852, gave the men welcome shelter from the storms.)

The eternally overoptimistic Franklin Richards had assured Grant that he would meet the Martin Company at Devil's Gate or farther west. When the express team reached the Gate and found no sign of the missing company, they grew deeply alarmed. Nonetheless, they obeyed orders and waited there for four days.

Meanwhile, having dispatched William Kimball and six wagons to shepherd the Willie Company toward the Valley, Grant pushed on eastward with ten wagons and about sixteen men on October 21. It was not until October 26 that this main rescue caravan reached Devil's Gate. There, consternation prevailed. Grant began to speculate that the companies lagging behind had stopped at Fort Laramie to winter over. His own horses were getting played out, and feed was increasingly hard to find in the snowdrifts. Grant thus came perilously close to calling off the rescue mission, or at least to waiting at Devil's Gate for the laggards to come to him.

As Daniel Jones wrote of this impasse, "At first we were at a loss what to do for we did not expect to go further than Devil's Gate." But, according to Jones, the five returning missionaries still in Grant's team had "many dear friends" among the missing companies, and thus "suffered great anxiety, some of them feeling more or less the responsibility resting upon them for allowing these people to start so late in the season across the plains."

As of October 26, the Martin Company had been stalled for six days in their squalid camp beneath Red Buttes, a full sixty-five miles east of Devil's Gate. With them was camped the Hodgetts wagon company, also unable to move. Even farther east lingered the Hunt wagon company.

At last, on October 27, Grant decided to send ahead yet another express scouting team, with fast horses and a pack mule, but carrying no flour, to search for the missing parties. The three-man mission was made up of Joseph Young, Abel Garr, and Daniel Jones. Jones would later claim that the scouts' orders were "to find where the people were and not to return until they were found," but Harvey Cluff, the young man who had posted the critical signboard on the trail near Willow Creek, contradicted that statement. In his journal, Cluff wrote, "Four days was the extent of time they were to be gone. If the emigrants were not found within that length of time the [three] men were to return and the conclusion would be that the companies had gone into winter quarters."

That second express train would spell the difference between life and death for hundreds of emigrants. According to Jones's account, the men rode at "full gallop," but lost half a day when their horses strayed off from camp to follow a herd of buffalo. Even so, the trio covered the sixty-five miles in the extraordinary time of two days. The first sign of the Martin Company came when the scouts discovered a "white man's shoe track in the road." Joseph Young called out, "Here they are." As Jones later recalled, "We put our animals to their utmost speed and soon came in sight of the camp at Red Bluff."

The Martin Company and the Hodgetts wagon party had not moved for seven days. Their rations had recently been reduced to four ounces of flour per day for adults, two ounces for children. Many of the Saints had reconciled themselves to impending death. "At last the Company gave up and decided they could go no further," remembered Louisa Mellor Clark years later. "We all gathered around and held a meeting, praying

God to help us, as we knew it was Him alone who could deliver us from death. We were happy and willing to die for a just cause."

Heber McBride, thirteen at the time, later reflected, "I have wondered many times since how it was we ever lived for my sister and I used [to] pray we could die to get out of our misery." The stalwart John Jaques insisted that the Saints did all they could to maintain morale: "The outlook was certainly not encouraging, but it need not be supposed that the company was in despair. . . . O no! A hopeful and cheerful spirit pervaded the camp, and the 'songs of Zion' were frequently heard at this time, though the company was in the very depths of its privations." But Jaques also admitted, "At the same time [the Saints] had become so accustomed to looking death in the face that they seemed to have no fear of it, nor of corpses either, the bodies of the dead having become such familiar sights as to lose their ordinary thrilling influence on beholders."

Both Patience Loader and Jane Griffiths later remembered that at Red Buttes, nineteen members of the company died in a single night. Among their number was John, the oldest brother of eight-year-old Jane Griffiths. Josiah Rogerson went even further, insisting many years later that after October 23 in the Red Buttes camp there were "six to eight and more deaths every twenty-four hours. The aged and worn-out seemed in an hour or two to relinquish all their desire for life, passing away like an infant in slumber."

By now, virtually none of the Martin Company diarists was still keeping a journal, and the reminiscences of others from years later tend to be cursory, as if that stalled week in the snow was too terrible a time to be remembered in detail. But twelve-year-old John Bond in the Hodgetts wagon company later re-created several memorable scenes from what he called the "Snow Bound Camp of Death." He recalled "the saints [w]ringing their hands and stamping their feet they were so cold." Bond described a mass burial, as hymns were sung and prayers spoken, while in the background "the wolves were howling around in all directions on the snow clad mountains." While the service was going on, "Captain Martin stood over the graves of the departed ones with his shot gun in hand firing at intervals to keep the crows from hovering around in mid air."

And Bond was able to confess to a shameful deed that he had perpetrated in the Red Buttes camp. After several days of waiting, the flour supply was so scanty that it would only "make a little thickning in poor ox soup." One day the bugler called the company to a prayer meeting.

> I had been to many of the prayer meetings previous, but as I had seen Sister Scott cooking a nice pot of dumplings just before the bugle sounded for prayers, she hid the dumplings nicely under the wagon and covered them up ready to eat on her return from the meeting and she being a very zelous woman went to the prayer meeting and I did not go with her this time and as I had been watching her cook the dumplings, I went to look for the same and found them, and being so hungry I could not res[is]t the temptation so I sat down and ate them all and duly admit that those dumplings did me more good than all the prayer that could have been offered, and for such an act, I have done a grevious wrong for which I regret going and ask God to forgive me in time of hunger. In time the old lady returned from the meeting and went to look for her dumplings, but to her surprise they were all gone, so she inquired of all to see if she could find out who had taken them, but was fruitless in fing[er]ing the one.

Patience Loader later wrote vividly about the trials of the Red Buttes camp. She remembered that she and her sister had to walk nearly a mile through knee-deep snow to find firewood, and then all she could get was "green ceder," i.e., juniper. The single repast that stuck in her memory was broth made by boiling "an old beef head": Patience

> chopt it in peices the best I could put it into the pot with some Snow and boiled for along time about four o clock in the after noon we was able to have some of this fine Made broath I cannot say that it tasted very good but it was flavord boath with Sage brush and from the smokey fire from the green ceder fire so after it was cooked we all enjoyed it and fealt very thankfull to have that much it would have tasted better if we could have alittle pepper and salt but that was aluxury we had been deprived of for along time.

Patience lavishes considerable detail upon the decline of a Saint she calls John Laurey—since "he had no friends with him he was alone," her family invited him into their tent. No Saint by that name is listed in the LDS Archives roster of the Martin Company, but scholar Lyndia Carter believes the unfortunate loner may have been a fifty-five-year-old man from London named George Lawley. Patience's family offered the man some of the beef-head broth: "We tryed to give him alittle with a tea-spoon but we could not get the spoon between his teeth poor dear Man he looked at us but could not Speak aword he was nearly dead frozen."

That night,

We rapt him up the best we could to try to get warm but he was two far gone we all laid down to try to get warm in our quilts the best we could My Mother and Myself and sister Jane in one bed My sister Tamar Maria sarah and my little brother Robert in the other bed and poor brother Laurey in his own bed poor Man hehad only one old blanket to rap him in we had a buflow roab this he had over him after we was in bed it was a dark loansome night he commenced to talk to himself he called for his wife and children he had previously told me that he had a wife and nine children in London and that they would come out as soon as he could make money enough to send for them.

It was indeed too late for Brother Laurey (or Lawley). As Patience amplifies,

In the night we could not hear him talking any more I said to Mother I think poor brother is dead I have not heard him for the last hour Mother ask me to get up and go to him I got up but everything in the tent seemed so silent and then was such a sadd feeling came over me it was so dark and drear that I said to Mother I cannot go to him She sais well get back in bed and try to get warm and wait untill daylight of course we did not Sleep early as it was alittle light I got up and went to the poor man found him dead frozen to the tent as I turned him over to look in his face never can I forget that Sight poor Man.

Wrapped in his single thin blanket, "Laurey" was buried that morning, according to Patience, in the mass grave with the eighteen others who had died during the night.

With the weather failing to moderate and their provisions almost gone, it is likely that the Martin Company would have been unable to start along the trail again without the timely intercession of the three-man scouting express sent out from Devil's Gate. Once more, a blessed event was presaged by prophetic dreams. Elizabeth Jackson, who had lain through the endless night beside the dead body of her husband, Aaron, a few days before, later claimed, "When I retired to bed that night, being the 27th of October, I had a stunning revelation. In my dream, my husband stood by me, and said, 'Cheer up, Elizabeth, deliverance is at hand.'"

Josiah Rogerson reported the prophetic vision of John Rodwell that same night: "He said: 'I dreamed that it was Tuesday or Wednesday, and about noontide, as near as I could judge. I saw a mule, packed with blankets and cooking utensils, come right in the middle of our camp, as we are now, followed by three Californians, wear[ing] blue soldier overcoats, riding mules or horses. They stopped and told us of teams and relief from the valley, after which we started again on our journey.'"

The best account of the Martin Company's deliverance on October 28 appears in the memoir of John Bond, the twelve-year-old in the Hodgetts party. "In the after part of the day," Bond remembered many years later, "I was playing in front of Sister Scott's wagon with her son Joseph, then seven years old and his mother was looking to the westward." It was Sister Scott whose dumplings the young lad had stolen and eaten.

All at once Sister Scott sprang to her feet in the wagon and screamed out at the top of her voice. I see them coming! I see them coming! Surely they are angels from heaven. At such being said, I looked the way she was looking, but could not see or perceive what she was looking at in the distance. . . . By this time, more of the Brethern and Sisters came from their tents and wagons, from over the camp anxious to observe what she saw in the distance.

All kept looking westward for the moving objects, when all commenced to see in the far distance at the curve of the hill what Sister Scott saw, and it was three men on horses driving another slowly in the deep crusted snow, and the wolves were howling in all directions. . . . [A] general cry rent the air. Hurrah! hurrah! Some of the voices choking with laughter and of tears down care worn cheeks. . . . When Sister Scott waved her shawl, "We are saved!" so loud that all in camp could hear her and still repeating, *"It is! It is surely the relief party from Utah."*

Joseph A. Young, Daniel W. Jones and Abraham Garr came into camp with a small dun colored mule packed with supplies when much rejoicing insued through camp with Hurrahs! Hurrahs! again and again as the broken hearted mothers ran clasping their emaciated arms around the necks of the relief party, kissing them time and time again and as do rush up in groups to welcome the brethern, fathers, mothers, brothers, and sisters fall on each others necks the tears falling from their eyes in profusion.

Also many years later, Albert Jones's recall of the joyous rendezvous was fresh:

I well remember the scene of then, Joseph A. Young & companion reached us, as the first noble band of rescuers from the vallies— Jos. A. rode a white mule down a snow covered hill or a dugway into our camp the white mule was lost sight of, on the white background of snow—and Jos. A. with his big blue soldiers overcoat, its large cape & capacious skirts rising & falling with the motion of the mule, gave the appearance of a big blue winged angel flying to our rescue.

The scene that presented itself on his arrival, I shall never forget; women crying aloud; on their knees, holding to the skirts of his overcoat as though afraid he would escape from their grasp & fly away.

Patience Loader remembered that the rescuers were as deeply moved as the rescued, as "with tears streaming down his face," Joseph Young asked her where Captain Martin's tent was. Locating the captain, Young asked him how many had died. Martin reported that fifty-six members of the company had perished since the Saints had left Florence nine weeks before.

Young then ordered the immediate disbursement of a pound of flour per adult from what must have been the last remnants of the company's supply, and the slaughter of all the remaining cattle, lean and unnutritious though they might be. And he "told the people to gather 'up' and move on at once as the only salvation was to travel a little every day." The Saints agreed to start the next morning.

From Martin, Young learned that the Hunt wagon company was marooned a good fifteen miles farther east, somewhere near the banks of the Platte. After tending to the Martin and Hodgetts Companies, the three express scouts rode on, once more at "full gallop," to locate the last of all the emigrant caravans. That same afternoon, the trio rode in sight of the Hunt Company camp. Daniel Jones's account of the meeting is strange in the extreme, giving perhaps a glimpse into the all-encompassing apathy that can descend on people as they approach death by starvation:

> On arriving no one noticed us or appeared to care who we were. Their tents were pitched in good shape, wood was plentiful, and no one seemed concerned. Joseph A. Young became offended, not expecting such a cool reception and remarked, "Well it appears we are not needed here." So we went down into the bottom and made camp for ourselves. After a while some one sauntered down our way, thinking probably we were mountaineers [i.e., non-Mormon mountain men heading east along the trail]. These recognized Brother Young and made a rush for camp, giving the word; soon we were literally carried in and a special tent was pitched for our use. Everything was done to make "amends" for the previous neglect.

The official journal of the Hunt Company is at odds with Jones's memory of a "cool reception," recording simply, "Bro. Joseph Young and two others arrived this evening, which caused generally rejoicing throughout the camp."

On the morning of the 29th, Daniel Jones and Abel Garr tried to rally the Hunt Company Saints to get them moving, while Joseph Young (for some reason that Jones's memoir does not explain) pushed on even farther east, to the bridge over the Platte for which the Martin Company had been too poor to pay the toll. Once more, Jones deplored "the spirit of apathy among the people." Instead of gathering up their cattle at once, they began to quarrel among themselves over who should take on that unpleasant chore. "This made us feel like leaving them to take care of themselves," reported Jones. "We saddled up to do so."

Meanwhile, an ominous storm was gathering in the west. Thick clouds amassed, with only a narrow hole of blue sky ahead. Abel Garr called the dilatory emigrants' bluff.

> We mounted our mules; Brother Garr, pointing to the bright spot in the heavens, said, "Do you see that hole? You had better all get out of here before that closes up, for it is your opening to the valley. We are going." The people, I believe, took this for a warning and soon started for their cattle.

By the time Jones and Garr had regained the Red Buttes camp, they found that the Martin Company had vacated it, while the Hodgetts wagon company was just starting out. Riding on, the two scouts overtook the caravan of handcarts. As Jones later recaptured the scene,

> The train was strung out for three or four miles. There were old men pulling and tugging their carts, sometimes loaded with a sick wife or children—women pulling along sick husbands—little children six to eight years old struggling through the mud and snow. As night came on the mud would freeze on their clothes and feet. There were two of us and hundreds needing help. What could we do?

What the scouts, with Joseph Young having caught them up, did do was to ride on as fast as they could to bring the news to George Grant's stationary rescue party at Devil's Gate. The morning after their return, Grant's whole team set off eastward again. The rescuers met the handcarts at Greasewood Creek, sixteen miles east of Devil's Gate.

In a letter to Brigham Young written on November 2 from Devil's Gate, Grant vividly evoked that meeting:

> We dealt out to br. Martin's company the clothing, &c., that we had for them; and next morning, after stowing our wagons full of

the sick, the children and the infirm, with a good amount of luggage, started homeward about noon. The snow began to fall very fast, and continued until late at night. It is now about 8 inches deep here, and the weather is very cold.

It is not of much use for me to attempt to give a description of the situation of these people, for this you will learn from your son Joseph A. and br. Garr, who are the bearers of this express; but you can imagine between five and six hundred men, women and children, worn down by drawing hand carts through snow and mud; fainting by the way side; falling, chilled by the cold; children crying, their limbs stiffened by cold, their feet bleeding and some of them bare to snow and frost. The sight is almost too much for the stoutest of us; but we go on doing all we can, not doubting nor despairing.

GRANT AT ONCE realized the impossibility of solving the crisis. Several of the participants put the number of nearly starving Saints in the three companies at 1,200, though nine hundred is probably a more accurate count. Grant's twenty-odd men with their ten wagonloads of flour could make only a tiny and temporary improvement in the emigrants' ordeal. As Grant wrote to Young, "Our company is too small to help much, it is only a drop to a bucket, as it were, in comparison to what is needed. I think that not over one-third of br. Martin's company is able to walk."

Nonetheless, for several days he boosted the daily ration to a pound of flour per adult. Even so, a few Saints died between Greasewood Creek and Devil's Gate, including six-year-old Herbert Griffiths, whose twelve-year-old brother, John, had died at Red Buttes. Their father, John Griffiths, reached camp one night during that painful march only by crawling on his hands and knees through the snow.

The Martin Company reached Devil's Gate on November 2, although the Hunt wagon company did not come in until November 5. The half-ruined stockade and cabins of Fort Seminoe could hardly give refuge to nine hundred Saints. Daniel Jones recalled that "All the people who could, crowded into the houses of the fort out of the cold and the s[t]orm. One crowd cut away the walls of the house they were in for fuel, until half of the roof fell in; fortunately they were all on the protected side and no one was hurt."

Patience Loader, however, remembered that emergency campfire differently. On arriving at Devil's Gate,

> We found several big fiars there was several log huts standing there and Several breathren from the valley was camping there. ... We was all so hungery and cold many ran to get to the fiar to warm but the breathren ask for all to be as patint as possable and that we should have Some wood to make us afiar so we could get warm brother George Grant was there he told us all to Stand back for he was going to Knock down one of those log hutts to make fiars for us for he sais you are not going to freeze to night.

Boasting that he had the strength of a giant, Grant

> raised his axe and with one blow he Knocked in the whole front of the building took each log and Split in four peices gave each family one peice oh such crowding for wood Some would have taken more than one piece but Bro grant told them to hold on and not to be greedy there was some that had not got any yet he Said there is one sister standing back waiting very patintly and She must have some I called out Yes brother grant My Name is Pati[e]nce and I have waited with patience he laugh and said give that sister some wood and let her go and make afiar I was very thankfull to get wood I had waited So long that my clothing stiff and my old stockings and shoes seemed frozen on my feet and legs.

That evening, however, the Saints were ordered out of the stockade, to pitch their tents on the ground surrounding it. This proved a herculean task. John Jaques recaptured the ordeal twenty-two years later:

> There was a foot or eighteen inches of snow on the ground which, as there were but one or two spades in camp, the emigrants had to shovel with their frying pans, or tin plates, or anything they could use for that purpose, before they could pitch their tents,

and then the ground was frozen so hard that it was almost impossible to drive the tent pegs into it. Some of the men were so weak that it took them an hour or two to clear the places for their tents and set them up. They would shovel and scrape away at the hard snow a few minutes and then rest, then shovel and scrape and rest again, and so on.

The next day, as another storm descended upon the pioneers, Captain Grant called a council meeting. Among the options he considered was having the whole nine-hundred-person throng halt at Devil's Gate and try to winter over. Common sense prevailed, however, as Grant realized that that effort would amount to a recipe for mass death. Meanwhile, Grant was vexed that none of the rescue teams that he knew had left Salt Lake shortly after his own had yet arrived.

One decision Grant made during the council was to send Joseph Young and Abel Garr back to Salt Lake City, riding as fast as they could, and carrying Grant's letter to Young. The two indefatigable scouts set off that very day. Among the benefits their mission might perform would be to intercept other rescue wagons and urge them forward at top speed. Young and Garr covered the 327 miles in the extraordinary time of ten days.

Although Grant's letter to the Prophet reported the desperate plight of the last three companies, and even though that letter was published in the *Deseret News* on November 19, in the same issue the official newspaper of the colony also published a short report from the scouts that defies credibility:

Elder Joseph A. Young and br. Abel Garr arrived, from the three immigrating companies yet due, at 4 a.m. on the morning of the 13th inst. Elder Young reported the condition of the immigration to be very favorable, considering the lateness of the season, and that abundant relief would reach them soon after he left Fort Bridger.

One wonders whether this absurdly rose-tinted glimpse of the impending disaster reflected Young's true belief, or simply mouthed the upbeat party line with which the *News* consistently wrote about the handcart emigration.

As well as flour, the relief wagons carried some five hundred articles of clothing. Robert Burton's list of these items includes 157 pairs of socks and stockings, 102 pairs of boots and shoes, one hundred coats and jackets, and even, bizarrely, twenty-seven handkerchiefs and fourteen neckties. This itemization meant, however, that only about one out of every two of the suffering Saints received any apparel at all. Those who did were eternally grateful for the gifts. Patience Loader remembered decades later "anice warm quilted hood which was very warm and comfortable I also got apar of Slippers as I was nearly bearfoot."

At the November 3 council, Grant and the other leaders made another momentous decision. If Grant's assessment that "not over one-third of br. Martin's company is able to walk" was not an exaggeration, it was obvious that most could no longer pull their handcarts. Thus the handcarts had to be abandoned. But there was not nearly enough room in the wagons to carry the ill and the lame. At first, Grant pondered the notion of caching at Devil's Gate every single personal belonging that was not vital to survival, to be recovered the following spring.

The cache plan evolved into something far more dramatic, as revealed in the tragicomic telling of Daniel Jones, the mountain man turned Mormon scout:

> Steve Taylor, Al Huntington and I were together when the question, "Why doesn't Captain Grant leave all the goods here with some one to watch them, and move on?" was asked. We agreed to make this proposal to him. It was near the time appointed for the meeting. As soon as we were together, Capt. Grant asked if anyone had thought of a plan. We presented ours. Capt. Grant replied, "I have thought of this, but there are no provisions to leave and it would be asking too much of anyone to stay here and starve for the sake of these goods; besides, where is there a man who would stay if called upon." I answered, "Any of us would." I had no idea I would be selected, as it was acknowledged I was the best cook in camp and Capt. Grant had often spoken as though he could not spare me.

With that noble but foolish slip of the tongue, Jones realized he had volunteered to winter over at Devil's Gate and guard the goods. The un-

loading of carts and wagons took three days. At the end of that task, sub-
captain Robert Burton informed Jones that he had demanded seventeen
men from the (relatively healthy) Hunt and Hodgetts teams to winter
over as well. Burton asked Jones to round out the party by choosing two
others from the rescue mission. He chose Thomas Alexander and Ben
Hampton, though in his memoir, after Burton urges him to make his
choice, saying "You are acquainted with the boys and whoever you want
will stay," Jones confesses that "I had a great mind to tell him that I wanted
Captains Grant and Burton." As Jones amplified his dismay, "There was
not money enough on earth to have hired me to stay. I had left home for
only a few days and was not prepared to remain so long away."

The goods to be guarded through the winter were deposited in the ruins of Fort Seminoe, which the twenty "volunteers" now occupied. Meanwhile, the stormy weather failed to relent, and the temperature plunged.
On November 4, the thermometer registered minus 6 degrees Fahrenheit.

It was obvious to Grant that in this weather the exhausted Saints
could not move on. The solution he arrived at was born of desperation.
About two and a half miles to the west of the fort, the low granite ridge
bordering the valley on the north bent like a horseshoe, forming a semi-
circular cove. That cove offered the best shelter anywhere nearby, with
the added advantage that the slopes of the ridge grew thick with pines
and junipers—potential firewood.

To get the company to what has become known as Martin's Cove,
however, required crossing the Sweetwater. Compared to the Platte,
this tributary was but a stream: at Devil's Gate, it ran only two to three
feet deep but thirty to forty yards wide. Now it was flowing thick with
cakes of ice. For the played-out Saints, the ford seemed more than they
could bear.

The crossing took the better part of the day of November 4. The
records of the Saints abound in horrors and heroism attending that passage. And for the last time, to get their gear and what was left of their
food to the cove, the emigrants had to pull their handcarts.

John Jaques later recalled a vignette of near hopelessness:

> In that rear part of the company two men were pulling one of
> the handcarts, assisted by two or three women, for the women

pulled as well as the men all the way, so long as the handcarts lasted. When the cart arrived at the bank of the river, one of these men, who was much worn down, asked, in a plaintive tone, "Have we got to go across there?" On being answered yes, he was so much affected that he was completely overcome. That was the last straw. His fortitude and manhood gave way. He exclaimed, "O dear? I can't go through that," and burst into tears. His wife, who was by his side, had the stouter heart of the two at that juncture, and she said soothingly, "Don't cry, Jimmy. I'll pull the handcart for you."

In the end, one of the "boys from the valley" among the rescuers carried the women across the Sweetwater on his back. He tried to carry Jimmy, too, but slipped and fell, dunking both men in the icy current.

Meanwhile, the stronger man was left to try to pull the cart across the stream singlehanded. Jaques:

He rolled up his pants as high as he could, pulled off his stockings and boots which he had happened to receive at Greasewood Creek, put on a pair of old shoes he carried with him, and all alone went into the river with naked legs and with his cart laden with pots and kettles. It was easy enough to go into the river, but not so easy to pull across it and get out again. . . . When in the water the narrow felloes of the cart wheels cut into the soft bottom of the river bed and he soon got stalled. Two of the "boys" in the water went to his help, and one soon exclaimed "D—n it, you don't pull an ounce!" So hard was the tugging at the cart that it required the utmost combined strength of the three to take the vehicle through safe to dry land. While in the river the sharp cakes of floating ice below the surface of the water struck against the bare shins of the emigrant inflicting wounds which never healed until he arrived at Salt Lake and the dark scars of which he bears to this day.

Jaques's sister-in-law Patience Loader had her own story of the crossing.

> There was quite a nomber of the breathren from the valley stand-
> ing in readyness to help us across the stream of water with our
> cart I was feeling somewhat bad that morning and when I saw
> this Stream of water we had to go through I fealt weak and *I could*
> *not Keep my tears back* I fealt ashamed to let those breathren see
> me sheding tears I pulled my old bonnet over my face as thay
> should not See my tears.

Several "boys from the valley" helped Patience and her sisters trundle
the family cart across the Sweetwater. Later, she could not accurately
remember their names, but she wrote, "Those poor breathren was in the
water nearly all day we wanted to thank them but thay would not listen."
One of the men, whom Patience identifies as "Br Kimble" [Kimball],
"Staid so long in the water that he had to be taken out and packed to
camp and he was along time before he recoverd as he was child through
and in after life he was allways afflicted with rhumetism."

Out of the undoubted courage of the "boys from the valley" during
this crossing of the Sweetwater grew one of the most persistent myths of
the whole Mormon migration to Utah. It was crystallized by Solomon
Kimball in 1914, in a church publication called *Improvement Era*:

> After [the company] had given up in despair, after all hopes had
> vanished, after every apparent avenue of escape seemed closed,
> three eighteen-year-old boys belonging to the relief party came
> to the rescue, and to the astonishment of all who saw, carried
> nearly every member of the illfated handcart company across the
> snowbound stream. The strain was so terrible, and the exposure
> so great, that in later years all the boys died from the effects of it.
> When President Brigham Young heard of this heroic act, he wept
> like a child, and later declared publicly, "that act alone will ensure
> C. Allen Huntington, George W. Grant [the captain's son] and
> David P. Kimball an everlasting salvation in the Celestial King-
> dom of God, worlds without end."

Since Solomon Kimball was David Kimball's younger brother, this
account might have met with a certain skepticism, but instead the story
was passed down from one Mormon generation to the next, like an ex-

emplum from a medieval saint's life. Kimball's text is quoted verbatim as the truth, for instance, in Hafen and Hafen's *Handcarts to Zion*.

It was not until 2006 that LDS historian Chad M. Orton demonstrated that none of the "boys" in the rescue mission was eighteen years old; that a number of the men, not just the stated three, helped the handcarters across the ford; and that many of the handcart pioneers crossed the Sweetwater unassisted. Most importantly, Orton found the true death dates of Grant, Kimball, and Huntington to be 1872, 1883, and 1896, respectively—sixteen, twenty-seven, and forty years after the supposedly fatal ford. Kimball and Huntington, in fact, outlived Brigham Young.

The Martin, Hodgetts, and Hunt Companies spent five days in Martin's Cove. Those days marked the nadir of their agonizing journey—indeed, of the whole handcart campaign of 1856. The cold was beyond brutal: on November 6, the thermometer plunged to a new low of minus 11 degrees Fahrenheit. In such conditions, with the Saints as poorly clad as they were, widespread frostbite became inevitable. A still, calm cold would have been bad enough, but several days were windy, and on the worst day the gusts blew down every single tent. Of this reversal, Peter McBride, only six at the time, could much later make an almost funny story:

> Later we had a terrible cold spell; the wind drifted so much I knew I would die. The wind blew the tent down. They all crawled out but me. The snow fell on it. I went to sleep and slept warm all night. In the morning I heard someone say, "How many are dead in this tent?" My sister said, "Well, my little brother must be frozen to death in that tent." So they jerked the tent loose, sent it scurrying over the snow. My hair was frozen to the tent. I picked myself up and came out quite alive, to their surprise.

The vigil in Martin's Cove was so grim that some of the Saints later remembered it as lasting much longer. Patience Loader thought she and her family had spent nine days snowbound in the cove. Samuel Openshaw, who had managed faithfully to keep a diary from the start of the trip through September 26, added a summary entry after he reached Salt Lake City in which he claimed, "We then went into a canyon where we camped for about three weeks."

The hundreds of Saints marooned in Martin's Cove quickly devoured the bulk of the relief party's flour. On November 5, the daily ration, which had been boosted to a pound a day per adult for about a week, was reduced once more to four ounces, two ounces for the children. Yet on that day James Bleak, one of the few Martin Saints still keeping a diary, could write a remarkable testament to the strength of faith: "Through the blessing of our Father we felt as contented, as when we had 1 lb per head."

Peter McBride remembered that during part of the vigil in the cove, "We had nothing to eat but some bark from trees." His thirteen-year-old brother, Heber, would later recall, "Nearly all the children would cry themselves to sleep every night my 2 little Brothers would get the sack that had flour in and turn it wrong side out and suck and lick the flour dust of it."

Fifty years later, Samuel S. Jones would summon up Martin's Cove: "I remember the pinched, hungry faces, the stolid absent stare, that foretold the end was near, the wide and shallow open grave, awaiting its numerous consignments." No one has ever accurately reckoned the death toll during the five-day stay in the cove, although several Saints later testified that thirteen or fourteen died in a single day and night. Most of those fatalities go virtually unnoticed in the collective record of the Martin Company, but here and there, the anguish of personal loss emerges in the later telling of a survivor. Thus Elizabeth Sermon, remembering many years later her last night with her husband:

> We went to bed about three o'clock. He put his arm around me and said, "I am done," and breathed his last. I called Brother John Oley. We sewed him up in a quilt with his clothes on, except his boots, which I put on my feet and wore them into Salt Lake City. . . . [My husband] was buried in the morning with two more in the grave. I stood like a statue, bewildered, not a tear; The cold chills, even now as I write, creep over my body, for I feel I can still see the wolves waiting for their bodies as they would come down to camp before we left.

As if the loss of her husband were not tribulation enough, Elizabeth's six-year-old son, Robert, now had severely frostbitten feet. As she would recall, "I had to take a portion of poor Robert's feet off which pierced my very soul. I had to sever the leaders with a pair of scissors. Little did I think when I bought them in old England that they would be used for such a purpose. Every day some portion was decaying until the poor boy's feet were all gone."

In the Hunt wagon company, the family of William and Mary Goble suffered excruciating losses. Their daughter, only two years old, had died in Iowa City. As another daughter, thirteen-year-old Mary, would remember later,

> While there [in Martin's Cove], an ox fell on the ice and the brethren killed it and the beef was given out to the camp. My brother James ate a hearty supper and was as well as he ever was when he went to bed. In the morning he was dead.
>
> My feet were frozen and also my brother Edwin and my sister Caroline had their feet frozen. It was nothing but snow.

Caroline would die before the party reached South Pass. Mother Mary, forty-three years old, would persevere until the day the company finally reached Zion, only to die just a few miles short of Salt Lake City.

Patience Loader paints an affecting picture of her mother trying to rally the family in Martin's Cove. Amy Loader and her daughters had gotten through a terribly cold and windy night, but

> Mother called to me come Patience get up and Make us afiar I told her that I did not feel like geting up it was so cold and I was not feeling very well So she ask My sister Tamar to get up and she said She was not well and she could not get up then she sais come Maria you get up and she was feeling bad and said that She could not get up with this Mother sais come girls this will not do I believe I will have to dance to you and try to make you feel better poor dear Mother she started to Sing and dance to us and she slipt down as the snow was frozen and in a moment we was all up to help our dear Mother up for we was afraid she was hurt she laugh and said I thought I could soon make you all jump up if I danced to you then we found that she fell down purposely for she Knew we would all get up to see if she was hurt.

Captain George Grant still expected more relief wagons to arrive any day. When they did not, he began to recognize that the only chance of survival for the three companies would be to rouse them to move on, no matter how exhausted, frostbitten, or ill the majority of the Saints might be. On November 9, he somehow got the emigrants moving again. The agony of that restart goes all but undocumented in the collective record. Robert Burton's journal says only, "Fine, warm morning. Hand-cart company and Capt. Hodgett's company moved on at 11 o'clock a.m. Capt. Hunt's company not yet done 'catching' goods."

Then, toward sunset on the following day, instead of a train of rescue wagons, a single man on horseback rode into view from the west. It was Ephraim Hanks, the scout and canny frontiersman who had heard the voice calling him in the middle of the night as he fished on Utah Lake. One man could hardly make a major difference to the welfare of the nine-hundred-odd refugees, and Hanks's advent is only tersely mentioned in the several journals that were still being kept. Yet it remains possible that Hanks appeared to the emigrants as another heaven-sent angel.

For Hanks's heroic mission has become part of the established folk-lore of the Martin Company. The story was told most fully by Hanks himself, thirty-five years after the fact, when he was interviewed by church historian Andrew Jensen. In this telling, riding alone through the snow on his horse, leading a second pack horse, Hanks ran into Joseph Young and Abel Garr, who were hurrying toward Salt Lake with the news. Young and Garr told Hanks where he might find the hundreds of Saints straggling along the Sweetwater.

That night Hanks camped alone near South Pass.

As I was preparing to make a bed in the snow with the few articles that my pack animal carried for me, I thought how comfortable a buffalo robe would be on such an occasion, and also how I could relish a little buffalo meat for supper, and before lying down for the night I was instinctively led to ask the Lord to send me a buffalo. Now, I am a firm believer in the efficacy of prayer.

Sure enough, when Hanks looked up, there was a buffalo only fifty yards from camp. Even though "I had certainly not expected so immediate an answer to my prayer," Hanks leapt up and felled the animal with one rifle shot. He slept that night with a full belly, his bedroll spread on his new buffalo robe.

The next day, near the Ice Slough on the Sweetwater, Hanks shot a second bison, a cow, which he skinned and dressed; then he loaded his pack horse with long strips of meat.

> I think the sun was about an hour high in the west when I spied something in the distance that looked like a black streak in the snow. As I got near to it, I perceived it moved; then I was satisfied that this was the long looked for hand-cart company. . . . I reached the ill-fated train just as the immigrants were camping for the night. The sight that met my gaze as I entered their camp can never be erased from my memory. The starved forms and haggard countenances of the poor sufferers, as they moved about slowly, shivering with cold, to prepare their scanty evening meal was enough to touch the stoutest heart.

Hanks then narrates his reception by the Saints as the heaven-sent angel of the legend this meeting would become.

> . When they saw me coming, they hailed me with joy inexpressible, and when they further beheld the supply of fresh meat I brought into camp, their gratitude knew no bounds. Flocking around me, one would say, "Oh, please, give me a small piece of meat"; another would exclaim, "My poor children are starving, do give me a little"; and children with tears in their eyes would call out, "Give me some, give me some."

It took only five minutes for all the buffalo meat to be unloaded from the pack horse and cooking on the fires. The next day, Hanks took some of the strongest men in the party back to the carcass of the buffalo, which they butchered and carried to camp.

In his own telling, Hanks was not only the prodigal supplier of meat, but a healer who moved through the Martin Company performing miraculous cures. They began with a brother Blair, whose prostrate body the leaders of the company had given up for dead. Inspired, Hanks ordered several men to build a fire, next to which they laid Blair. He then washed the apparently lifeless man "from head to foot" and anointed him with consecrated oils. Several men laid hands on Blair and "commanded him in the name of Jesus Christ to breathe and live."

> The effect was instantaneous. The man who was dead to all appearances immediately began to breathe, sat up in his bed and commenced to sing a hymn. His wife, unable to control her feelings of joy and thankfulness, ran through the camp exclaiming: "My husband was dead, but is now alive. Praised be the name of God. The man who brought the buffalo meat has saved him."

During the next several days, according to Hanks, he went "from tent to tent administering to the sick." Scores of moribund Saints recovered, as Hanks "rebuked the diseases in the name of Jesus Christ. . . . I believe I administered to several hundreds in a single day." The scout further rallied the company by promising them that more rescue wagons were not far ahead along the trail.

Hanks, however, had no cure for frostbite. As he recalled in 1891,

> Many of the immigrants whose extremities were frozen, lost their limbs, either whole or in part. Many such I washed with water and castile soap, until the frozen parts would fall off, after which I would sever the shreds of flesh from the remaining portions of the limbs with my scissors. Some of the emigrants lost toes, others fingers, and again others whole hands and feet; one woman who now resides in Koosharem, Piute, Co., Utah, lost both her legs below the knees, and quite a number who survived became cripples for life.

WHERE, DURING THESE days, were the rest of the rescue teams sent out from Salt Lake City? The question vexed Grant at the time, and it has vexed historians ever since. In *Rescue of the 1856 Handcart Companies*, Rebecca Bartholomew and Leonard Arrington offer a cogent if dismaying explanation. The essence of it is that the rescue teams themselves found the going so arduous, they had to worry about their own survival. "These later rescuers," the historians write, "were in as much danger of frozen limbs and starvation if they pushed too far too fast as were the immigrants." They quote one rescuer as recording snow on Big Mountain, only eighteen miles out of Salt Lake, as "up to the tops of our wagon bows."

In the face of this early winter, some of the rescue teams turned back. The hardier ones fought through to Fort Bridger, 113 miles from Salt Lake City. But there, according to Bartholomew and Arrington, they found "no word on what to do next." Two rescue leaders pushed a single day farther east, but decided against crossing South Pass to look for the refugees on the Sweetwater. Returning to the fort, they persuaded all the other potential rescuers to give up the search. Seventy-seven wagons started west again along the trail back to Salt Lake City.

Meanwhile, Brigham Young had learned by express courier of this failure to pursue the mission. He sent out a fast team under William Kimball and Hosea Stout to turn the rescue wagons back eastward again. Stout's diary gives the clearest account of the thinking of the fainthearted rescuers, as he summarizes the excuses offered by John Van Cott, one of the leaders of the returning teams.

> Van Cott justified himself for returning and abandoning the Hand Cart Company as he could get no information of them and had concluded they had returned to the states, or Stopt at Larimie, been killed by the Indians or other wise gone to the devil and for him to have gone further was only to loose his own team and starve to death himself & do no good after all.

Van Cott and his colleagues knew that Grant's team of rescuers was somewhere out there to the east, still searching. But, in Stout's withering paraphrase, Van Cott thought that "as for G. D. Grant and those with him who had gone to meet [the Martin Company] they had probably stoped at Ft. Larimie. So on these vague conclusions he had not only turned back but had caused all the rest of the teams to return and thus leave the poor suffering Hand carters to their fate."

Meeting the returnees on the trail on November 12, Kimball and

Stout turned them around once again. Those wagons would save the lives of scores of Saints.

The lack of resolve of Van Cott and his colleagues eventually became general knowledge, for Daniel Jones, wintering over at Devil's Gate, learned of it. In *Forty Years Among the Indians*, he would write of these so-called rescuers, "I will not mention their names for it was always looked upon by the company as cowardly in the extreme."

The chief credit for the rescue, however, must go to the vanguard party led by Grant and Burton, and reinforced by the doughty Ephraim Hanks. In getting the Saints to shake off the deadly torpor of Martin's Cove and start moving west again, Grant turned the corner of an ordeal that could have proved far worse than what in fact ensued after November 9. At last the Martin Saints were able to abandon their handcarts, as the weakest of them now rode in the wagons supplied not only by Grant but by the Hunt and Hodgetts Companies. Not everyone could ride, however. About a dozen years later, Heber McBride, thirteen at the time, recalled that after Martin's Cove "all the small children and the old and those that [were] weak and worn out had the privilege of riding in the wagons so my Sister and me would see Mother and Peter and Maggie fixed in the wagon then Ether Jennetta and me would walk along with others." As John Jaques later indicated, "One perplexing difficulty was to determine who should ride, for many must still walk, though . . . the cart pulling occupation was gone. There was considerable crying of women and children, and perhaps of a few of the men, whom the wagons could not accommodate with a ride."

Some of the Saints actually chose to walk because, exhausted though they were, the exercise warmed their bodies as sitting stationary in a wagon could not. And indeed, the temperatures remained brutally cold through the middle of November.

From the 9th of that month on, however, virtually every day at least two or three Martin Saints died. It is curious that Robert Burton's diary mentions not a single one of those deaths. It is almost as though the whitewash that church leaders would soon apply to the tragedy began with the very entries the sub-captain of the rescue allowed himself to write. The only time Burton touches on the question is in an entry on November 14: "No deaths in camp tonight."

For decades afterward, however, the Martin Saints vividly recalled the losses of their brothers and sisters who almost made it all the way to Zion. From the collective record, poignant vignettes emerge. Fifty-eight years later, Jane Griffiths Fullmer, eight at the time of the emigration, could say, "I remember two women that died while sitting by me. My mother was cooking some cakes of bread for one of them. When she had passed one to her she acted so queer then tossed it in the fire and dropped over dead."

Some of the Saints effectively gave up on life. As nineteen-year-old George Housley later remembered:

At this time I was permitted to sleep in a tent with two of my companions. Each of them dying by my side where I slep by them 'till morning when they were taken away and buried. . . . At the time of my companions death I became despondent through weakness that I longed for death and tried to hide myself from the company that I might die, but one of the brethren returning back for something, found me sitting behind the rock where I had hoped to die. He took me along with him for a day before we caught up with the company. I was permitted to sleep in a wagon that night, where I slep with a dead man all night.

In a stormy camp on the Sweetwater, Elizabeth Scrmon reached kindred depths of hopelessness, as she mused, "My eldest boy John's feet decaying, my boys both of them losing their limbs, their father dead, my own feet very painful, I thought, 'Why can't I die?'"

Twenty-two years later, John Jaques could not clearly distinguish one Sweetwater camp from another, except for the site where the party spent the night in a grove of "quaking aspens." There, he remembered, "sixteen corpses were interred, the largest number at any one camp."

On November 16, the refugees prepared to cross Rocky Ridge, the series of bare, stony swales where the Willie Company had had their most desperate day three weeks before. Providentially, it was here that the first additional wagon train of rescuers met the party. It was led not by John Van Cott or any of the other halfhearted missionaries who had previously given up and started back toward Salt Lake City, but by Anson Call.

With his ten wagons, Call had met the Willie Company at Fort Bridger on November 3, and had realized at once that the Martin Company must be in an even more wretched condition. As Call later described his meeting with the Martin Saints, "We found them starving and freezing and dying, and the most suffering that I ever saw among human beings."

Call's intervention meant that more of the weaker Saints could ride in wagons, and it meant more food for all. That day, the ration of flour per adult was doubled, from eight ounces to a pound. Yet during this time, hunger continued to aggrieve the Saints. Elizabeth Sermon remembered "asking one of the drivers to give me a cob of corn to eat."

> He looked so pitiful and said, "Oh, sister, I hate to refuse you but my horses haven't enough to eat now, and I do not know how we will get back to Salt Lake."
>
> I said, "I ought not to have asked you, but myself and children are so hungery."
>
> He said, "Keep up your faith, sister."

Many of the Saints were allowed to sleep in the wagons, rather than on the ground. This proved a mixed blessing. As Patience Loader recalled one such night,

> We made our bed there but we only had one old quilt to lie on and in the night I woke up and called to Mother I am freezing the side I had laid on was so benomed with cold Mother got up and helped me out of the wagon there was some big fiars burning in several places in the camp and lots of the sisters siting and Sleeping near the fiar to Keep warm So I went to the fiar and staid there the remainer of the night.

Patience's family finally figured out a sleeping system: "After we baked our bread we put the hott coles in our bake kittle and took in the wagon and that made it quite comfortable and warm for us to sleep in."

John Jaques had his own system, which was to sleep on the ground on top of the extinguished campfire. Unfortunately, "In the morning the same spot was found to be the most available for a graver use—it was the easiest place in which to dig a grave to bury the night's dead. No pun is here intended."

Twenty-two years later, Jaques was still shocked to recall the change in character that the ordeal wrought among his colleagues: "Worn down by the labors and fatigues of the journey, and pinched by hunger and cold, the manliness of tall, healthy, strong men would gradually disappear, until they would grow fretful, peevish, childish, and puerile, acting sometimes as if they were scarcely accountable beings."

At South Pass, the refugees were met by more rescue teams, and again by even more at Fort Bridger. At last, every Saint could ride, and the daily pace increased until the whole party was averaging over twenty miles a day. Yet some had grown so weak that even this abundance of aid came too late. At Fort Bridger, John and Zilpah Jaques lost their two-year-old daughter, Flora. The couple carried the dead baby through to Salt Lake, so she could be buried in Zion.

From near Fort Bridger, Joseph Simmons wrote a letter to his brother in Salt Lake:

I am setting . . . on a sack of oats with the paper on my knee, by the side of a blazing Camp fire, surrounded by some eight hundred persons, one old lady lays dead within twenty feet of me, babies crying. . . . The suffering of the camp from frozen feet and various other causes, I will not attempt to describe, suffice to say bad. *bad.*

Joseph Wadsworth, one of the rescuers, later recalled,

The next morning after leaving Fort Bridger I was called on to help bury children that had died during the night. We were camped in a big cedar grove and buried the children on the side of the mountain.

Everything went along all right as there was plenty of fuel and provisions, until we came to East Canyon stream. There I was called on again to bury two more children.

In Echo Canyon, less than forty-five miles from Salt Lake, on November 27 Sarah Squires gave birth to a girl. The successful delivery seemed something of a miracle to the Saints. How Sarah managed to persevere through Martin's Cove and the last three hundred miles of the deadly trek while in her ninth month of pregnancy is but one more instance of the heroism of the everyday Saints. The parents named their infant Echo Squires. She would live to the ripe old age of eighty-six, dying only in 1943.

The last stretch of the Mormon Trail was the ruggedest of all, as the Saints had to climb and descend narrow canyons in the Wasatch Range, crossing over high passes called Big Mountain and Little Mountain. By now the snow was so deep that a special team out of Salt Lake had been ordered to pack down the "road" and to greet the emigrants with established camps and fires.

Finally, on November 30, the Martin Company entered Salt Lake City. The meeting with the residents, John Jaques later reported, was "not very joyous." Years later, Louisa Mellor Clark remembered that "President Young met us, and when he saw us he was so melted down with grief at sight of our condition he had to go home sick, but he blessed us first."

But eighteen-year-old Langley Bailey, who for weeks had been unable to walk, experienced a more momentous reception: "I was lifted up in the wagon, more dead than alive, and saw in the distance houses. . . . When [*illegible*] the city the people were coming out of meeting. Hundreds came and viewed us with much amazement."

The Saints who had relatives in the city were taken into their homes; others were more or less arbitrarily assigned to families to nurse them back to health. From much previous experience with near-starvation, the Saints knew that they could not let the refugees gorge themselves on the food that was suddenly available in abundance. Remembered George Housley many years later, "Brother Slack, our kind friend, would not allow me only a limited amount of bread as he was afraid it would kill me. But after they had gone to meeting I finished up the whole pot pie which had been prepared for the family, and I am alive yet and I have been hungry to this day."

At least three of the Martin Saints made it all the way from Liverpool to Zion, only to die the day after they arrived. Half a century later, Josiah Rogerson remembered seventeen-year-old Alice Ollorton, "whose feet and back became so badly frozen between the Red Buttes and Bridger that she was brought into Salt Lake more dead than alive, expiring the next day."

Rescuer Thomas Steed had been overjoyed to meet his good friend from England John Bailey (Langley's father) among the Martin Saints a day's drive east of Fort Bridger. But he would later report, "Brother Bailey was so severely frost bitten that his daughter had to carry him." Instead of accompanying Bailey the rest of the way to Salt Lake, Steed pushed on eastward to rescue others still in the rear. "We wept together when I had to tell them of that decision. My poor friend Bailey died in arriving to Salt Lake."

And in the plainest of language, Margaret Griffiths later recorded, "My father died the next morning after we got in to Salt Lake. He was frozen to death, He was 47 years of age."

Because the rescuers had concentrated their efforts on the handcart Saints, the two wagon companies lagged well behind in the home stretch. The Hunt and Hodgetts wagons trickled in through the first two weeks of December. The last of all the Saints in the monumental 1856 emigration did not arrive in Zion until December 15.

WITH FAR GREATER uncertainty than that attending the Willie Company, the true death toll among the Martin Company can never be reckoned. The Saints themselves in the party could not keep count. Their retrospective estimates range from a low of one hundred to a high of three hundred. Hafen and Hafen cite 135 to 150. LDS archivist and historian Mel Bashore, who has carefully studied the question, sets the toll at 150 to 170.

If we take the range of the death toll in the Willie Company as between sixty-six and seventy-seven, and the range in the Martin Company as between 135 and 170, then the total mortality count in the last two handcart companies amounts to between about 200 and 240. In contrast, the toll in the much more famous Donner Party disaster of 1846–47 was forty-two—only from one-fifth to one-sixth the number of deaths incurred by the handcarters. The conclusion is inescapable: the Mormon catastrophe of 1856 remains far and away the most deadly in the history of westward migration in the United States.

At once, however, the propaganda machine of church publications began to cover up the disaster. Only four days after the Martin Company's arrival, the *Deseret News* acknowledged, "As was to be expected, they have suffered considerably from storms and inclement weather, and several have had their feet and hands more or less frosted, but are now comfortably housed and cared for." But the Lord was watching over even this ill-fated caravan of Saints, for "we can plainly recognize the kind hand of an overruling Providence in opening a way of escape for so many." In that peculiarly Mormon vein, with its sense of collective persecution, the brief newspaper notice closed with a defiant vaunt: "Let the world oppose the gathering of Israel, let the wicked scoff, rage and imagine vanity, so long as the Saints give diligent heed to the counsels of those placed to direct, the gathering will progress as shall please the Most High."

By the time the tidings of the last handcart company reached John Taylor's office in New York, the disaster had been further sanitized. In *The Mormon*, Taylor quoted a letter from Brigham Young written in early December:

> "The weather for some time has been and continues to be cold, but through the blessings of the Lord, all our immigrating companies have arrived, except two independent ox train companies, which are now safely quartered at Fort Bridger, and will probably arrive in eight or ten days. . . .
>
> "Notwithstanding the companies now out and the two last arrived hand-cart companies were caught in the cold and storms, owing to far too late a start from Florence, yet the relief so promptly, freely, liberally, and timely sent from here was so blest in rescuing them, that but few comparatively, have suffered severely, though some had their feet and hands more or less frosted; yet the mortality has been much less than often attends well fitted animal trains travelling in good season."

That letter closed with a characteristic Young flourish: "Business remains dull; money is scarce and becoming scarcer, which will prove a great blessing to the people, if they wisely improve the lesson."

In early December, however, the streets of Salt Lake City were abuzz with gossip that no amount of presidential rhetoric could stifle. Even before the Willie Company came in, news of the terrible suffering of the last two handcart companies had been broadcast through the city. Moreover, the blame was being laid squarely on the Prophet's shoulders. Heber Kimball acknowledged as much as he spoke in the Tabernacle on November 2 (a week before the Willie party's arrival) to complain about the people's "murmuring":

> Some find fault with and blame br. Brigham and his Council, because of the sufferings they have heard that our brethren are enduring on the plains. A few of them have died, and you hear some exclaim, 'what an awful thing it is! Why is it that the First Presidency are so unwise in their calculations? but it falls on their shoulders.' Well, the late arrival of those on the plains cannot be helped now, but let me tell you, most emphatically, that if all who were entrusted with the care and management of this year's immigration had done as they were counseled and dictated by the First Presidency of this church, the sufferings and hardships now endured by the companies on their way here would have been avoided. Why? Because they would have left the Missouri river in season, and not have been hindered until into September.

This had already become the party line. In all of Young's correspondence, there is not a single word before November 1856 indicating that he explicitly warned the handcart companies not to set out from Florence too late in the season. From that date on, however, Young would insist that that had always been his counsel. The disaster (insofar as he could admit that a disaster had occurred) would not be laid to his account: it was entirely the fault of his shortsighted lieutenants.

In particular, the Prophet singled out Franklin Richards and Daniel Spencer for his most scathing comments. At that same meeting in the Tabernacle, a month before the worst of the suffering would become known, Young outlined the ideal handcart trek as starting from the Missouri River on June 1. (The Willie Company had left Florence on August 16, the Martin Company on August 25.) Then he turned his famous

talent for scorn on the returning missionaries, who, he would insist, had
botched the 1856 emigration:

> Here is br. Franklin D. Richards who has but little knowledge
> of business, except what he has learned in the church; he came
> into the church when a boy, and all the public business he has
> been in is the little he has done while in Liverpool, England;
> and here is br. Daniel Spencer, br. Richards' first counselor and
> a man of age and experience, and I do not know that I will at-
> tach blame to either of them. But if, while at the Missouri river,
> they had received a hint from any person on this earth, or if
> even a bird had chirped it in the ears of brs. Richards and Spen-
> cer, they would have known better than to rush men, women
> and children on to the prairie in the autumn months, on the 3d
> of September, to travel over a thousand miles. I repeat that if a
> bird had chirped the inconsistency of such a course in their ears,
> they would have thought and considered for one moment, and
> would have stopped those men, women and children there until
> another year.

As for those who wished to blame the Prophet instead of his lieutenants: "If any man, or woman, complains of me or of my Counselors, in
regard to the lateness of some of this season's immigration, let the curse
of God be on them and blast their substance with mildew and destruction, until their names are forgotten from the earth."

CHAPTER EIGHT

THE MORMON
MAYFLOWER

One day in August 2006, I wandered into the Downtown Marriott hotel in Salt Lake City. In a nook just to the right of the front door, I was surprised to stumble across a small bronze sculpture. It was a replica, about one-fourth size, of the original, called *The Handcart Pioneer,* cast in 1926 by Torleif S. Knaphus. Just the day before, I had carefully studied that original work where it stands, in the open air in the southwest corner of Temple Square, the center of sprawling Salt Lake City and the spiritual hub of today's flourishing LDS church.

The cynosure of the ten-acre square is the soaring Temple, built of quartz monzonite quarried in Little Cottonwood Canyon, twenty miles to the southeast. Begun in 1853 with a groundbreaking ceremony presided over by Brigham Young, the Temple was not completed until 1893, sixteen years after the Prophet's death.

Temple Square also encloses the rotunda-shaped Tabernacle, where the celebrated Mormon Tabernacle Choir performs virtually every Sunday; two of Young's residences dating from the 1850s, the Beehive House and the Lion House, the former restored as a National Historic Site, the latter converted into a popular "pantry" where luncheon crowds feast on Mormon home-cooking; the towering Church Office Building (housing the LDS Archives, where I spent weeks doing research); and the Joseph Smith Memorial Building, home of the FamilySearch Center, arguably the world's leading genealogical resource. The square is also festooned with statuary, including not only Knaphus's tribute to the handcart emigrants but a colossal sculpture of Brigham Young facing south from the center of the southern gateway to the square. (Even faithful Saints joke that Young's hand is raised in salute not to the Temple, which stands behind him on the right, but toward Zions Bank across the street.)

Knaphus's skillful sculpture powerfully evokes the grit and the pathos of the handcart pioneers during the 1856 ordeal. Inside the yoke, a tired but determined man pulls the cart's burden. A young lad with a brimmed hat pushes gamely from the rear. The wife, walking on the left side of the cart, holds her hand to her breast as she turns to gaze anxiously at her tiny daughter, who, with a resigned look on her face, rides the box on top of the family's baggage.

In the Marriott lobby, however, what caught my attention was not the Knaphus replica, but a laminated plaque affixed to it. In bold print, the caption named six ancestors of J. Willard Marriott, the founder of the hotel chain, who had "crossed the plains" to Salt Lake City during the pioneer days. Two names leapt out at me:

ELIZABETH STEWART MARRIOTT, J. Willard Marriott's grandmother, pulled a handcart from Kirtland, Ohio to Salt Lake City in 1853.

WILLIAM MORRIS, J. Willard Marriott's maternal grandfather, crossed the plains with a handcart company in 1855.

By this point in my research, I knew that neither claim could be true. No Mormon handcart company was ever organized before Edmund Ellsworth's in 1856. And no Mormon ever pulled a handcart from Kirtland, for that erstwhile LDS stronghold had been abandoned by 1838.

I walked to the front desk and told the clerk the reasons that I doubted the claims on behalf of William Morris and Elizabeth Stewart Marriott. He was dumbfounded. "You're the first person who's ever brought anything like this to our attention," he told me. Then a wan smile crossed his face. "But you can be sure," he confided, "they're never going to change it."

It was Saturday night, and all the higher-ups were enjoying their weekend elsewhere. I turned to go, resolved to file away the erroneous captions as just one more example of apocryphal signage—of which I had discovered an abundance over the years all across the West, as well as elsewhere. But the impasse nagged at me. It was always possible that Marriott's two ancestors had indeed performed their handcart feats, but that the dates and origin points had gotten garbled in the retelling. A quick check of the partial rosters of the 1856 handcart companies revealed no William Morris and no Elizabeth Stewart [Marriott], but that still could not rule out the participation of those shadowy pioneers.

Thus began eight frustrating months of e-mail exchanges between me and the Marriott corporate headquarters in Washington, D.C. As the hotel clerk had predicted, corporate headquarters was not amenable to correcting the captions on the plaques. The Marriott corporation's reluctance sprang not merely from institutional inertia, but also from wounded pride. After a century and a half of hindsight, having a handcart pioneer as an ancestor had been transformed from a semisecret family tragedy into a badge of courage, and even beyond that, into a seal of authenticity. By this time, the handcart was no longer John Ahmanson's "two-wheeled man-tormentor" or "infernal machine." It had become the Mormon *Mayflower*.

Half-jokingly, I shared my insight with Ardis Parshall, a freelance researcher and devout Mormon whom I had hired to guide me through the labyrinth of the LDS Archives. I was surprised to receive her wholehearted agreement. "Mormons are proud of our pioneer ancestors," Parshall told me. "Most of us secretly feel that having ancestors who came by wagon is better than having ancestors who came by train. It's even better when your ancestors came by handcart. And of course you're practically royalty if you can claim someone in the Martin or Willie Companies."

I asked Parshall to apply her formidable talents to a genealogical ferreting out of William Morris and Elizabeth Stewart. In only a day or two, she came back to me with the definitive results. Elizabeth Stewart, born in 1829 in Bedfordshire, England, was indeed J. Willard Marriott's grandmother. She had in fact come across the plains in 1853—not by handcart, but in the fifty-six-wagon Moses Clawson Company. Parshall confirmed this finding with three published sources.

Marriott's maternal grandfather was harder to find, but the indefatigable Parshall came up with some solid facts:

William Morris cannot yet be placed with any specific overland company. He and his family (a wife previous to the one we are concerned with) are on the 1850 census living in Alton, Madison County, Illinois. He appears on the Utah 1856 territorial census, living in Weber County, suggesting that he had emigrated at least by 1855. . . . Whichever company he traveled with, he cannot have come by handcart because no handcarts were used by Mormons prior to 1856.

By now I had given up on the Marriott corporation bureaucrats. Instead, I did what I should have done in the first place. I telephoned the hotel in Salt Lake City and asked to speak to the general manager. Within minutes, a man named Steve Lundgren was on the line. I summarized Parshall's research, offering to send him her report. If he was dismayed by the news, Lundgren didn't let on. Instead, he emphasized that J. Willard Marriott, Jr., son of the founder and CEO of the corporation, who Lundgren said was his good friend, would be the first to insist that the laminated plaque in the lobby, if untruthful, be corrected. Lundgren, in fact, would be meeting with the CEO in a couple of weeks and would be glad to share my findings.

I forwarded Parshall's report. A few weeks later, I received an e-mail from Lundgren:

I spoke with Bill Marriott regarding the research you presented regarding his family and their travels to Utah. He acknowledged that Elizabeth Stewart did not cross the plains in a handcart company; he did not have recollection of William Morris. He was also unaware of the specifics on the caption on the handcart statue in the hotel lobby. We have removed the caption and will replace it with a corrected one regarding Elizabeth Stewart and William Morris. Thank you for sharing this information.

As of this writing, a revised plaque has been installed.

FOR MORE THAN two decades the handcart catastrophe of 1856 was swept under the Mormon rug. At the time, the Prophet used his formidable talents to put the most positive possible spin on the debacle. The death toll was minimized, while Young insisted again and again that the 1856 emigration had proved the handcart plan fundamentally sound. As a gratuitous demonstration of this tenet, in April 1857 Brigham sent seventy handpicked missionaries eastward from Salt Lake along the Mormon Trail, pushing and pulling better-designed handcarts than the ones carpentered out of green wood from the forests around Iowa City.

It was not until 1878 that any survivor of the 1856 tragedy publicly disputed the official version. Fittingly, the veteran who spoke out was John Jaques, the former associate of Franklin D. Richards in the Liverpool office of the church. No longer the zealot who had shamed his in-laws, the James Loader family, into undertaking the handcart pilgrimage by printing Patience's timorous letter in the *Millennial Star*, Jaques had become a thoughtful witness to the history he had helped create. What drove him to publish a seven-part memoir of the Martin Company's ordeal in the *Salt Lake Daily Herald* between December 1, 1878, and January 19, 1879, was Jaques's indignation that twenty-two years later, the church was still trying to collect from the battered survivors the Perpetual Emigration Fund loans that had launched them on the handcart trail. With Swiftian eloquence, at the end of his seventh installment, he made his own modest proposal. He couched that proposal in an ironic anticipation of the objections he knew would greet it. "In conclusion," Jaques wrote, "I have a benevolent suggestion to offer. I may be blamed for it by some persons, but I cannot help that. Namby-pamby sycophancy may deem the suggestion rashly presumptuous."

To lend authority to the proposal, before he spelled it out Jaques conjured up his own suffering in the Martin Company, as one who "for weeks together stood face to face with Death in the repulsive aspects outlined in these papers, who witnessed his victories daily under heart-rending circumstances, who saw those near and dear to me succumb to his attacks under such circumstances and fall helpless victims to his all-conquering power, and who at that time would scarcely have cared the toss of a button to avoid a decisive wrestle with the grim monster myself."

Now the proposal:

The suggestion is this: It would be entirely proper for the president of the Perpetual Emigration Fund company and his assistants to be asked to freely and fully cancel the indebtedness for passage, if any remains, of every member of this unfortunate and sorely tried emigrant company, and it would be a righteous, beneficent and graceful act for those gentlemen to readily accede to such a request. For if anybody ever worked his passage, to the uttermost farthing, these poor emigrants did. They paid not only the principal, but the interest also, with the latter rigorously compounded. They paid it in the hardest and most precious and most costly coin—by enduring daily hard labor, wasting fatigue, and pinching privations, by passing through untold hardships, by suffering cold and hunger, wretchedness and starvation, nakedness and famine, by frozen limbs and injured health and broken constitutions and many by giving their earthly all. Most of them lost old and valued friends and near relatives, and not a few sacrificed their own lives. In this most painful and most rigorous manner did these poor creatures pay dearly for the privilege of being brought over land and sea. Methinks that even stern Justice herself, inflexibly rigid and relentlessly exacting as she is, if she were to speak, would say, with no uncertain voice, that they had paid enough, and much more than enough.

Whether Jaques succeeded in getting the handcart pioneers' debts to the PEF annulled is not a matter of record. It seems, however, that many an overdue loan was quietly forgotten.

In Jaques's seven vivid installments, there is no hint yet of turning the handcart tragedy into a Mormon *Mayflower*. Instead (as the many quotations from those newspaper dispatches cited earlier attest) he unblinkingly recorded the suffering, the losses, and the horror of the Martin Company's trial by starvation and cold. Jaques gave a cogent explanation for the two-decade veil of silence that had settled over the disastrous emigration:

This is the first time that the story of this handcart expedition has been written from beginning to end, so far as I know. It was not

done before, partly for the reason that, for years after the journey was made, nobody wished to say or hear much about it, and
those who were in the company cared to remember little of it.
The affair was one of those disagreeable things, like some hate-
ful dream, or dreadful vision, or horrible nightmare, that people
seem indisposed to refer to but rather tacitly agree to forget, as
much as possible, at least for a time.

Yet, in a famous conclusion that is often quoted today by apologetic
historians, Jaques wrote in his last installment, "The question may be
asked, whom do I blame for the misadventures herein related. I blame
nobody. I am not anxious to blame anybody. I am not writing for the
purpose of blaming anybody, but to fill up a blank page of history with
matters of much interest."

Brigham Young had died the year before Jaques published his
testament. Perhaps when the Prophet was still alive, it would have
been heretical to argue for cancellation of the PEF indebtedness. Perhaps even after Young's death, it was still dangerous to blame any of
the high-ranking officials involved for the outcome of the handcart
"experiment"—even the officially scapegoated Franklin Richards. Yet
Jaques's disavowal of blame sounds sincere, as he credits Captain Martin for his ceaseless care and vigilance, cites the "most commendable
spirit of liberality . . . manifested by the residents of this valley" who
took in the ill and maimed after they arrived in Salt Lake, and gives
the highest marks to the rescuers, saluting "the self-denying exposure,
privations, and labors of those who went with the teams from this city
to help the emigrants along."

Jaques's outpouring remained, however, an isolated evocation of
the 1856 debacle. In the 1870s and 1880s, exposés written by apostates
sometimes summarized the disastrous campaign. The most scathing account emerged in the pages of Ann Eliza Young's sensational *Wife No. 19*.
Young devoted two chapters of her tell-all book to the handcart episode,
announcing her thesis at the start: "In the history of any people there
has never been recorded a case of such gross mismanagement as that
of gathering the foreign Saints to Zion in the year 1856." There was no
doubt in Ann Eliza's mind as to who was to blame for that mismanage-

ment, as she excoriated her ex-husband for "one of the very worst blunders that the Prince of Blunderers, Brigham Young, ever made."

By the 1890s, chroniclers had begun to record the reminiscences of the pioneers who had gathered to Zion in the early years. These records included some stories of handcart emigrants from 1856. Yet according to independent historian Lyndia Carter, "Fifty years go by before people really are willing to talk about the handcart expeditions. And it's not until the 1920s and the 1930s that Mormon pioneer history begins to be glorified."

In 1906, several survivors of the Willie and Martin Companies decided to organize a fiftieth reunion. Even at that remove from the disaster, those men felt they had to petition the church for permission to hold such a gathering.

The reunion was held on October 4, 1906, in the 14th Ward assembly hall in Salt Lake City. The organizer was Samuel Jones, who had been a nineteen-year-old in the Martin Company half a century before. By 1906, Jones and others calculated, only twenty-three members of the Willie Company were still alive, fifty-eight veterans of the Martin Company, and fourteen of the rescuers. It was noted that some of the survivors who had been bound so tightly together during their ordeal had not seen each other in more than thirty years.

Jones's brother Albert, three years younger than Samuel, gave a stirring address. He relived for his colleagues some of the more poignant and pivotal episodes in the Martin Company's travails, such as the near-miraculous appearance of rescuer Joseph Young on his white mule as the company lay stalled beneath Red Buttes. Then, in his peroration, Jones explicitly drew the uplifting moral lesson of the ordeal that would serve as the church's official version during the century to come:

In all the labors of your frontier life you have nobly taken your post of duty—& this day you feel in your hearts that the toils and labors of the past are amply rewarded in the blessings of today. . . . [T]hough the handcart episode is one of the unpleasant expirences of our lives, the schooling that it gave, & the training of our unpleasant episodes in our lives since then—all have tended to make our faith in our religion the stronger—& our appreaceation of Gods own hand dealing to us as a people, more easily discerned.

The tone of the reunion was not exactly jubilant, but a fierce pride in having gone through their terrible ordeal united the survivors in a solidarity they had not previously enjoyed. A few years later, in a published reminiscence, Samuel Jones would underline the sense the veterans shared of having been singled out for a special blessing: "While the journey was a hard one, we have nothing but the best of feelings for the men who advised us to make the trip. The purpose was a glorious one."

From 1906 on, the survivors were formally united in the Handcart Veterans Association. But when Samuel Jones proposed the erection of a monument to those who had died along the handcart trail, church leaders became skittish. In a 1908 letter to Jones from the First Presidency (headed now by Prophet Joseph F. Smith, nephew of the founder), those leaders unctuously insisted, "But while we feel tenderly towards [the handcart martyrs] we hesitate to give our consent to the erection of a monument in their honor, believing the time is hardly ripe for it. . . . It is clear to us that this important suggestion of yours be deferred for the present." Any such monument would be deferred for another nine decades.

The year after the fiftieth reunion, Josiah Rogerson, fifteen at the time he traveled in the Martin Company, determined to write the first comprehensive history of his own party's 1856 emigration. He assiduously gathered and transcribed what unpublished diaries he could locate (relying primarily on James Bleak's journal) and melded them with reminiscences by other pioneers and with his own memories of the ordeal. Between October 13 and December 8, 1907, Rogerson published nine weekly installments of his patchy but admirably rich account in the *Salt Lake Herald*. What drove Rogerson to distraction, however, was his inability to find the diary kept by Captain Edward Martin, who had died in 1882. As Rogerson wrote in his fifth installment:

> To make the record as full as possible, I have spared neither time nor pains to get Captain Edward Martin's journal and diary, which I know he kept daily throughout the entire journey that

year, of over 1,350 miles, for I many times saw him writing, and read his entries in his journal, and it contains the names of all that died and fell by the way, and where buried, yet notwithstanding the search of his relict and children, who are quite willing these names should be had therefrom, as yet it has not been found.

To this day, Martin's diary, which scholars would give much to be able to read, has never been found. A persistent rumor has it that after Martin's death, the diary was "consigned to the flames." Historian Lyndia Carter discusses this murky business: "Martin's wife later said the diary was 'accidentally burned.' But was it burned while he was still on the trail? Or only after his death? Because he was the leader of the party, he always bore a certain blame and sense of guilt. One descendant whom I interviewed said that the Martin family has always had a taint because of the tragedy. His widow might have burned the diary on purpose."

In the end, Rogerson never managed to put his newspaper articles together as a book. The Harold B. Lee Library at Brigham Young University holds a poignant testimonial to that failed effort: a sheaf of clippings of the original *Herald* articles with Rogerson's penciled-in corrections and second thoughts.

The loss of Martin's diary raises the question of censorship and expurgation in the handcart record. Beginning in the late 1930s, Kate B. Carter, an editor and chronicler for the Daughters of Utah Pioneers, published multivolume miscellanies of memoirs and historical sketches under such titles as *Heart Throbs of the West* and *Treasures of Pioneer History*. These books contain relentlessly upbeat, sentimental, and pious homilies based on historical fact, as gathered over the years in the voluminous DUP archives. Another persistent rumor has it that Kate Carter made it a regular practice to destroy documents that fell into her hands that could be construed as casting an unflattering light on the church. If the rumor is true, we shall never know what other accounts of the 1856 handcart campaign disappeared into Carter's wastebasket.

The first book-length history of the handcart emigration did not appear until 1960, when LeRoy and Ann Hafen published *Handcarts to Zion*. As noted earlier, the Hafens were spurred to their effort in part by the fact that their mother, as a girl of six emigrating from Switzerland, had come to Salt Lake City with the last of all the handcart companies in 1860. The Hafens honestly concede that the Willie and Martin exodus ended up as "the worst disaster in the history of Western migration." But they subscribe to the myth first propagated by Brigham Young that the handcart plan was basically sound: "Taken in its normal operation, with adequate preparations and proper scheduling, the handcart plan was an economical, effective, and rather beneficent institution."

The last paragraph in the Hafens' narrative (not counting their substantial and useful appendices) amounts to a ringing affirmation of the spiritual boon of handcart travel:

> Like Israel of old, these modern "Children of God" responded to a Prophet's voice. From their zeal for a new religion, they drew strength. From an abiding faith in God and his overruling care, and from a firm belief in the divinity of the command for Latter-day Saints to gather to Zion, they were enabled to gird up their loins and walk the long scourging trail.

The first non-Mormon historian seriously to chronicle the handcart campaign was Wallace Stegner, in *The Gathering of Zion* (1964). More than half the book is devoted to the pioneer trek of 1846–47, but Stegner allocates three chapters to the handcart campaign and its aftermath. Fascinated all his life by the Latter-day Saints, and on the whole an admirer of them as people, Stegner colors his chronicle with the ironic style he learned from Bernard DeVoto, which in this instance has the odd effect of lightening the tragedy with an almost jaunty overtone. As its title indicates, the third handcart chapter, called "The Man That Ate the Pack Saddle," treats the desperate wintering-over at Fort Seminoe by Daniel Jones and his nineteen fellow "volunteers" as a swashbuckling saga in the vein of Davy Crockett or Daniel Boone.

IN THE 1960S, when Stegner was writing, he received no help from church authorities. So uncooperative, in fact, were the Mormon archivists that Stegner complained in his Acknowledgments, "Several libraries have helped to compensate for the fact that the most logical source of information, the library of the Church of Jesus Christ of Latter-day Saints, is opened to scholars only reluctantly and with limitations."

As I began my own research, I was fearful that the same sort of road-block would bar my path to the Mormon truth. Making my first visit to the LDS Archives in April 2005, I thought it best to slip in, as it were, under the radar, registering at the desk as if I were simply another out-of-towner curious about his ancestors in Utah. To my great surprise, I found that the archivists not only knew I was coming, but welcomed me with open arms. During the subsequent two years, they went out of their way to aid my research, even putting me on the track of documents I would not otherwise have known existed.

This new generation of archivists, partly in reaction to their prede-cessors' obstinacy, practices a truly enlightened and disinterested open-ness even to non-LDS scholars. Furthermore, under the direction of Mel Bashore, the diaries and reminiscences of all the pioneer emigrat-ing parties between 1847 and 1868 have been faithfully transcribed by volunteers and posted online under the subheading "Mormon Pioneer Overland Travel" on the official church Web site (http://www.lds.org/churchhistory). This matchless resource saved me (as it will save other scholars to come) countless hours of squinting at microfilm and tran-scribing in pencil, word for word, documents that are all but unreadable in the original.

As I would do in 2005 and 2006, in the early 1960s Wallace Stegner retraced much of the Mormon Trail by automobile. At the time, how-ever, virtually no plaques or monuments called attention to the hand-cart saga. Standing before the granite cirque in western Wyoming where so many Saints had died, Stegner conjured up the scene out of thin air: "At Martin's Cove, just above Devil's Gate, the pilgrim may stop and try to imagine how that cliff-backed river-bottom might have looked to a shivering, exhausted, starving handcart emigrant in November, 1856."

By the time I began my own research, I knew that a visitors' cen-ter—opened in 1997, to mark the sesquicentennial of the pioneer trek of 1847—had been built near Martin's Cove. The first of my three trips to the Mormon Handcart Visitors' Center, however, in August 2005, was full of surprises.

I had not expected such an ambitious operation. The church had bought and refurbished the Sun Ranch, an assemblage of buildings erected in 1872 by a French-Canadian settler at the southern entrance to Devil's Gate. Nothing remains of nearby Fort Seminoe, where Daniel Jones and his fellow sufferers had wintered over in 1856–57 to guard the handcart pioneers' possessions, though an archaeological crew out of the University of Wyoming had excavated the site in 2001. (In the following year, a faithful reconstruction of the old fort was begun.) Nearby, the main Sun Ranch building had been turned into a handsome museum. I started my visit with a leisurely tour.

By now, having already spent considerable time in the LDS Archives in Salt Lake City, I was prepared for the sanctifying platitudes with which the visitors' center converted a needless tragedy into a saga of perseverance and faith. A sign at the entrance to the museum formed a précis of the center's purpose:

> In 1856 . . . portions of the ground were made sacred by the sacrifices of a company of handcart pioneers who struggled through the snow of Wyoming enroute to the Valley of the Great Salt Lake. This is the story of those stirring events and the legacy of courage and faith wrought by all ten companies of handcart pioneers. This visitors' center is dedicated to honor their courage, faith, and triumphs in the face of terrible adversity.

Like Mormon docents everywhere, the "elders" and "sisters" staffing the museum were eager to give me help and information. I politely fended them off so I could concentrate on the displays. As the visitor wends his way from room to room, the story of the westward migration unfolds. The captions emphasized the persecution of the Saints in the East and Midwest: they had chosen to head for Utah to thrive in a place "free of injustice, bigotry and malice." One panel acknowledged that the handcart plan was Brigham Young's scheme for saving money, but insisted in bold print, "The Poor Welcomed Less Expensive Travel." Moreover, "The plan was received with rejoicing by needy Saints in Great Britain and throughout Europe. It was the answer to fervent prayers."

Likewise, the exhibits acknowledged the seventeen-pound weight limit for personal goods, "including bedding and clothing." But as things started to go wrong, it was as if an unforeseeable fate had jinxed the plan: "Church emigration officials at Iowa City could not keep up with the demand for handcarts."

I was beguiled and puzzled by the medley of pious obfuscation and frank admission of suffering that the museum presented. A glass case holding a day's ration of flour made vividly clear how little food the Saints were forced to subsist on. One caption granted, "Children chewed rawhide to quiet their pains of hunger." Yet the rescue came across as a deus ex machina: "But President Young was true to his word"; "Martin Handcart Company Found and Saved."

Most conspicuous by its absence was any count of the total number of dead in the Willie and Martin Companies. The only retrospective quotations from survivors were blindly loyal ones, such as that of Francis Webster, a twenty-five-year-old pilgrim in the Martin Company in 1856: "We came through with the absolute knowledge that God lives for we became acquainted with him in our extremities. . . . I knew that the Angels of God were there."

Somehow the museum curators realized they had to account for the tragedy. A single display case accomplished this task by stacking ten oversized dominoes beside each other, frozen in the moment that the chain started to topple. From left to right, the dominoes were labeled thus: "Left England Late," "Many Elderly & Children," "Handcarts Not Built," "Frequent Repairs to Carts," "Oxen Lost in Storm," "Flour Transferred to Carts," "Clothes Left to Lighten Load," "Rations Cut, then Gone," "Cattle Weaken & Die," "October 19 Storm."

So that was it: the whole handcart tragedy was the result of a bad alignment of dominoes. As many a literary critic and scholar has pointed out, the passive voice is a handy structure for evading the question of human responsibility. According to the visitors' center museum, it was not the agents in Iowa City who grievously erred by failing to have handcarts ready for the Saints; it was "Handcarts Not Built." It was not the foolhardy decision by Captain Martin and his lieutenants to burn extra clothing and baggage at Deer Creek that plunged the company into a more desperate plight; it was "Clothes Left to Lighten Load." And the last and fatal domino was the most impersonal of all: an early snowstorm that no one saw coming.

The Mormon Handcart Visitors' Center, however, amounts to far more than a museum. My chief aim in stopping there that August, like that of 90 percent of the 32,000-odd visitors who arrive each summer, was to pull and push my own handcart. The church has purchased hundreds of handcart wheels built by Amish craftsmen in Pennsylvania, then used its own carpenters to build the boxes and yokes that complete a veritable fleet of modern handcarts. From slow beginnings in 1997, the Handcart Visitors' Center has become quite the place to spend a few summer days or even a week, as whole Mormon stakes make the pilgrimage from their far-off hometowns to this lonely place in western Wyoming to pull their own handcarts, visit Martin's Cove, camp together, and sing songs and tell tales about their ancestors. The most serious groups dress for the occasion in 1850s garb.

Before launching out with my cart, I chatted with Elder Hadley in the compound's machine shop. An expert on the design of the "replicas," Hadley pointed out the differences between the carriages furnished visitors today and the ones Chauncey Webb and his helpers cobbled out of green wood in 1856. The modern handcarts are considerably bigger and heavier than the originals (about 150 pounds each, compared to the 60 or 65 pounds of the pioneers' carts), but they also have the inestimable advantages of iron rims on the wheels, ball bearings in the hubs, and steel axles. The trail leading west from the visitors' center, moreover, is a dirt road today, far smoother and easier than the sodden track of 1856.

Finally I approached the headquarters where the handcarts were stabled. I was surprised that no one charged me a rental fee, or even required an ID as deposit. A cheerful elder assigned me handcart No. 155. Knowing that a typical load for an 1856 handcart manned by five emigrants was about two hundred to three hundred pounds, I threw what I considered an equivalent load of sixty pounds of backpack and duffel bag into my cargo box and set out.

Even along the gravel road, I was shocked by how hard it was to move my handcart. I alternated pushing and pulling, unable to get the hang of either. When I stood inside the yoke and pushed, the crossbar banged uncomfortably against my hips or my chest, depending on whether I grasped it with an underhand or overhand grip. When I stood in front of the yoke, reached back for the crossbar and pulled, my forearms grew sore from the unnatural twisting the act required.

Apparently a solo handcarter at the visitors' center was an anomaly. I had gone only a few hundred yards when a white-shirted missionary standing sentinel along the trail called out, "Looks like you lost your family!"

Just before I had started out, in fact, a throng of two hundred Saints from the town of Parowan, in southwestern Utah, had streamed out of the headquarters with their caravan of handcarts. They were costumed to the teeth in period outfits, and they exuded a Sunday-picnic exuberance that seemed strangely at odds with the somber chapter of history they were reliving.

It was only 1.3 miles by the dirt road to a second visitors' station, from which a paved walking trail loops up into the cove. It took me half an hour to cover that distance with my handcart, and I arrived sore and tired. The effort had given me a profound new respect for the courage and hardiness of the Saints in 1856. I was, after all, in good health, well fed, and in shape from a summer of hiking—not emaciated from weeks of undernourishment, nor trudging through snow wearing tattered shoes, nor played out from day after day of hypothermic bivouacs.

I parked my cart at the visitors' station, then hiked the trail into Martin's Cove. It was an 80 degree day with a cooling wind out of the west, pushing high cumulus clouds across the sky. The cove itself is protected by a cone-shaped mound of earth that fronts it—a sand dune stabilized by natural grasses. The granite slabs that backed the cove gleamed in the sun, and groves of piñons and junipers gentled the place with swaths of deep green boughs. It was impossible on this August day to see Martin's Cove as anything other than a beautiful landscape. To conjure up the misery of November 1856 required an effort of imagination.

At the apex of the trail, midway between the fronting dune and the backing granite slabs, a group of thirty or forty visitors in period clothing sat on several rows of bleachers while a "sister" addressed them. They were members of a Mormon stake from Lehi, a small town midway between Salt Lake City and Provo. I sat at some distance from the group and unpacked my picnic lunch, not without a certain guilt about munching on cheese, crackers, and nuts while the Saints from Lehi sat in rapt and sober attention to the woman's lecture.

"When President Hinckley was here," she said, "he asked if he could go alone over to where they thought they buried their dead." She gestured at a hollow to the north, covered with grasses and low bushes. Gordon Hinckley, ninety-five years old that August of 2005, was Joseph Smith's fourteenth successor as President, Prophet, Seer, and Revelator of the Church of Jesus Christ of Latter-day Saints.

The speaker suddenly choked up, then began weeping. Several of the Lehi Saints stifled sobs themselves. Eventually, their lecturer regained control and finished her talk. Slowly, lingering in small groups, the modern-day pilgrims set out along the back trail toward the visitors' station to the south. I waited till they were all gone, then read the plaque that alluded to the fifty-six Martin Company members who had died in the cove. The back trail passes close to the supposed burial ground. A sign indicates, "Fragile Soil and Vegetation—Please remain on Developed Trail."

Some of the most assiduous students of the Oregon and Mormon Trails believe the Mormon Handcart Visitors' Center has mislocated Martin's Cove—that the cirque where the ordeal transpired is actually a similar cove a couple of miles farther west. To me at the moment, the question did not seem very important. What mattered was that the Saints of the twenty-first century have a "sacred place" along the Wyoming trail where they can gather and contemplate the fate of their ancestors.

Back at the visitors' station, I chatted with another volunteer, whose nametag identified him as Elder Whittier. "A week ago," he said, "I was giving a Cove talk up there. You know, it's pretty hard not to cry. You know the Spirit's working on them." (By "them," I wasn't sure whether Elder Whittier meant the dead or the present-day visitors.) "One guy sat there for five or ten minutes after everybody else had left. Later he told me, 'Between the cove and your talk, I'm going to change my whole life.'"

The standard loop for modern handcarters pushes a little farther west, crosses the Sweetwater without a bridge, then trundles along the south bank of the stream back to the headquarters—two more miles, making a round trip of 3.3. I got back inside the yoke of my two-wheeled man-tormentor and trudged on. As I came to the Sweetwater crossing, I saw the Parowan stake sitting on the far bank, taking its lunch break. It was very close to here that the Martin Company Saints had made their desperate ford on November 4, 1856, as they headed for Martin's Cove— and here that the myth of the three eighteen-year-old "boys from the valley" who carried scores of Saints across the river, only to die shortly afterward as a result of their heroic service, was first crystallized.

My cart rolled easily down into the river bottom. The current was only calf-deep, and in sandals I found it almost pleasant to splash my way across the cobblestoned streambed. But the incline up to the bank on the far side was made of soft sand. With all my might, I couldn't get my cart up that mere ten-foot rise.

As I struggled in place, a freckle-faced redheaded boy of about fourteen jumped up from his lunch and ran over to help me. With him pushing and me pulling, we got the cart up to level ground. "Good boy, Cody!" sang out an elder in the Parowan stake.

"Thanks, Cody," I said, sweat pouring down my face as I shook the lad's hand. But then I was surprised to see that the boy's nametag read "Ephraim Hanks." Was he Cody or Ephraim? It took me a moment to remember the lone 1856 scout who had brought the buffalo meat to the starving Martin Saints. A sister at the handcart headquarters had told me that modern-day pilgrims often assume the identity of figures from the 1856 pageant. What Mormon boy could resist the temptation to play Ephraim Hanks on the Sweetwater?

I trudged on along the south bank. Here there was no gravel road, but only a sandy track, and the going was correspondingly tougher. On a last twenty-foot rise, I could proceed only by unloading my cart, pulling it empty up the slope, then returning for my duffel bag and backpack.

By the time I reached the visitors' center I was, in the modern epithet, "wasted," and my arms and thighs would ache for several days. Thanks to my timid loop, however, the handcart emigration had become shockingly real. With a cart far superior to the rickety, poorly lubricated vehicle of 1856, I had covered precisely 1/394th of the journey the successful Martin and Willie Saints had accomplished a century and a half before me.

• • •

A YEAR LATER, ONCE again in August, I made my second trip to the Mormon Handcart Visitors' Center. I had had enough of handcart-hauling: this time I simply hiked from the headquarters to the station below Martin's Cove. I had hoped to fall in with some party of modern-day Mormon pilgrims, rather than lurk on the periphery like a voyeur, as I had in 2005 with the Lehi stake. I was in luck: a small group of eleven women and two men from West Valley, a Salt Lake suburb, promptly welcomed me into their midst.

Each had chosen a pioneer to impersonate. In some cases, the pres-ent-day Saints had ancestors who had come across the plains, either by wagon or by handcart. Thus Trish Wade was calling herself Minerva Wade, after an ancestor whose mother, as she lay dying in Florence, had made her promise to go on to Zion so that someone in the family would complete the gathering. Minerva, according to Trish, had also had the distinction of marrying Bill Hickman, the notorious Danite who late in life had dictated his memoir, *Brigham's Destroying Angel*. Others had no such ancestors, so they chose whatever personae they wished among the real pilgrims of the 1850s.

The day before, the West Valley group had pulled their handcarts three miles to the visitors' center campground on Cherry Creek. There, around the campfire, they had told the tales of the pioneers whose iden-tities they had assumed.

The West Valley women were only too glad to explicate for me the period clothing they were wearing. Their colorful blouses were made of calico, their long ruffled skirts and aprons of cotton ("It was considered immoral to show your ankles," one woman giggled). They were further garbed with bonnets, shawls, and bandannas. Despite a temperature in the high 80s, the day before one sister had worn two skirts, to get into the spirit of the exigencies the seventeen-pound handcart limit had im-posed. The only discordant note in the women's apparel was the Nikes and Adidases that peeked out from below the hems of their skirts. (The handcarts likewise carried the anachronistic freight of box lunches and coolers filled with Gatorade.)

We hiked together up to the Lower Cove, a way station on the path to the scene of the grim vigil of 1856. There a husband-and-wife team of missionaries, Elder and Sister Schlappi, outlined the history of Martin's Cove (with which by now the thirteen members of the West Valley ward were thoroughly conversant). "In April," said Elder Schlappi, almost jovially, "the Sweetwater runs five feet deep. We still do baptisms in the river. It's quite an experience for an eight-year-old to be baptized in Martin's Cove."

The elder's tone modulated. "This is the Lower Cove. This is one of the most touching spots for me." Suddenly he could not go on, as he fought down tears.

A West Valley woman intervened, asking to lead a prayer. As everyone but me knelt, in a soft voice she thanked the Lord "for all that was sacrificed here on our behalf." Elder Schlappi recovered, and recited the canonic myths about the place: that no one had ever seen a snowstorm strike western Wyoming as early as October 19, how the three young men had sacrificed their health by carrying the Saints across the Sweetwater.

Sister Schlappi took over. "The amazing miracle," she averred, "is that *anybody* in the Martin Company made it from the last crossing of the Platte to Martin's Cove.

"This is sacred ground," she continued, "hallowed by the pioneers. The Spirit will speak to you, if you listen. Open your heart, and the Spirit will speak to you."

After a closing prayer, we moved on to the Upper Cove, where I had eavesdropped on the Lehi stake the summer before. Here another docent, Elder Harper, reeled out anecdotes from the Martin party that by now were familiar tales to me—about the tent collapsing on Peter McBride and keeping him warm, about young George Housley, who wanted only to die. "'Young man, go cut me down three trees!'" Elder Harper dramatized an order from one of the leaders of the Martin Company. "Later, George said, 'That man saved my life.'" At this point, Elder Harper collapsed in a fit of weeping.

Without missing a beat, Harper's wife took up the baton. "I get to tell a love story," she announced almost smugly, and I knew the oft-told tale that was about to ensue. In *The Price We Paid*, Andrew Olsen succinctly summarizes the story:

Sarah Franks and George Padley were engaged when they left England and planned to be married when they arrived in Salt Lake City and raise their family in Zion. George died at Martin's Cove, however, and Sarah was extremely ill and weak even before the grief she felt in George's death.

Sarah survived the journey but had no relatives or friends to meet her.

Now Sister Harper added some embellishments. "Sarah couldn't bear the thought of the wolves getting to George. They hung his body from a tree to keep it from the wolves. Sarah left her shawl with her fiancé.

"The rescue party later went back and got it. It's said that the family still owns a piece of that shawl."

I felt uncomfortable witnessing these tableaux of piety and romance: the temptation was to retreat into cynical resistance. But the deep emotion Martin's Cove elicited from these devout Saints moved me, despite my own agnostic distance.

Later, back at the picnic tables beside the visitors' station over lunch, Marsha Herbert, one of the West Valley pilgrims, told me her ancestral tale. Her great-great-grandparents were David and Jane Bowen, members of the Hunt wagon company, which had trailed the Martin Company all the way to Zion. And yet, according to Herbert, their inclusion in that party was "a blessing in disguise."

"They had planned to come to Zion two years earlier," Herbert told me. "But as they got off the ship in New York harbor, David dropped his money bag accidentally into the sea. It was all he had. He had to work for two years in Pennsylvania to earn enough money for the trek. But Jane was extremely weak when she arrived in the New World, and later she gave birth. Their one-year-old came across with the Hunt Company. Two years earlier, Jane probably wouldn't have made it."

David Bowen (thirty-three), Jane Bowen (thirty-six), and John Bowen (one) are indeed listed in the official roster of the Hunt Company in the LDS Archives. But no anecdotes or reminiscences are linked to their names.

"Is that story in the Archives?" I asked Herbert.

"No."

"How did you learn it, then?"

"It came down in the family," she replied. "My grandmother had a copy, parts of which were in David Bowen's handwriting. I typed the story out from her copy."

When I had first launched my research for this book, I had fantasized about crisscrossing Utah soliciting unpublished, uncollected memoirs from the handcart pioneers. It had not taken me long to realize what an impossible task that would prove. Yet, as rich as the archival record is in Salt Lake City, there surely remain untold further riches squirreled away in attics such as Marsha Herbert's.

A little later, though, one of the West Valley women repeated the story about the three eighteen-year-olds carrying the Saints across the Sweetwater. I could not bite my tongue. "You know, that's a myth," I blurted out. "Chad Orton has written a paper that completely debunks the story. It didn't happen."

This was not welcome news to the West Valley ward. An awkward silence ensued, as I began to feel like a drunken guest at a party who has just committed some unforgivable faux pas.

"How do we know what's really the truth?" asked Trish Ward, in conciliatory tones. I started to utter some piety of my own about relying on authentic primary sources, but instead, a young woman who had previously spoken not a word mused out loud, "Maybe we could pray."

THE MORMON HANDCART Visitors' Center stands about thirty miles west of the small town of Alcova, on State Highway 220. The road is not heavily traveled, although it serves as the truck route for rigs barreling between Rawlins and Casper. After bidding goodbye to the West Valley ward, I got back on the highway and headed west. At Muddy Gap, where a lone gas station (the only one for miles around) marks the junction with U.S. Highway 287, I took the northwest fork, still following the Sweetwater toward its headwaters below South Pass. The ambitiously named Jeffrey City proved a ghost town of some six or eight derelict buildings.

Low ridges with granite outcrops and swaths of forest marched along on either side of the Sweetwater basin. On my left, a small herd of ante-lope bounded with consummate grace across the grassland, as if racing my rental car. There was no shaking the perception that this was one of the most beautiful places in Wyoming. A perfect August day was inter-fering with my attempt to see the Mormon Trail as the gauntlet of suf-fering and death it had proved in 1856.

About ten miles west of Jeffrey City, I stopped at the Ice Slough. It was here, on October 19, 1856, in the middle of the snowstorm, that the Willie Company had been met by the advance rescue team of Young, Wheelock, Taylor, and Garr. The roadside sign, however, made no allu-sion to that propitious rendezvous, restricting its information to the fact that Oregon Trail emigrants counted on the slough for fresh water even in the heat of summer.

Nine miles farther west, I came to the Sixth Crossing. It was here that the Willie Company, buoyed by the arrival of the quartet from the Valley, camped as they prepared for their hardest day of all—the storm-lashed ascent of Rocky Ridge. Back at the Handcart Visitors' Center, Elder Had-ley had told me that more vigorous modern pilgrims than those who loop the 3.3-mile trail to Martin's Cove and back pull handcarts over Rocky Ridge, taking two days to cover the twenty-eight miles between the Sixth Crossing and Rock Creek Hollow, where the Willie Company had met up with the main rescue party led by George Grant.

In recent years, the church has built another (much smaller) visitors' center at the Sixth Crossing, just off Highway 287. A small flotilla of handcarts rested in a yard behind the tiny museum. I parked and read the plaque out front, which proclaimed in part about the Willie Saints,

> With much faith in each footstep, they struggled on through thick dust, mud, and snow. . . . Bound together in faith and with tears of joy and sorrow, mothers, daughters, and sisters worked together for one cause and one purpose. They walked on, endur-ing one of the most tragic, yet most heroic events of the pioneers going west. They left a treasured legacy to their descendants.

Inside the museum, I perused a replica of an 1856 handcart (sig-nificantly smaller and frailer than the ones parked out back), another display case holding a day's ration of flour, and a case that laid out a typical handcart woman's seventeen pounds of belongings: besides clothing and a blanket, a dish, cup, fork, spoon, and knife; a button case, with thread and thimble; and a Bible.

It was hard for me to concentrate on these artifacts, however, because the docent assigned to the place, having seized on her first visitor of the day, was oozing with inspirational chatter. As she started from scratch to explain the significance of the Sixth Crossing, I tried to let her know that I was familiar with the story, but failed to stanch the flow of her spiel. I noticed that her nametag read "Sister Willie." Was she related, then, to the captain of the ill-fated fourth handcart company? Yes, she said proudly, a direct descendant by marriage. Then on she chattered: Wasn't it inspiring to stand here where—?

Suddenly I couldn't take any more. "Yes," I interrupted, "but who was to blame?"

That stopped her cold. Sister Willie's eyes seemed to bulge with incomprehension. "Blame?" she repeated.

"After all," I went on, "more than two hundred people died."

"But they came to know God. And not one of them ever left the church."

I fled without signing the guest register.

A few miles farther west, I turned off Highway 287, which here abandons the Sweetwater as it vectors north toward Lander. I headed down the old dirt road to Atlantic City, a gold rush town near South Pass. I had no desire to pull a handcart over Rocky Ridge, but I wanted to hike part of it. Thirty-one miles down the lonely road, I came to a corral and parking lot. Here the Saints who undertake only the one-day handcart pull over Rocky Ridge (as opposed to the two-day trek from the Sixth Crossing) begin their journeys with carts trucked in on trailers.

A four-wheel-drive road follows the path the Willie Saints struggled to ascend on October 23, but the Bureau of Land Management has wisely prohibited motor vehicle travel along it. At the starting point, a monument erected in 1992 identifies the place as the "Willie Rescue Site." "This monument," the plaque reads, "is constructed to the memory of those courageous pioneers of the Willie Handcart Company and the brave men who rescued them." Yet the plaque also names nineteen Saints who died in the vicinity.

That August morning, there was no one else on the trail. The heat was cut by a twenty-five-mile-an-hour wind right in my face—the wind that seems perpetual in western Wyoming. The views were spectacular: to the northwest, I saw the Wind River Range (where I had often climbed) stretching like a blue crest across the sky; on my left, to the south, I could glimpse the impassable Sweetwater gorge that forced the emigrants up onto the swales of Rocky Ridge. What a barren place! Scarcely a bush protruded from the stony soil, and there was not a tree in sight.

Stretching ahead of me, the trail looked gentle enough, but as I hiked it, I climbed grade after grade inclined at 15 to 20 percent—tough enough in a Jeep, I thought, and agony with a laden handcart. One false summit after another added discouragement to the tedious ascent, and I stepped over countless sharp-edged bedrock shelves, the ridges that had broken many a handcart wheel or axle. Every mile, a simple concrete pillar stood beside the trail, engraved on either side: "Oregon Trail, Mormon Trail." Here and there, beside the modern two-wheel track of the road, I saw vestiges of narrow ruts in the tundralike ground cover—the remnants of the wagon and handcart trail of the 1840s to 1860s.

With only my daypack, Rocky Ridge was an easy hike, but it nonetheless brought home to me the ordeal of the Willie Saints. This would have been the steepest, roughest, most dangerous stretch since Iowa City. In a snowstorm, with men, women, and children on the verge of death, pulling handcarts up this grade seemed unthinkable.

After several miles of trudging up the track, I turned around. On the way back to my car, my only companions were antelope, flitting along in groups of three and five.

Later that day, I made my way by back roads to Rock Creek Hollow, where the Willie Company struggled into Grant's camp after dark on October 23, 1856. As mentioned, trail historians argue over whether the rendezvous took place here, or two miles farther west, on Willow Creek. Once again, the true location of the camp seemed to me not terribly important. I had pictured the meeting place as a sheltered refuge, guarded perhaps by a grove of cottonwoods, nestled beneath cliffs that would block the piercing wind. Rock Creek Hollow was nothing so auspicious. A thick stand of willows offered the only shelter, and the "cliff" I had pictured was only a thirty-foot-high bank of gravel and shale—on the east side of the tributary stream, moreover, where it would have done nothing to block the west wind.

To my surprise, the monument here, identifying the fifteen who died that night and the next morning, had been erected way back in 1933. And for once the motto adorning it avoided pieties about faith and heroism, as it stated with admirable plainness, "In memory of those members of the Willie Handcart Co. whose journey started too late and ended too early."

A far more grandiose granite monument a hundred yards to the south commemorated the visits between 1992 and 1997 of the church's First Presidency—Prophet Gordon Hinckley and leading Apostles Thomas Monson and James Faust. Under the boldly capitalized injunction "REMEMBER" were graved the dates of their several visits, followed by a citation from the *Book of Mormon*, Helaman 10:4–5. The text in question has the Lord blessing Nephi for his good deeds—Nephi being the leader of the true Saints whose followers were wiped out by the Lamanites (ancestors of today's Native Americans, cursed with dark skin for their perfidy). Verse 5 begins, "And now, because thou hast done this with such unwearyingness, behold, I will bless thee forever; and I will make thee mighty in word and in deed, in faith and in works."

Not far from this granite memorial, a crude fence made of boards and cables enclosed a scattering of anonymous graves, marked not with headstones but with piles of shale. I was left to wonder whether those were the actual graves of the fifteen Willie Saints who had died here, or the graves of later pioneers, or merely symbolic mounds evoking a tragic place. Whichever the truth, I found those mounds more moving than all the monuments, plaques, signboards, and museum captions whose earnest legends I had read between the visitors' center and Rock Creek Hollow.

I SUPPOSE THE sentimentalization of the handcart disaster should have come as no surprise to me. All cultures mythologize their pasts. No episode in American history was more brutal or tragic than the Civil

War, but do the reenactors who dress up in blue and gray uniforms and shoot each other with blanks as they re-create Bull Run or Antietam honor the terrible losses of life in those battles, or trivialize them? Do the armchair generals who argue into the night about Stonewall Jackson's flanking maneuver against Joseph Hooker at Chancellorsville treat the men who lived and died there as anything more real than toy soldiers?

The courage and perseverance of most of the handcart Saints are beyond question. Some of them, as well as some of the rescuers, emerged from the ordeal as genuine heroes. What seems to have been lost in the mythmaking is the fact that those Saints were also victims—and not of some domino topple of impersonal causes, but of colossal mismanagement and negligence on the part of LDS leaders.

For a people as devout as the Mormons, the question of why the handcart disaster happened takes on a deep teleological significance. On my first visit to the Handcart Visitors' Center, a docent named Elder Merrill, standing outside the museum, raised the question in its simplest form. "Some people get upset when they come here," Elder Merrill told me. "Why did the Father in heaven let them [the handcart pioneers] do that?"

But Merrill's answer, like that of most of his colleagues, was far too pat for me to swallow. The handcart Saints had died, he insisted, to turn the trail into "sacred ground" (on my three visits, I heard and read that phrase ad nauseam). They had died in order to inspire today's Saints to improve their lives. Particularly youths, according to Elder Merrill: "Kids come here leading troubled lives. Some aren't even in the church. They go home and get baptized. They say it changed their lives forever."

Historian Lyndia Carter, who regularly speaks to school groups about the handcart tragedy, was more skeptical. "That kind of reenactment is delusionary history," she told me. "It gives you no sense of what day after day of cold and short rations really meant. The kids get into doing it, but it's just fun and games for them. At most, a rite of passage. The school groups I talk to aren't very interested in history."

The struggle to make sense of the tragedy is natural and human. For believers, it is the profound dilemma wrestled with by such pop psychologists as Harold S. Kushner in *When Bad Things Happen to Good People* and by such deep thinkers as C. S. Lewis in *The Problem of Pain* (or, for that matter, by John Milton, who wrote *Paradise Lost* to "justify the ways of God to man"). But the simplistic formula of Sister Willie at the Sixth Crossing visitors' center—"They came to know God"—cannot satisfy any but the most credulous.

To be sure, many of the Saints who survived the Willie and Martin catastrophe later uttered that very formula. All their tribulations and losses, many testified, were worth it, to be able to come to Zion and to know that God had saved them via a miraculous rescue effort. For Mormons seeking to justify the disaster, the locus classicus is a short article written by William R. Palmer (the Harold Kushner of his day, at least within the LDS church) in *The Instructor* in May 1944. Under the rubric "Pioneers of Southern Utah," it purports to relate the very words spoken in a Sunday school class many years before by Francis Webster, a survivor of the Martin Company, twenty-five years old at the time of the emigration.

Palmer's reminiscence is perforce suspect, for Webster had died in 1906, thirty-eight years before Palmer's piece appeared in *The Instructor*. Moreover, the only memoir in Webster's own hand that has survived is a four-sentence résumé of the ordeal, whose sole vivid line is the following: "I had the diarrhea all the way from Ioway City to Florance so bad that I have sat down on the road and been administered to by the Elders and got up and pulled my hand cart with renewed vigor."

In Palmer's 1944 telling, he was sitting in an adult Sunday school class in Cedar City with about fifty other men and women. The discussion was about the handcart expeditions of 1856. "Some sharp criticism of the Church and its leaders was being indulged in," Palmer related.

An old man in the corner sat silent and listened as long as he could stand it then he arose and said things that few of those who heard him will ever forget. His face was white with emotion, but he spoke slowly, deliberately, but with great earnestness and sincerity.

He said in substance, "I ask you to stop this criticism for you are discussing a matter you know nothing about."

The old man, Francis Webster, then revealed that he had been a survivor of the very debacle that the church group was analyzing.

"Mistake to send the handcart company out so late in the season? Yes. . . . But did you ever hear a survivor of that company utter a word of criticism? Not one of that company ever apostatized or left the Church because everyone of us came through with the absolute knowledge that God lives for we became acquainted with him in our extremities.

"I have pulled my handcart when I was so weak and weary from illness and lack of food that I could hardly put one foot ahead of the other. I have looked ahead and seen a patch of sand or a hill slope and said I can go only that far and there I must give up for I cannot pull my load through it. I have gone on to that sand and when I reached it, the cart began pushing me. I have looked back many times to see who was pushing my cart but my eyes saw no one. I knew then that the angels of God were there.

"Was I sorry that I chose to come by handcart? No. Neither then nor one moment of my life since. The price we paid to become acquainted with God was a privilege to pay and I am thankful that I was privileged to come to Zion in the Martin Handcart Company."

I had not been surprised to find this canonic affirmation inscribed on a wall of the handcart museum, where it was attributed not to Palmer's reminiscence but directly to Francis Webster. According to Palmer, "When he sat down there was not a dry eye in the room. We were a subdued and chastened lot." As for Palmer himself, Webster's testimony "made me tingle to the roots of my hair."

The oft-repeated claim that no veteran of the Willie and Martin Companies ever apostatized is easily refuted, starting with such prominent sub-captains as John Chislett and John Ahmanson, and extending to such "ordinary" Saints as Elizabeth Sermon. Because of the spotty record, the actual number of survivors who left the church is impossible to calculate. According to Lyndia Carter, substantial numbers in the Hunt and Hodgett wagon companies—especially women—later apostatized. "Records show that they went back East or to England," says Carter. "And there were the dropouts in Iowa City and Florence. In general, among all the Saints who came to Utah in the pioneer years, about one-third ended up leaving the church. And Brigham liked to say that only one-third [of the pioneers] were worth keeping. Another third weren't worth the salt, and a further third just left Utah."

Whether or not Palmer's vignette of the old man speaking up in the Sunday school classroom is a fairy tale, it strikes me as both puzzling and yet inevitable that so many of the handcart survivors, in their memoirs and reminiscences, expressed conclusions not unlike those that Palmer puts so eloquently in Webster's mouth—that the journey was worth it; that God's providence saw the survivors through; and that their subsequent lives were enriched by the ordeal. When evil works its harm in the world—when "bad things happen to good people"—there is an insatiable need, especially among the devout, to find some metaphysical and moral explanation for that harm. It is simply a human propensity that the victims of tragedy grasp at what to the skeptic seem trite and overliteral "lessons."

To my agnostic sensibility, the mechanism at work here is brilliantly elucidated in Robert Frost's late, dark poem, "The Draft Horse." That seemingly simple verse of five quatrains is at once blatantly allegorical and characteristically sly, inviting, as Frost so often does, the very sort of misinterpretation it is his aim to puncture. In "The Draft Horse" a couple rides through "a pitch-dark limitless grove" with a sputtering lantern, in too frail a buggy, drawn by too heavy a horse. Suddenly a man—otherwise unidentified and unexplained—comes out of the trees and stabs the horse in the side. The beast collapses, dead; the man apparently disappears.

The fifth stanza is set up by the fourth, the one that few readers pay close attention to:

> The most unquestioning pair
> That ever accepted fate
> And the least disposed to ascribe
> Any more than we had to to hate,

We assumed that the man himself
Or someone he had to obey
Wanted us to get down
And walk the rest of the way.

To me, most of the handcart Saints were like that "unquestioning pair," unwilling to attribute their own ordeal to the failings of church leaders. (The questioners, like John Ahmanson, could not accept Young's answer and so left the church.) The evil done to the handcart pilgrims must have some purpose: God must want them to learn something infinitely valuable from their sufferings. Frost's couple grasp at the homiletic answer—self-reliance, getting down and walking the rest of the way. But Frost himself (if I read the poem correctly) does not buy that moral: the calamity in the forest is ultimately senseless, and there is no lesson to be learned from it, except that evil is abroad in the world.

So, in a century and a half, the greatest disaster in westward migration history was transformed from a campaign so terrible that no one wanted to talk or write about it into the Mormon *Mayflower*. In the last decade and a half, the retrospective gilding of tragedy with moral uplift has reached its frenzied zenith.

That transformation goes beyond such shrines as the Handcart Visitors' Center. Within the past few years, a pair of documentary films have grappled with the handcart story. *In Their Footsteps of Faith: The Story of the Willie and Martin Handcarts* invites the viewer to step back into "a time when faith and endurance were needed to survive." Brigham Young is absolved of all responsibility for the disaster; as one expert asserts, "They planned on three handcart companies. Brigham Young did not know about the other two." A voice-over elaborates, "Organizers in Salt Lake City assumed [the Willie and Martin Companies] would spend the winter in the East."

The film reckons the toll of dead in the Martin Company alone as 156, but reassures us that the survivors "almost all remained in Salt Lake, stronger in faith, with proven courage, and dedicated to the church lifestyle." *In Their Footsteps of Faith* ends with an omniscient voice-over: "But whether they lived or died, they left a legacy of teamwork, self-sacrifice, and devotion, a legacy just as valid today as it was in 1856."

Sweetwater Rescue: The Willie and Martin Handcart Story is a little more balanced. The film makes the standard effort to paint Brigham Young as the hero of the rescue effort, quoting LDS archivist Mel Bashore to the effect that the Prophet's intervention was the single most significant factor in the survival of the Saints who made it through to Zion, historian Howard Christy as claiming that Young's "fury" started the massive rescue effort, and that "The timing of the rescue is stunning."

But the film also quotes Lyndia Carter's demurral. Of the Martin Company's starting out too late from Florence, Carter says, "In my opinion, they were doomed from the beginning." And rather than absolve the Prophet, Carter asserts, "Brigham Young *was* aware that there were probably a lot of people coming. He had been informed by Daniel Spencer, who was the superintending agent at Iowa City, that he had sent off three groups, and that two more were expected."

Sweetwater Rescue, however, reverts to platitudes: "In a word, it was heroic." "The trail was consecrated in blood." And the film ends with John Jaques's famous exoneration, "I blame nobody."

Andrew Olsen's comprehensive and well-researched *The Price We Paid: The Extraordinary Story of the Willie and Martin Handcart Pioneers* (2006) is the best book yet written about the exodus. Yet Olsen, too, shies away from blame: for him, Brigham Young is a paragon of conscience and good judgment. Olsen's concluding chapter strives mightily to turn catastrophe into heroic pageant. The chapter's sectional subtitles give Olsen's game away: "A Story of Countless Miracles," "After Much Tribulations Come the Blessings," and "A Trail of Tears, a Trail of Hope." Olsen's final paragraph dwells only on the positive: "But the experiences of the Willie and Martin handcart pioneers show that faith and hope will triumph over the worst days on the trail. Faith and hope kept these Saints stepping forward when their strength was gone."

DURING MY TWO August forays in western Wyoming, the weather had been sublime. It had thus been almost impossible to plunge into an empathic appreciation of what the trail had been like for the played-out Saints in the snows of October and November 1856. Finally I decided to take three days to traverse the trail from Salt Lake City to eastern Wyoming in early February 2007, retracing by automobile in reverse the latter half of the Martin and Willie Companies' journey, and also seeking out those odd locales where the dire and momentous events of a century and a half before were commemorated by no plaques or visitors' centers.

My trip began at This Is the Place Heritage Park, on the northeastern outskirts of Salt Lake. The spacious grounds, crowning a low hill, enclose a splendid replica of the city as it looked during the early years, wide dirt streets, wooden sidewalks, quaint clapboard shops, and all. The park— named after the most famous pronouncement Brigham never uttered— is dominated by a sixty-foot-tall pylon atop which the Prophet stands flanked by his two faithful Apostles, Heber C. Kimball and Wilford Woodruff. Nearby, of far humbler stature, yet another handcart sculpture strikes its poignant and heroic pose, annotated by a plaque derived from Hafen and Hafen's *Handcarts to Zion* detailing the statistics from the handcart companies. I was amused also to find a latter-day attempt at PC rehabilitation of the Lamanites: a statue of the great Shoshone chief Washakie, with the legend: "Known all over the western country as one of the most intelligent and able of the Indian chiefs. . . . Sometimes referred to as the 'George Washington' of the western tribesmen."

Heading up Emigration Canyon into the Wasatch Mountains, I found the road, which I had twice driven in summer, closed on account of winter snows. I was forced to resort to the soulless detour of Interstate 80. I pulled off at the Castle Rock Observation Point and surveyed Echo Canyon below me. Somewhere near here, on November 26, 1856, Echo Squires had been born, in what the Martin Saints regarded as one of the last miracles along the home stretch of their journey.

The canyon is a dreary place today. Under a leaden sky, I surveyed the semi–ghost town of Castle Rock below me and the grim railroad workers' camp, first established as part of the effort to push the transcontinental track toward the golden spike that would revolutionize westward emigration after 1869. The birthplace of Echo Squires, who would live to the age of eighty-seven, is annotated by no roadside sign.

Six miles on from Castle Rock, I crossed the Wyoming border. For the fifth or sixth time, I stopped at Fort Bridger, which has been superbly reconstructed as a Wyoming historic monument. A reconstructed stockade, authentic to the last detail, stands near where the original was built, the foundations of which are gradually emerging from the ground in an ongoing archaeological dig.

The trading post was erected by the great mountain man Jim Bridger in 1843. Four years later, Brigham Young's pioneer company passed through. The Prophet pumped Bridger for all that he knew about the Great Basin to the southwest, but from that first meeting on, bad blood coursed between these haughty antagonists. In 1853, Young sent a party of armed men, some of them Danites, to arrest Bridger, ostensibly for inciting the Utes against the Mormons. The mountain man feared very few enemies, but rather than shoot it out with the Saints, he went into hiding in the hills. Whereupon the Mormons essentially stole the fort from its founder. Later, Young paid $4,000 to Bridger's partner, Louis Vasquez, but for the rest of his life, Bridger claimed he had been cheated by the Mormons and never paid anything for the fort.

By the time the handcart Saints passed through, then, Fort Bridger was in Mormon hands. It was to be an important locus both of hope and disappointment—the latter, when Franklin Richards's promised resupplies never materialized, the former, when the numerous rescue teams that met the Martin Company there at last allowed every Saint to ride on to the Valley in a wagon.

From Fort Bridger, I followed Interstate 80 east toward Rock Springs, but turned off north on U.S. Highway 30 to visit the town of Granger. The little hamlet (population 125) seems all but forgotten by history, but the site, at the junction of Blacks Fork and Hams Fork (which combine as a western tributary of the Green River), was once an important place. An orgiastic mountain man rendezvous took place here in 1834, the celebrants including such luminaries as Jim Bridger and Kit Carson. And a carefully researched guidebook informed me that both the Willie and Martin Companies had camped here in 1856. No monument in Granger records those one-night layovers, but the gentle river bottom must have seemed a refuge after the rigors of crossing South Pass and ferrying across the Green River.

Oddly enough, that same guidebook cannot identify with certainty where the last two handcart companies crossed the Green River. To get a feeling for that pivotal step westward, I made my way along State Highway 28 to its bridge over the river, in the middle of the Seedsakee National Wildlife Refuge. Here, we do know, the first two handcart parties, under Captains Ellsworth and McArthur, crossed the Green at what was then called the Lombard Ferry. For the impoverished Saints, the charge levied by the mercenary ferrymen—from $3 to $16 per wagon—must have been hard to bear.

My February outing was at last paying empathic dividends. I stood on the west bank of the river, shivering in a stiff wind at 36 degrees. A few ducks gliding on the current advertised the wildlife refuge, but cakes of ice floating downstream conjured up the ordeal of the November fords of the Sweetwater that the Martin Company had been forced to perform.

I crossed South Pass and rejoined U.S. Highway 287 south of Lander. The Sixth Crossing visitors' center was closed for the winter. At the Ice Slough, I saw generous pans of ice peeping through the grasses. The Handcart Visitors' Center stays open year-round, but on this chilly day—the wind up to forty miles an hour, the temperature in the low 40s—I was only the fourth visitor of the day. Remembering the throngs of the previous two Augusts, I found a quiet delight in the emptiness of the place. "We had eight visitors yesterday," the elder on duty told me. "But not a single one on the four days before that." I didn't bother hiking the trail up to Martin's Cove.

East beyond Devil's Gate, the trail was new to me. On my second afternoon, I stopped beneath the Red Buttes, on the Bessemer Bend of the North Platte. Here the Martin Saints had been marooned for ten terrible days and nights, as they began to give up hope. And here, Joseph Young had ridden into sight on his white mule, with his two companions—the vanguard of the rescue effort that got the company moving again. Even in winter, the river bottom looked like a nice place to camp, nestled in a cottonwood grove, with the ruddy buttes to the south catching the golden light of late afternoon. Once again, no sign or plaque signaled the ordeal of 1856.

I pushed on and by dusk reached Casper, where I rented a motel room. In the morning, there was frost coating every vacant lot, and the temperature was a raw 24 degrees under an overcast sky. I had hoped to find the site of the desperate Martin Company ford of the North Platte, the one narrated so vividly years later by Patience Loader. Gradually I realized that the ford lay today smack in the middle of downtown Casper.

From Casper east for some eighty miles, Interstate 25 follows the Mormon Trail along the North Platte. Careening along at seventy miles an hour, I stared at the bleak, treeless landscape on either side. I turned off at Exit 165 and trundled two miles north into the town of Glenrock. This middling burg (population 2,200) sports a welcome sign boasting "Big enough to enjoy—small enough to care."

At Glenrock, Deer Creek flows into the Platte from the south. The cozy, tree-lined basin that enfolds the town today makes it evident why this had been one of the favorite campsites for the pioneers, as the shelter, abundant firewood, and clear drinking water afforded a welcome respite from the agoraphobic emptiness of the plains. It was here that the first two handcart companies, under Edmund Ellsworth and Daniel McArthur, had been overjoyed to meet the resupply wagons from the Valley. But it was also here, on October 17, that the Martin Company had made its desperate and ultimately foolhardy decision to burn its "excess" baggage and reduce the handcart load to ten pounds per adult.

In the center of town stands diminutive Deer Creek Station Historic Monument. The signage, however, says nothing about the handcart parties, choosing instead to celebrate a trading post and saloon established in 1857 by former mountain man Joseph Bissonette and a Pony Express station built a few years later.

I pushed on past Douglas and the Glendo Reservoir, then left Interstate 25 to branch east on U.S. Highway 26, which rejoins the Platte at Guernsey. South of town, I spent some time surveying the best-preserved trail ruts anywhere along the 1,300 miles between Iowa City and Salt Lake. Here, the wagons inexplicably left the meandering valley bottom to crest a hill where shelves of soft sandstone protrude as bedrock. In places the ruts are shoulder-deep. It seemed unlikely, however, that handcarts had contributed much to the depressions worn by hundreds of heavy wagons rumbling west, not only toward Zion but to Oregon.

Near the trail ruts looms a sandstone bluff called Register Rock, where the finest collection of pioneer inscriptions anywhere along the trail covers two sides of the cliff. The bitter weather continued, with temperatures in the low 20s and that relentless wind out of the west, but I spent an hour walking the base of Register Rock as I struggled to decipher signatures and initials, many eroded almost into illegibility. The earliest date I found was 1850. I discovered only a single 1856 inscription, that left by a pioneer named Caffey—not, so far as I could ascertain, a handcarter.

Eleven miles farther east, I came to Fort Laramie National Historic Site. The wind had picked up, and the reconstructed fort, spread across a bare hill, felt like a Hudson's Bay outpost in the Arctic. Here I was the only visitor of the day, and my advent seemed to startle Sandra Lowry, the librarian staffing the headquarters.

Historians of the handcart emigration have long wondered whether Fort Laramie might preserve records that could cast a new light on the 1856 campaign—explaining, for instance, why Richards's promised resupply had failed to materialize, or following up on the subsequent lives of the backouts who had chosen to stay here rather than push on to Zion. Yet none of those scholars had visited the place. Lyndia Carter had made many an inquiry by mail and telephone, only to come up with nothing new—a failure she attributed to bureaucratic confusion, not to the absence of records.

In a few minutes, however, Lowry dashed all my hopes. "We know that the traders kept journals," she explained. "But the fort today doesn't have any of their day books or logs. We have no idea what happened to them. Remember that this was a privately owned trading post in 1856."

From 1867 to 1877, the U.S. Army took over the fort to use as a base in its campaign against the Sioux. Then in 1890, the fort was closed and abandoned.

"The old-timers," Lowry continued, "reported finding all kinds of stuff here that the army had just walked off and left. A lot of records probably ended up in private hands. When the National Park Service took over in 1937, there was nothing left."

Lowry helped me identify the only three reconstructed buildings that had stood in 1856. Leaning into the wind, my parka hood closed tight around my face, clutching my notebook clumsily with gloved hands, I made a quick tour of the Magazine (1850), the Trader's Store (1849), and a prisonlike edifice called Old Bedlam (1849)—the oldest standing building in Wyoming, a sign proclaimed. In 1856, Fort Laramie must have seemed to the handcart pioneers an immensely appealing haven of civilization. I recalled Josiah Rogerson's wistful evocation of the place: "The comfortable adobe quarters, and the snug and warm log rooms were quite tempting for a winter's rest, with plenty to eat."

But on that grim February day, Fort Laramie seemed to me only a forlorn collection of shuttered and locked historic buildings, exposed naked on its hilltop to the lashing west wind. Even the headquarters where Sandra Lowry stood vigil was barely warmed by its potbellied stove. I was glad to get back in my car and crank up the heater.

I could, I supposed, push on across Nebraska and into Iowa. But at Torrington, eight miles from the border, I turned south, with visions in my head of the cozy motel room and the hearty steak dinner that awaited me in Cheyenne. The February traverse of Wyoming had served its purpose. I had gained a minimal but intensely visceral sense of what the trail had been like in the early winter of 1856. And that was enough to make me profoundly glad that I would never go backpacking (let alone crossing the plains) with only seventeen pounds of baggage, that my camp meals would always be richer and more varied than a single pound of flour, and that in my whole life the farthest I would ever pull a handcart was 3.3 miles.

THE PREVIOUS AUGUST, to plumb what I considered the most bizarre and misguided of all the modern responses to the handcart tragedy, I had left the Sweetwater valley of western Wyoming to drive north to the town of Riverton. Here, between 1991 and 1992, had unfolded what the local stake leaders called the Second Rescue.

The campaign, in which virtually every member of the stake, including young children, got passionately caught up, is well documented in Susan Arrington Madsen's book *The Second Rescue* (1998). It began with a chance conversation among three Riverton church leaders and a visitor from Salt Lake City, who told them about some groundbreaking new computer technology being developed in the Utah capital that vastly simplified and sped up the process of compiling genealogical information. The computers, the software, and the CD-ROMs were, however, still in the experimental stage.

One of the Riverton counselors, Kim McKinnon, became fascinated by the news. The Riverton stake had two family history centers, but no computers. McKinnon launched a series of appeals to Salt Lake City to get Riverton on the waiting list for the requisite equipment and software. For two months, he received no response. Frustrated, he took a day off work to drive to Salt Lake—twelve hours round-trip—and plead his case in person. "We really need those computers!" McKinnon exhorted the head of the Church Purchasing Department. As Madsen writes, "Two weeks later, on April 24, 1991, two computers, two printers, and two full sets of family history CDs arrived in Riverton." McKinnon was told that they were the only family history systems operating outside of northern Utah.

Greatly excited, McKinnon set up the systems, one in the library in Riverton, the other in nearby Lander (part of the Riverton stake). But as he drove one evening with stake president Scott Lorimer toward Fort Washakie on the Wind River Reservation, McKinnon began to muse out loud. "Why have I felt so pushed about obtaining these computers? Why the great sense of urgency?"

President Lorimer did not at first answer. Then, suddenly, he burst out, "It's the Willie people!"

"What?" replied McKinnon. "What made you think of them?"

"That's why we have the computers. Their temple work has not been done."

Growing up in Casper, Lorimer had heard stories told by his mother about the handcart exodus, for her Danish grandfather had been a member of the McArthur Company. In 1977, Lorimer had first visited Rock Creek Hollow, where the 1933 monument commemorates the fifteen Willie Company Saints who had died there on the night of October 23–24, 1856. He had been deeply moved by the visit.

What Lorimer now meant by his revelatory outburst during that evening drive toward Fort Washakie depends on a complicated and (to outsiders) arcane Mormon doctrine, called "baptism for the dead." As theologian Bruce R. McConkie explains it, "The Lord has ordained *bap-*

tism for the dead as the means whereby all his worthy children of all ages can become heirs of salvation in his kingdom." McConkie elaborates:

> Obviously, during the frequent periods of apostate darkness when the gospel light does not shine, and also in those geographical areas where legal administrators are not found, hosts of people live and die without ever entering in at the gate of baptism so as to be on the path leading to eternal life. For them a just God has ordained baptism for the dead, a vicarious-proxy labor.

The sudden, alarming insight Lorimer had in the car that April night was that the Saints who had died in the Willie Company, working-class poor from Britain and Scandinavia, might never have been baptized into the LDS church. McKinnon's obsession with the computers must have been a divine urging to the Riverton stake to rectify the problem.

To enter heaven, a Saint must have performed a series of what are called temple ordinances. These rituals, which include "washings, anointings, endowments, sealings," and the like, "pertain to exaltation within the celestial kingdom."

In Riverton, during two separate visits, I met with Lorimer and McKinnon, and with the current president of the stake, Lloyd Larsen. As Larsen explained to me the plight of the unbaptized handcart Saints, "These folks who died without ordinances are in Paradise waiting, but they can't progress. We feel a great responsibility to seek out kindred dead, and vicariously do the work for them. That work can only be done in the temple."

In other words, a living Saint could stand in as "proxy" for the unbaptized dead, even a century and a half later, and perform the ordinances for him or her, ushering the lost soul into the celestial kingdom. But to perform baptism for the dead, a certain list of facts had to be ascertained. As Larsen told me, "We need the birth date, where the person was born, if he or she was married, if he or she had children, and where and when he or she died."

Whence the computers and their software, with their power to ferret out the most obscure and far-flung genealogical data. In 1991, Lorimer and McKinnon put the stake to work researching the handcart victims, starting with the fifteen who had died at Rock Creek Hollow. This was no easy task, given how poor the records were (and are) of the thousands of Saints in the 1856 migration, how complete rosters of the five parties will never be compiled. But the stake was soon swept up in its messianic mission. Each Riverton Saint was assigned a handcart pioneer. A record form was drafted, with blanks to be filled in for everything from "Name, Last" to "Year of Birth" to "Sealed to Spouse" to "Baptism: Date" to "Research Date Completed."

The work went on nonstop for fourteen months. When enough facts became known about the unbaptized pilgrim, his or her proxy was ready to perform the necessary temple ordinances. Riverton has no temple, so the ceremonies had to be performed in Ogden, Utah. The details of those rituals are not readily disclosed to Gentiles, although Lorimer assured me, "The ordinances are not secret, but sacred. They have to do with being sealed for eternity. The endowments allow you to go through the veil. This life is a progression. We have the potential to be where God is, even to be like Him. As Christ on the Cross said to the thief, 'Tomorrow I'll be with you in Paradise.'"

By the end of this orgy of effort, some 4,200 temple ordinances had been vicariously performed. The scope had expanded from the Willie Company to the Martin Company, the rescuers, and the families of all of the above. Lloyd Larsen told me, "I would say we rescued 97 percent [of the unbaptized Saints involved in the handcart campaign]."

Madsen's *The Second Rescue* contains a chapter titled "Testimonials." It reproduces drawings of handcarts pulled by pioneers executed by Riverton kids as young as five. The most charming testimonials, of course, are those of youngsters. A good example is that of Heika Lorimer, the president's eleven-year-old daughter:

> I went to church with just my scriptures but walked out with a huge smile and a packet with James Alfred Peacock's name written on it. My Dad and I could not find him on the computer so we ordered some microfilm. We searched for a very long time and we did not find him. Just when we were about to stop we both felt that we should keep going. We were both so excited when we finally found him that we both let out a big happy yell.

Twelve-year-old Kristen Gard wrote:

> The youth got to go to the temple and got baptized for the dead.
> The spirits of the pioneers were really strong and encouraging.
> Once we got out of the temple their spirits seemed to evaporate.
> I wanted to go back into the temple.

Before traveling to Riverton, I was aware that the LDS archivists in Salt Lake took a fairly dim view of the Second Rescue. Lyndia Carter was even more blunt. "The Riverton folks are very sincere. From inside their culture, the Second Rescue makes sense. The whole effort was very unifying for the stake. But I went through all their records. Their documentation is very poor. I have to dismiss a lot of their history."

I was also aware that, in the name of baptism for the dead, Mormons had enraged Jewish groups by performing temple ordinances for victims of the Holocaust, without bothering to ask the families of those who had died at Dachau and Auschwitz whether their martyred relatives wanted to spend eternity in the heaven of the Latter-day Saints.

Before arriving in Riverton, I had told Lorimer and McKinnon that I was not a member of the church. In view of my skepticism, I thought it was gracious of them to meet with me. And it was obvious that both men were thoroughly used to the incredulity that the Second Rescue tends to provoke in nonbelievers.

Toward the end of our interview, Lorimer acknowledged the doubters. "Some people get upset about all this," he admitted. "But for us it's a gift. We don't have to fake it." He paused as he peered deeply into my agnostic eyes, then said softly, "And what if we're right?"

CHAPTER NINE

A DAY OF RECKONING

On November 9, 1856, George Grant's rescue party had finally gotten the Martin Company moving again. As the Saints staggered westward from the death trap of Martin's Cove, they left behind, in the ruins of Fort Seminoe, the twenty "volunteers" appointed to guard the goods of the Martin, Hunt, and Hodgetts parties through the long winter.

That we know much at all about the experience of those twenty men during their perilous wintering over is thanks almost exclusively to Daniel Jones's lively memoir, *Forty Years Among the Indians*. And given the details of that vigil, it is not surprising that Jones waited until after Brigham Young's death to tell his story, publishing only in 1890.

Early on, Jones was voted by his peers to be one of three leaders of the band. If his memoir is not unduly self-serving, the former mountain man also emerged as the sturdiest and most useful member of the entourage. Given the scarcity of provisions that November near Devil's Gate, that men were expected to perform such a desperate service is testimony to what a premium the church put on material possessions—an emphasis that trickled down from Young himself.

According to Jones,

Captain Grant asked about our provisions. I told him they were scant, but as many [among the handcart emigrants] were suffering and some dying, all we asked was an equal chance with the rest. He told us there would be a lot of worn out cattle left; to gather them up and try to save them.

Scant indeed:

> On taking stock of provisions, we found about twenty day's rations. No salt or bread excepting a few crackers. There was at least five months of winter before us and nothing much to eat but a few perishing cattle and what game we might chance to kill. The game was not very certain, as the severe storms had driven everything away.

During the first few days after the Martin Company left its cove, Jones rode out to see how the Saints were faring, and he witnessed "deaths occurring often" along the trail. Back at the fort after the first such foray, he offered his fellow volunteers the chance to back out. (Whether this option was sanctioned by Grant, Jones does not say.)

> I told them in plain words that if there was a man in camp who could not help eat the last poor animal left with us, hides and all, suffer all manner of privations, almost starve to death, that he could go with me the next day and overtake the trains. No one wanted to go. All voted to take their chances.

Finally Jones had to sever his tenuous connection with the Martin Saints whom he had helped to save. As he later wrote, "I left the company feeling a little downcast, to return to Devil's Gate. It was pretty well understood that there would be no relief sent us."

Grant's advice to the volunteers to live off the "worn out" cattle left behind by the emigrants would prove far too sanguine. The hope of Jones's men to get the cattle "on good feed and recruit them a little" was dashed in the first few days. Some two hundred dead cattle strewed the trail for a day's march either side of Fort Seminoe, and their carcasses emboldened the wolves to a terrible ferocity. These predators came right into camp and killed twenty-five living but emaciated cows within the first week. Remembered Jones, "In fact, it became dangerous to face these wolves, they were at times almost ready to attack men."

The only solution was to slaughter the last fifty living cattle before the wolves could devour them. As Jones wryly put it, "We killed them to keep them from dying." One of the charms of *Forty Years Among the Indians* is a certain Bunyanesque irony, a tone that had become the stock-in-trade for the yarn-spinning mountain men who had met and wildly celebrated at the yearly mountain men rendezvous between 1825 and 1840. Thus:

> We had a first-class butcher from London, who dressed every-thing in the best style. Everything was saved that we thought might be eaten. We hung the meat up. The poorest of it we did not expect to eat, but intended to use it for wolf bait . . . provided we could get traps.

As Jones had feared, the hunting proved lean. Day after day, men went out looking for wild game, but saw none. Sometime in December, twelve miles away from the fort, Jones felled a buffalo that was charging him with a single shot. So cumbersome was the toil in the snow, the men by then so weakened, that "it took all hands three days to get [the buffalo meat] into camp." By then, the little store of "bread" had given out, and the men were living on cattle carcasses alone.

A day or two before Christmas, the men had their first visitors— the indefatigable Ephraim Hanks and Feramorz Little, Brigham Young's nephew, who were engaged in a mind-boggling two-man effort to carry the mail from the Valley to the eastern settlements in midwinter. They carried a letter written on December 7 by Brigham Young, which ad-dressed the guardians of the cached goods. Jones published the letter in full in *Forty Years* (as he would not likely have done when the Prophet was still alive).

It is a rather astonishing document. Micromanaging in his fussiest style, the Prophet offered "suggestions and words of counsel" that the Saints who received the letter took as inflexible orders. "You are in an Indian country," Young reminded the men, from a distance of 330 miles, "few in number, blockaded by the snows, and far from assistance at this season of the year." Therefore it was vital to be "constantly on the alert, to be firm, steady, sober-minded and sober-bodied, united, faithful, and watchful, living your religion." (One wonders what the men at Fort Seminoe would have drunk had they felt the temptation to lapse from a sober-bodied state.) More particularly,

> Do not go from your fort in small parties of one, two or three at a time. But when game is to be sought, wood got up, or any other operation to be performed requiring you to travel from under the protection of the fort guns, go in bands of some ten or twelve together, and let them be well armed; and let those who stay by the stuff be watchful while their comrades are out. And at all times and under all circumstances let every person have his arms and ammunitions ready for active service at a moment's warning, so you cannot be surprised by your foes nor in any way taken advantage of.

Brigham's fears of Indian attack are curious. As he must have known by December 7, among the thousands of far more vulnerable handcart emigrants who had crossed the plains that year, not one had been assaulted by Indians. The "stuff" cached at Seminoe might have been a tempting target for raiders, but it had never been the indigenous nomads' style—whether Sioux, Cheyenne, Ute, or Shoshone—to attack a fort guarded by well-armed men.

On with the counsel, in the tone of a sergeant addressing raw recruits: "Always have plenty of water about the buildings, and be very careful about fires. . . . You had better kill some of the cattle than run much risk in quest of game. . . . Try to so ration out your flour as to have it last until we can send you relief."

What flour? Had Grant failed to inform the Prophet about the actual scarcity of the provisions left the men who were wintering over?

As Jones dared to write in 1890, "From this letter it is plain to see that Brother Brigham was not apprised of our condition." Yet because it was the Prophet who so addressed them, the men at Fort Seminoe tried to follow his commands to the letter. Though it became absurdly inconvenient to do so, for weeks the men never ventured from the fort in groups of fewer than ten.

As for "relief," Young's promises were vague and even contradictory.

"We will send teams to your relief as early as possible in the spring," he vowed; but they "may not reach you until May, depending somewhat on the winter snows and spring weather."

As winter deepened, the hunting grew hopeless: "Game soon became so scarce we could kill nothing." In a vivid passage laced with self-deprecating humor, Jones evokes the onset of starvation:

> We ate all the poor meat [from the slaughtered cattle]; one would get hungry eating it. Finally that was all gone, nothing now but hides were left. We made a trial of them. A lot was cooked and eaten without any seasoning and it made the whole company sick. Many were so turned against the stuff that it made them sick to think of it.
>
> We had coffee and some sugar, but drinking coffee seemed to only destroy the appetite, and stimulate for only a little while. One man became delirious from drinking so much of it.
>
> Things looked dark, for nothing remained but the poor raw hides taken from starved cattle. We asked the Lord to direct us what to do. . . . We had cooked the hide, after soaking and scraping the hair off until it was soft and then ate it, glue and all. This made it rather inclined to stay with us longer than we desired. Finally I was impressed how to fix the stuff and gave the company advice, telling them how to cook it; for them to scorch and scrape the hair off; this had a tendency to kill and purify the bad taste that scalding gave it. After scraping, boil one hour in plenty of water, throwing the water away which had extracted all the glue, then wash and scrape the hide thoroughly, washing in cold water, then boil to a jelly and let it get cold, and then eat with a little sugar sprinkled on it. . . .
>
> We asked the Lord to bless our stomachs and adapt them to this food. We hadn't the faith to ask him to bless the raw-hide for it was "hard stock."

In such grim conditions, with nothing to do most of the day but sit and wait, guarding the stored belongings against an enemy who never came, the morale of the men inevitably plunged. Jones only hints at the dissension that broke out among the ranks: "During meeting we became impressed that there were some wrongs existing among the brethren in camp that should be corrected, and that if we would make a general cleaning up, and present our case before the Lord, He would take care of us."

By March 4, "the last morsel had been eaten for breakfast." The men took stock of anything in the fort that could be considered edible. "We were now in a tight place," writes Jones dryly. "There was a set of harness and an old pack saddle covered with rawhide still on hand, that some of the boys considered safe to depend on for a few days." The company actually "were getting the pack saddle soaked up ready for cooking," when a fortuitous event saved them from this extreme measure, with the sudden arrival of a second midwinter express mail team from the Valley, led by the Danite Bill Hickman. "Of course we were rejoiced to see them," records Jones, "especially so when we learned they had a good supper for us. . . . I remember about the first thing I did after shaking hands, was to drink a pint of strong salty broth, where some salt pork had been boiled."

With mock indignation, Jones refutes the rumor that emerged from this timely arrival of the mail team. "[George] Boyd [a member of the express] always calls me the man that ate the pack saddle. But this is *slander*. The kindness of him and others prevented me from eating my part of it. I think if they had not arrived, probably I would have taken a *wing* or *leg*, but don't think I would have eaten the whole of it. As it was, the saddle was allowed to dry up again, and may be in existence yet and doing well so far as I know." (From this jaunty paragraph, Stegner took his chapter title in *The Gathering of Zion*, "The Man That Ate the Pack Saddle.")

The arrival of Hickman's mail team, however, did not save the faithful cache-guarders from starvation. The crowning irony of that wintering over is that, for all of Young's warnings to the men to be on guard against Indian attack, in the end it was Indians who saved the twenty men.

It was not until February that the first Indian arrived at Fort Semi-noe. He was a solitary man from the Snake tribe, and one must read between the lines of Jones's narrative to appreciate the courage born of desperation that allowed this wanderer to approach the outpost guarded by twenty Mormons. He, too, was starving. Out of pity, according to Jones, "Some of the boys hunted up a small piece of raw hide and gave it to him. He said he had eaten it before. None of us were able to talk much with him; we invited him to remain with us over night." The volunteers were able, however, to glean the information that the main Snake band was camped a day's travel up the Sweetwater; that their own efforts to hunt had proved fruitless; and that they lived in daily fear of attack by their enemies, the Crows. The next morning, "The Indian went away saying he would tell his people about us, and if they could find any meat they would divide."

Jones's account of the solitary Indian visitor also reminds us that in the nineteenth century (and no doubt in pre-contact times), every winter posed the threat of mass starvation for most if not all of the nomadic tribes ranging across the West. In the weeks to come after the February encounter the peaceful interchange bore dividends, as groups of Snakes and Bannocks dared to approach the fort. And as Jones was the first to admit, the Indians were better hunters with bows and arrows than the Saints were with their rifles. From his mountain man days, he recalled that

These Indians of the plains years back killed a great many buffalo with arrows. They would stick two arrows into a buffalo's heart, crossing their direction so that as the buffalo ran these arrows would work and cut his heart almost in two. This would soon bring the poor brute down; whereas with a single arrow in the heart they would run a long distance.

By March, the Snakes and Bannocks in the Sweetwater valley had in fact succeeded in killing numerous bison. Now they entered into a wary trade with the strangers ensconced in the decrepit fort. Jones himself organized the barter, weighing each pound of buffalo meat on a scale and establishing its value in nonedible goods. "We exchanged various articles with them, many of the company trading shirts, handkerchiefs and such things as they could spare. We had some coffee, for which the Indians traded readily." Jones records the purchase of three hundred pounds of buffalo meat on one occasion, of "hundreds of pounds" on another. Thanks to the skill of the Indian hunters, the Fort Seminoe volunteers turned the corner of their starving winter. As Jones admiringly noted, "An Indian will manage to kill game where it is so scarce and wild that but few white men would even see it."

Finally, in late spring (Jones does not give a date), with the trail opened up again, the long-awaited relief train arrived—twenty men from the Valley carrying "a ton of flour and other provisions." These blessed emissaries also brought startling news: that a party of more than fifty apostates fleeing Salt Lake City was close on their heels.

In the debate about how many of the handcart emigrants later apostatized, this crucial passage in *Forty Years Among the Indians* seems to have been overlooked by historians. The apostate exodus, Jones makes clear, included quite a number of Saints from the Martin, Hunt, and Hodgetts Companies:

> The goods we were guarding belonged to the last season's emigrants. . . . Some of the owners had become dissatisfied with "Mormonism" and were going back to the States. As their goods had not arrived in Salt Lake City, they demanded that they should be delivered at Devil's Gate. Quite a number settled their freight bills and brought orders for their goods and received them all right. Others refused to settle, but threatened that if the goods were not given up they would take them by force.

Jones recounts the ensuing showdown as a classic dime-novel drama, with his allies stationed inside the fort, their rifles cocked and aimed through "port holes" in its walls, as he himself faces down the angry leader of the apostate throng. "We have been here all winter eating poor beef and raw hide to take care of these goods," Jones tells the leader. "We have had but little fun, and would just as soon have some now as not. . . . If you think you can take the fort just try it. But I don't think you can take me to commence with; and the first one that offers any violence to me is a dead man."

Jones's bluster does the trick: the apostates back down, and no blood is shed. Whether the disillusioned Saints abandoning Zion ever received their belongings, the chronicler does not say. Jones's account proves that a sizable number of apostates among the last three 1856 parties turned their backs on Mormonism only months after arriving in Salt Lake City. But it also makes clear another condition of their plight: that on top of their debt to the Perpetual Emigration Fund, the always dollar-conscious

Brigham Young expected the handcart pioneers to pay "freight bills" to recover the very belongings the handcart plan itself had made them too weak to carry beyond Devil's Gate.

Remarkably enough, not one of the twenty "volunteers" perished during their interminable winter at Fort Seminoe. By early summer 1857, they had returned to Salt Lake City. If Jones expected to be greeted as a hero, he was in for a rude shock. In his absence, he learned, "strange stories had been put in circulation about me." He was "accused of stealing and hiding away thousands of dollars' worth of goods." One indignant family went so far as to come to Jones's house to search for the purportedly stolen belongings. And a "teacher" visited Jones's wife in Provo, "telling her that she ought to leave me and marry some good man." Mrs. Jones's answer: "Well I will not leave Daniel Jones. I cannot better myself, for if he will steal there is not an honest man on earth."

With these sorts of rumors flying about, Jones felt understandably "stiff" as he had in his first audience with the Prophet. Young asked him if he had left everything in order upon leaving the fort. "I hope I did but do not know," Jones answered.

"Well, you acted according to my instructions, did you not?"

"I don't know. I did not get any instructions, and it was pretty hard on me." Jones then handed the Prophet a "book" in which he had recorded the doings of the twenty men during their near-starvation winter. In front of its author, Young began to read the book. As he did so, he murmured, "This is right; this is right. Well, you seemed to get along all right."

It was as close to an encomium as Daniel Jones would receive for his heroic job of guarding the emigrant belongings. As he wrote of that day in the Prophet's office more than thirty years later, "I began to feel pretty good."

AS MENTIONED EARLIER, even before the last two handcart companies arrived in Salt Lake City, Young launched a strenuous campaign to minimize the disaster. The Prophet himself never publicly reckoned the number of dead in the Willie and Martin parties; instead, he found ingenious ways to imply that the toll was not very high. Thus, speaking in the Tabernacle on November 16, when the Martin Company was limping across Rocky Ridge, still 260 miles and two weeks away from Salt Lake, the Prophet reassured his congregation,

> Count the living and the dead, and you will find that not half the number died in br. Willie's hand-cart company, in proportion to the number in that company, as have died, in past seasons by the cholera in single companies traveling with wagons and oxen. ... With regard to those who have died and been laid away by the roadside on the plains, since the cold weather commenced, let me tell you that they have not suffered one hundredth part so much as did our brethren and sisters who have died with the cholera.

And even as he acknowledged the snuffing out of lives in the hand-cart companies, Young painted the most romantic picture possible of death on the Wyoming plains:

> Some of those who have died in the hand-cart companies this season, I am told, would be singing and, before the tune was done, would drop over and breathe their last; and others would die while eating, and with a piece of bread in their hands. I should be pleased, when the time comes, if we could all depart from this life as easily as did those our brethren and sisters. I repeat, it will be a happy circumstance, when death overtakes me, if I am privileged to die without a groan or struggle, while yet retaining a good appetite for food. I speak of these things, to forestall indulgence in a misplaced sympathy.

That "misplaced sympathy," of course, was not so easily squelched, for the streets of Salt Lake were coursing with scuttlebutt about a colossal mismanagement of the handcart migration by the Prophet himself. As noted earlier, Young deflected the blame in his fiery oration of November 2, when he scapegoated Franklin Richards and Daniel Spencer for letting the last two companies leave Florence too late in the season.

It was not only Young who perpetrated the myth that he had long counseled against too late a start from the Missouri River. At the same November 2 meeting, Apostle Jedediah Grant credited both himself and the Prophet with that convenient hindsight-as-foresight:

In relation to hand-cart companies, I have said, and I say it again, that they should start by the first of May, and then they can travel leisurely according their strength and feelings; they can then have May, June, July and August for the accomplishment of their journey....

The grand difficulty with a portion of our immigration this year has been in starting in the forepart of September instead of the first of May....

Br. Brigham has invariably advised early starts, and he gave his reasons for so doing this morning, and I do not wish to reiterate them.

Even as he spoke in the Tabernacle that day, Grant had less than a month to live. On December 1, Young's "sledgehammer," the "Mormon Thunder," the architect of the Reformation, died of pneumonia and/or typhoid, probably contracted by performing one too many baptisms in freezing mountain streams. He was only forty years old.

Within weeks of the arrival of the last emigrants in 1856, the Prophet was baldly asserting the soundness of the handcart plan. In a typical letter, he reassured an official in England, "The Hand Cart scheme of immigrating the poor, is now no longer a problem. But a happy & important reality, we now know that by this mode much time and means can be saved, and the poor more numerously gathered."

As willfully deaf to the tragedy as such a pronouncement rings, there is no reason to believe that the Prophet was cynically twisting the truth. He sincerely believed that the handcart plan was the solution to the vexing problem of gathering the foreign-born poor to Zion. And to demonstrate the efficacy of that plan, he devised an unnecessary but symbolically freighted exercise. On April 23, 1857, seventy handpicked missionaries set out from Salt Lake City to push and pull handcarts toward Florence. This team, a "Crack Company" if ever there was one, completed the journey in the remarkable span of forty-eight days, averaging almost twenty-two miles a day. Upon the missionaries' arrival in Florence, the local newspaper proclaimed, "They were feeling fine after their trip and expressed themselves to be on hand for a foot race or wrestling match with any one in Florence who might feel inclined to indulge."

This return mission has entered Mormon folklore as a vindication of the "divine" handcart plan. LeRoy and Ann Hafen call it "a dramatic and successful demonstration of the efficiency of handcart travel." Yet, as historian Will Bagley was the first to point out, an eyewitness account of the missionaries' journey flatly contradicts the Florence newspaper's jaunty boast. On his own way from Salt Lake City to Chicago, Chauncey Webb overtook the handcart train at Devil's Gate. Webb had been the master carpenter who had superintended the building of the 1856 handcarts in Iowa City, and his had been the sole voice arguing against the launching out from Florence of the Martin Company in late August.

The account of Webb's observation of the missionaries appears in the pages of his daughter's *Wife No. 19*, an apostate screed so embittered that it may be suspect. But there is no a priori reason to doubt Webb's assessment of the condition of the handcarters at Devil's Gate. (Chauncey Webb was still alive when *Wife No. 19* was published in 1875. One assumes that he would have objected to a misrepresentation of his testimony on his daughter's part.)

According to Ann Eliza Young, at Devil's Gate her father found the handcart missionaries "completely jaded and worn out."

> In truth, they were almost dead from weariness. They travelled slowly, making long stops to rest, and finally they reached the Missouri River in a perfect state of exhaustion. They left their carts there with the utmost willingness. . . . To this day they all aver they cannot bear to hear the word "Hand-cart" mentioned.

Meanwhile, Young was busy organizing two more handcart expeditions to bring European and British Saints to Zion in the summer of 1857. Eventually they would be complemented by a single handcart train in 1859, and by two more in 1860. In all, then, ten handcart caravans crossed the plains between 1856 and 1860. The fact that none of the subsequent five suffered a major disaster akin to that of the Willie and Martin Companies has solidified the myth, current today among Mormons, that the handcart plan was fundamentally sound and benign. Thus Andrew Olsen, in *The Price We Paid*, argues that the Willie and Martin catastrophe should not "be seen as an indictment of the handcart plan. Three companies before them made the journey successfully, and five companies after them would do the same."

The diaries and reminiscences of the participants in those last five handcart parties, so assiduously collected in the LDS Archives, tell a different story. They are full of the same kinds of heart-wrenching testimonies to exhaustion and near-starvation as the more oft-quoted Willie and Martin sources. Thus, in the 1857 company led by Israel Evans, Robert Fishburn complained, "We could not help but feel that somebody was at fault for the scanty supply of provisions furnished us." Of the same expedition, Susan Witbeck remembered forty years later, "There could not have been a more difficult mode of travel. We would push and pull these carts across more than a thousand miles of trackless plains, barren desert, and towering mountains. I knew when I left England that ours was to be an handcart company, but it was impossible for me to realize the hardships I had to meet."

In the second 1857 company, led by Christian Christiansen, twenty-year-old Kersten Erickson, who left her parents and grandmother behind in Florence, later recalled:

> About the fifth day out, I was so worn out pulling over the rough roads—up hills—and through the sand and discouraged because I did not believe that I could stand the journey, and I came to the conclusion that I might as well die there as suffer longer—and I was lonely for I had no relatives in the company.
>
> So I purposely staid behind while the company were travelling and laid down in the grass expecting to die there.

Captain Christiansen discovered the young woman and rallied her to continue the journey.

There is good evidence that the death toll among the last five handcart expeditions has been seriously undercounted by Mormon historians. Andrew Olsen asserts, "In those five companies, totaling 1,071 people, only 12 deaths were recorded." Hafen and Hafen list the death toll in the Israel Evans Company as "(?)." Annotating the Christian Christiansen party, the Hafens claim "6 (?)" deaths.

The Christiansen expedition is the most sketchily documented among all ten handcart companies, largely because most of its members were Scandinavian. Yet two participants in the party later swore that "One tenth of the company died for want of care and nourishment." Since 330 emigrants set out from Iowa City in the Christiansen Company, that rate of attrition would put the death toll in the vicinity of thirty-three—not "6 (?)."

Will Bagley calculates the death rate among all ten handcart companies at 10 percent, versus a rate of 4 percent among all Mormon wagon companies. His characteristically acerbic conclusion: "There were more than two handcart disasters: there were ten handcart disasters, plus the comedy that the handcart missionaries staged in the spring of 1857."

THE CHRISTIANSEN COMPANY arrived in Salt Lake City on September 13. Two days earlier, the Evans Company had come in. And on that very day, September 11, 1857, an unfathomable tragedy befell another emigrant party, camped in a high basin 280 miles southwest of the capital.

That party, made up of some 140 men, women, and children, was not made up of Mormons but of Gentiles, most of them hailing from Arkansas. They had passed through Utah along the Mormon and old Spanish Trails, en route to California, where they hoped to begin new lives. Some accounts have them trading insults with the Mormons as they traversed the territory, but no violence had yet broken out.

On September 6, the Baker-Fancher party (named after its leaders) had stopped to camp in a lush, well-watered valley bottom known today as Mountain Meadows. The emigrants were some forty miles beyond Cedar City, the southwesternmost Mormon settlement in the Utah Territory, and the simmering tensions between themselves and the hostile and suspicious Saints whose villages they had passed through seemed to have diffused. The party anticipated a peaceful journey onward to California.

As the emigrants gathered for breakfast, a shot broke the tranquil scene, and one of the children collapsed, struck by a bullet. Assuming they were being attacked by Indians—the emigrants caught glimpses of dark-skinned gunmen wearing war paint—the Baker-Fancher party quickly circled its wagons and returned fire.

So began a five-day siege. The attackers probably included Paiutes, but they were organized and led by Mormons who had dressed up as Indians and painted their faces. The Arkansans defended themselves well, and the siege dwindled into a stalemate. On September 11, a Mormon hoisting a white flag warily approached the makeshift wagon fortress. He told the leaders of the besieged party that the Mormons had interceded with the Indians, and would now guarantee the emigrants safe passage out of Mountain Meadows, if the Arkansans would turn over their guns.

The women and children were led away from the camp first, followed by the Baker-Fancher men, each guarded by an armed Saint. Half an hour into this procession, Major John Higbee, on horseback, fired his rifle, then uttered the command, "Halt! Do your duty!"

In a matter of seconds, every man in the Baker-Fancher party was gunned down from point-blank range. The women and older children were slaughtered with guns, knives, and gunstocks used as clubs. Only seventeen were spared, all of them children five years old or younger, under the presumption that they would not remember enough of the carnage to testify credibly against its perpetrators.

The Mountain Meadows Massacre—a depredation unmatched before or since in Western annals—remains all but inexplicable today. What was the motive? Theories range from simple greed (the Arkansans had a thousand head of livestock, as well as handsome wagons full of valuable possessions) to an apocalyptic spasm of the mass paranoia first engendered by the Reformation. By September 1857, hatred of Gentiles had reached a new pitch in the Utah Territory, whose inhabitants lived with the nagging fear that Zion was about to be invaded by federal troops. Such a denouement indeed unfolded during the coming winter, as President James Buchanan sent 2,500 soldiers west to Fort Bridger, in the opening act of what would eventually become the relatively bloodless Utah War.

And who commanded the massacre? Both then and now, suspicion fell on the Prophet himself. Whether or not Brigham Young ordered the carnage, there is no doubt that he covered it up and hindered federal investigations into it. Only one participant was ever tried and executed for the massacre, and that only twenty years later, as John D. Lee, stepson of Young and one of his most reliable lieutenants, stood before a firing squad and took the bullets that scapegoated him as the alleged master-mind of the massacre.

The first comprehensive account of this dark episode was published in 1950, as *The Mountain Meadows Massacre*, by Mormon historian Juanita Brooks. In 2002, that treatise was superseded by Will Bagley's definitive *Blood of the Prophets*. Bagley labors to demonstrate that Young himself commanded the slaughter, but if so, the Prophet was careful not to leave behind a smoking gun. Still, *Blood of the Prophets* amasses a powerful circumstantial case against Brigham Young. The book is so disturbing to the faithful that during the last five years, a triumvirate of high church officials has spent millions of dollars and collected bookshelves full of "evidence" in support of a book intended to refute Bagley at every turn.

FOR THE MODERN student of the handcart exodus, a striking feature of its written legacy is the paucity of later reflection upon or analysis of the experience by the Saints who survived. To be sure, the average working-class Danish or Scottish convert was perhaps not temperamentally inclined to such reflection, or if he or she was, it did not issue in written form.

Once they arrived in Salt Lake City, the veterans from the Willie and Martin Companies seemed only to want to get on with their lives. Patience Loader, otherwise so vivid a memoirist, recounts her first days in Salt Lake as a forlorn business, as her extended family was broken up so that various residents could take in its members as boarders. Within a few weeks she found work in her old occupation as seamstress. Not once in "Reccolections of past days" does Patience stop to ask herself whether the whole desperate journey had been worth it.

Levi Savage, who had faithfully kept his journal from the start of the trek through October 25, when he grew too exhausted to continue writing, appended a final entry after his company's arrival in the capital. The last line reports, "We overtook Bro Smoot's Com. in emegration, in the a.m. that afternoon arrived in G.S.L. City, deposited the people among the Saints w[h]ere they were made comfortable."

The next entry in Savage's journal (which he would again keep through October 1858) does not appear until January 1, 1857. Neither that brief note nor any subsequent entry contains a single word of judgment on the Willie Company's ordeal—not even the hint of an "I told you so" in reference to his tearful, prescient, and finally fruitless plea to winter over in Florence rather than risk the snows of Wyoming.

It may well be that for the majority of Saints in the two decimated handcart companies, the experience was too traumatic even to call to mind. Sarah Hancock Beesley, a veteran of the 1859 handcart party, which came through relatively unscathed (Hafen and Hafen list only a single death), was interviewed years later. Before her interrogator could finish the first question, Sarah burst out:

"Don't ask me anything about that. You should go and talk to Mrs. Lapish. She can tell you all about it. . . . Those are dreadful stories and I don't see why we shouldn't try to forget them. I say 'Bury them with the dead who died on the plains.' My children have often tried to get me to write my handcart story but I will not."

The advent of the Willie and Martin Companies in the capital presented every citizen who greeted them with the most appalling evidence of frostbite suffered by scores of survivors. Even the Prophet could not ignore the ravages inflicted by the cold and snow. On November 30, the day of the Martin Company's arrival, he preached to his audience in the Tabernacle, "Some you will find with their feet frozen to their ankles; some are frozen to their knees and some have their hands frosted. They want good nursing, and if you do not know how to treat frozen flesh, let me inform you that the same treatment is needed as in a burn, and by pursuing that method you can heal them."

In his pragmatic way, Young went on:

The afternoon meeting will be omitted, for I wish the sisters to go home and prepare to give those who have just arrived a mouthful of something to eat, and to wash them and nurse them up. You know that I would give more for a dish of pudding and milk, or a baked potato and salt, were I in the situation of those persons who have just come in, than I would for all your prayers, though you were to stay here all the afternoon and pray. Prayer is good, but when baked potatoes and pudding and milk are needed, prayer will not supply their place.

There is no record of the number and severity of amputations performed on the Willie and Martin survivors. The stories that have endured lean toward the miraculous, like the saga of seven-year-old Mary Hurren recorded almost a century later by a descendant. As recounted earlier, George Reeder, greeting his brother-in-law James Hurren, suddenly asked, "What is this odor I can smell?"

"Little Mary's legs are frozen," replied James.

Mary was placed on a bed in the Tithing Office and a doctor was sent for. He examined her frozen limbs and said he could do nothing for her as mortification had already set in. He returned the next morning with his instruments expecting to amputate her legs. "She will die easier," he said.

Her father protested, "This little [girl] didn't walk a thousand miles to have her legs cut off. If she dies, she will die with her legs on."

The family was loaded into a wagon and taken to Brigham City (Box Elder). A pioneer nurse, Mrs. Snyder, looked at the limbs and recommended trying fresh raw-beefsteak on them. Fresh meat was not obtainable at Box Elder so her father walked to Ogden and obtained some round steak. This was placed on the frozen parts and in several days the rotten flesh dropped off. They trimmed the sinews and applied a home-made ointment to assist in the healing. She was able to walk again in two years. When she grew up she married Joseph Wight and became the mother of ten children. She was a great nurse in Brigham and surrounding areas.

In the gilding mirror of decades of retrospect, even the horrors of frostbite could be turned into a parable of uplift. The most famous case is that of Nellie Pucell Unthank, whose panegyrist was the same William Palmer who remembered the long-ago Sunday school class in which the old man in the corner, Francis Webster, had spoken out so passionately to defend the handcart emigration against its gossiping critics.

In *The Instructor* for April 1944, Palmer published "She Stood Tall on Her Knees," a short biography of a woman whose story, claimed Palmer, was "unlike any other and surpassing most of them in the qualities of sheer heroism," of "a woman who, in spite of crushing handicaps, carried on the highest mission of womanhood." At age nine, Nellie was the youngest of five children who crossed the ocean with their parents on the *Horizon* to gather to Zion. (Palmer implies that all five children joined the Martin Company, but Andrew Olsen clarifies that three of them stayed in Boston.)

Both parents died in the Wyoming storms. Nellie and her sister were saved by the rescue party that found the company marooned beneath Red Buttes. They rode in wagons, claims Palmer, all the way to Salt Lake City. But:

Poor little Nellie, nothing could be done to save her feet. When they took off her shoes and stockings the skin with pieces of flesh came off too. The doctor said her feet must be taken off to save her life. They strapped her to a board and without an anesthetic the surgery was performed. With a butcher's knife and a carpenter's saw they cut the blackened limbs off. It was poor surgery, too, for the flesh was not brought over to cushion the ends. The bones stuck out through the ends of the stumps and in pain she waddled through the rest of her life on her knees.

Nellie ended up in Cedar City, where she became the plural wife of William Unthank. A poor man, William could afford to build only a small adobe house with a dirt floor. "Nellie kept damping and scraping that dirt floor until she had it as hard and smooth as pavement," Palmer wrote. "That floor was never swept. It was mopped up every day with a damp rag and no spot of dust or stain was ever left upon it."

Meanwhile, Nellie never really healed from her amputations.

Those stumps were festering, running sores as long as she lived. She never knew a moment of freedom from pain. . . . Dr. George W. Middleton offered to fix her legs by cutting the bones off farther up and bringing the flesh down over the ends so they would heal and enable her to wear artificial limbs, but the horrors of that first amputation were so vivid in her memory that she could never consent to another operation.

Despite being crippled, Nellie raised six children. She helped support the family by "taking in washing" and knitting stockings. Stoically, she "never asked for favors of pity or charity because of her tragic handicap."

Nellie died in 1915, at the age of sixty-eight. Palmer closes his tribute with a glowing reminiscence:

> In memory I recall her wrinkled forehead, her soft dark eyes that told of pain and suffering, and the deep grooves that encircled the corners of her strong mouth. But in that face there was no trace of bitterness or railings at her fate. There was patience and serenity for in spite of her handicap she had earned her keep and justified her existence. She had given more to family, friends and to the world than she had received.

In 1991 a bronze statue of Nellie Unthank was erected on the campus of Southern Utah University in Cedar City. The work, by sculptor Gary Anderson, depicts Nellie as a young girl who still has her feet. With a radiant, uplifted face, she dances on her toes, arms outspread, fingers extended in joy. The dedicatory ceremony was attended by the governor of Utah and by LDS president Gordon Hinckley. According to a Southern Utah University archivist, whenever a snow falls, today's students brush the drifts off the statue's toes.

A handful of Saints in the two stricken companies went on to attain a minor celebrity in the Utah Territory. The most remarkable may have been Jens Nielson, a Dane in the Willie Company who was thirty-six at the time of the trek. Nielson nearly died crossing Rocky Ridge, saved only by the gritty effort of his wife, Elsie, who pulled him for some distance in their handcart. The couple lost their six-year-old son on Rocky Ridge. Jens was crippled by frostbite, and though he suffered no amputations, he walked the rest of his life with one foot at a right angle to the other.

Despite this handicap, twenty-three years after the handcart journey, Jens became one of the leaders of the legendary Hole-in-the-Rock

Expedition, charged with settling southeast Utah to forestall Gentile in-
trusions. Setting out from Escalante in the late fall of 1879, the expedition—230 men, women, and children in eighty-three wagons—expected
to take six weeks to blaze a trail eastward to a pre-scouted settlement on
the San Juan River. Instead, the journey took the party six months.

The tour de force of this extraordinary mission was the lowering of
all eighty-three wagons down a thousand-foot chasm in the cliff above
the Colorado River (the "hole in the rock"), then floating them across the
current. The pioneers pulled off this feat without losing a single wagon,
and completed their journey without a single death in the party.

In April 1880, these emigrants founded the town of Bluff. Jens Nielson,
fifty-nine years old during this arduous journey, became the town's first
bishop, a post in which he served for the next twenty-six years, until his
death in 1906, two days before his eighty-sixth birthday. He is buried on
Cemetery Hill above the town, and his pioneer house is a local landmark.

Another Saint in the Willie party, twenty-year-old Emily Hill, had a
talent for versifying. In Utah, as Emily Hill Woodmansee, she became a
kind of unofficial poet laureate of the territory. Though she apparently
kept no diary during the trek, in 1881 Emily composed a long poem
about the journey, titled "Hunger and Cold." Narrating the nadir of the
expedition, in the Wyoming snows just before the arrival of the rescue
express, she wrote:

> At length came the climax—how well I remember—
> That cold, dismal night in the month of November.
> Faint and fasting, we camped by a hard frozen stream
> Here nothing we had, but of plenty could dream.
> Our rations eked out with discretion and care,
> Had utterly vanished, "the cupboard was bare,"
> Not a morsel to eat could we anywhere see,
> Cold, weary and hungry and helpless were we.
>
> Our woes were pathetic and everywhere round
> Every inch of the prairie was snow covered ground,
> Shut off from the world as in ocean's mid waves,
> The desolate plains offer nothing but graves.

Death seemed but a question of limited time.
Yet the faith of these faint ones was truly sublime!
On the brink of the tomb few succumbed to despair,
Our trust was in God, and our strength was in prayer.

Just as William Palmer could repackage the ordeal of the Willie and Martin Companies into an idealized Saint's life of Nellie Unthank, so in the twentieth century the tragedy would serve as the yarn-spinning fodder for a children's adventure book. Cedar City historian Howard R. Driggs seized upon a character named George "Beefsteak" Harrison, whom Driggs knew as the proprietor and cook of a hotel in Springville. "Beefsteak was one thing in which he took pride," Driggs wrote in a 1944 reminiscence. "He could cook this royal meat to a queen's taste. Beside there would be tempting salads, creamy potatoes with gravy, and peas, carrots and turnips. Of course, there were pies and cakes, and sometimes a plum pudding."

According to Driggs's memoir, George Harrison had been a boy in the Martin Company. Somewhere in Wyoming, overcome by the handcart trial, he slipped away from the party, so as to burden his family with one fewer mouth to feed. Rather than perish, George was rescued by a band of Indians, with whom he flourished in the finest Fenimore Cooper fashion, before eventually making his way to Utah as part of a later army train.

A fourteen-year-old named George Harrison is listed in the roster of the Martin Company in the LDS Archives, with little biographical information save his 1921 date of death. In Driggs's long memoir, presented as nonfiction, the story is quoted verbatim from Beefsteak Harrison's lips. Eight years later, Driggs converted and expanded the tale into a novel for children, told in the third person, called *George, the Handcart Boy.*

A sample—the moment when the starving George reaches the first Indian "teepee":

Lifting the flap of elkskin at the opening, he saw the astonished Indian family—a mother and several children seated round a fire. On the embers was a kettle with something cooking in it.

Pointing to the kettle, George pleaded, "Give me some! Give me some!"

The mother understood. Reaching for a tin plate, she filled it with pieces of boiled buffalo meat. George seized it and began to eat ravenously.

When it was gone, he again handed the empty plate to the Indian mother, saying, "Give me some more! Give me some more!"

"Oo-oo!" she exclaimed in sympathy as she began to refill the plate.

The handcart tragedy also gave birth to an epic novel, in Gerald N. Lund's *Fire of the Covenant*, published in 1999. A kind of Mormon James Michener, Lund is immensely popular among LDS readers for his sprawling works of historical fiction, supposedly buttressed by prodigious research. In his 758-page *Fire of the Covenant*, Lund tries to have it both ways, arguing in a prefatory note that "This story is true. Most of the characters in the book were real people.... A few fictional characters are created to help convey to the reader the fulness of the experience, but *the story is not fiction.*"

The fullness of the experience requires Lund to center his novel on a pair of made-up characters, the winsome Hannah McKensie in the Martin Company and the doughty rescuer, David Granger. Their slow-burning love affair culminates, we are promised on the last page, in a proposal of marriage and the prospect of happily-ever-after in Zion. Meanwhile, the Danish Saints in the companies, far from being isolated in their monolingual vacuum, are taught English along the trail by their British brothers and sisters. They cannot cure themselves of uttering "Yah" instead of "Yes," but they express their gratitude to their tutors in accents like "Olaf's": "We learn music? That is good."

Many Mormon readers, impressed perhaps by the bibliographical notes Lund appends to each chapter, believe that the novel, dialogue and all, is a faithful reconstruction of the Willie and Martin Companies' ordeal. Lund's saga, however, reads not as tragedy so much as a patchwork of back-to-back episodes in which brave men and women perform one selfless and heroic deed after another, all in the fulfillment of their "covenant" to gather to Zion. Thus on October 20, 1856, as Captain Willie

and Joseph Elder set out to cross Rocky Ridge to scout for the rescue wagons:

"It's you two that we're worried about," John Chislett said softly. "Do you think you can find the trail in the snow? If that wind picks up again . . ." He just shook his head.

James Willie nodded slowly, his eyes dark and brooding. "We ride with the Lord, firm in the faith that He has not forsaken us. Brethren, Brother Elder and I will not be alone. Nor will you. We ask that you and the camp pray to God with all the energy of your souls that the Lord will hear our cries in this our extremity and bring us deliverance. *We must find those wagons.*"

Then, suddenly determined, he turned to Brother Elder. "Are you ready?"

"Yes, sir. Let's do it."

He handed Captain Willie the reins of his mule and they both swung up. "May God be with you, brethren," Brother Willie said as he wheeled his mule around.

"And with you," Levi Savage said quietly.

MORE THAN A century and a half after the handcart expeditions of 1856, it remains an elusive challenge to affix responsibility for the greatest disaster in Western migration history. The toppling dominoes on display at the Mormon Handcart Visitors' Center do not give an adequate answer.

Despite his many retrospective claims that he had always counseled against too late a departure from Florence, Brigham Young in fact never dictated firm cutoff dates until after the catastrophe. That he did not do so is all the more puzzling in view of the experience of the company led by George A. Smith in 1849. This party, made up of between 370 and 447 emigrants riding in 120 wagons, set out from Kanesville, Iowa (present-day Council Bluffs), on July 14. The advance guard of the company did not arrive in Salt Lake City until October 26.

On October 2, near the summit of South Pass, the company was engulfed by a severe snowstorm. Smith himself published only a sani-

tized version of the ravages of that storm, in a letter to the *Frontier Guardian*, but even that dispatch was given an alarming subhead: "Account of travel—tremendous snow storm—60 head of Cattle Perished—Chickens and Pigs froze to death—no person died on the journey."

In his 1889 *History of Utah*, the magisterial historian Hubert Howe Bancroft, who probably got the details directly from Smith, elaborated on the story:

> Toward night on the 2d a strong wind set in from the north-east, accompanied with driving snow. The company encamped on a branch of the Sweetwater, driving their cattle into a willow copse near by, as to build a corral was impossible. The wind freshened into a gale, and then into a hurricane, howling incessantly for thirty-six hours, and drifting the snow in every direction. For two nights women and children lay under their frail covering, exposed to the blast, with no food but a morsel of bread or biscuit. Tents and wagon-tops were blown away, and the wagons buried almost to the tops of their wheels in the snow-drifts. . . .
>
> At length the storm abated, and making their way toward the willow copse, the men found nearly half their cattle lying stiff amid the snow-banks, while others died from the effects of the storm. Not a single human life was lost, however.

The difference between the survival rate in the George Smith party and that in the Willie and Martin Companies derives from several obvious causes. As handcarts never could, the wagons themselves shielded the 1849 emigrants from the brunt of the storm; they presumably had adequate clothing and bedding; and they had not arrived at South Pass weakened by months of undernourishment.

Even so, Smith took the occasion to make a firm suggestion that, had it been acted on seven years later, might have averted the Willie and Martin tragedy altogether. In his letter to the *Frontier Guardian*, Smith (and his co-signer, William Appleby) urged, "We would earnestly recommend to all emigrating companies hereafter, coming to the Valley, not to attempt to leave the Missouri river after the middle of June, for if they start later, they will almost be certain to encounter severe snow storms as we have, in crossing these everlasting snow capped, and rock bound mountains. By starting early they will be apt to miss the snows, and have time and opportunity for recruiting a few days."

Even seven years afterward, the close call of Smith's party must have been common knowledge throughout Zion. And since Smith was Joseph Smith's cousin, it seems unlikely that Brigham Young would have lightly dismissed his fervent recommendation against too late a start from the Missouri.

In the light of history, Young's public scapegoating of Franklin Richards and Daniel Spencer to deflect blame away from himself was a brilliant stroke. A century and a half later, the blame has stuck where the Prophet flung it. At a 2005 session of the Mormon History Association, a panel of experts debated who was ultimately responsible for the Willie and Martin tragedy. The majority unhesitatingly chose Richards, while no panelist blamed the Prophet himself.

Although he continued as an Apostle and leader of the church, Richards was lastingly devastated by the Prophet's mocking denunciation. According to Hannah S. Lapish, herself a veteran of the ninth handcart expedition in 1860, "Sister Richards said that for 4 yrs. Pres. Young would not speak to Bro. Richards. Sister Richards told Bro. Young that if he did not speak to her husband it would break his heart. Pres. Young said he could not speak without condemning him."

Just as brilliant was the Prophet's vigorous call, as soon as the missionary party had brought the bad news to Salt Lake, for a massive rescue mission to set out immediately to find the last two handcart companies of 1856. A century and a half later, the Prophet is widely viewed by Mormons as the hero of the handcart story.

Even among church historians who hold that view, there are some who concede that there is a certain logic in holding the Prophet accountable, on the blanket principle that the general of an army is responsible for what his troops carry out. But the most thoroughgoing modern effort to focus the blame squarely on Brigham Young resides in the pages of an unpublished article by that sharpest of all thorns in the side of the Mormon history establishment, Will Bagley.

An independent scholar living in Salt Lake City, Bagley grew up Mormon but became disillusioned with the church early on. In an informal lecture about the handcart emigration that would serve as a précis for the eventual article, he said, "I have a deep and passionate connection to this story. Fifteen of my sixteen great-grandparents crossed the plains to Utah, one of them in 1857."

Concentrating on what he calls the Prophet's "obsessive penny-pinching," Bagley takes the tack of analyzing the handcart saga in economic terms. In the 1850s, according to Bagley, Brigham had squandered hundreds of thousands of church dollars on failed development schemes. These were

> based on importing industrial machinery to manufacture iron, sugar, pottery, paper, wool, and salt. After the LDS Church—or, more exactly, Brigham Young—took over managing these enterprises, it lost $12,000 invested in pottery in 1853, at least $8,500 spent on a paper mill by 1857, and more than $100,000 on the failure of the effort of the "Damn Miserable Company"—the Deseret Manufacturing Company—to make sugar from beets in 1856. By the time it folded in 1858, the Deseret Iron Company had made direct expenditures of at least $150,000 "to produce nothing more than a few andirons, kitchen utensils, flat irons, wagon wheels, molasses rolls, and machine castings."

At the same time that his schemes were threatening to bankrupt the church, Bagley argues, the Prophet had amassed a personal fortune worth more than $150,000. The great appeal of the handcart plan was economic—to gather thousands of foreign-born Saints to Zion at a fraction of the cost of bringing them in wagons. Yet so poor were those working-class converts from Britain and Europe that the Perpetual Emigration Fund sank deeper and deeper in debt. Shockingly, Young blamed the poor themselves. In an angry speech, he told his Salt Lake congregation, "It is the poor who have got your money, and if you have any complaints to make, make them against the Almighty for having so many poor. I do not owe you anything. I cannot chew paper and spit out bank notes."

Bagley was the first historian to point to one of Brigham's far-fetched development schemes as a leitmotif crucially interwoven with the handcart debacle. This involved the procurement of a gigantic and ultimately useless steam engine. In early 1855, the Prophet ordered Apostle Erastus Snow to buy an engine in St. Louis and ship it overland to Salt Lake. The ultimate purpose of the contraption remains uncertain, but Bagley believes it was intended to power a steamboat to navigate the Great Salt Lake.

Against his better judgment, Snow purchased an engine weighing 13,000 pounds. It was loaded in pieces into five separate wagons. A "church train" under Isaac Allred lugged the onerous burden to thirty miles west of the Missouri River, where the team gave up and deposited the steam engine in a farmer's yard.

Furious, the Prophet ordered another party under Abraham Smoot to retrieve the engine and get it to Salt Lake City during the summer of 1856. This new train labored mightily to perform the task. In western Wyoming, as noted earlier, Smoot's team met and interacted with the rescue party looking for the Willie and Martin Companies. Finally Smoot, too, gave up on the debilitating job and cached the cumbersome baggage at Fort Bridger.

This only further infuriated Brigham. Incredible though it may seem, the Prophet ordered some of the rescue teams to divert their resources from saving handcart emigrants to gather up the "freight" at Fort Bridger. Proof of these orders is preserved in the LDS Archives. Thus in a report filed in the capital on December 12, 1856, Caleb Grant, a member of Smoot's team, wrote, "On [November] 3rd inst, we met an express from the Governor, stating that some one was to return & bring on from Bridger the wagons & freight we had left there as well as several useless & tired out cattle left there by us."

Even more explicitly, another member of Smoot's team, Franklin Woolley, recorded,

At Fort Ridges [Bridger] we left 8 waggons and their loads as it was impossible for our teams to take them all, through to the valley when at the mouth of Echo Kanyon Bro Smoot received a letter from Bro Young directing him to bring all the goods in and if he had not enough team to call upon the brethren who were out in the mountains with ox teams to assist the hand cart emmigrations, to assist in bring the waggons that we left at Bridges.

The Willie Company was made aware of this diversion of teams to haul freight instead of save lives, for on November 4, William Woodward recorded in the company's official journal,

Franklin B. Woolley came on from A.O. Smoot's train informing the company that President B. Young had sent word that some freight still lying at "Fort Bridger" was to be brought in this season & that some teams and men of our company were needed to go on to "Bridger." Several teams & men were selected for the trip.

The ultimate fate of the steam engine was as bathetic as Young's plans for it were grandiose. As Bagley writes,

Exactly what Young intended to do with a steamboat on the Great Salt Lake is not clear. It might have been part of an ambitious plan to transport coal from San Pete County, across Utah Lake, and down the Jordan River. It may be that the prophet had no clear idea what he wanted to do with the contraption for on March 1857, Young sent the engine south to the iron works at Cedar City, where like the many crippled handcart veterans he dispatched to the remote settlement it would be out of sight. The machinery replaced two existing 30-horsepower engines that had arrived a year earlier "but had not worked well." Later that year, the Deseret Iron Company paid Brigham Young $2,181 for the engine.

Bagley grants that Franklin Richards's sending on the last two handcart parties from Florence was "the key blunder" in the tragedy. But in his view, the whole debacle was caused not by mismanagement on the part of officials in Liverpool, New York, or Iowa City; it was a classic case of "top-down bungling." Brigham Young was almost solely responsible for designing the emigration of 1856, and for setting in motion the machinery that would send almost two thousand Saints from Liverpool to Iowa City and thence by handcart to Zion. But once this ambitious campaign was launched, the Prophet—quite uncharacteristically, for the habitual micromanager—seemed to lose track of the details. As we have seen, Young knew full well by July 30 that there were more than a thousand handcart Saints who had crossed the ocean on the *Thornton* and the *Horizon* preparing to set out from Iowa City in the Willie and Martin Companies. It is almost as though the Prophet lost interest in these late-arriving converts, preoccupied as he may have been by such distractions as the steam engine.

Bagley was also the first historian to argue, as he put it in his public lecture, that "If there's anyone in the story who's a hero, it's John Taylor." The record bears out this assertion. Months of correspondence between Taylor in New York and the Prophet in Salt Lake reveal that the former was constantly worried about the logistics of the massive operation—and in those worries, he anticipated many of the problems that would contribute to the catastrophe. As early as January 18, 1856, Taylor wrote to Young, "I have ordered one hundred carts made at Saint Louis I have done this, as good seasoned timber can be had there for wheels. I am afraid of these new countries for wheel making. . . . If the wheels should break down on the road the company would be ruined."

By March 4, Taylor was so disturbed by the lack of explicit instructions from those in charge of the emigration that he offered to resign as president of the New York office. "I asked Bro.s Grant & Kimball in council if they had any private instructions from you," Taylor complained to Franklin Richards. "They informed me that they had not; but that they were perfectly free to carry out any measure that I wished. . . . I really felt sorry that our blundering should have placed them in such a position."

In April, Taylor began to feel overwhelmed by the sheer numbers of emigrants streaming into New York from the old countries. "We have had a great many calculations about the hand cart operations and sometimes have felt almost at a loss what course to pursue," he wrote to the Prophet. "Whilst on the one hand we have felt an ardent desire to do what we could and forward as many as possible with as little outlay, on the other hand we have been afraid of throwing a great many into the wilderness in a helpless condition."

A June 30 letter from Young to Taylor promises relief trains to meet the handcart parties: "We expect to start teams with provisions to meet the emigration so soon as we can get flour from the present harvest." Those relief trains would prove vital in seeing the Ellsworth, McArthur, and Bunker Companies through to Salt Lake, but they never materialized to come to the aid of the Willie and Martin Companies. Was this one more detail of the handcart emigration of which the Prophet somehow lost track?

Taylor's letters make it clear that some kind of power struggle between himself and Franklin Richards was hindering the organization of the exodus. In August he pleaded with the Prophet for explicit orders as to who was in charge.

On September 18, in phrases that mingle exasperation and relief, Taylor wrote, "The emigration is now beyond my bounds." He hopes for the best, but "I must confess that I felt a little fearful, as to its practicability with so many weak aged & infirm."

Having ignored all the warning flags hoisted by Taylor over the months, on October 30, as the disaster began to loom on the Salt Lake horizon, the Prophet wrote an angry letter to Taylor scolding him for not better superintending the emigration. And for the first time, Young blamed others—in this case, Taylor—for the lateness in setting out of the last thousand emigrants. Young's harshest criticism, however, was an attack on Taylor as fiscally irresponsible: "We . . . feel gratified at the exertions you have made . . . but you are aware Bro Taylor that we do not hold in very high estimation your financial talent and ability. You must not blame us for this, as we do not attach any to you, beleiving it to be a natural weakness. But you must excuse us for not wishing to pay two or three extra dollars on each passenger."

For Taylor, this must have been the last straw. In February 1857, he sent the Prophet a letter that came as close to outright criticism as any high church official would get away with during Young's lifetime. That letter also adumbrates the first cogent critique of what had gone wrong in 1856. Among other sharp remarks, Taylor wrote,

On the death of br. Spencer and in the absence of br. Snow, without being able to obtain communications from you, I knew that the responsibility rested somewhere. . . . I would give $500 for

five minutes conversation with you. You must here excuse me Br.
Young, I may be obtuse and so may those who were with me; but
however plain your words might be to yourself on this matter,
neither I nor my associates could understand them.

With barely contained sarcasm, Taylor added,

The Hand-Cart system was to me, and to us all a new operation.
I considered that the utmost care and prudence was necessary.
I wanted if a train started, to know that it would go through. I
knew of the weakness and infirmity of many women, children
and aged persons that were calculated to go, I did not consider
that a few dollars were to be put in competition with the lives of
human beings.

A CONSISTENT THEME THROUGHOUT the thirty-three years of
Young's tenure as Prophet is what we would regard today as the under-
valuing of human life. Apostates who wanted to flee Zion were better
off dead. To be sure, Young sincerely believed that it was preferable for a
Saint to die on the handcart trail than to languish in Babylon.

Like all despots, Young found himself virtually incapable of admitting that he was wrong or had committed a mistake. He never acknowledged the handcart disaster for the tragedy it was. Yet in his blithe
pronouncements that the handcart scheme was not only fundamentally
sound, but had already proved by the end of 1856 to be the best way of
gathering the poor to Zion, there may be something more than the spin
of a master propagandist. A modern psychologist might call it denial; a
good Mormon would call it faith.

The baldest expression of that bedrock conviction came in the Fourteenth General Epistle, Young's state of the union address disseminated
to all of Zion on December 10, 1856.

This season's operations have demonstrated that the Saints, being
filled with faith and the Holy Ghost, can walk across the plains,
drawing their provisions and clothing on hand-carts. The expe-

rience of this season will of course help us to improve in future operations; but the plan has been fairly tested and proved entirely successful.

It was widely predicted by skeptical observers at the time that with the Prophet's death, the Latter-day Saints would collapse as a church. By far the greatest of Brigham Young's achievements was that he not only ensured the survival of the church after his death, but propelled it toward its current status as the most successful homegrown religion ever spawned in the United States, as well as one of the fastest growing faiths in the world, with twelve million adherents all over the globe.

Even a critic as acerbic as Will Bagley can see Young's virtues. "He was a great American and a great leader," says Bagley. "But he was a man with horrific flaws. In some sense, he was a victim of his own history. He always lived with the fear that he couldn't do what Joseph Smith had done."

To the Prophet's skeptical 1925 biographer Morris Werner, "It is my conviction that without Brigham Young the Mormons would never have been important after the first few years of their institutional life, but without the Mormons Brigham Young might have been a great man." For Bernard DeVoto, Young's cardinal achievement was the pilgrimage to Utah. "Without him, the church must have perished," DeVoto wrote in 1930. "He did not originate the idea of going west, but he did make the decision and carry it out. That emigration saved Mormonry." Yet "His genius was commercial shrewdness, and only that. He was not a statesman. He devised the hand-cart emigration, a bitter and gratuitous tragedy."

In concurrence with Bagley and DeVoto, I must conclude that, far from being the hero of the handcart saga, Brigham Young was the architect of an emigration plan so ill-conceived that it had built into it the fatal flaws—chiefly the seventeen-pound baggage limit and the ration of a pound per day of flour—that would ineluctably lead to unbearable hardships and scores of deaths. And further, that in failing competently to supervise the emigration once he had set it in motion, or even coherently to delegate that supervision, the Prophet compounded a disaster that has no parallel in American history.

In concurrence with Ann Eliza Young, I have to conclude that the 1856 handcart debacle was the worst blunder of the Prophet's long career—worse in terms of human suffering even than his dogged championing of polygamy, a diehard clinging to a hopeless cause that delayed Utah statehood until 1896 and helped bring the territory to the brink of war against the United States.

The most pernicious of all the myths about the handcart campaign—a myth still cherished every summer by the throngs of reenactors who flock to the Mormon Handcart Visitors' Center in western Wyoming—is that "because they came to know God," all the tribulations of the Saints in the Willie and Martin Companies were "worth it." That myth effectively annuls the terrible realities of starving to death, of dying from exposure to the cold, of incurring frostbite so severe as to cripple one for life.

It is a testament to the power of myth to rationalize senseless evil that many of the Saints in the Willie and Martin Companies apparently subscribed to that justification for their suffering. Yet not all the victims so believed. Across the century and a half that separates us from the handcart tragedy, a few voices still ring out in protest.

John Bond, the twelve-year-old in the Hodgetts wagon company, conjured up decades later the "untold hardships, broken hearts and so many deaths of loved ones" he witnessed along the trail. "Whatever was on the agents minds"? he wondered out loud, before inveighing, "The men in high standing with high priesthood power are yet to meet the innocent ones before the bar of God to answer to Him for the atrocities of inhuman advice."

And John Chislett mused upon the tragedy for a decade and a half, before writing in the early 1870s, "Whether Brigham was influenced in his desire to get the poor of Europe more rapidly to Utah by his sympathy with their condition, by his well-known love of power, his glory in numbers, or his love of wealth, which an increased amount of subservient labour would enable him to acquire, is best known to himself. But the sad results of his Hand-Cart scheme will call for a day of reckoning in the future which he cannot evade."

ACKNOWLEDGMENTS

For a non-Mormon, the intricacies of LDS doctrine and history present a labyrinthine challenge. As I began to conduct research for this book, I felt seriously lost on more than one occasion. I would have remained lost had I not hired the services of Ardis Parshall, a Mormon historian, newspaper columnist, and freelance researcher. Parshall's command of the documents in the LDS Archives in Salt Lake City, as well as of published sources, proved to be utterly masterful (an inside joke has it that Ardis knows the Archives better than the official church archivists).

Besides being delightful to work with—a woman with a keen sense of humor and a powerful intelligence—Parshall impressed me as by far the most talented researcher I have ever collaborated with on any book or magazine article. As a devout Mormon, Ardis realized early on that my conclusions about the handcart tragedy, nineteenth-century Mormon history, and Brigham Young himself would be seriously at odds with hers. Yet she never hesitated in supplying me documents that I thought I needed, even when they cast a less than flattering light on LDS leaders or events. Far and away my greatest debt in writing *Devil's Gate* is thus to her, and I admire her integrity in persevering in her invaluable labors even after she recognized that she disagreed with my narrative argument.

In the middle of my research, as I visited Boulder, Colorado, my brother Alan, a genealogy buff, caught sight of the unusual name Woodmansee in my notes, and recognized it from our own family tree. With much help from Ardis Parshall, Alan figured out that Emily Hill Woodmansee, a survivor in the Willie Company and later author of the poem "Hunger and Cold" (quoted in Chapter Nine), was my second cousin five times removed. For me, this discovery furnished a fugitive but beguiling personal link to the story.

I had anticipated a diffident or even suspicious reception when I started work in the LDS Archives in 2005. To my great surprise, the archivists, librarians, and historians in the Church History Library could not have been more welcoming and helpful. In 1964, Wallace Stegner had complained that the LDS library and archives were "open to scholars only reluctantly and with limitations." Nothing could be further from the truth today. To my mind, the Archives now set a shining example of disinterested service to writers and researchers who will inevitably quarrel with and criticize "orthodox" Mormon history.

Within the Church History Library, especially helpful to me were Bill Slaughter, Mel Bashore, and Andrew D. Olsen, who regularly dropped whatever they were doing to help me solve a knotty dilemma or fill in a gap in my understanding. I also benefited from consultation with Chad Orton, Michael Landon, and Richard Turley.

A number of dissident or skeptical Mormon historians helped me fix my bearings on the complicated handcart saga. By far the most helpful was the brilliant iconoclast Will Bagley, whose *Blood of the Prophets* is the definitive work on the Mountain Meadows Massacre. David Bigler likewise came to my aid, both over the telephone and through the pages of his scrupulously researched and very readable books. Gary Bergera shared his thoughtful conclusions with me over lunch in Salt Lake City. Bureau of Land Management archaeologist Terry Del Bene took time out to give me some valuable lessons on overland travel on the Mormon Trail. Steve Lundgren, general manager of the Downtown Marriott hotel in Salt Lake City, went out of his way to correct the erroneous information that had been laminated into the caption on a replica of a famous handcart sculpture that rests in the hotel lobby. And independent historian Lyndia Carter, who knows more about the handcart expeditions than anyone else alive, spent half a day bringing me up to speed on all kinds of arcana, even though she is in the process of writing her own pair of books about the handcart story.

In Riverton, Wyoming, I was also surprised and grateful to be granted meetings with Scott Lorimer, Kim McKinnon, and Lloyd Larsen, even though I'm sure they knew I was bound to be skeptical of the Second Rescue mission they had launched and carried out. Those stake leaders also gave me free run of their own archives, through which I was guided by the savvy Gary Anderson.

Every elder or sister whom I met at the Mormon Handcart Visitors' Center near Alcova, Wyoming, was unfailingly kind and helpful. And I was pleased to be invited briefly into the fold of the West Valley, Utah, stake as they carried out their own pilgrimage in honor of their ancestors at the Visitors' Center and Martin's Cove. Likewise, I received nothing but assistance from the staffers at Fort Bridger and Fort Laramie.

Research carried out in other libraries supplemented my core work in the LDS Archives. I am particularly grateful to Janet Seegmiller of the Special Collections department of Southern Utah University in Cedar City. I wish also to thank the staffs of Special Collections at Brigham Young University, the Missouri Historical Society, the Beinecke Library at Yale, and the Houghton, Widener, and Tozzer Libraries at Harvard.

Long before I started writing, I talked through some of my theses with several close friends, who reacted candidly. These sounding boards included Greg Child, Vaughn Hadenfeldt, Jon Krakauer, and my wife, Sharon Roberts. Jon's superb *Under the Banner of Heaven* did not serve as the immediate impetus for *Devil's Gate,* but his hard-earned expertise in matters Mormon helped set me back on my own path time and again.

As usual, my agent, Stuart Krichevsky, put in long hours helping me craft a proposal and was a constant source of good advice when it came to the writing itself. In many details, I was admirably aided by Stuart's longtime colleague, Shana Cohen, and by his assistant, Kathryne Wick.

At Simon & Schuster, Gypsy da Silva and Fred Chase performed the kinds of careful reading and querying I have almost taken for granted. And Johanna Li was, as ever, on top of every stray detail.

This is my tenth book for my Simon & Schuster editor, Bob Bender, in what for me has been an ideal relationship spreading across fifteen years. I'm sure Bob is sick of hearing it by now, but I cannot resist the temptation once more to salute the best damned editor I know of, and the best I ever hope to have.

NOTES

CHAPTER 1: PATIENCE

Page

1 *Up to that point, for Patience Loader:* Archer, *Recollections*, 62–63, 209.

1 *Florence, a fledgling community:* Berrett et al., *Sacred Places: Iowa and Nebraska*, 216–18.

1 *Averaging ten miles a day:* http://www.lds.org/churchhistory.

1 *Yet even as the emigrants:* Archer, 62, 165.

1 *Patience, her father, her mother:* http://www.lds.org/churchhistory.

1 *what historians LeRoy and Ann Hafen call:* Hafen and Hafen, *Handcarts*, 11.

2 *A few ox-drawn wagons:* http://www.lds.org/churchhistory.

2 *The handcart "experiment":* Millennial Star, December 22, 1855.

2 *By 1856, Young's virtually autonomous empire:* Hirshson, *Lion of the Lord*, 116–20.

2 *"those twin relics of barbarism":* Nevins, *Frémont*, 433–34.

2 *Not only to strengthen: Millennial Star,* December 22, 1855.

3 *The handcart of 1856:* Rogerson, "Martin's Handcart Company, 1856," *Salt Lake Tribune,* January 4, 1914; Olsen, *Price We Paid,* 25–26; Elder Hadley, Mormon Handcart Visitors' Center, Wyoming.

3 *From Iowa City to Florence:* Archer, 62–63, 165–66.

4 *August 1: About 9 aclock:* Joseph Beecroft, http://www.lds.org/church history.

4 *Unlike Beecroft, Patience Loader:* Archer, 14–15.

5 *Thus, describing James Loader's collapse:* Ibid., 63.

5 *On the thousand miles:* Berrett et al., *Sacred Places: Iowa and Nebraska,* 283–87; Berrett and Anderson, *Sacred Places: Wyoming and Utah,* 16–23, 157–75.

5 *In that last week of August:* Archer, 62–63.

5 *In 1846, Brigham Young's vanguard party:* Slaughter and Landon, *Trail of Hope,* passim.

5 *In her memoir, Patience bitterly rues:* Archer, 56–57.

6 *Born in 1827:* Ibid., 21, 165.

6 *By the time she wrote:* Ibid., 11–14.

6 *Thus the gardener's cottage:* Ibid., 22–23, 25–27.

8 *No photograph of Patience:* Ibid., 100.

8 *The Loaders were staunch Anglicans:* Ibid., 21–22, 31, 34.

8 *One day in 1851:* Ibid., 35.

9 *Accepting what she could not change:* Ibid., 39–41.

10 *Yet something "took":* Ibid., 42.

11 *At some point, a new housekeeper:* Ibid., 44–45.

11 *Patience was even castigated:* Ibid., 45.

11 *Patience promptly found another job:* Ibid., 45–46.

12 *Within a year after founding his church:* Brodie, *No Man Knows,* 111, 120–21.

12 *By 1855, Zion had been relocated:* Hirshson, *Lion,* 102–3.

12 *As early as 1848: Millennial Star,* March 15, 1848.

12 *And in September 1855:* Ibid., September 22, 1855.

13 *By December 9, 1855:* Archer, 49.

13 *There must have been some confusion:* Ibid.

14 *A semiofficial report: The Mormon,* March 1, 1856.

14 *In her memoir, Patience left an account:* Archer, 50–54.

17 *In her memoir, Patience recalls that President John Taylor:* Ibid., 55–56.

18 *The grand scheme had been announced: Millennial Star,* December 22, 1855.

18 *It had likewise been published in* The Mormon: *The Mormon,* December 1, 1855.

18 *There is no getting around the family's shock:* Archer, 56–57.

19 *Not only did John Jaques answer it: Millennial Star,* June 14, 1856.

20 *The impact on James Loader:* Archer, 57.

21 *The Loaders left New York:* Ibid., 58–60.

21 *Thirty-three years old that July:* http://www.lds.org/churchhistory.

22 *The Loaders arrived in Iowa City:* Archer, 58–61.

22 *Thirty-seven years old, born in Lancashire:* http://www.lds.org/churchhistory.

23 *Decades later, Patience would look back:* Archer, 62–63.

23 *In a reminiscence published:* Jaques, "Some Reminiscences," *Salt Lake Daily Herald,* December 1, 1878.

24 *John Jaques also kept a diary:* Jaques, [Diary and Reminiscences], http://www.lds.org/churchhistory.

24 *As Wallace Stegner writes in his pithy history:* Stegner, *Gathering,* 221.

24 *Built in 1846 as Winter Quarters:* Berrett et al., 208–16.

25 *On August 25, the company started off:* Archer, 62–68.

26 *Before they could catch up with the company:* Ibid., 66–67.

27 *(In his 1878 reminiscence):* Jaques, "Some Reminiscences," *Salt Lake Daily Herald,* December 8, 1878.

27 *James Loader's strength held up:* Archer, 68–71.

27 *John Jaques's otherwise mundane diary:* Jaques, [Diary and Reminiscences], http://www.lds.org/churchhistory.

27 *The 1878 reminiscence amplifies:* Jaques, "Some Reminiscences," *Salt Lake Daily Herald*, December 8, 1878.

27 *The fort, established in 1848:* Berrett et al., 283–86.

28 *Wrote Jesse Haven:* Haven, Journals, http://www.lds.org/churchhistory.

28 *And Samuel Openshaw recorded:* Openshaw diary, ibid.

28 *It was now that James Loader began to fail:* Archer, 70–73.

30 *John Jaques tersely recorded the gravesite:* Jaques, [Diary and Reminiscences], http://www.lds.org/churchhistory.

30 *After that, for the Loaders:* Archer, 73, 215n.

30 *The team's few oxen were forced to swim:* Ibid., 73–74.

CHAPTER 2: FINDING ZION

Page

32 *What is today by far:* Riess and Bigelow, *Mormonism*, 10.

32 *In his 1930 essay:* DeVoto, "The Centennial of Mormonism," 2.

32 *Indeed, during the 1860s:* E.g., T. B. H. Stenhouse, *Rocky Mountain Saints*, 668; Beadle, *Life in Utah*, 524–26; *New York Times*, August 30, 1877.

33 *Driven by poverty and illness:* Brodie, 7–10.

33 *Born on June 1, 1801:* Hirshson, *Lion*, 5–6.

33 *During the first decades:* Werner, *Brigham Young*, 56.

33 *The region centering on Palmyra:* Brodie, 14.

34 *The Mormons would do better:* Werner, 20.

34 *She sees her subject:* Brodie, 16.

34 *"He was known among the young men":* Daniel Hendrix, *St. Louis Globe Democrat*, February 2, 1897, quoted in Linn, *Story*, 13.

34 *Among them is an affidavit:* Brodie, 16, 18. Italics in original.

34 *Smith himself, in a church publication:* *Latter-day Saints Messenger and Advocate*, November 6, 1840, quoted in ibid., 17.

34 *In any event, while still a teenager:* Brodie, 16, 18.

35 *He was big, powerful:* Ibid., 32.

35 *In the best-known portrait:* By Adrian Lamb, National Portrait Gallery.

35 *At the age of nineteen:* Brodie, 29–32.

35 *At some point, while still a teenager:* Ibid., 20–21, 30–31.

36 *In 1820, a latent religious instinct:* B. H. Roberts, ed., *History of the Church*, vol. 1, 5–7. Italics in original.

36 *The second vision:* Ibid., vol. 1, 11–12.

37 *The very next day:* Ibid., vol. 1, 14–16; Brodie, 39–40.

37 *The hill, named Cumorah:* Krakauer, *Under the Banner of Heaven,* 63–64.

38 *The golden plates were densely inscribed:* Brodie, 42–43, 50.

38 *"seemed to be pliable":* Saints Herald, October 1, 1879, quoted in ibid., 43.

38 *Eventually Smith collaborated:* Brodie, 53, 60–62, 80, 87.

39 *To Bernard DeVoto:* DeVoto, "Centennial," 5.

39 *"Perhaps in the beginning":* Brodie, 41.

39 *"It was like taking":* Shirley E. Stephenson interview, November 30, 1975, quoted in Bringhurst, *Fawn McKay Brodie,* 58.

40 *In 1946, the year after:* Bringhurst, "Fawn Brodie and Her Quest," 79.

40 *It is impossible to determine:* Werner, 31.

40 *"intellectually the most eminent":* Sterling McMurrin, in B. H. Roberts, *Studies of the Book of Mormon,* xviii.

40 *"the greatest Mormon thinker":* Rea, *Devil's Gate,* 226.

40 *The terms upon which the debates:* B. H. Roberts, *Studies,* 3–4.

40 *Then, late in his own life:* Ibid., xvi–xviii, 94–115.

41 *There is a school of Mormon thought:* Ardis Parshall, personal communication, February 18, 2007.

41 *Mark Twain famously called:* Twain, *Roughing It,* 110–11.

41 *One of the antagonists:* B. H. Roberts, *Studies,* 7.

42 *From almost the time:* E.g., Brodie, 46–47, 444–52.

42 *Neither plagiarism claim:* B. H. Roberts, *Studies,* 321–44.

42 *Quite aside from allegations:* E.g., Hyde, *Mormonism,* 100.

42 *In the face of such early criticism:* Brodie, 77–80.

43 *One of his first and most important converts:* Pratt, quoted in ibid., 103.

43 *One of the first to fall:* Hirshson, 7.

43 *Young, however, was no instant convert:* Werner, 10–12.

43 *By his own admission:* Hirshson, 6.

43 *Some skeptical visitors:* E.g., Hyde, 155–56.

44 *"He loses his temper":* Young, *Wife No. 19,* 520.

44 *On April 15, 1832:* Werner, 13.

44 *"He was happy to see us":* B. H. Roberts, ed., *History of the Church,* vol. 1, 295–97.

44 *"It consisted of a babble":* Werner, 14.

44 *The duty of every Saint:* Doctrine and Covenants, 29: 7–8; 28: 9; 47: 67, 71.

44 *According to the* Book of Mormon: Book of Mormon, 43–46, 250–61; Riess and Bigelow, 157–61.

45 *The new faith got off:* Brodie, 87, 94–97.

45 *To persuade the recalcitrant:* Howe, *Mormonism Unvailed,* 111.

46 *Kirtland lasted as the Mormon stronghold:* Brodie, 102, 111–13.

46 *They stripped him:* Journal of Discourses, vol. 11, 3–4, paraphrased in ibid., 119.

46 *For one thing, the Mormon colony:* Stegner, viii–ix.

47 *As early as 1831:* Brodie, 108.

47 *One of them delivered:* Ludlow, ed., *Encyclopedia*, vol. 2, 533–34.

47 *Frictions with neighbors:* Stegner, vii–viii.

47 *Arriving there two years later:* Ibid., 19.

47 *Even as the Kirtland colony:* Ibid., ix.

47 *In January, Smith abandoned:* Ibid.

48 *There is good evidence:* Brodie, 184.

48 *"Inasmuch as this Church":* B. H. Roberts, ed., *History of the Church*, vol. 2, 247.

48 *"a remarkable series of evasions":* Brodie, 321.

48 *Brodie offers a list:* Ibid., 335–36.

48 *The man, of course:* Ibid., 339–41.

48 *As late as the early 1850s:* Fanny Stenhouse, *"Tell It All,"* 103–4.

49 *Brodie imagines "a man":* Brodie, 186.

49 *"Whenever I see a pretty woman":* Werner, 130.

50 *"Within the state raged":* Hirshson, 30.

50 *By 1838 the numbers:* Arrington, *Great Basin Kingdom*, 15; Brodie, 209.

50 *One of Smith's closest associates:* Brodie, 213–14.

50 *Both Smith and Young would aver:* Ibid., 215–16.

50 *In 1859, the famous journalist:* Hirshson, 252.

50 *Greeley pressed the Prophet: New York Tribune*, August 20, 1859.

51 *Leonard J. Arrington, whose* Brigham Young: Arrington, *Brigham Young*, 250.

51 *One of the most notorious:* Beadle, ed., *Brigham's Destroying Angel*.

51 *"to go out on a scout":* B. H. Roberts, ed., *History of the Church*, vol. 3, 180–81.

51 *In the middle of 1838:* Werner, 101–2.

52 *John D. Lee, who was Brigham Young's stepson:* Lee, *Mormonism Unveiled*, 58–60; Journal History of the Church of Jesus Christ of Latter-day Saints, August 6, 1838.

52 *The conflict culminated:* B. H. Roberts, ed., *History of the Church*, vol. 3, 182–86; Brodie, 237.

53 *What followed remains uncertain:* Brodie, 239–40; Lee, 82.

53 *With his five hostages:* Werner, 103.

53 *The upshot was that Smith:* Brodie, 242–55.

54 *Without hesitation, he chose:* Ibid., 256.

55 *Within months, however, malaria:* Ibid., 256–57.

55 *According to a reporter: Peoria Register and Northwestern Gazette*, April 17, 1840, quoted in Hirshson, 38–39.

55 *And only months after choosing:* Hirshson, 35.

55 *Brigham Young, one of the Twelve:* Ibid., 35–36, 190.

55 *In their penury:* Ardis Parshall, personal communication, December 11, 2006.

55 *Young had left Illinois:* Hirshson, 35–36.

56 *George A. Smith, Joseph's cousin: Times and Seasons,* November 15, 1840, quoted in Brodie, 264.

56 *During the single year:* Hirshson, 36.

56 *The newspaper made honeyed promises: Millennial Star,* February 1, 1842.

56 *The first British converts:* Brodie, 265.

56 *By 1844, Nauvoo's population:* Ibid., 362–63.

56 *On a windy, rainy night:* Schindler, *Orrin Porter Rockwell,* 67–69.

57 *Rockwell's appearance was enough:* Hirshson, 64.

57 *The dates of Rockwell's temporary absence:* Brodie, 266, 314, 323–24.

58 *That denial failed to satisfy:* Ibid., 324–25.

58 *Disheartened by exile, Rockwell:* Schindler, 88–94.

58 *When he finally returned:* Brodie, 332.

58 *Experts, including Rockwell's sympathetic biographer:* Schindler, 72–73; Brodie, 330–31.

59 *For his part, Smith soon wearied:* Brodie, 327–29.

59 *The final unraveling began:* Ibid., 367–72.

60 *Rather than leave Nauvoo:* Ibid., 372–75.

60 *The retaliation Smith wreaked:* Ibid., 377.

60 *At a signal from the prophet:* Schindler, 116.

61 *This violent episode:* Ibid., 117–18.

61 *The* Warsaw Signal *editorialized:* Brodie, 378.

61 *Governor Ford, whose role:* Ibid., 382–83.

61 *In any event, we know:* B. H. Roberts, ed., *History of the Church,* vol. 6, 548.

62 *Smith was in tears:* Brodie, 383–84.

62 *The retrospective account:* B. H. Roberts, ed., *History of the Church,* vol. 6, 551.

62 *I am going like a lamb:* Ibid., 555. Italics in original.

63 *The journey was uneventful:* Ibid., 559.

63 *According to Krakauer:* Krakauer, 131–33.

64 *The men who had murdered:* Stegner, 35.

65 *Brigham Young's biographer:* Hirshson, 50.

65 *Fawn Brodie ponders this question:* Brodie, 380–81.

65 *Brigham Young, who had risen:* Hirshson, 48.

66 *"The death of the modern Mahomet": New York Herald,* July 8, 1844, quoted in Brodie, 397.

66 *One of the most cherished:* Hirshson, 51.

66 *One historian calls Young's oration:* Ibid., 53.

66 *Well, he spoke, and his words:* Hyde, in *Journal of Discourses,* vol. 13, 181.

67 *(Indeed, a bishop who listened)*: Hirshson, 53.

67 *Desperate to be anointed*: Ibid., 52.

67 *Young, who did in fact speak last*: Werner, 191.

67 *Not once did Young*: Ibid., 191–92.

67 *Like Stalin deposing Trotsky*: Hirshson, 53–54; Werner, 194.

68 *Rigdon indeed decamped for Pittsburgh*: Werner, 194–95.

68 *As late as 1871*: Hirshson, 308–9.

68 *Besides the challenge briefly posed*: Ibid., 56–58.

68 *In the aftermath of the Prophet's murder*: Werner, 195.

68 *John D. Lee, in his late*: Lee, 161.

69 *The feud between William and Young*: Hirshson, 59.

69 *Finally, in 1860*: Werner, 195.

69 *They were brought to the flash point*: Hirshson, 64.

69 *though Harold Schindler, Rockwell's biographer*: Schindler, 138–40.

69 *In response, Gentiles attacked*: Werner, 200.

69 *"Every Saint, mongrel or whole-blood"*: *Madison Express*, [n.d.], quoted in Werner, 200.

69 *The temple, which Mormons claimed*: Werner, 201–2.

70 *During the last weeks*: Ibid., 202.

70 *Among them was Brigham Young*: Hirshson, 65.

70 *"It was the first time"*: *Journal of Discourses*, vol. 3, 266.

70 *No doubt there were dutiful aspects*: Hirshson, 65–66.

70 *Yet if Young initially obeyed*: See, e.g., Hirshson's chapter "The Seventy Wives of Brigham Young," 184–223.

70 *Early in February 1846*: Werner, 202.

71 *On the other hand*: Ibid., 204–5.

71 *We know that Young*: Hirshson, 80.

71 *In fact, as it headed west*: Slaughter and Landon, *Trail of Hope*, 50.

71 *Much speculation has gone*: Bagley, *Pioneer Camp*, 45.

72 *As early as October 1845*: Slaughter and Landon, 23.

72 *It did not take long*: Ibid., 24.

72 *Adding to the pilgrims' difficulties*: Ibid., 28–38.

73 *As it was, even an elite cadre*: Stegner, 73.

73 *Garden Grove and Mount Pisgah*: Berrett et al., 72–75, 87–88.

73 *Yet the Prophet still keenly hoped*: Stegner, 84.

74 *In later years, Young would rail*: *Journal of Discourses*, vol. 5, 231–32.

74 *The army pay*: Stegner, 78, 83.

74 *Some orthodox histories*: Ibid., 78.

74 *In the fall of 1846*: Berrett et al., 121–24, 207–8, 212–15.

74 *A year-end census*: Stegner, 106.

75 *There were 538 wooden houses*: Berrett et al., 214.

75 *No accurate death count:* http://www.lds.org/placestovisit.

75 *Winter found me bed-ridden:* Margaret Phelps, quoted in Slaughter and Landon, 46–47.

75 *That number resonated:* Slaughter and Landon, 50–51.

75 *"the most extensively reported":* Stegner, 111.

75 *South Pass in western Wyoming:* Berrett and Anderson, 116.

76 *In 1843 alone:* Unruh, *Plains Across*, 5.

76 *In 1813 the* Missouri Gazette: Ibid., 28–29.

76 *The first Anglo women:* David Roberts, *Newer World*, 31.

76 *The few encounters with Indians:* Slaughter and Landon, 61.

76 *In fact, that spring and summer:* Unruh, *The Plains Across*, 252.

76 *The trail was so crowded:* Slaughter and Landon, 53.

77 *the Mormon pioneer trek is well documented:* http://www.lds.org/church history.

77 *It comes as no surprise:* Stegner, 132–34; Clayton, *Emigration Guide*, 10.

78 *Sandy Bluffs, west foot:* Clayton, 54.

78 *The cavalcade on the Mormon Trail:* Stegner, 119.

78 *To bring order:* Ibid., 119–20.

78 *On May 29, Young blew his stack:* Slaughter and Landon, 61.

79 *When I wake up in the morning:* unnamed source, quoted in Stegner, 137.

79 *By June 12, the trekkers:* Stegner, 127, 147–48; Slaughter and Landon, 67.

79 *Ascending the Sweetwater:* Stegner, 148–50.

80 *"men, women and children":* Wilford Woodruff, quoted in Stegner, 150.

80 *The Mormon caravan:* Stegner, 153.

80 *Two decades before, leading:* Berrett and Anderson, 157–58.

80 *Another Mormon legend hovers:* E.g., John Steele, quoted in Slaughter and Landon, 68.

81 *"there was but one thing":* Woodruff, *Woodruff's Journal*, 220.

81 *On June 30, as the Saints lingered:* Stegner, 157–58.

81 *Another Mormon legend:* Ibid., 158.

82 *Br Brannan fell in:* Norton Jacob, June 30, 1847, http://www.lds.org/church history.

82 *Once across the Green River:* Clayton, 74.

82 *But in that home stretch:* Stegner, 164.

82 *It was characterized:* Ibid., 157.

82 *"The sagebrush through which":* Terry Del Bene, interview, February 11, 2007.

82 *No one was stricken more seriously:* Stegner, 162–63.

82 *On July 21, Pratt's team:* Ibid., 167.

83 *Alas, Young never uttered:* Ibid., 168.

83 *Wilford Woodruff's journal:* Woodruff, http://www.lds.org/churchhistory.

CHAPTER 3: THE DIVINE HANDCART PLAN

Page

84 *On June 9, 1856, a party:* http://www.lds.org/churchhistory.

84 *Though still in poor health:* Bigler, *Forgotten Kingdom*, 40–41.

85 *In March 1849, Brigham Young:* Morgan, *Deseret*, 125.

85 *The grandiosity of Mormon ambitions:* Unruh, 303; Bigler, *Kingdom*, 46.

85 *In an uneasy 1850 compromise:* Bigler, 48–49.

85 *Young tried at first to divert:* Unruh, 303, 307–8.

86 *The official U.S. census for 1851:* Ibid., 303.

86 *In a typical 1855 pronouncement: Journal of Discourses,* vol. 2, 317, quoted in Bigler, *Kingdom*, 43.

86 *The government surveyor and explorer:* Gunnison, *Mormons*, 26, 67–71.

87 *Yet because of the revelations:* See, e.g., Fielding, *Unsolicited Chronicler.*

87 *Those dark suspicions:* Hirshson, 144–45.

87 *As part of his statehood effort:* Bigler, *Kingdom*, 102.

88 *John Unruh, whose The Plains Across:* Unruh, 408–9.

89 *By the mid-1850s, a wagon:* Olsen, 29.

89 *To solve this problem:* Slaughter and Landon, 106–9.

89 *What those backers failed to mention:* Bagley, "Two-Wheeled Torture Devices," 4–6.

89 *In sheer practical terms:* Ibid., 5–6.

90 *"Many men have traveled the long": Millennial Star,* December 22, 1855, 811.

90 *Adding urgency to Zion's looming:* Olsen, 21–22.

90 *In 1848, a similar infestation:* Werner, 240–41.

90 *On October 29, 1855:* Hafen and Hafen, 34–35.

90 *A month before that, the Prophet had written: Millennial Star,* December 22, 1855, 809–815.

91 *"I have been thinking how we should":* Ibid., 813–14.

92 *Unlike Joseph Smith:* Hirshson, 81.

92 *"The plan is the device of inspiration": Millennial Star,* December 22, 1855, 809.

92 Oh, our faith goes with the hand-carts: "Hand-cart Song," quoted in Hafen and Hafen, 275.

92 *In his December 22 editorial: Millennial Star,* December 22, 1855, 809–12.

93 *LDS scholar Andrew D. Olsen:* Olsen, 29.

94 *At once he dispatched:* Ibid., 53.

94 *More mythologizing:* http://www.lds.org/churchhistory.

94 *In this case, the source: Deseret News,* October 8, 1856, 243.

94 *Most of the British Saints:* Hafen and Hafen, 43–44, 56.

95 *Daniel Spencer had arrived:* Spencer journal, LDS Archives, quoted in Olsen, 55.

95 *Thus Archer Walters, a skilled carpenter:* Archer Walters diary, http://www .lds.org/churchhistory.

95 *It is a testimony either to the converts' loyal obedience:* Ibid.

95 *His team earned the nickname:* Ibid.

96 *On July 1, Archer Walters:* Ibid.

96 *Archer Walters, whose duty it was:* Ibid.

97 *In a memoir written:* Daniel McArthur, Reminiscences, ibid.

97 *"June 9th, 1856. At 5 P.M.":* Edmund Ellsworth Emigrating Company journal, ibid.

97 *As John Oakley, a sub-captain:* John Oakley journal, ibid.

98 *That pressure from peers and leaders:* Patrick Twiss Bermingham journal, ibid.

98 *Combing genealogical records:* Hafen and Hafen, 199n.

98 *In a letter to the New York newspaper:* J. H. Latey, "Correspondence," http:// www.lds.org/churchhistory.

99 *John Oakley, Ellsworth's sub-captain:* Oakley journal, ibid.

99 *Thus on June 20, in Oakley's diary:* Ibid.

100 *Heartless though it seems:* Ibid.

100 *The main daily staple for adults:* Edmund Ellsworth Company narrative, ibid.

100 *Archer Walters's clipped diary entries:* Walters diary, ibid.

101 *John Oakley dutifully recorded:* Oakley journal, ibid.

101 *Apparently the pilfering continued:* Walters diary, ibid.

101 *In an iconoclastic study:* Bagley, "Two-Wheeled Torture Devices," 5.

101 *Archer Walters thought:* Walters diary, http://www.lds.org/churchhistory.

101 *The punitive John Oakley:* Oakley journal, ibid.

102 *Nineteen-year-old Mary Ann Jones:* Mary Ann Jones Ellsworth diary, ibid.

102 *"On the arrival of the company":* Bermingham journal, ibid.

102 *While in Florence:* Oakley journal, ibid.

103 *(As a Swiss girl of six):* Hafen and Hafen, 12.

103 *In the McArthur Company:* Thordur Didriksson, "A brief story," http://www .lds.org/churchhistory.

104 *They are glancingly referred to:* Ellsworth Company narrative, ibid.

104 *e.g., an emigrant recorded as "Peter Stalle":* Ellsworth Company list of individuals, ibid.

104 *Their addition to the party:* Ellsworth Company journal, ibid.

104 *The cold-eyed John Oakley:* Oakley journal, ibid.

104 *It would remain for a single informant:* Margaret Stalle Barker, "Reminiscences," ibid.

105 *Yet even the loyal sub-captain John Oakley:* Oakley journal, ibid.

105 *The toil was terrible:* Bermingham diary, ibid.

105 *Wrote Archer Walters:* Walters diary, ibid.

106 *On August 16, the McArthur party:* Bermingham diary, ibid.

106 *"Before half an hour," Bermingham averred:* Ibid.

106 *In his account of the journey:* McArthur, "Reminiscences," ibid.

106 *Another member of the party:* Mary B. Crandal, "Autobiography," ibid.

107 *As the word was given:* McArthur, "Reminiscences," ibid.

107 *Retrospect may have added a rosy glow:* Crandal, "Autobiography," ibid.

108 *On August 31, near Deer Creek:* Oakley journal, ibid.

108 *He was buried at Deer Creek:* Ellsworth company, list of individuals, ibid.

108 *A few months later, McArthur would remember:* McArthur, "Reminiscences," ibid.

109 *Thus, farther west along the trail:* Ibid.

109 *now a mere 228 miles short:* Clayton, 72.

109 *On September 11, having pushed hard:* Ellsworth Company narrative, ibid.

109 *With laconic resignation:* Ellsworth Company journal, ibid.

109 *But that it was a dramatically orchestrated coup:* Phyllis Hardie Ferguson, "Reminiscences," ibid.

110 *McArthur's own report has his company:* McArthur, "Reminiscences," ibid.

110 *Archer Walters, the Ellsworth Company coffin-maker:* Walters diary, ibid.

111 *Writing later for the* Millennial Star: Thomas Bullock, "Letter," ibid.

111 *On September 17, another English Saint:* Ellsworth Company journal, ibid.

111 *"one man of the Italian brethren":* Oakley journal, ibid.

111 *John Oakley, who had pitilessly attributed:* Ibid.

111 *With the scent of Zion in his nostrils:* Ellsworth Company journal, ibid.

111 *Just how dangerous a passage this was:* William Butler, "Autobiography," ibid.

112 *Charles Treseder, a young man living:* Charles Treseder, "Correspondence," ibid.

113 *Mary Powell Sabin, a twelve-year-old:* Sabin, "Autobiography," ibid.

114 *William Aitken, a thirty-six-year-old dentist:* William Aitken, "Adventures," ibid.

114 *The official Ellsworth journal lists:* Ellsworth Company journal, ibid.

114 *McArthur acknowledged "only the loss":* McArthur, "Reminiscences," ibid.

114 *Hafen and Hafen fix the number:* Hafen and Hafen, 193.

115 *Without citing sources, the company narratives:* Ellsworth Company narrative, McArthur Company narrative, http://www.lds.org/churchhistory.

115 *The* Deseret News *baldly asserted: Deseret News*, October 1, 1856.

115 *In an emotional speech: Deseret News*, October 8, 1856.

116 *At the same meeting:* Ibid.

117   *If anything, at that bowery meeting:* Ibid.

118   *In a speech given two weeks after:* Deseret News, November 26, 1856.

118   *Mary McCleve, a sixteen-year-old:* Mary Meeks, "Reminiscences," http://www.lds.org/churchhistory.

118   *But William Butler, who had staggered:* Butler, "Autobiography," ibid.

119   *Twiss Bermingham, the scrupulous diarist:* Twiss Bermingham, "To Utah," ibid.

119   *William Aitken, that much angrier apostate:* Aitken, "Adventures," ibid.

119   *As for Archer Walters, the loyal carpenter:* Archer Walters, "The Journal," ibid.

119   *In New York City, President John Taylor:* Hafen and Hafen, 91.

120   *On June 11, from Iowa City, William Woodward:* William Woodward to Heber C. Kimball, 11 June 1856, http://www.lds.org/churchhistory.

120   *Normally the arrival dates of such documents:* Ardis Parshall, personal communication, May 30, 2007.

CHAPTER 4: SAVAGE ADVICE

Page

121   *"Dont you think I had a pleasant":* Priscilla Evans, Autobiography, http://www.lds.org/churchhistory.

121   *Edward Bunker, thirty-four years old:* Hafen and Hafen, 81.

122   *In mid-June of 1856, a church official:* William Woodward, "Iowa Correspondence," http://www.lds.org/churchhistory.

122   *Bunker himself wrote almost nothing:* Edward Bunker, Autobiography, ibid.

122   *Priscilla Evans claimed many years later:* Evans, Autobiography, ibid.

122   *Yet David Grant, a sub-captain:* Millennial Star, November 29, 1856, 767.

122   *A delay of three weeks ensued:* Evans, Autobiography, http://www.lds.org/churchhistory.

123   *It contains this cryptic avowal:* Elizabeth Lane Hyde, "Autobiagraphy of Elizabeth L. Hyde," ibid.

123   *Priscilla Evans paints a woeful picture:* Evans, Autobiography, ibid.

123   *Thomas Evans had lost his leg:* Ibid.

123   *Elizabeth Lane elaborates: "He soon gave out":* Hyde, "Autobiagraphy," ibid.

123   *A slightly different version:* Kate B. Carter, Heart Throbs of the West, vol. 6, 355, quoted in Hafen and Hafen, 85.

124   *Elizabeth Lane wrote that after rheumatism:* Hyde, "Autobiagraphy," http://www.lds.org/churchhistory.

124   *Several sources report:* John Parry, Reminiscences and diary, ibid. Also Robert David Roberts, Reminiscences, ibid.

124   *Even this, reported John Parry:* Parry, Reminiscences and diary, ibid.

124   *Only Parry's account even mentions:* Ibid.

124   *"Indians met us some times":* Ibid.

124 *Priscilla relates how it backfired:* Evans, Autobiography, ibid.

125 *one diary mentions a six-inch snowfall:* Roberts, Reminiscences, ibid.

125 *One emigrant, Samuel Orton:* Samuel Taylor Orton, Record book, http://www.lds.org/churchhistory.

125 *Twenty-three-year-old Eleanor Roberts:* Carter, *Heart Throbs of the West*, vol. 6, 357, quoted in Hafen and Hafen, 87–88.

125 *By his own account, Robert Roberts's boots:* Roberts, Reminiscences, http://www.lds.org/churchhistory.

125 *(The actual distance from Independence Rock):* Clayton, 70.

125 *As late as August 30: Millennial Star*, November 29, 1856, 767.

125 *The loner Elizabeth Lane later recalled:* Hyde, "Autobiagraphy," http://www.lds.org/churchhistory.

126 *Thomas Giles, one of the blind men:* Carter, *Heart Throbs of the West*, vol. 10, 325–26, quoted in Hafen and Hafen, 86–87.

126 *After the daily ration had been reduced:* Orton, Record book, http://www.lds.org/churchhistory.

127 *Without citing their sources:* Hafen and Hafen, 193.

127 *One of the emigrants, Robert Roberts:* Roberts, Autobiographical sketch, http://www.lds.org/churchhistory.

128 *By early 1856:* David L. Bigler, *Kingdom*, 121.

128 *He was known to the faithful as "the sledgehammer":* Ibid., 122.

128 *Historian David L. Bigler describes:* Ibid.

128 A New York Times *reporter: New York Times*, September 21, 1857, quoted in Hirshson, 155.

128 *Grant was attending a church meeting:* Fanny Stenhouse, *"Tell It All,"* 313. See also Young, 184–85.

129 *"call[ing] upon everybody to repent":* Young, 185.

129 *Grant's "spirit of fiery denunciation" sparked:* Fanny Stenhouse, *"Tell It All,"* 313–14.

129 *Indeed, Grant would suddenly die:* Bigler, *Kingdom*, 129.

129 *In a speech on September 14, just twelve days: Deseret News*, September 24, 1856, quoted in ibid., 123.

130 *Gustive Larson, an LDS scholar:* Gustive O. Larson, "Reformation," 45.

130 *"The Church needs trimming up": Journal of Discourses*, vol. 3, 60–61, quoted in ibid.

130 *Larson and others see the Reformation:* Ibid.

130 *The bishops were "whipped" for dereliction:* T. B. H. Stenhouse, *Saints*, 294.

130 *On November 3, in dramatic fashion:* Autobiography of John Powell, quoted in Larson, "Reformation," 53–54.

131 *Later the catechism would be expanded:* Diary of John Moon Clements, quoted in Sessions, *Mormon Thunder*, 220–21.

131 *(The Prophet himself was obliged to confess):* Journals of Hannah Tapfield King, quoted in Bigler, *Kingdom,* 128.

131 *The catechism was no mere laundry list:* Hirshson, 156.

131 *At one all-male meeting:* T. B. H. Stenhouse, *Saints,* 295–96.

132 *One scholar demonstrated:* Stanley S. Ivins, "Notes on Mormon Polygamy," 231, quoted in Larson, "Reformation," 48.

132 *On September 21, he announced:* Deseret News, October 1, 1856, quoted in Bigler, *Kingdom,* 126.

132 *On November 5, 1856:* Deseret News, November 5, 1856, quoted in Larson, 57–58.

132 *In one tirade:* Hirshson, 155–56.

133 *According to historian David Bigler:* Bigler, *Kingdom,* 124.

133 *At the bowery meeting, Young urged the Saints:* Journal of Discourses, vol. 4, 219–20.

133 *Grant then elaborated on this doctrine:* Deseret News, October 1, 1856.

134 *The wife of one Elder:* Fanny Stenhouse, *"Tell It All,"* 318.

134 *Yet one LDS theologian:* Bruce R. McConkie, *Mormon Doctrine,* 92, quoted in Bigler, *Kingdom,* 124n.

134 *In matter-of-fact prose:* Beadle, ed., *Brigham's Destroying Angel,* 47.

135 *In Salt Lake City, Hickman continued:* Ibid., 82–83, 87.

135 *"The satisfied point and undoubted fact":* Ibid., 96.

135 *Sometimes the victim was a Gentile:* Ibid., 97–98.

136 *The memoir, which was published in 1872:* Ibid., 193.

136 *That very imprisonment throws a monkey wrench:* Ibid., 122–26.

136 *On Christmas Eve 1856:* Garland Hurt to Alfred Cumming, December 17, 1857, Territorial Papers, quoted in Bigler, *Kingdom,* 131n.

136 *Even at the time, there were suspicions:* Bigler, 131–32.

137 *There is quite a reformation springing up:* Brigham Young to George Q. Cannon, October 4, 1856, CR1234/1, Letterbook 3, LDS Archives.

137 *Morris Werner, Brigham Young's skeptical 1925 biographer:* Werner, 404–5.

138 *"The call to repentance in the Reformation":* Larson, *Prelude to the Kingdom,* 63.

138 *Leonard J. Arrington manages:* Arrington, *Brigham Young,* 300.

138 *On May 4, 1856, the sailing ship* Thornton: John Ahmanson, *Secret History,* 27.

139 *The Atlantic crossing was largely uneventful:* [Information on Thomas and Susannah Stone Lloyd], http://www.lds.org/churchhistory.

139 *According to a Danish passenger, John Ahmanson:* Ahmanson, 28.

139 *Yet another Danish passenger, Peter Madsen:* Peter Madsen diary, May 21, 1856, LDS Archives.

139 *Despite the lapses of the English young people:* Ibid., June 11, 1856.

139   *With some misgivings:* John Taylor to Brigham Young, June 18, 1856, CR1234/1, Box 43, Folder 4, LDS Archives.

139   *"I wish the passengers":* The Mormon, April 26, 1856, quoted in Olsen, 59.

140   *According to forty-six-year-old emigrant William James:* Loleta Wiscombe Dixon, [Willie Handcart Company and William James], http://www.lds.org/churchhistory.

140   *"There was a scarcety of seasoned wood":* Ibid.

140   *The agents all talked economy:* Young, 207.

140   *One of the men in the company:* "J. R.," The Mormon, August 16, 1856.

141   *According to Peter Madsen:* Peter Madsen journal, http://www.lds.org/churchhistory.

141   *The hardship that this unforeseen restriction:* Ibid.

141   *"The health of the company is good":* Ibid.

142   *This fourth handcart company:* Olsen, 66.

142   *Apparently he never wrote a word:* Hafen and Hafen, 92n.

142   *The official journal of the company:* Olsen, 68.

142   *In one of the few extant photographs:* Ibid., 66.

142   *Willie's second-in-command, Millen Atwood:* Ibid., 66–67.

142   *Only a week after arriving in Salt Lake City:* Millen Atwood, "Account of His Mission," Deseret News, November 26, 1856.

143   *Ahmanson's lot was a particularly hard one:* Ahmanson, 28–29.

144   *After he left the church:* Olsen, 186.

144   *In 1876, he wrote in Danish a memoir:* Ahmanson, 9–10.

144   *Diaries and memoirs recount the occasional kindness:* James G. Willie Emigrating Company Journal, http://www.lds.org/churchhistory.

145   *According to George Cunningham:* George Cunningham, Reminiscences, ibid.

145   *On July 25, near Muddy Creek:* James G. Willie Emigrating Company Journal, ibid.

145   *The official company journal did its best:* Ibid.

145   *Within five days of starting from Iowa City:* Ibid.

145   *The most curious of them:* Ibid.

146   *"the first 200 miles":* Mary Ann James Dangerfield, Autobiographical sketch, ibid.

146   *Another, Sarah Moulton:* Sarah Moulton to Mark H. Forscutt, August 13, 1856, ibid.

146   *More typical, though:* Agnes Caldwell Southworth, [Autobiographical sketch], ibid.

146   *Even the blindly partisan Millen Atwood:* Atwood, Deseret News, November 26, 1856.

146   *John Chislett later cogently appraised:* T. B. H. Stenhouse, Saints, 316.

147 *According to the official journal:* James G. Willie Emigrating Company Journal, http://www.lds.org/churchhistory.

147 *In the end, about a hundred:* Cunningham, Reminiscences; Dixon, ibid.

147 *About these backouts:* Atwood, *Deseret News,* November 26, 1856.

147 *Many years later, the granddaughter:* Margaret Bennett, [Interview], http://www.lds.org/churchhistory.

148 *Among the Saints remaining in the Willie Company:* T. B. H. Stenhouse, *Saints,* 317.

148 *Born in Ohio, Savage was thirty-six years old:* Olsen, 67–68.

148 *With tears streaming down his face:* Cunningham, Reminiscences; Ann Jewell Rowley, [Autobiography], http://www.lds.org/churchhistory.

148 *In his own journal:* Levi Savage journal, ibid.

149 *For his pains:* T. B. H. Stenhouse, *Saints,* 317.

149 *As one emigrant later recalled:* James Sherlock Cantwell, Autobiography, http://www.lds.org/churchhistory.

149 *Savage himself recorded the captain's rebuke:* Savage journal, ibid.

149 *Heaping further scorn on Savage's misgivings:* Ahmanson, 29–30; see also T. B. H. Stenhouse, *Saints,* 317.

149 *It would be left to John Chislett:* T. B. H. Stenhouse, *Saints,* 317.

150 *The recurrent problem:* Ibid., 318.

CHAPTER 5: TROUBLES ON THE PLATTE

Page

151 *On July 9, 1856, as the Willie Company Saints:* James G. Willie Emigrating Company Journal, http://www.lds.org/churchhistory.

151 *The* Horizon *had departed from Liverpool:* Olsen, 219.

151 *Some two hundred emigrants:* Langley A. Bailey, [Reminiscences], http://www.lds.org/churchhistory.

151 *as the Saints rode by train:* Olsen, 227.

151 *Eventually a company of about 650 emigrants:* Ibid., 274.

152 *Born in Preston:* Ibid., 231–35.

152 *In a letter to a friend in England:* Edward Martin to John Melling, *Our Pioneer Heritage,* vol. 12, 356–57, quoted in Olsen, 233.

152 *A poignant letter from his eleven-year-old daughter:* Mary Ellen Martin to Edward Martin, September 29, 1855, Edward Martin correspondence, LDS Archives, quoted in Olsen, 235.

153 *Recruited by President Franklin D. Richards:* Ibid., 235.

153 *He certainly had the hardest job of all:* Ibid., 243.

153 *President Richards, who would see them off: Journal History,* October 4, 1856, quoted in Olsen, 243.

153 *A few of the Martin Company Saints:* Margaret Ann Griffiths Clegg, Autobiographical sketch, http://www.lds.org/churchhistory.

154 *Yet the diary of Jesse Haven:* Haven, Journals, ibid.

154 *On July 22, Jesse Haven's thermometer:* Ibid.

154 *More than half a century later:* John William Southwell, Autobiographical sketch, ibid.

155 *As Samuel Openshaw described it:* Openshaw diary, ibid.

155 *Some of the Saints regarded the meteor:* Olsen, 279.

155 *Fifteen-year-old Aaron Giles:* Aaron Barnet Giles to Brigham Young, December 3, 1856, http://www.lds.org/churchhistory.

155 *More than sixty years later:* Langley Allgood Bailey, Reminiscences and journal, ibid.

156 *Even Webb's daughter:* Young, 207.

156 *One member of the assembly later recalled:* John Bond, "Handcarts West in '56," http://www.lds.org/churchhistory.

156 *A fifteen-year-old boy in the crowd:* Josiah Rogerson, "Martin's Handcart Company, 1856," *Salt Lake Herald*, October 27, 1907.

157 *By the time the Martin party set out:* James G. Willie Emigrating Company Journal, http://www.lds.org/churchhistory.

157 *The fourth handcart company was thus 133 miles:* Clayton, 48.

157 *The William B. Hodgetts Company:* http://www.lds.org/churchhistory.

157 *now reduced to 404 individuals:* Olsen, 86.

157 *Many years later, Mary Ann James:* Loleta Wiscombe Dixon, [Willie Handcart Company and William James], http://www.lds.org/churchhistory.

157 *Even John Chislett:* T. B. H. Stenhouse, *Saints*, 317–18.

157 *The Saints invented many songs:* Hafen and Hafen, 272–73.

158 *Along with "The Handcart Song":* Louisa Mellor Clark, "A Record," http://www.lds.org/churchhistory.

158 *which after its composition in 1846:* Clayton, 101.

158 *In today's hymnal: Hymns of the Church*, 30.

159 *"Our carts were more heavily laden":* T. B. H. Stenhouse, *Saints*, 317.

159 *"would like to see all the grumblers":* James G. Willie Emigrating Company Journal, http://www.lds.org/churchhistory.

159 *The official journal records:* Ibid.

159 *Seventeen-year-old Joseph Wall:* Kate B. Carter, *Heart Throbs of the West*, vol. 4, 79, quoted in Olsen, 88.

160 *The official journal tersely notes:* James G. Willie Emigrating Company Journal, http://www.lds.org/churchhistory.

160 *Levi Savage's journal routinely recorded:* Levi Savage journal, ibid.

160 *John Chislett would later eloquently analyze:* T. B. H. Stenhouse, *Saints*, 318.

160 *By their own reckoning, they had covered:* James G. Willie Emigrating Company Journal, http://www.lds.org/churchhistory.

160 *Many years later, Emma James:* Dixon, ibid.

161 *Chislett describes the woeful solution:* T. B. H. Stenhouse, *Saints*, 318.

161 *On September 7, a Sunday:* James G. Willie Emigrating Company Journal, http://www.lds.org/churchhistory.

162 *By September 12, the Willie Company:* Ibid.

163 *The next morning, with the wagons hitched:* Savage journal, ibid.

163 *Before riding onward:* T. B. H. Stenhouse, *Saints*, 319.

164 *And also before departing:* Ibid.

164 *James Bleak (pronounced "Blake"):* Olsen, 270–72.

165 *On the trail, Bleak kept a journal:* James Bleak Journal, http://www.lds.org/churchhistory.

165 *Like James Bleak, thirty-seven-year-old Elizabeth Sermon:* Olsen, 264–65.

166 *Though she apparently did not keep a journal:* Elizabeth Whitear [Sermon] Camm, Reminiscence, http://www.lds.org/churchhistory.

167 *In his diary for September 21:* Stella Jaques Bell, *Life History and Writings of John Jaques*, 136.

167 *In an 1879 reminiscence:* Jaques, "Some Reminiscences," *Salt Lake Daily Herald*, January 12, 1879.

168 *"We saw a great many buffalo":* Peter Howard McBride, [Life sketch], http://www.lds.org/churchhistory; see also E. E. McBride, Autobiographical sketch, ibid.

168 *Many years later, Josiah Rogerson:* Rogerson, "Martin's Handcart Company, 1856," *Salt Lake Herald*, November 3, 1907.

169 *Also many years later:* John William Southwell, Autobiographical sketch, http://www.lds.org/churchhistory.

169 *About a dozen years after the trek:* Heber Robert McBride, Autobiography, ibid.

169 *On September 7, twenty-two-year-old Samuel Openshaw:* Openshaw diary, ibid.

170 *"lower limbs were paralyzed":* Southwell, Autobiographical sketch, ibid.

170 *The count is uncertain:* Rogerson, "Martin's Handcart Company, 1856," *Salt Lake Herald*, October 27, 1907.

171 *"A man fell down dead":* Openshaw diary, http://www.lds.org/churchhistory.

171 *"An old sister died this morning":* Ibid.

171 *"A change for worse occurred":* Southwell, ibid.

171 *Perhaps the strangest of all the deaths:* Rogerson, "Martin's Handcart Company, 1856," *Salt Lake Herald*, October 27, 1907.

172 *The report was probably accurate:* Schindler, 232n.

172 *Babbitt had been a leading member:* Hirshson, 72–73.

172 *In 1851, he himself emigrated:* http://www.lds.org/churchhistory.

172 *Even before that, in 1849:* Bigler, *Kingdom*, 47.

172 *In Utah, Babbitt became one of the first:* Hilton, *"Wild Bill" Hickman*, 20, 25.

172 *In 1851, he was disfellowshiped from the church:* Schindler, 230n.

172 *Despite that disgrace:* Ibid., 230.

172 *In the summer of 1856:* Ibid., 231.

172 *On August 29, the Willie's Saints:* James Cantwell, Autobiography, http://www.lds.org/churchhistory.

173 *The next day, the Willie Company:* Ibid.

173 *Another diarist recorded:* William Woodward Journal, ibid.

173 *According to Cantwell:* Cantwell, Autobiography, ibid.

173 *Despite warnings from the Willie Company:* Schindler, 231–32.

173 *Arriving at Fort Kearny:* Ibid., 232–34.

173 *(When the Martin Company came upon the site):* Jaques, "Some Reminiscences," *Salt Lake Daily Herald*, December 8, 1878.

174 *Harold Schindler, Rockwell's sympathetic biographer:* Schindler, 233–36.

174 *When Babbitt's small party failed to show up:* N. H. Felt, Correspondence, http://www.lds.org/churchhistory.

174 *Enter, at this point:* Caleb Green Diary, Missouri Historical Society.

174 *When Rockwell arrived in Fort Laramie:* Schindler, 236.

174 *Caleb Green's diary adds:* Green Diary, MHS.

175 *In 1862, Brigham Young cast:* New York Times, August 30, 1877, quoted in Hirshson, 160.

175 *Levi Savage recorded his disappointment:* Savage journal, http://www.lds.org/churchhistory.

175 *It was not a military establishment:* Berrett and Anderson, 18–20.

175 *At the fort, there was a very limited amount:* Olsen, 106.

175 *Levi Savage wrote in his diary:* Savage journal, http://www.lds.org/church history.

176 *In the end, Captain Willie:* Olsen, 109.

176 *Salt Lake City was still 509 miles away:* Clayton, 60.

176 *He called a meeting of the whole company:* T. B. H. Stenhouse, *Saints*, 319.

176 *"It was resolved to reduce":* Ibid., 319.

176 *Historians struggle to come up with an explanation:* See, e.g., Olsen, 108–9.

176 *In a diary entry on October 3:* Openshaw diary, http://www.lds.org/church history.

176 *On October 4, the Willie Company:* James G. Willie Emigrating Company Journal, ibid.

176 *Jesse Haven's diary recorded the death:* Haven journals, ibid.

177 *Unlike the vast majority of the Saints:* Olsen, 227–28.

CHAPTER 6: ROCKY RIDGE

Page

179 *We know that the Prophet's protestation:* William Woodward to Heber C. Kimball, 11 June 1856, http://www.lds.org/churchhistory.

179 *For example, as Andrew Olsen writes:* Olsen, 115. See also Bartholomew and Arrington, *Rescue,* 5, and Hafen and Hafen, 119.

179 *The very next day: Deseret News,* October 15, 1856.

180 *(The Martin Company at that moment):* Clayton, 56.

180 *"That is my religion": Deseret News,* October 15, 1856.

180 *After Young finished:* Ibid.

180 *And then, after Spencer:* Ibid.

181 *in the Prophet's formula:* Ibid.

181 *The minutes of the conference:* Ibid.

181 *(After the pioneer trek to the Great Basin):* Bigler, *Fort Limhi,* 135ff.

181 *Yet even as the colony awoke: Deseret News,* October 15, 1856.

182 *On October 7, the first rescue wagons:* Olsen, 121–22.

182 *Some LDS historians and scholars:* For example, William Slaughter and Michael Landon, personal communication, February 2006.

182 *Even T. B. H. Stenhouse:* T. B. H. Stenhouse, *Saints,* 339.

182 *Leonard Arrington, author of* Brigham Young: Arrington, *Brigham Young,* 404–5.

183 *"About this time Captain Willie":* T. B. H. Stenhouse, *Saints,* 320.

184 *At the times of those encounters:* Clayton, 56, 70, 72, 74.

184 *Richards and Spencer's account: Deseret News,* October 22, 1856.

184 *Tackling this thorny problem:* Olsen, 107–8.

184 *But Olsen also points to the diary:* Robert T. Burton, [Journal], http://www.lds.org/churchhistory, quoted in Olsen, 108.

185 *At Fort Laramie in the beginning of October:* Olsen, 110; James G. Willie Emigrating Company Journal, http://www.lds.org/churchhistory.

185 *On October 4, the day the rations:* Levi Savage journal, http://www.lds.org/churchhistory.

187 *John Oborn, then twelve:* John Oborn, Reminiscences and diary, ibid.

187 *Michael Jensen, an eleven-year-old Dane:* Michel [Michael] Jensen, [Interview], ibid.

187 *On October 12, Levi Savage recorded:* Savage journal, ibid.

187 *Five days later, a calf gave out:* Willie Company Journal, ibid.

187 *Fifteen-year-old George Cunningham:* George Cunningham, Reminiscences, ibid.

188 *Eighteen-year-old Sarah James:* Loleta Wiscombe Dixon, [Willie Handcart Company and William James], ibid.

188   *Ann Rowley was a forty-eight-year-old English widow:* Ann Jewell Rowley, [Autobiography], ibid.

188   *According to one emigrant:* Dixon, [Willie Handcart Company and William James], ibid.

188   *On October 15, Willie convened a council:* Willie Company Journal, ibid.

188   *"It was unanimously agreed":* Ibid.

188   *In the first week of October:* Olsen, 111.

188   *Within eight days:* Robert Reeder, History of Robert Reeder, http://www.lds.org/churchhistory.

189   *Also within days, the Gadd family:* Olsen, 111–12.

189   *Ann Rowley, the matriarch traveling:* Rowley, [Autobiography], http://www.lds.org/churchhistory.

189   *Susannah Stone, twenty-five at the time:* [Information on Thomas and Susannah Stone Lloyd], ibid.

190   *Ann Rowley witnessed an instance:* Rowley, [Autobiography], ibid.

190   *On October 14, the Willie Company:* Olsen, 110, 125.

190   *(An old legend had it):* Clayton, 67–68.

190   *Robert Reeder swore that James Hurren:* Adolph Madsen Reeder, Writings, http://www.lds.org/churchhistory.

190   *The pious Ann Rowley:* Rowley, [Autobiography], ibid.

191   *By contrast, William Woodward's official journal:* Willie Company journal, ibid.

191   *It would remain for John Chislett:* T. B. H. Stenhouse, *Saints,* 320–22.

192   *On October 19, the Willie Company:* Olsen, 131–32; T. B. H. Stenhouse, *Saints,* 322–23.

193   *Bond remembered his shock:* Bond, "Handcarts West in '56," http://www.lds.org/churchhistory.

194   *As John Jaques remembered in 1878:* Jaques, "Some Reminiscences," *Salt Lake Daily Herald,* December 8, 1878.

194   *Peter McBride, only six years old:* Susan Madsen, *I Walked to Zion,* 45.

194   *Josephine Hartley remembered:* Josephine Hartley Zundle, Biography of Josephine Hartley Zundle, http://www.lds.org/churchhistory.

194   *The most harrowing testimony to hunger:* Sarah Crossley Sessions, Autobiographical sketch, ibid.

195   *"The hardship on the men having":* Alice Welsh Strong, Autobiographical sketch, ibid.

195   *Fifteen-year-old Albert Jones:* Albert Jones, [Reminiscences], ibid.

195   *Margaret Clegg remembered:* Margaret Ann Griffiths Clegg, Autobiographical sketch, ibid.

196   *If his own testimony is to be believed:* Aaron Barnet Giles, to Brigham Young, December 3, 1856, ibid.

196 *Samuel Openshaw's diary places:* Openshaw diary, ibid.

197 *According to John Jaques:* Jaques, "Some Reminiscences," *Salt Lake Daily Herald*, December 8, 1878.

197 *Elizabeth Sermon would later claim:* Elizabeth Whitear [Sermon] Camm, Letter, http://www.lds.org/churchhistory.

197 *As Josiah Rogerson remembered:* Rogerson, "Martin's Handcart Company, 1856," *Salt Lake Herald*, November 3, 1907.

197 *Their presence is explained by John Bond:* Bond, "Handcarts West in '56," http://www.lds.org/churchhistory.

197 *At the fort, several backouts:* Rogerson, "Martin's Handcart Company, 1856," *Salt Lake Herald*, November 3, 1907.

198 *"Laramie's Peak, in the distance":* Jaques, "Some Reminiscences," *Salt Lake Daily Herald*, December 8, 1878.

198 *John Bond took in the same view:* Bond, "Handcarts West in '56," http://www.lds.org/churchhistory.

198 *As John Jaques remembered twenty-two years later:* Jaques, "Some Reminiscences," *Salt Lake Daily Herald*, December 8, 1878.

198 *Half a century later:* Rogerson, "Martin's Handcart Company, 1856," *Salt Lake Herald*, November 10, 1907.

199 *In his journal, William Binder wrote:* William Binder, Journal, quoted in Olsen, 316.

199 *The reminiscence of one Saint:* John Watkins, Reminiscences, http://www.lds.org/churchhistory.

199 *Five miles east of where the Saints waded:* Olsen, 317.

200 *Wrote John Jaques in 1878:* Jaques, "Some Reminiscences," *Salt Lake Daily Herald*, December 8, 1878.

200 *Thomas Durham wrote in his journal:* Thomas Durham journal, http://www.lds.org/churchhistory.

200 *Twelve-year-old John Bond:* Bond, "Handcarts West in '56," ibid.

201 *The snowstorm was no passing squall:* Durham journal, ibid.

201 *Heber McBride, thirteen years old at the time:* Heber Robert McBride, Autobiography, ibid.

201 *Years later, his wife recounted:* Elizabeth Horrocks Jackson Kingsford, [Autobiographical sketch], ibid.

202 *Other Saints confirmed that fourteen:* Watkins, Reminiscences, ibid.; Rogerson, "Martin's Handcart Company, 1856," *Salt Lake Herald*, November 10, 1907.

203 *As John Jaques pithily put it twenty-two years later:* Jaques, "Some Reminiscences," *Salt Lake Daily Herald*, December 8, 1878.

203 *Most of the volunteers:* Bartholomew and Arrington, 8.

203 *Ephraim Hanks was a footloose frontiersman:* Hanks and Hanks, *Scouting for the Mormons on the Great Frontier*, 116–19.

203   *The process by which Daniel W. Jones signed on:* Daniel W. Jones, *Forty Years Among the Indians,* 60.

204   *After uttering his soon-to-be infamous phrase:* Bartholomew and Arrington, 10.

204   *Traveling fast, Grant's entourage:* Ibid., 10–11.

204   *Meanwhile the main caravan pushed on:* Olsen, 122.

205   *We began to feel great anxiety:* Jones, *Forty Years,* 61–62.

205   *Although there was no way to know it:* Olsen, 123.

205   *Daniel Jones later remembered:* Jones, *Forty Years,* 62.

205   *But Robert Burton, one of the few men:* Robert T. Burton, [Journal], http://www.lds.org/churchhistory.

205   *But in any event, by the 18th:* Bartholomew and Arrington, 11.

205   *With all the advantages of hindsight:* Ibid., 11.

206   *in Robert Burton's dry diary entry:* Burton, [Journal], http://www.lds.org/churchhistory.

206   *On the morning of October 18:* Loleta Wiscombe Dixon, [Willie Handcart Company and William James], ibid.

207   *The party had reached a marshy lowland:* Berrett and Anderson, 84.

207   *In the midst of the storm:* Dixon, http://www.lds.org/churchhistory.

207   *George Cunningham, fifteen years old:* George Cunningham, Reminiscences, ibid.

208   *The Dane Michael Jensen:* Michael Jensen, "The Story of My Life," ibid.

208   *And John Chislett averred:* T. B. H. Stenhouse, *Saints,* 322.

208   *Euphemia Bain remembered:* Euphemia Mitchell Bain, "Pioneer Sketch," http://www.lds.org/churchhistory.

208   *In the official journal:* Willie Company Journal, ibid.

208   *According to Chislett:* T. B. H. Stenhouse, *Saints,* 323.

208   *Chislett recorded, "They informed us":* Ibid., 322.

209   *The official journal dutifully recorded:* Willie Company Journal, http://www.lds.org/churchhistory.

209   *Chislett elaborated on that stormy bivouac:* T. B. H. Stenhouse, *Saints,* 323.

209   *In the morning, new snow lay heavy:* Ibid., 323; Willie Company Journal, http://www.lds.org/churchhistory.

209   *The last ration of flour had been issued:* T. B. H. Stenhouse, *Saints,* 323.

209   *Wrote Chislett, "Being surrounded":* Ibid., 323–24.

210   *Robert Burton's noncommittal journal notes:* Burton, [Journal], http://www.lds.org/churchhistory.

210   *Ann Rowley, the widowed matriarch:* Rowley, [Autobiography], ibid.

210   *Levi Savage's journal entry for October 20:* Savage journal, ibid.

210   *Twelve-year-old John Oborn:* John Oborn, Reminiscences and diary, ibid.

210   *But after covering twelve miles:* Joseph B. Elder journal, quoted in Allphin, *Tell My Story, Too,* 38.

210 *Ahead of them loomed Rocky Ridge:* Berrett and Anderson, 94.

211 *Wrote Elder later:* Elder journal, quoted in Allphin, 38.

211 *Elder swore that he and Willie rode:* Ibid.

211 *But it occurred to one rescuer:* Harvey Cluff journal, quoted in Olsen, 138.

211 *"When they saw us":* Elder journal, quoted in Allphin, 38.

211 *Church historian Andrew Olsen:* Olsen, 139.

212 *John Chislett, who had been put in charge:* T. B. H. Stenhouse, *Saints*, 324.

212 *Chislett records the momentous return:* T. B. H. Stenhouse, *Saints*, 325.

213 *Even historians succumb:* Hafen and Hafen, 127.

213 *Daniel Jones, the former mountain man:* Daniel Jones, *Forty Years*, 62.

214 *(In fact, at the moment):* Clayton, 66, 70.

214 *In John Ahmanson's private memoir:* Ahmanson, 34.

214 *In his journal, Levi Savage:* Savage journal, http://www.lds.org/churchhistory.

215 *Savage, again, in his longest journal entry:* Ibid.

215 *Its last entry:* Ibid.

216 *Michael Jensen, only eleven at the time:* Jensen, "The Story of My Life," ibid.

216 *As usual, John Chislett had the most comprehensive:* T. B. H. Stenhouse, *Saints*, 327–29.

217 *William Woodward, in the official journal entry:* Willie Company Journal, http://www.lds.org/churchhistory.

217 *Chislett described the mass grave:* T. B. H. Stenhouse, *Saints*, 329.

218 *Only seven years old at the time:* Mary Hurren Wight, [Reminiscences], http://www.lds.org/churchhistory.

218 *Nineteen-year-old Robert Reeder:* Robert Reeder, History of Robert Reeder, ibid.

218 *In addition to the fifteen dead:* Mettie Mortensen Rasmussen, Reminiscences, ibid.

218 *despite the arrival on October 24:* Willie Company Journal, ibid.

218 *And according to Chislett:* T. B. H. Stenhouse, *Saints*, 329.

219 *Yet from that date on:* Ibid., 330.

219 *Woodward's official journal records:* Willie Company Journal, http://www.lds.org/churchhistory.

219 *On top of all their other miseries:* William Woodward, 1907 letter to Joseph F. Smith, ibid.

219 *Years later, the eleven-year-old Danish boy:* Jensen, "The Story of My Life," ibid.

220 *Also years later, Agnes Caldwell:* Madsen, *I Walked to Zion*, 58–59.

220 *During these onerous days:* Ahmanson, 33–35.

221 *As usual, John Chislett had the keenest eye:* T. B. H. Stenhouse, *Saints*, 330.

222 *A cherished piece of Mormon folklore:* Stegner, 255–56.

222 *Thirty-one-year-old Margaret Dalglish:* http://www.lds.org/churchhistory.

222 *Church historian Andrew Olsen believes:* Andrew Olsen, personal communication, August 28, 2007.

222 *Susannah Stone, twenty-five during the journey:* Susannah Stone Lloyd, Lloyd family sketches, http://www.lds.org/churchhistory.

222 *Woodward's journal systematically records:* Willie Company Journal. ibid.

223 *Chislett would later write:* T. B. H. Stenhouse, *Saints*, 331.

223 *Euphemia Bain recalled:* Euphemia Mitchell Bain, "Pioneer Sketch," http://www.lds.org/churchhistory.

223 *Susannah Stone later remembered:* Lloyd family sketches, ibid.

223 *As the Saints entered the city:* Ahmanson, 35.

223 *But Susannah Stone remembered:* Lloyd family sketches, http://www.lds.org/churchhistory.

223 *Of both bishops and families:* T. B. H. Stenhouse, *Saints*, 331.

223 *Captain Willie, the proud leader:* Adolph Madsen Reeder, Writings, http://www.lds.org/churchhistory.

223 *The horror of the toll that frostbite:* Ibid.

224 *Saints in the party put the toll:* Bain, "Pioneer Sketch," ibid.; Willie Company Journal, ibid.; Adolph Reeder, Writings, ibid.; T. B. H. Stenhouse, *Saints*, 331.

224 *though Robert Reeder:* Robert Reeder, History of Robert Reeder, http://www.lds.org/churchhistory.

224 *In Handcarts to Zion:* Hafen and Hafen, 193.

224 *After careful research, church historian:* B. H. Roberts, ed., *A Comprehensive History of the Church*, vol. 3, 94.

224 *Andrew Olsen, in his recent:* Olsen, 172.

224 *The already embittered Danish sub-captain:* Ahmanson, 34.

224 *Millen Atwood, Willie's fanatical second-in-command:* Deseret News, November 26, 1856.

224 *And on November 12:* Deseret News, November 12, 1856.

CHAPTER 7: MARTIN'S COVE

Page

225 *A curious footnote to the rescue mission:* Bartholomew and Arrington, 31.

225 *A brief notice of this aborted expedition:* Deseret News, October 22, 1856.

225 *A much more elaborate and bizarre version:* Earl S. Paul, "The Handcart Companies of 1856 and Arza Erastus Hinckley," 8–9.

226 *possibly Hinckley was the "doctor":* Bartholomew and Arrington, 31.

227 *George Grant had ordered:* George D. Grant to Brigham Young, Deseret News, November 19, 1856.

227 *the half-decrepit remains of Fort Seminoe:* Olsen, 337–38.

227 *The eternally overoptimistic Franklin Richards:* Ibid., 337.

227 *Meanwhile, having dispatched William Kimball:* Bartholomew and Arrington, 21.

227 *Grant began to speculate:* Ibid., 21.

227 *As Daniel Jones wrote of this impasse:* Daniel Jones, *Forty Years*, 64.

228 *Jones would later claim:* Ibid., 64.

228 *Harvey Cluff, the young man who had posted:* Harvey H. Cluff, Journal, quoted in Hafen and Hafen, 235.

228 *According to Jones's account:* Daniel Jones, *Forty Years*, 64.

228 *Their rations had recently been reduced:* Margaret Ann Griffiths Clegg, Autobiographical sketch, http://www.lds.org/churchhistory; Heber Robert McBride, Autobiography, ibid.; Jaques, "Some Reminiscences," *Salt Lake Daily Herald*, December 15, 1878.

228 *"At last the Company gave up and decided":* Louisa Mellor Clark, Reminiscences, http://www.lds.org/churchhistory.

229 *Heber McBride, thirteen at the time:* Heber Robert McBride, "Tongue nor Pen Can Never Tell the Sorrow," ibid.

229 *The stalwart John Jaques insisted:* Jaques, "Some Reminiscences," *Salt Lake Daily Herald*, December 15, 1878.

229 *Both Patience Loader and Jane Griffiths:* Archer, 76; Jane Griffiths Fullmer, [Reminiscence], http://www.lds.org/churchhistory.

229 *Josiah Rogerson went even further:* Josiah Rogerson, "Martin's Handcart Company, 1856," *Salt Lake Herald*, November 17, 1907.

229 *But twelve-year-old John Bond:* John Bond, "Handcarts West in '56," http://www.lds.org/churchhistory.

229 *And Bond was able to confess:* Ibid.

230 *She remembered that she and her sister:* Archer, 74.

230 *The single repast that stuck in her memory:* Ibid., 75.

231 *Patience lavishes considerable detail:* Ibid.

231 *scholar Lyndia Carter believes:* Ibid., 215 n38.

231 *Patience's family offered the man:* Ibid., 75–76.

232 *Elizabeth Jackson, who had lain:* Elizabeth Horrocks Jackson Kingsford, [Autobiographical sketch], http://www.lds.org/churchhistory.

232 *Josiah Rogerson reported the prophetic vision:* Rogerson, "Martin's Handcart Company, 1856," *Salt Lake Herald*, November 17, 1907.

232 *The best account of the Martin Company's deliverance:* Bond, "Handcarts West in '56," http://www.lds.org/churchhistory.

233 *Also many years later:* Albert Jones, Address, ibid.

233 *Patience Loader remembered:* Archer, 76.

233 *Martin reported that fifty-six members:* Rogerson, "Martin's Handcart Company, 1856," *Salt Lake Herald*, November 17, 1907.

234   *Young then ordered the immediate disbursement:* Bartholomew and Ar-
      rington, 23.

234   *And he "told the people":* Daniel Jones, *Forty Years,* 65.

234   *Daniel Jones's account of the meeting:* Ibid., 65.

234   *The official journal of the Hunt Company:* Dan Jones Emigrating Company
      Journal, http://www.lds.org/churchhistory.

234   *On the morning of the 29th:* Daniel Jones, *Forty Years,* 66.

235   *By the time Jones and Garr:* Ibid., 66–67.

235   *In a letter to Brigham Young:* George D. Grant, "The Companies Yet on the
      Plains," *Deseret News,* November 19, 1856.

236   *though nine hundred is probably a more accurate count:* Olsen, 364.

236   *As Grant wrote to Young:* Grant, "The Companies Yet on the Plains," *Deseret
      News,* November 19, 1856.

236   *Even so, a few Saints died:* Olsen, 350–51.

236   *The Martin Company reached Devil's Gate:* Ibid., 352.

236   *Daniel Jones recalled:* Daniel Jones, *Forty Years,* 68.

237   *Patience Loader, however, remembered:* Archer, 81.

237   *John Jaques recaptured the ordeal:* Jaques, "Some Reminiscences," *Salt Lake
      Daily Herald,* December 15, 1878.

238   *The next day, as another storm descended:* Olsen, 355.

238   *Meanwhile, Grant was vexed:* Daniel Jones, *Forty Years,* 68.

238   *Young and Garr covered the 327 miles:* Olsen, 356.

238   *the official newspaper of the colony also published:* "Express," *Deseret News,*
      November 19, 1856.

239   *As well as flour:* Robert Burton, [Journal], quoted in Olsen, 357.

239   *Patience Loader remembered:* Archer, 79.

239   *The cache plan evolved into something:* Daniel Jones, *Forty Years,* 69–70.

240   *On November 4, the thermometer registered:* Jesse Haven, Journals, http://
      www.lds.org/churchhistory.

240   *at Devil's Gate, it ran only two to three feet deep:* Jaques, "Some Reminis-
      cences," *Salt Lake Daily Herald,* December 15, 1878.

240   *John Jaques later recalled a vignette:* Ibid.

241   *He rolled up his pants:* Ibid.

241   *Jaques's sister-in-law Patience Loader:* Archer, 83–84.

242   *It was crystallized by Solomon Kimball:* Kimball, "Belated Emigrants of 1856,"
      Improvement Era, February 1914, 288.

243   *Chad M. Orton demonstrated:* Orton, "The Martin Handcart Company at
      the Sweetwater: Another Look," *BYU Studies* 45, no. 3 (2006), 5–37.

243   *The cold was beyond brutal:* Robert T. Burton, [Journal], http://www.lds
      .org/churchhistory.

243   *on the worst day the gusts blew down:* Samuel S. Jones, Reminiscences, ibid.

243 *Of this reversal:* Susan Arrington Madsen, *I Walked to Zion*, 46.

243 *Patience Loader thought:* Archer, 84.

243 *Samuel Openshaw, who had managed faithfully:* Openshaw diary, http://www.lds.org/churchhistory.

244 *On November 5, the daily ration:* James Godson Bleak, Journal, ibid.

244 *Peter McBride remembered:* Susan Arrington Madsen, *I Walked to Zion*, 46.

244 *His thirteen-year-old brother:* Heber McBride, Autobiography, http://www.lds.org/churchhistory.

244 *Fifty years later, Samuel S. Jones:* Samuel S. Jones, Reminiscences, ibid.

244 *several Saints later testified:* E.g., James Cantwell, Autobiography, ibid.; Louisa Mellor Clark, Reminiscences, ibid.

244 *Thus Elizabeth Sermon:* Elizabeth Whitear [Sermon] Camm, Reminiscence, ibid.

244 *As if the loss of her husband were not tribulation:* Ibid.

245 *Their daughter, only two years old:* Olsen, 368.

245 *As another daughter, thirteen-year-old Mary:* Mary Goble Pay, Life of Mary Goble Pay, http://www.lds.org/churchhistory.

245 *Patience Loader paints an affecting picture:* Archer, 86–87.

246 *Robert Burton's journal says only:* Burton, [Journal], http://www.lds.org/churchhistory.

246 *The story was told most fully by Hanks:* Hanks and Hanks, *Scoutings*, 122–23, 131–39.

248 *Hanks, however, had no cure for frostbite:* Ibid., 140.

248 *In* Rescue of the 1856 Handcart Companies: Bartholomew and Arrington, 32–33.

249 *But there, according to Bartholomew and Arrington:* Ibid., 33.

249 *Stout's diary gives the clearest account:* Juanita Brooks, *Diary of Hosea Stout*, vol. 2, 605–6, quoted in Bartholomew and Arrington, 33.

250 *In* Forty Years Among the Indians: Daniel Jones, *Forty Years*, 72.

250 *About a dozen years later:* Heber McBride, Autobiography, http://www.lds.org/churchhistory.

250 *As John Jaques later indicated:* Jaques, "Some Reminiscences," *Salt Lake Daily Herald*, December 22, 1878.

250 *Some of the Saints actually chose to walk:* Ibid.

250 *From the 9th of that month on:* Bartholomew and Arrington, 35.

250 *It is curious that Robert Burton's diary:* Burton, [Journal], http://www.lds.org/churchhistory.

251 *Fifty-eight years later:* Jane Griffiths Fullmer, [Reminiscence], ibid.

251 *As nineteen-year-old George Housley:* George Frederick Housley, [Reminiscences], ibid.

251 *In a stormy camp on the Sweetwater:* Elizabeth Whitear [Sermon] Camm, Reminiscence, ibid.

251 *Twenty-two years later:* Jaques, "Some Reminiscences," *Salt Lake Daily Herald*, December 22, 1878.

251 *Providentially, it was here:* Olsen, 391–92.

252 *As Call later described his meeting:* Anson Call, Autobiography and Journal, quoted in Olsen, 392.

252 *That day, the ration of flour per adult:* Bleak, Journal, http://www.lds.org/churchhistory.

252 *Elizabeth Sermon remembered:* Camm, Reminiscence, ibid.

252 *As Patience Loader recalled one such night:* Archer, 87.

252 *John Jaques had his own system:* Jaques, "Some Reminiscences," *Salt Lake Daily Herald*, January 5, 1879.

253 *Twenty-two years later:* Ibid.

253 *At South Pass, the refugees were met:* Olsen, 392–94.

253 *At Fort Bridger, John and Zilpah Jaques:* John Jaques, [Letter], http://www.lds.org/churchhistory; Archer, 219 n67.

253 *From near Fort Bridger:* Lola Simmons Hunter, History of Joseph Marcellus Simmons, http://www.lds.org/churchhistory.

253 *Joseph Wadsworth, one of the rescuers:* Joseph Warren Wadsworth, [Autobiography], ibid.

253 *In Echo Canyon:* Jaques, "Some Reminiscences," *Salt Lake Daily Herald*, December 22, 1878.

254 *She would live to the ripe old age of eighty-six:* http://www.lds.org/churchhistory.

254 *By now the snow was so deep:* Wadsworth, [Autobiography], ibid.

254 *The meeting with the residents:* Jaques, "Some Reminiscences," *Salt Lake Daily Herald*, December 22, 1878.

254 *Years later, Louisa Mellor Clark:* Louisa Mellor Clark, Reminiscences, http://www.lds.org/churchhistory.

254 *But eighteen-year-old Langley Bailey:* Langley A. Bailey, [Reminiscences], ibid.

254 *Remembered George Housley:* Housley, [Reminiscences], ibid.

254 *Half a century later, Josiah Rogerson:* Josiah Rogerson, "Martin's Handcart Company, 1856," *Salt Lake Herald*, December 1, 1907.

255 *Rescuer Thomas Steed:* Thomas Steed, "The Life of Thomas Steed from His Own Diary," http://www.lds.org/churchhistory.

255 *And in the plainest of language:* Margaret Ann Griffiths Clegg, Autobiographical sketch, ibid.

255 *The last of all the Saints:* http://www.lds.org/churchhistory.

255 *Their retrospective estimates:* Benjamin Platt, Reminiscences, ibid.; Mary Soar Taylor Moore, Biography of Mary Soar Taylor Moore, ibid.

255 *Hafen and Hafen cite:* Hafen and Hafen, 193.

255 *LDS archivist and historian Mel Bashore:* Mel Bashore, personal communication, September 2007.

256 *Only four days after the Martin Company's arrival:* "Arrival," *Deseret News,* December 3, 1856.

256 *By the time the tidings of the last handcart company:* "Arrival of the Hand-Carts at Great Salt Lake City," *The Mormon,* February 21, 1857.

257 *Heber Kimball acknowledged as much:* Heber C. Kimball, "Remarks," *Deseret News,* November 12, 1856.

257 *At that same meeting in the Tabernacle:* Brigham Young, "Remarks," *Deseret News,* November 12, 1856.

CHAPTER 8: THE MORMON *MAYFLOWER*

Page

259 *The cynosure of the ten-acre square:* http://www.ldschurchtemples.com.

259 *Temple Square also encloses the rotunda-shaped Tabernacle:* http://www.visit templesquare.com.

260 *(Even faithful Saints joke):* Ardis Parshall, personal communication, May 2007.

261 *John Ahmanson's "two-wheeled man-tormentor":* Ahmanson, 33, 35.

261 *"Mormons are proud of our pioneer ancestors":* Ardis Parshall, personal communication, April 2007.

261 *Elizabeth Stewart, born in 1829:* Ardis Parshall, [Marriott Grandparents], unpublished typescript.

261 *Marriott's maternal grandfather was harder to find:* "Autobiography of Elizabeth Stewart Marriott" [unpublished], quoted in ibid.

262 *I spoke with Bill Marriott regarding the research:* E-mail, Steve Lundgren to David Roberts, [April 2007].

263 *"In conclusion," Jaques wrote:* Jaques, "Some Reminiscences," *Salt Lake Daily Herald,* January 19, 1879.

264 *This is the first time that the story:* Ibid.

265 *"The question may be asked":* Ibid.

265 *"In the history of any people":* Young, 200.

265 *There was no doubt in Ann Eliza's mind:* Ibid., 221.

266 *"Fifty years go by before people":* Lyndia Carter, personal communication, September 2006.

266 *Even at that remove from the disaster:* Ibid.

266 *The reunion was held on October 4, 1906:* Handcart Veterans Association Scrapbook, LDS Archives.

266 *Jones's brother Albert:* Albert Jones, Address, http://www.lds.org/church history.

267 *A few years later, in a published reminiscence:* S. S. Jones, "Personal Reminiscence," in "The Martyrs of the Plains," *The Christmas News,* 1910.

267 *In a 1908 letter to Jones:* Joseph F. Smith (First Presidency) to S. S. Jones, April 18, 1908, LDS Archives.

267 *To make the record as full as possible:* Rogerson, "Martin's Handcart Company, 1856," *Salt Lake Herald,* November 10, 1907.

268 *A persistent rumor has it:* William Slaughter, personal communication, April 2006.

268 *Historian Lyndia Carter discusses this murky business:* Lyndia Carter, personal communication, September 2006.

268 *The Harold B. Lee Library at Brigham Young University:* Josiah Rogerson Handcart Collection, Harold B. Lee Library, Brigham Young University.

268 *Another persistent rumor has it:* Lyndia Carter, personal communication, September 2006; Ardis Parshall, personal communication, April 2006.

268 *As noted earlier, the Hafens were spurred:* Hafen and Hafen, 12, 190.

269 *The Hafens honestly concede:* Ibid., 140.

269 *"Taken in its normal operation":* Ibid., 194.

269 *Like Israel of old:* Ibid., 195.

269 *So uncooperative, in fact:* Stegner, vi.

270 *Standing before the granite cirque in western Wyoming:* Ibid., 306.

273 *like that of 90 percent of the 32,273-odd visitors:* Elder Hadley, personal communication, August 2005.

273 *An expert on the design of the "replicas":* Ibid.

275 *Some of the most assiduous students:* Lyndia Carter, personal communication, September 2006.

278 *In* The Price We Paid, *Andrew Olsen:* Olsen, 444.

283 *As mentioned, trail historians argue over whether:* Lyndia Carter, personal communication, September 2006; Terry Del Bene, personal communication, February 2007.

285 *Historian Lyndia Carter, who regularly speaks:* Lyndia Carter, personal communication, September 2006.

285 *For Mormons seeking to justify the disaster:* Palmer, "Pioneers of Southern Utah: Vol. 6, Francis Webster," *The Instructor,* May 1944, 217–19.

286 *Moreover, the only memoir in Webster's own hand:* Francis Webster, Reminiscences, http://www.lds.org/churchhistory.

286 *In Palmer's 1944 telling:* Palmer, "Pioneers of Southern Utah," 217–19.

287 *According to Lyndia Carter, substantial numbers:* Lyndia Carter, personal communication, September 2006.

289 *a pair of documentary films:* Jack Hubbell, *In Their Footsteps of Faith: The Story of the Willie and Martin Handcarts,* 2006; Lee Groberg, *Sweetwater Rescue,* 2006.

292 *The trading post was erected:* Fort Bridger Historic Monument; Vestal, *Jim Bridger,* 182–91; Alter, *Jim Bridger,* 223–57.

292 *And a carefully researched guidebook:* Berrett et al., 147–48.

293 *Here, we do know, the first two handcart parties:* Ibid., 144.

295 *In a few minutes, however, Lowry dashed:* Sandra Lowry, personal communication, February 2007.

295 *From 1867 to 1877:* Berrett et al., 20.

296 *I recalled Josiah Rogerson's wistful evocation:* Rogerson, "Martin's Handcart Company, 1856," *Salt Lake Herald*, November 3, 1907.

296 *It began with a chance conversation:* Susan Arrington Madsen, *The Second Rescue*, 12–13, 21–24.

297 *As theologian Bruce R. McConkie explains it:* McConkie, 72–73.

298 *To enter heaven:* Ibid., 779.

298 *As Larsen explained to me the plight:* Lloyd Larsen, personal communication, August 2005.

299 *"The ordinances are not secret":* Scott Lorimer, personal communication, August 2006.

299 *By the end of this orgy of effort:* Madsen, *Second Rescue*, 47.

299 *"I would say we rescued":* Lloyd Larsen, personal communication, August 2005.

299 *A good example is that of Heika Lorimer:* Madsen, *Second Rescue*, 61–62.

300 *Twelve-year-old Kristen Gard wrote:* Ibid., 57.

300 *Lyndia Carter was even more blunt:* Lyndia Carter, personal communication, September 2006.

CHAPTER 9: A DAY OF RECKONING

Page

301 *Early on, Jones was voted by his peers:* Daniel Jones, *Forty Years*, 70.

301 *Captain Grant asked about our provisions:* Ibid., 71.

302 *On taking stock of provisions:* Ibid., 72.

302 *During the first few days:* Ibid., 71–72.

302 *Finally Jones had to sever:* Ibid., 74.

302 *The hope of Jones's men:* Ibid.

303 *The only solution was to slaughter:* Ibid., 74–75.

303 *Sometime in December:* Ibid., 76, 78.

303 *A day or two before Christmas:* Ibid., 76.

303 *It is a rather astonishing document:* Ibid., 76–77.

305 *"Game soon became so scarce":* Ibid., 79–80.

305 *Jones only hints at the dissension:* Ibid., 80.

306 *By March 4, "the last morsel":* Ibid., 84, 86.

306 *It was not until February that the first Indian:* Ibid., 80–81, 83–84.

307 *These Indians of the plains years back:* Ibid., 83.

307 *By March, the Snakes and Bannocks:* Ibid., 87–88, 91–92.

308 *Finally, in late spring:* Ibid., 102–3.

308 *The goods we were guarding belonged:* Ibid., 102–5.

309 *If Jones expected to be greeted as a hero:* Ibid., 109.

309 *With these sorts of rumors flying about:* Ibid., 107–8.

309 *"I began to feel pretty good":* Ibid., 108.

309 *Thus, speaking in the Tabernacle:* Young, "Remarks," *Deseret News,* November 26, 1856.

310 *At the same November 2 meeting:* Grant, "Discourse," *Deseret News,* November 12, 1856.

311 *On December 1, Young's "sledgehammer":* Bigler, *Forgotten Kingdom,* 129.

311 *In a typical letter:* Brigham Young to Ezra T. Benson, January 26, 1857, LDS Archives.

311 *And to demonstrate the efficacy of that plan:* Hafen and Hafen, 144–47.

311 *"They were feeling fine after their trip":* Florence Courier, [n.d.], quoted in ibid., 148.

312 *LeRoy and Ann Hafen call it:* Hafen and Hafen, 144.

312 *According to Ann Eliza Young:* Young, 227, quoted in part in Bagley, "Two-Wheeled Torture Devices," 41.

312 *Thus Andrew Olsen:* Olsen, 477.

312 *Thus, in the 1857 company led by Israel Evans:* Robert Leeming Fishburn, "Pioneer Autobiographies," http://www.lds.org/churchhistory.

313 *Of the same expedition, Susan Witbeck remembered:* Susan Melverton R. Witbeck, Autobiographical sketch, ibid.

313 *In the second 1857 company:* Kersten Erickson Benson, Kersten E. Benson biographical file, ibid.

313 *"In those five companies":* Olsen, 477–78.

313 *Hafen and Hafen list the death toll:* Hafen and Hafen, 193.

314 *Yet two participants in the party later swore:* C. C. N. Dorius, [Journal], http://www.lds.org/churchhistory. See also James Jensen, [Reminiscences], ibid.

314 *Will Bagley calculates the death rate:* Bagley, "Two-Wheeled Torture Devices," speech at Sunstone Conference, Salt Lake City, August 2006.

314 *His characteristically acerbic conclusion:* Bagley, "Two-Wheeled Torture Devices," 47.

314 *And on that very day, September 11, 1857:* For the Mountain Meadows Massacre, see Brooks, passim, and Bagley, *Blood,* passim.

316 *The book is so disturbing to the faithful:* Richard Turley, personal communication, August 2006.

316 *Patience Loader, otherwise so vivid a memoirist:* Archer, 89–92.

316 *Levi Savage, who had faithfully kept his journal:* Savage journal, http://www.lds.org/churchhistory.

317 *Sarah Hancock Beesley, a veteran of the 1859 handcart party:* Sarah Hancock Beesley, [Reminiscences], ibid., quoted in Bagley, "Two-Wheeled Torture Devices," 46.

317 *(Hafen and Hafen list only a single death):* Hafen and Hafen, 193.

317 *On November 30, the day of the Martin Company's arrival:* Young, "Remarks," *Deseret News,* December 10, 1856.

318 *As recounted earlier:* Adolph Madsen Reeder, Writings, http://www.lds.org/churchhistory.

319 *In* The Instructor *for April 1944:* William R. Palmer, "She Stood Tall on Her Knees," 152–55.

319 *(Palmer implies that all five children):* Olsen, 256.

320 *Nellie died in 1915:* http://www.lds.org/churchhistory.

320 *Palmer closes his tribute:* Palmer, "She Stood Tall," 155.

320 *According to a Southern Utah University archivist:* Janet Seegmiller, personal communication, February 2007.

320 *The most remarkable may have been Jens Nielson:* Olsen, 206–8.

320 *Despite this handicap:* David Roberts, *Sandstone Spine,* 128–33.

321 *Narrating the nadir of the expedition:* Emily Hill Woodmansee, "Hunger and Cold," http://www.lds.org/churchhistory.

322 *"Beefsteak was one thing":* Howard R. Driggs, "Handcart Boy," *The Children's Friend,* July 1944, 291.

322 *According to Driggs's memoir:* Ibid.; also *The Children's Friend,* September and November 1944.

322 *A fourteen-year-old named George Harrison:* http://www.lds.org/churchhistory.

322 *Lifting the flap of elkskin at the opening:* Driggs, *George, the Handcart Boy,* 42.

323 *In his 758-page* Fire of the Covenant, *Lund tries:* Lund, *Fire of the Covenant,* xix.

323 *They cannot cure themselves of uttering "Yah":* Ibid., 196.

323 *Many Mormon readers:* Personal communication, several women from West Valley ward, August 2006.

323 *Thus on October 20, 1856:* Lund, 543.

324 *This party, made up of between 370 and 447 emigrants:* http://www.lds.org/churchhistory.

325 *In his 1889* History of Utah: Bancroft, *History of Utah,* 421–22.

325 *In his letter to the* Frontier Guardian: "Letter from G. A. Smith," *Frontier Guardian,* December 26, 1849, http://www.lds.org/churchhistory.

326 *At a 2005 session:* W. H. Bagley, personal communication, August 2006.

326 *According to Hannah S. Lapish:* Hafen papers, Brigham Young University.

326 *Even among church historians who hold that view:* Michael Landon and Chad Orton, personal communication, May 2006.

327 *In an informal lecture about the handcart emigration:* Bagley, "Two-Wheeled Torture Devices," speech at Sunstone Conference, Salt Lake City, August 2006.

327 *Concentrating on what he calls:* Bagley, "Two-Wheeled Torture Devices," 5.

327 *In the 1850s:* Ibid., 7. The quotation is from Leonard Arrington, *Great Basin Kingdom,* 146.

327 *At the same time that his schemes were threatening:* Bagley, "Two-Wheeled Torture Devices," 7.

327 *In an angry speech:* Arrington, *Great Basin,* quoted in Bagley, "Two-Wheeled Torture Devices," 5–6.

328 *Bagley was the first historian:* Ibid., 12–13.

328 *Thus in a report filed in the capital:* Caleb Grant, [Report], http://www.lds.org/churchhistory.

328 *Even more explicitly, another member of Smoot's team:* Franklin Benjamin Woolley, Autobiography, ibid.

329 *The Willie Company was made aware:* James G. Willie Emigrating Company Journal, ibid.

329 *Exactly what Young intended to do with a steamboat:* Bagley, "Two-Wheeled Torture Devices," 30–31.

329 *Bagley grants that Franklin Richards's sending on:* Ibid., 21.

329 *But in his view, the whole debacle was caused:* Ibid., 13.

330 *Bagley was also the first historian to argue:* Bagley, Sunstone speech, August 2006.

330 *As early as January 18, 1856:* John Taylor to Brigham Young, January 18, 1856, LDS Archives.

330 *By March 4, Taylor was so disturbed:* John Taylor to Franklin Richards, March 4, 1856, ibid.

330 *"We have had a great many calculations":* John Taylor to Brigham Young, April 16, 1856, ibid.

330 *A June 30 letter from Young to Taylor:* Brigham Young to John Taylor, June 30, 1856, ibid.

331 *In August he pleaded with the Prophet:* John Taylor to Brigham Young, August 18, 1856, ibid.

331 *On September 18, in phrases that mingle exasperation:* John Taylor to Brigham Young, September 18, 1856, ibid.

331 *Having ignored all the warning flags:* Brigham Young to John Taylor, October 30, 1856, ibid.

331 *In February 1857, he sent the Prophet a letter:* John Taylor to Brigham Young, February 24, 1857, ibid.

332 *The baldest expression of that bedrock conviction:* Fourteenth General Epistle, *Millennial Star,* April 18, 1857.

333 *It was widely predicted by skeptical observers:* See, for example, Germiquet, *Brigham Young et la Secte Mormone,* 173–74; or Beadle, *Life in Utah,* 524–26.

333 *"He was a great American":* Will Bagley, personal communication, August 2006.

333 *To the Prophet's skeptical 1925 biographer:* Werner, v.

333 *For Bernard DeVoto:* DeVoto, "Centennial of Mormonism," 9–10.

334 *John Bond, the twelve-year-old:* John Bond, "Handcarts West in '56," http://www.lds.org/churchhistory.

334 *And John Chislett mused upon the tragedy:* T. B. H. Stenhouse, *Saints,* 313.

BIBLIOGRAPHY

Ahmanson, John, translated by Gleason L. Archer. *Secret History: A Translation of Vor Tids Muhamed*. Chicago: 1984.

Allphin, Jolene S. *Tell My Story, Too*. Ogden, Utah: 2001.

Alter, J. Cecil. *Jim Bridger*. Norman, Oklahoma: 1962.

Archer, Patience Loader Rozsa. *Recollections of Past Days*. Logan, Utah: 2006.

Arrington, Leonard J. *Brigham Young: American Moses*. New York: 1985.

———. *Great Basin Kingdom: An Economic History of the Latter-day Saints*. Cambridge, Massachusetts: 1958.

The Alantic Monthly, December 2006

Bagley, Will. *Blood of the Prophets: Brigham Young and the Massacre at Mountain Meadows*. Norman, Oklahoma: 2002.

———. *The Pioneer Camp of the Saints: The 1846 and 1847 Mormon Trail Journals of Thomas Bullock*. Spokane, Washington: 1997.

———. "Two-Wheeled Torture Devices: The Handcart Disasters" [in ms].

Bancroft, Hubert Howe. *History of Utah*. San Francisco: 1889.

Bangerter, Howard K., and Cory W. Bangerter. *Tragedy and Triumph: Your Guide to the Rescue of the 1856 Willie and Martin Handcart Companies*. Provo, Utah: 2004.

Bartholomew, Rebecca, and Leonard J. Arrington. *Rescue of the 1856 Handcart Companies*. Provo, Utah: 1992.

Beadle, J. H., ed. *Brigham's Destroying Angel*. New York: 1872.

———. *Life in Utah; or, The Mysteries and Crimes of Mormonism*. Philadelphia: 1871.

Bell, Stella Jaques. *Life History and Writings of John Jaques*. Rexburg, Idaho: 1978.

Berrett, LaMar C., and A. Gary Anderson. *Sacred Places: Wyoming and Utah*. Salt Lake City: 2007.

Berrett, LaMar C., William G. Hartley, and A. Gary Anderson. *Sacred Places: Iowa and Nebraska*. Salt Lake City: 2006.

Bigler, David L. *Forgotten Kingdom: The Mormon Theocracy in the American West, 1847–1896*. Logan, Utah: 1998.

———. *Fort Limhi: The Mormon Adventure in Oregon Territory, 1855–1858*. Spokane, Washington: 2003.

Bond, John. "Handcarts West in '56." http://www.lds.org/churchhistory.

Brigham Young Collection, LDS Archives, Salt Lake City.

Bringhurst, Newell G. "Fawn Brodie and Her Quest for Independence," in John Sillitto and Susan Staker, eds., *Mormon Mavericks*. Salt Lake City: 2002.

———. *Fawn McKay Brodie: A Biographer's Life*. Norman, Oklahoma: 1999.

Brodie, Fawn M. *No Man Knows My History: The Life of Joseph Smith*. New York: 1945.

Brooks, Juanita. *The Mountain Meadows Massacre*. Stanford, California: 1950.

Burton, Sir Richard. *The City of the Saints and Across the Rocky Mountains to California*. London: 1862.

Chandless, William. *A Visit to Salt Lake*. London: 1857.

Christensen, Allen C. *Before Zion: An Account of the 7th Handcart Company*. Springville, Utah: 2004.

Christensen, C. C. A., translated by Richard L. Jensen. "By Handcart to Utah: The Account of C. C. A. Christensen." *Nebraska Historical Quarterly* 66, no. 4 (Winter 1985).

Christy, Howard A. "Weather, Disaster, and Responsibility: An Essay on the Willie and Martin Handcart Story." *BYU Studies* 37, no. 1 (1997–98).

Clayton, W., edited by Stanley B. Kimball. *The Latter-day Saints' Emigrants' Guide*. Tucson, Arizona: 1983.

Deseret News. Salt Lake City: 1853–60.

DeVoto, Bernard. "The Centennial of Mormonism." *The American Mercury* 19, no. 73 (January 1930).

———. *Forays and Rebuttals*. Boston: 1936.

———. *The Year of Decision: 1846*. Boston: 1943.

Doctrine and Covenants. Liverpool: 1845.

Driggs, Howard R. *George, the Handcart Boy*. New York: 1952.

———. "Handcart Boy." *The Children's Friend*, July 1944.

Ferris, Benjamin G. *Utah and the Mormons*. New York: 1854.

Ferris, Mrs. B. G. *The Mormons at Home: With Some Incidents of Travel from Missouri to California, 1852–3*. New York: 1856.

Fielding, Robert Kent. *The Unsolicited Chronicler: An Account of the Gunnison Massacre*. Brookline, Massachusetts: 1993.

Gallaher, Ruth. "The Handcart Expeditions." *The Palimpsest* (July 1922).

Germiquet, J. *Brigham Young et la Secte Mormone*. Paris: 1879.

Glazier, Stewart E., and Robert S. Clark, editors. *Journal of the Trail*. Sandy, Utah: 2005.

Grayson, Donald K. "Human Mortality in a Natural Disaster: The Willie Handcart Company." *Journal of Anthropological Research* 52, no. 2 (Summer 1996).

Green, Caleb. Diary. Missouri Historical Society, St. Louis.

Groberg, Lee. *Sweetwater Rescue: The Willie and Martin Handcart Story* (DVD). 2006.

Gunnison, J. W. *The Mormons, or, Latter-day Saints, in the Valley of the Great Salt Lake*. Philadelphia: 1860.

Hafen, LeRoy, papers. Harold B. Lee Library, Brigham Young University, Provo, Utah.

Hafen, LeRoy R., and Ann W. Hafen. *Handcarts to Zion: The Story of a Unique Western Migration, 1856–1860*. Glendale, California: 1960.

Hafen, Mary Ann. *Recollections of a Handcart Pioneer of 1860*. Lincoln, Nebraska: 2004.

Handcart Veterans Association Scrapbook. LDS Archives, Salt Lake City.

Hanks, Sidney Alvarus, and Ephraim K. Hanks. *Scouting for the Mormons on the Great Frontier*. Salt Lake City: 1948.

Harris, Sr., James Roy. *Southwestern American Indian Rock Art and the Book of Mormon*. Orem, Utah: 1991.

Hastings, Lansford W. *The Emigrants' Guide to Oregon and California*. Cincinnati: 1845.

Hawthornthwaite, Samuel. *Mr. Hawthornthwaite's Adventures Among the Mormons*. Manchester, England: 1857.

Hilton, Hope A. *"Wild Bill" Hickman and the Mormon Frontier*. Salt Lake City: 1988.

Hirshson, Stanley P. *The Lion of the Lord: A Biography of Brigham Young*. New York: 1973.

Howard R. Driggs Collection. Southern Utah University, Cedar City, Utah.

Howe, Eber D. *Mormonism Unvailed, or, a Faithful Account of That Singular Imposition and Delusion from Its Rise to the Present Time*. Painesville, Ohio: 1834.

Hubbell, Jack R. *In Their Footsteps of Faith: The Story of the Willie and Martin Handcarts* (DVD). 2006.

Hyde, Jr., John. *Mormonism: Its Leaders and Designs*. New York: 1857.

Hymns of the Church of Jesus Christ of Latter-day Saints. Salt Lake City: 1985.

Jaques, John. "Some Reminiscences." *Salt Lake Daily Herald*, December 1, December 8, December 15, December 22, 1878; January 5, January 12, January 19, 1879.

Jarman, W. *U.S.A., Uncle Sam's Abscess, or Hell upon Earth for U.S., Uncle Sam*. Exeter, England: 1884.

Jenson, Andrew. "Church Emigration." *The Contributor*, vol. 14, 1893.

Jones, Daniel W. *Forty Years Among the Indians*. Los Angeles: 1960 [originally Salt Lake City: 1890].

Jones, S. S. "Personal Reminiscence," in "The Martyrs of the Plains," *The Christmas News*, 1910.

Josiah Rogerson Handcart Collection. Harold B. Lee Library, Brigham Young University, Provo, Utah.

Journal History of the Church of Jesus Christ of Latter-day Saints. LDS Archives, Salt Lake City.

Journal of Discourses. Liverpool: 1854–86.

Kimball, Solomon F. "Belated Emigrants of 1856." *Improvement Era*, February 1914.

Krakauer, Jon. *Under the Banner of Heaven: A Story of a Violent Faith*. New York: 2003.

Larson, Gustive O. "The Mormon Reformation." *Utah Historical Quarterly* 26 (1958).

———. *Prelude to the Kingdom: Mormon Desert Conquest*. Westport, Connecticut: 1978.

Lee, John D. *Mormonism Unveiled: or, The Life and Confessions of the Late Mormon Bishop*. St. Louis: 1877.

Linn, William A. *The Story of the Mormons*. New York: 1902.

Ludlow, Daniel, ed. *Encyclopedia of Mormonism*. New York: 1992.

Lund, Gerald N. *Fire of the Covenant*. Salt Lake City: 1999.

Madsen, Carol Cornwall. *Journey to Zion: Voices from the Mormon Trail*. Salt Lake City: 1997.

Madsen, Susan Arrington. *I Walked to Zion: True Stories of Young Pioneers on the Mormon Trail*. Salt Lake City: 1994.

———. *The Second Rescue: The Story of the Spiritual Rescue of the Willie and Martin Handcart Pioneers*. Orem, Utah: 1998.

Martin, Charles W. "John Ahmanson vs. Brigham Young: A Nebraska Legal Controversy, 1859–1861." *Nebraska History* 64 (1983).

McConkie, Bruce R. *Mormon Doctrine*. Salt Lake City: 1966.

Millennial Star. Liverpool: 1842–60.

Monaghan, Jay. "Handcarts on the Overland Trail." *Nebraska History* 30 (1949).

Morgan, Dale L. *The State of Deseret*. Logan, Utah: 1987.

The Mormon. New York: 1855–60.

Mulder, William. *Homeward to Zion: The Mormon Migration from Scandinavia*. Minneapolis: 1957.

Mulder, William, and A. Russell Mortensen. *Among the Mormons: Historic Accounts by Contemporary Observers*. Lincoln, Nebraska: 1958.

Nevins, Allan. *Frémont, Pathmarker of the West*. New York: 1961.

New York Times. New York: 1853–77.

New York Tribune. August 20, 1859.

Olsen, Andrew D. *The Price We Paid: The Extraordinary Story of the Willie and Martin Handcart Pioneers*. Salt Lake City: 2006.

Orton, Chad M. "Francis Webster: The Unique Story of One Handcart Pioneer's Faith and Sacrifice." *BYU Studies*, 45, no. 2 (2006).

————. "The Martin Handcart Company at the Sweetwater: Another Look." *BYU Studies* 45, no. 3 (2006).

Palmer, William R. "Pioneers of Southern Utah: Vol. 6, Francis Webster." *The Instructor*, May 1944.

————. "She Stood Tall on Her Knees." *The Instructor*, April 1944.

Parkman, Jr., Francis. *The Oregon Trail*. New York: 1849.

Parshall, Ardis. [Marriott Grandparents] [unpublished typescript].

Paul, Earl S. "The Handcart Companies of 1856 and Arza Erastus Hinckley." LDS Archives, Salt Lake City [unpublished typescript].

Rea, Tom. *Devil's Gate: Owning the Land, Owning the Story*. Norman, Oklahoma: 2006.

Remember: The Willie and Martin Handcart Companies and Their Rescuers—Past and Present. Salt Lake City: 1997.

Riess, Jana, and Christopher Kimball Bigelow. *Mormonism for Dummies*. Hoboken, New Jersey: 2005.

Roberts, B. H., edited by Gary James Bergera. *The Autobiography of B. H. Roberts*. Salt Lake City: 1990.

————, ed., *A Comprehensive History of the Church of Jesus Christ of Latter-day Saints*. Salt Lake City: 1948.

————. *The Life of John Taylor*. Salt Lake City: 1892.

————. *Studies of the Book of Mormon*. Urbana, Illinois: 1985.

Roberts, David. *A Newer World: Kit Carson, John C. Frémont, and the Claiming of the American West*. New York: 2000.

————. *Sandstone Spine*. Seattle: 2006.

Rogerson, Josiah. "Martin's Handcart Company, 1856." *Salt Lake Herald*, October 13, October 20, October 27, November 3, November 10, November 17, November 24, December 1, December 8, 1907.

————. "Strong Men, Brave Women and Sturdy Children Crossed the Wilderness Afoot." *Salt Lake Tribune*, January 4, 1914.

Schindler, Harold. *Orrin Porter Rockwell: Man of God/Son of Thunder*. Salt Lake City: 1966.

Sessions, Gene A. *Mormon Thunder: A Documentary History of Jedediah Morgan Grant*. Urbana, Illinois: 1982.

Slaughter, William W., and Michael Landon. *Trail of Hope: The Story of the Mormon Trail*. Salt Lake City: 1997.

Smith, Jr., Joseph, translator. *Book of Mormon*. 1830.

Sonne, Conway B. *Saints on the Seas*. Salt Lake City: 1983.

Stegner, Wallace. *The Gathering of Zion: The Story of the Mormon Trail*. New York: 1964.

Stenhouse, Mrs. T. B. H. [Fanny]. *"Tell It All": The Story of a Life's Experience in Mormonism*. Hartford, Connecticut: 1875.

Stenhouse, T. B. H. *The Rocky Mountain Saints: A Full and Complete History of the Mormons*. London: 1874.

Stephenson, Shirely E. "Biography of Fawn McKay Brodie." Oral history collection, Fullerton State University, Fullerton, California.

Swinton, Heidi, and Lee Groberg. *Sweetwater Rescue: The Willie and Martin Handcart Story*. American Fork, Utah: 2006.

Taylor, John, Letters. LDS Archives, Salt Lake City.

Taylor, P. A. M. *Expectations Westward: The Mormons and the Emigration of Their British Converts in the Nineteenth Century*. Ithaca, New York: 1966.

Taylor, Samuel W. *The Last Pioneer: John Taylor, a Mormon Prophet*. Salt Lake City: 1976.

Turner, Lynne Slater. *Emigrating Journals of the Willie and Martin Handcart Companies and the Hunt and Hodgett Wagon Trains*. Taylorsville, Utah: 1996.

Twain, Mark [Samuel Clemens]. *Roughing It*. Hartford, Connecticut: 1872.

Unruh, Jr., John David. *The Plains Across: The Overland Emigrants and the Trans-Mississippi West, 1840–1860*. Urbana, Illinois: 1979.

Vestal, Stanley. *Jim Bridger: Mountain Man*. New York: 1946.

Walker, Ronald W. "The Stenhouses and the Making of a Mormon Image." *Journal of Mormon History* 1 (1974).

Werner, M. R. *Brigham Young*. New York: 1925.

West, Jr., Ray B. *Kingdom of the Saints: The Story of Brigham Young and the Mormons*. New York: 1957.

Wilson, Timothy B. *A Plain English Reference to the Book of Mormon*. Springville, Utah: 1998.

Woodruff, Wilford, edited by Scott G. Kenney. *Wilford Woodruff's Journal, 1833–1898*. Midvale, Utah: 1983.

Young, Ann Eliza. *Wife No. 19, Or the Story of a Life in Bondage*. Hartford, Connecticut: 1876.

WEB SITES

http://www.chipublib.org.
http://www.ldschurchtemples.com.
http://www.lds.org/churchhistory.
http://www.lds.org/placestovisit.
http://www.visittemplesquare.com.

INDEX

A CENTURY OF JUVENILE JUSTICE

A CENTURY OF
JUVENILE JUSTICE

EDITED BY

Margaret K. Rosenheim

Franklin E. Zimring

David S. Tanenhaus

and

Bernardine Dohrn

With a Foreword by

Adele Simmons

THE UNIVERSITY OF CHICAGO PRESS

CHICAGO AND LONDON

345
C397

Margaret K. Rosenheim is the Helen Ross Professor Emerita in the School of Social Service Administration of the University of Chicago. **Franklin E. Zimring** is professor of law and director of the Earl Warren Legal Institute at the University of California, Berkeley. **David S. Tanenhaus** is assistant professor of history and law at the University of Nevada, Las Vegas. **Bernardine Dohrn** is director of the Children and Family Justice Center of Northwestern University Law School.

The University of Chicago Press, Chicago 60637
The University of Chicago Press, Ltd., London
© 2002 by The University of Chicago
All rights reserved. Published 2002
Printed in the United States of America
11 10 09 08 07 06 05 04 03 02   5 4 3 2 1

ISBN (cloth): 0-226-72783-1

Library of Congress Cataloging-in-Publication Data

A century of juvenile justice / edited by Margaret K. Rosenheim . . . [et al.].
     p.   cm.
   Includes bibliographical references and index.
   ISBN 0-226-72783-1 (cloth : alk. paper)
   1. Juvenile justice, Administration of—United States.   2. Child welfare—United States.   3. Juvenile corrections—United States.   4. Juvenile justice, Administration of—United States.—History.   5. Child welfare—United States—History.
6. Juvenile corrections—United States—History.   I. Rosenheim, Margaret K. (Margaret Keeney), 1926–

KF9779 .C46   2002
345.73'08—dc21

                       2001043723